Information Systems
and Decision Processes

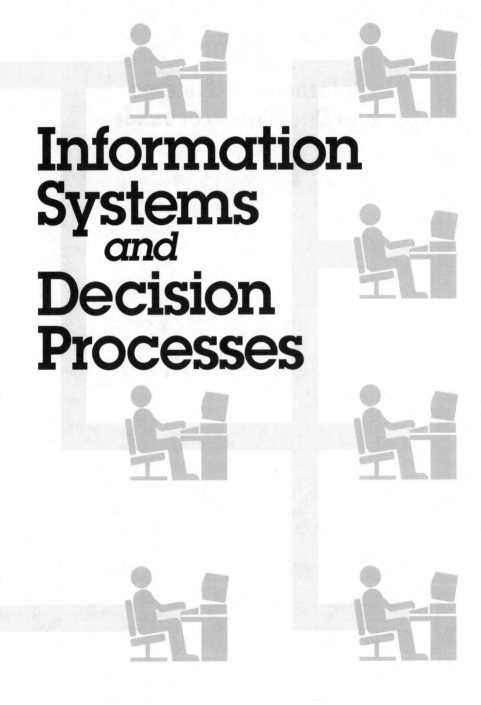

Information Systems *and* Decision Processes

Information Systems and Decision Processes

Edward A. Stohr and Benn R. Konsynski

IEEE Computer Society Press
Los Alamitos, CA
Washington • Brussels • Tokyo

IEEE Computer Society Press Monograph

Library of Congress Cataloging-in-Publication Data

Stohr, Edward A., 1936-
  Information systems and decision processes/ Edward A. Stohr
and Benn R. Konsynski
       p.   cm.
  Includes bibliographical references.
  ISBN 0-8186-2802-2 (case). -- ISBN 0-8186-2801-4 (microfiche)
  1. Management information systems. 2. Decision support systems.
I. Konsynski, Benn R., 1950- . II. Title.
T58.6.S745 1992
658.4'038--dc20

92-12137
CIP

Published by the
IEEE Computer Society Press
10662 Los Vaqueros Circle
PO Box 3014
Los Alamitos, CA 90720-1264

IEEE Computer Society Press Order Number 2802
Library of Congress Number 92-12137
IEEE Catalog Number EH0356-6
ISBN 0-8186-2801-4 (microfiche)
ISBN 0-8186-2802-2 (case)

Additional copies can be ordered from

IEEE Computer Society Press
Customer Service Center
10662 Los Vaqueros Circle
PO Box 3014
Los Alamitos, CA 90720-1264

IEEE Service Center
445 Hoes Lane
PO Box 1331
Piscataway, NJ 08855-1331

IEEE Computer Society
13, avenue de l'Aquilon
B-1200 Brussels
BELGIUM

IEEE Computer Society
Ooshima Building
2-19-1 Minami-Aoyama
Minato-ku, Tokyo 107
JAPAN

Consulting Editor: Ralph Sprague
Technical Editor: Barry Johnson
Production Editor: Lisa O'Conner
Copy Editor: Tom Culviner
Cover Artist: Joe Daigle
Printed in the United States of America by Braun-Brumfield, Inc.

 THE INSTITUTE OF ELECTRICAL AND ELECTRONICS ENGINEERS, INC.

Foreword

This text launches the IEEE Computer Society Press Information Systems Series, which will address the use of communication and computer technology to operate and manage organizations. First labeled as business data processing, and later as management information systems, the field is now known as information systems (IS). "Systems" is the operative word, since the field includes not only technologies, but people, processes, and organizational mechanisms as well, combined as systems to improve organizational performance.

In effect, management becomes the dominant use of information technology. While we use communication and computer technologies in space exploration, weapons systems, medicine, entertainment, and most other aspects of human activity, the major use of information technology is to run and manage organizations.

The IEEE Computer Society Press Information Systems Series will provide an ongoing stream of high-quality, up-to-date books on information technologies and their use in organizations. Drawing on the best papers from conferences and special research projects, this series will select, combine, and disseminate valuable material that is otherwise difficult to find and assemble. It will focus simultaneously on the technology and its organizational usage. Most publications emphasize a single technology or application in a specific industry. The unique emphasis of this series, viewing both areas simultaneously, represents a significant contribution to the literature.

This book is ideally suited to begin the Information Systems Series. It is the result of a five-year project, involving more than 40 academic leaders in information systems, to develop an agenda for future research on the intersection of information systems and decision processes. The ISDP project evolved from work on decision support systems, executive information systems, group decision support systems, expert systems, expert support systems, and other uses of information technology to support the performance of managers and executives. The main objective of the ISDP project was to rise above labels and focus on a new research agenda. A major result is this valuable compendium of original work, which will give direction to researchers in this field throughout the 90s.

Gordon B. Davis, Honeywell Professor of Management Information Systems at the University of Minnesota, provided valuable commentary during the preparation of this text. His insightful summary follows.

Ralph H. Sprague, Jr.
Consulting Editor

Reviewer Comments

Information Systems and Decision Processes — Charting New Directions for DSS Research: A Multidisciplinary Approach — edited by Edward A. Stohr and Benn Konsynski — is an impressive study. It results from the ISDP project, funded by TIMS College on Information Systems and the National Science Foundation, which employed five research teams with a total of 37 members (all recognized leaders in information systems research). The teams used traditional meeting formats and group decision support facilities at the University of Arizona in formulating their ideas, and wrote five substantial chapters summarizing the state of knowledge in the area and opportunities for research. Stohr and Konsynski have added two introductory chapters and two concluding chapters, plus an extensive reference bibliography — probably the most complete listing available on information systems in support of decision processes.

Each chapter explains the domain's nature, existing frameworks, and taxonomies. This provides a useful introduction. But the most valuable part of each chapter is the discussion of research ideas, containing commentary on priorities for research and methods of research applying to each chapter's topic. Each chapter was prepared by separate committees; therefore, the chapters differ in organization and (somewhat) in depth of presentation. However, Stohr and Konsynski have enhanced the basic chapters, thereby providing consistency throughout.

I strongly recommend this sourcebook of ideas on (1) how information systems are being used to support decision processes, and (2) what research needs to be done to increase effectiveness. Software developers and scholarly practitioners analyzing and designing such systems will find it a valuable source of ideas and direction.

Gordon B. Davis

Preface

In the last decade, the use of computers has advanced from the province of relatively few technicians to a daily activity of literally millions of people. Over one half of the work force in a modern industrialized nation is engaged in information work. Computer and communication systems are directly changing the nature of these people's work and reshaping the business world. Among other things, we are witnessing the introduction of new ways of doing business that avoid traditional paper transactions, new market forms that link buyers and sellers worldwide 24 hours a day, "strategic" uses of information systems that provide a sustainable economic advantage to the firm, electronic messaging systems linking thousands of employees in dynamically changing information networks, voice response systems that replace traditional human interfaces, and expert systems that encapsulate human knowledge and experience and replace or supplement human experts.

The list of new information technologies is large and the list of potential applications even larger. Furthermore, we are driven by a technological imperative. Every three or four years, computer-based hardware becomes twice as powerful and half as costly. The technological pipe dreams of only a few years ago are feasible and economic today. Companies that fail to exploit the new technologies take a grave risk of losing out to their competitors. Moreover, we may only be in quite an early stage of the information age. New technologies, new and more powerful machines, and, more importantly, new ways of using the technology and new organizational structures in which traditional business processes are modified or even eliminated entirely, seem just around the corner.

Like all revolutions, however, the information revolution has its costs and casualties. Information work is eliminating whole categories of workers. Bookkeepers and engineering draftsmen, for example, are suffering the fate of the telephone operators of the last generation. What will happen to information workers when the emerging communication and imaging technologies that really seem to strike at the heart of the office work problem (rather than compound it, as traditional information systems may have done) become commonplace? Will layers of middle management disappear or will there be newer forms of information work, perhaps requiring higher levels of skill, that will keep the work force employed?

Information technology is also costly to implement. Many organizations, particularly those in information-intensive sectors such as the financial services, are spending up to 10 percent of their total revenues on information technology. There is a growing concern among top management that this money may not be spent wisely. Strategic applications of information technology are difficult to find, and all too often the gains are transitory because competitors are forced to emulate the new information-based products and services. To many executives it seems as if they are in a "damned if we do, damned if we don't" position in which the main concern shifts from competitive advantage to competitive disadvantage.

There can be no doubt that the information revolution will continue. The important management issues are how to develop organizations that are responsive to change and capable of using the technologies to the best advantage. But this is not easy. Information systems are complex; organizations are even more so. Introducing information technology necessarily means organizational change. But our knowledge of the interaction between technology and organizations is scant if it exists at all. Moreover, change is of the essence. Information systems researchers and management theorists face a moving target. Thousands of software developers are carrying out experiments, and the shape of the technology seems to be subject to some form of Darwinian evolution. The current debates about appropriate operating systems and information architectures will probably be resolved as much by trial and error as by careful design and experiment. Appropriate organizational forms and processes may evolve similarly.

Yet the role of the information systems researcher is to understand and guide this process of change, and to help management realize the benefits of technology and avoid unfruitful ventures to the extent that this is possible. This book attempts to help readers understand some of these research issues. It is the outcome of a process that lasted several years and sought inputs from roughly fifty leading researchers representing a broad spectrum of backgrounds. Briefly, the objective was to seek out promising directions for research on issues that can provide definite and lasting benefits to management.

A major objective of the Information Systems and Decision Processes (ISDP) effort was to elicit ideas from researchers in other fields. The field of information systems and the subfield of decision support systems (DSS), out of which many of the ideas in this book were born, involve both technical and managerial issues and are inherently multidisciplinary. Behavioral scientists, management scientists, social scientists, computer scientists, and cognitive scientists have all become interested in the applications of computers in organizations and the impact of information technology at the individual, group, industry, and national levels. The different approaches of these groups of scientists are important to a full understanding of information systems in organizations. A major aim of the ISDP project was to develop a dialogue between these different research groups and to attempt a synthesis of ideas from these different fields.

Our hope is that this book will be useful to everyone interested in research in the application of technology in organizations. Because of the multidisciplinary nature of the problem, we are particularly hopeful that researchers from fields other than MIS and DSS will find the research issues and framework developed in this book to be of interest. The research issues are rich and the problems diverse and important. We are convinced that the best way to make progress is to cross-fertilize ideas from many fields.

We are particularly hopeful that this book will be useful to people working toward or holding PhDs in computer science, information systems, and other management disciplines. Many suggestions and interesting research ideas are presented that should provide fruitful dissertation topics and, indeed, fruitful areas for whole research careers.

While we have tried to cover a broad area of research interests, we cannot hope to cover the whole field. It is inevitable and desirable that other researchers will find our approach and framework lacking in many respects. A good framework and interesting research directions will only evolve over time and will soon outwear their usefulness to be replaced by other ideas and research opportunities. That this process occurs with such inevitability and rapidity is part of the fascination and challenge of the information systems field. The framework in this book should at least provide a focus for discussion and experimentation over a limited period of time.

Information technology has enormous potential for changing our lives. The research topics posed in this book are therefore of great importance. We hope readers will be stimulated to work on some of the research themes presented, to write papers that augment and criticize our approach, and to join with us in helping to forge new directions of importance for the field.

Acknowledgments

The initial idea for this book surfaced at a meeting of the ISDP organizing committee in Hawaii at the HICSS Conference in January, 1987. Since then, a great deal of work has been done and many organizations and people have generously provided support.

First, we wish to express our gratitude for the financial support given to us by our sponsoring organizations, the TIMS/ORSA DSS-XX Surplus Committee, and the National Science Foundation. We also wish to thank the Pacific Research Institute for Information Systems and Management at the University of Hawaii for helping to finance interim meetings of ISDP members at several academic conferences, and the Center for the Management of Information Systems at the University of Arizona at Tucson for hosting our ISDP workshop and for allowing us to use the CMI meeting room facilities.

The following individuals deserve thanks for helping us organize the workshop: Eileen Dennis and Betty Albert, from the University of Arizona, for their administrative assistance and for managing local arrangements; Kendall Cliff and numerous PhD students, from the University of Arizona's Management Information Systems Department, for staffing the CMI room and providing general assistance at the conference; Carole Larson and Anne Seaton, from the Center for Research in Information Systems at New York University — and Dianne Shapiro, from Harvard Business School — for their administrative support. Our special thanks go to ISDP team members for their hard work, collegiality, and great ideas.

Finally, we wish to thank Doug Engelbart for serving as our keynote speaker, and all of our other guests for taking time out from their busy schedules to attend the workshop and provide us with their comments and suggestions. Their ideas and comments helped shape subsequent work by the ISDP teams and our overview. Truly, this book was a joint effort.

Edward A. Stohr and Benn Konsynski
July 7, 1992

Table of Contents

Introduction

Benn Konsynski and Ted Stohr

Origins and objectives of the ISDP project

The decision support systems (DSS) field has focused attention on some important issues in the application of information technology to decision making. First conceived in the early 1970s, decision support systems were a new class of information system intended for direct use by managers and their staffs. These systems incorporated analytic capabilities, database access, interactive interfaces, and reporting capabilities. They were designed to aid decision making in "semistructured" decision situations where it is not possible to provide preprogrammed solutions. By the mid-1970s, efforts to understand and to apply this new concept were under way, and reports of these efforts began to appear in the literature as DSS began to be developed and used in organizations. Today, DSS has become established in the mainstream of information systems research and practice.

Although considerable progress has been made, we feel that there is a need to develop new research directions and to focus on those problems and opportunities that have the most practical significance to organizations. We wish to identify critical issues that either haven't been addressed by past research or that are just emerging as new areas that need further investigation.

An opportunity to fund a multidisciplinary effort to explore research directions for DSS arose when the DSS-XX Surplus Committee indicated in 1986 that it would consider a proposal to fund a DSS workshop. A group of researchers that included all the present members of the ISDP Committee met at the Hawaii International Conference on System Sciences (HICSS) in January 1986 to develop a proposal for the workshop. This proposal was subsequently accepted by the DSS-XX Committee (which was headed at that time by Professor John Little of MIT). A companion proposal submitted to the National Science Foundation's Decision, Risk and Management Science Program, award no. 8722257, was also accepted.

The proposal called for a collaborative research effort involving DSS researchers in universities around the country as well as researchers in reference disciplines such as cognitive psychology and organizational behavior. To emphasize the idea that we wanted to break with the traditions of DSS, the project was called Information Systems and Decision Processes (ISDP).

The objectives were

1. To develop a program of collaborative, multidisciplinary research.
2. To discover the important opportunities and problem areas in the application of information systems to the decision-making process in organizations.
3. To raise the standards of intellectual debate and research in this area.

There were three main phases in the ISDP process:

1. Work over a period of approximately 12 to 18 months on specific research themes by interdisciplinary teams of researchers.
2. A workshop at which the teams exchanged information and ideas and to which eminent researchers from related disciplines were invited. These researchers acted as discussants for the team presentations and offered constructive criticism on the proposed research agendas.
3. A period of consolidation and reconstruction of the teams' work based on the inputs received at the workshop and subsequent written comments and suggestions from many of the participants.

The summary and conclusions of this work are contained in this book and in the many research papers produced by the teams, as noted more fully throughout the book.

ISDP teams and research themes

At the original meeting in Hawaii, ISDP research activities were organized into five areas. These areas and the members of the ISDP group who chaired the research teams were as follows:

• Behavioral and Normative Decision Theory (Joyce Elam)
• Group Decision Support Systems (Paul Gray)
• Organizational Decision Support Systems (Jay Nunamaker)
• Information Technology Support Environments (Ralph Sprague)
• Modeling and Model Management (Bob Blanning and Andy Whinston)

The research areas were not meant to cover all of the areas of interest to DSS research. However, they span a broad spectrum of DSS research activities and proved to be very fruitful areas for research (as we hope will be evident from later chapters).

Altogether, 42 researchers served on the research teams and contributed to the chapters in this book; an additional 16 researchers served as discussants at the workshop. These individuals are listed in the Acknowledgments. Each research team had the following objectives:

1. Characterize the relevant literature from more than one academic discipline.
2. Suggest significant research issues and relate them to real-world problems and opportunities.
3. Describe one or more programs of research to investigate the significant issues.
4. Present a paper for the book and receive feedback from the workshop participants.

We expected that there would be differences in the approaches taken by the teams and also that common themes and problems would emerge that would help us get a better conceptual understanding of the field. Both of these expectations were realized.

Each team met several times during the 12 months prior to the workshop (usually at academic conferences) to discuss their topic area and to organize their work. The research strategies followed by the teams varied from a tightly focused and organized small-team approach (Behavioral Decision Making and DSS) to a wide-ranging large-team approach (Organizational DSS). The four larger teams (other than Behavioral Decision Theory) decided to break into smaller groups (usually of two people) to study separate facets of their topic. Chapters 3 through 7 of this book contain summaries of the papers submitted by these teams.

ISDP workshop

The ISDP workshop, held at the University of Arizona, Tucson, October 5 to 7, 1989, was the culmination of several years of effort by the research teams. The workshop provided the first opportunity for team members to review their own work; it was also the first opportunity for them to see the work done by the other teams. In addition to the ISDP team members, we invited a number of leading researchers to comment on the work done by the teams and to suggest new directions for research. Douglas Engelbart, inventor among other things of windows and the mouse, gave an inspiring keynote speech.

The workshop was an interesting experience in its own right. Each team had a half day devoted to presentations by team members and discussion of results. All of the sessions were videotaped. The discussion involved two forms—traditional and electronic. The traditional discussion involved discussants for each team who gave short prepared statements followed by a period of open discussion.

Electronic meeting sessions

The electronic discussion involved the use of the electronic meeting facilities of the University of Arizona. There were 24 terminals in the room, allowing (roughly) one terminal for every two attendees. Doug Vogel from the University of Arizona acted as moderator. Each research team posed one or two research questions at the start of the electronic session for their team. These questions were displayed on the screens of participants, who then typed in their responses. The responses varied in length from one or two sentences to five- or six-line position statements. The participants were able to send their responses to the system at the push of a button and, in turn, were (randomly) sent some of the responses from other participants. All of the comments were anonymous. Several rounds of this electronic exchange occurred in sessions that typically lasted about half an hour. Two software modules were used to capture the ideas and positions of attendees: Brain Storming and Topic Commenter. (These techniques have been described elsewhere [Nunamaker et al., 1988].) The electronic discussions were recorded on diskettes that were distributed to the attendees at the end of the meeting.

To some extent, our use of the electronic meeting facilities was experimental, and it is therefore appropriate to say a few words here about our experience. About half of the participants had not been involved previously in an electronic meeting. Learning to use the system, however, was no problem—generally one or two minutes of explanation from the moderator was sufficient for each type of software. All of the participants used the system, some more diligently than others. While the electronic sessions were in progress, conversation was generally limited to the researchers at each terminal. Discussion took place through the electronic media and was treated seriously (notwithstanding several humorous comments). While the electronic discussion was generally focused on the issues at hand, some of the comments concerned the electronic meeting technology itself rather than the research question. Some participants felt concern at the apparent randomness and inconclusiveness of the process. Ideas and comments were suggested in a bewildering variety, and it was sometimes difficult to follow the train of thought of other researchers. Some participants were concerned that there was no time to integrate and synthesize the ideas from the electronic discussion in the time that we had available. (However, this was a problem generated by lack of time rather than being an inherent problem of the technology.)

On the positive side, we have no doubt that the electronic discussion was useful. For example, the total number of ideas that were generated by the participants at the conference for the one team that substituted a verbal discussion for the electronic session as a "control measure" was smaller than the number generated for the other teams, with no difference in quality as far as we could tell. Altogether, we were able to identify approximately 200 distinct ideas from the one and a half hours of electronic discussion at the conference. We were able to gather more ideas in a shorter space of time because, effectively, 24 voices were able to speak at once.

In summary, while traditional forms of discussion are more enjoyable and can be less confusing to participants, we believe from our experience at Tucson that electronic discussions can have real benefits.

Concluding phase and outputs of the ISDP process

The video tapes, the records of the electronic discussions, and subsequent written comments sent to us by the discussants and others provided a unique and diverse database, sometimes confusing but always interesting and challenging, from which to write the conclusions of this book. We are grateful to all of the participants for so freely giving their time and ideas. We have done our best to attribute these ideas correctly throughout the discussion in this book.

The final outputs from the ISDP process are as follows:

1. This book, which contains the papers contributed by each of the five research teams, together with our conclusions regarding new research directions in the field.
2. Papers produced by the team members and published in scholarly journals. We have tried to identify and reference these papers at relevant points in the text.

Finally, we hope that the research associations formed among members of the teams will continue in the future to make valuable contributions to the field. We also hope, after a suitable interval of time, to repeat this process, perhaps in a different form.

Overview of this book

The book is organized in three parts. Part I starts with a brief review of the current status of DSS research and practice as a way of providing background for readers who may not be familiar with the field. Chapter 2 provides a rationale for our focus on decision processes rather than decision support systems and provides a perspective for the rest of the book.

Part II (Chapters 3 through 7) is the heart of the book. These five chapters contain summaries of the work of each of the teams. Each chapter contains a brief overview of the research area, suggests significant research problems and relates them to real-world problems and opportunities, and provides many specific research suggestions. An appendix to each chapter summarizes the verbal and electronic discussion that occurred at the Tucson workshop. The discussion was both lively and useful. Many divergent views were represented and many issues that were raised remain unresolved. We state these viewpoints and issues as well as we can based on the extensive records that were kept from the workshop. They serve as a useful reminder that the work of the ISDP process is incomplete and that much remains to be done before we can obtain a clearer view of appropriate research directions.

Part III of the book presents our conclusions and proposals for future research. Chapter 8, "Research Challenges," describes a framework that places the work of the teams in a larger perspective, summarizes the major conclusions from the previous five chapters, and ends with a discussion of recommended research directions. While Chapter 8 is concerned with issues of substance (what should be done), Chapter 9 is concerned with how the work should be carried out. It starts with an overview of research methodologies and ends by making some specific suggestions for the ISDP research program.

The summary and discussion in Part III are based on our observations and a review of the record of the activities at the workshop, the revised submissions from the teams, and comments submitted by the discussants. Summarizing and drawing conclusions from this vast amount of material was a challenging and exciting research project in its own right. While we have done our best to find the common themes and to discover and describe issues that were raised—and not raised—during the ISDP process, there are enough diversity and richness in the material for other interpretations and conclusions.

Finally, we end this introduction with a call for further collaborative research along the lines of the ISDP effort. We have made a start in a difficult but exciting area for multidisciplinary research, but much remains to be done.

Chapter 1

Review and Critique of DSS

Benn R. Konsynski, Edward A. Stohr, and James V. McGee

This chapter provides a brief overview of the decision support systems field and places the ISDP project in historical perspective. The second section of the chapter is provided for readers who are unfamiliar with the field of DSS. In the space available, we cannot give a complete overview of the field. Instead, we describe the origins and objectives of the DSS field, discuss several significant areas of past and present research and reference some of the key literature. We overview the following: DSS definitions, classification schemes and frameworks, model management systems, artificial intelligence and DSS, development methodologies, user interface research, human information processing and decision aids, executive information systems, group decision support systems, organizational decision support systems, empirical evaluations of DSS performance, and DSS in practice.

In the third section we provide a critique of DSS research to date. We argue that although DSS has been relatively successful, there are now both the need and the means to broaden its scope and objectives. This need to revisit some of the basic principles that have governed DSS research was the primary motivation for the ISDP project.

Overview of research in decision support systems

Origins of DSS. The concept of decision support systems, or DSS, was born in the early 1970s and prospered through the 1970s and 1980s. It developed at the intersection of two trends. The first was a growing belief that existing information systems, despite their success in automating operating tasks in organizations, had failed to assist management in many higher level tasks. The second was a continuing improvement in computing hardware and software that made it possible to place meaningful computing power (powerful, usable, etc.) directly in the hands of managers and executives. DSS systems were meant to be decision focused, supportive of higher levels of management, adaptive, and user initiated and controlled. While not always fulfilling the dreams of their sponsors, DSS applications have burgeoned and the study of DSS has grown into an important and accepted subfield of information systems theory and practice.

Two seminal articles in the early 1970s defined DSS and have had a major influence on the field ever since. The first of the articles, "Models and Managers: The Concept of a Decision Calculus" [Little, 1970], had its roots in management science. It opened with the observation that "the big problem with management science models is that managers practically never use them." Little pointed out the difficulty of developing effective computer implementations of management science models and stressed the importance of the model interface. Moreover, he argued that the interface requirements had implications for the design of the model itself. He then described the concept of a "decision calculus" as a "model-based set of procedures for processing data and judgements to assist a manager in his decision-making." The requirements for such a system to be successful were that it be simple, robust, easy to control, adaptive, complete on important issues, and easy to communicate with [Little, 1970, p. B470]. Each of these requirements has been a recurring issue in the DSS field over the last 20 years.

The second of these articles, "A Framework for Management Information Systems," by Gorry and Scott Morton, defined the term "decision support system" and has been widely recognized as the foundation paper for the field [Gorry and Scott Morton, 1971]. Gorry and Scott Morton were motivated by the failure of management information systems (MIS) practitioners to understand the range of possible applications of computers in organizations. In particular, they argued that a greater proportion of MIS resources should be devoted to the development of systems to support "decision processes" in organizations. They felt not only that the technology (time-sharing systems and relatively cheap minicomputers) was available, but that enough was understood about how human beings solve problems and how to build models that capture aspects of the human decision-making process. Moreover, the authors felt that much greater payoffs were possible in this area.

Because this paper has had such an influence on the field, it is worth further explanation at this point. The Gorry and Scott Morton framework maps potential computer support for management activities on two dimensions (see Figure 1). Each axis in the figure represents a continuum rather than a discrete classification. The horizontal axis consists of Anthony's three levels of managerial activity: operational control, management control, and strategic planning [Anthony, 1965]. The vertical axis contains three classes of decision situation: structured, semistructured, and unstructured.

To understand the latter terms, we need to regress slightly. The structured and unstructured decision situations correspond roughly to Simon's "programmed" and "unprogrammed" decisions, respectively [Simon, 1960]. According to Simon, decisions are programmed to the

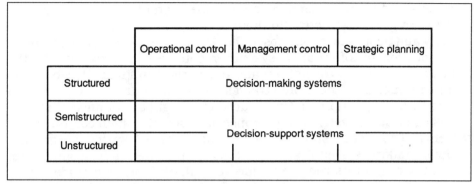

Figure 1. The Gorry and Scott Morton framework.

extent that a definite procedure can be worked out beforehand to be invoked whenever the decision situation occurs. Decisions are unprogrammed to the extent that they are novel and no cut-and-dried method for handling the problem exists, that they are important enough to warrant special treatment, or that the decision structure is elusive and complex. Programmed decision situations can be fully automated; in unprogrammed situations, the system must fall back on "whatever general capacity it has for intelligent, adaptive, problem-oriented action." Simon also proposed three phases of decision making: intelligence, design, and choice. Intelligence involves a search of the environment for conditions calling for a decision. Design involves the development and analysis of alternative courses of action. Choice involves a selection from the alternatives generated by the design activity.

Returning to the Gorry and Scott Morton framework, it is significant that they include human decision-makers in the loop with the computer system. Decision tasks could be divided between human decision-makers and a computer system in any number of ways. According to their definitions [Gorry and Scott Morton, 1971, p. 60], in a fully structured situation, all of the above three phases of decision making are structured and therefore potentially automatable. That is, we

> can specify algorithms, or decision rules, that will allow us to find the problem, design alternative solutions, and select the best solution. An example here might be the use of the classical economic order quantity (EOQ) formula on a straightforward inventory control problem. An unstructured problem is one in which none of the three phases is structured. Many job-shop scheduling problems are of this type.

Gorry and Scott Morton further define the semistructured case as one in which one or more of the design, intelligence, and choice stages are unstructured. Furthermore, they assert that the line between structured and unstructured decision situations moved over time as management scientists and users understood management problems better and were able to bring more structure to them.

Gorry and Scott Morton proposed that their framework be used to guide the allocation of information systems resources—in particular, in the situations shown on the bottom and to the right in Figure 1, which are more unstructured and more strategic, and where greater payoffs from systems that support management activities might be obtained. The term "decision support systems" was proposed to describe such computerized systems. The word "support" is key here. These systems were not decision-making systems (after all, the assumed decision situation was at least partially unstructured), nor were they simply to provide higher quality information from the use of models and databases. These systems were meant to improve the quality of the managerial decision process itself. They were to be an adjunct to decision-makers—to extend their capabilities but not to replace them.

Following these two articles, there was significant growth in the literature related to DSS during the 1970s and 1980s. Elam et al. review DSS research from 1975 to 1985 [Elam et al., 1987]. A number of books devoted to DSS [Scott Morton, 1971; Keen and Scott Morton, 1978; Alter, 1980; Bonczek et al., 1981; Sprague and Carlson, 1982; Bennett, 1983; Turban, 1988; Silver, 1991] have helped formalize and popularize the field. DSS is now accepted as a course within undergraduate and graduate business school programs and as a topic area at academic meetings throughout the world. DSS software is an important and growing component of the software industry. While many developments have taken place both in practice and in theory over the last 20 years, it is remarkable how well the central message of the above two papers has stood the test of time.

DSS definitions. A significant amount of soul searching has taken place regarding definitions of the DSS field. Two definitional issues have been especially pertinent. The first concerns the definition of "structuredness." The second issue has been the effort to distinguish DSS systems from other MIS applications or operations research models.

Several authors have defined the structured-unstructured dimension in a way somewhat different from Gorry and Scott Morton's approach. Rather than considering the unstructuredness of a task as a whole, the detailed decision-making activities associated with each of the three stages of decision making associated with the task can be assessed individually on a structured-unstructured dimension [Lerch and Mantei, 1984]. A number of authors have defined unstructuredness in terms of a traditional decision theory model: A decision situation is considered unstructured to the extent that objectives are difficult to determine or conflicting, the alternative actions that might be taken are hard to determine, and their effect on outcomes is uncertain [Stabell, 1979]. To some, computerized DSS are useful on the "structurable" part of a decision problem, while the (truly) unstructured part of a problem is that which, given current modeling and conceptual capabilities, must be left for resolution by the decision-maker or group of decision-makers using the DSS [Ginzberg and Stohr, 1981]. From a psychological viewpoint, it is supposed that the human memory contains strategies that can be brought to bear in such situations, but that these are not understood well enough to be susceptible to automation [Bonczek et al., 1981].

Turning to the second definitional question (characterizing DSS software), it is useful to consider three classes of software [Sprague, 1980]:

- DSS tools: The underlying technical building blocks (graphics packages, database management systems, and so on) for both the generators and applications [Sprague and Watson, 1989].
- DSS generator: A combination of hardware and software that facilitates the construction of DSS applications (Lotus 1-2-3 is a popular example).
- Specific DSS: A DSS application, the hardware and software system actually used by a decision-maker or group of decision-makers.

DSS generators and tools are relatively easy to recognize. The debate over the definition of DSS software focuses on how DSS applications can be recognized. Writers have offered a range of attributes as defining necessary characteristics of a DSS application. For example, according to various writers, a DSS application

- supports decision-makers rather than replaces them,
- is used in semistructured or unstructured decision situations,
- is focused on the effectiveness rather than the efficiency of decision processes,
- supports all phases of decision making,
- is interactive and easy to use,
- is controllable by the user,
- is used by managers and executives,
- uses data and/or models,
- is developed by an evolutionary design process, and
- facilitates learning.

In our view, only the first two attributes are required in a basic definition of a DSS. The other eight items may sometimes be characteristics of DSS but are by no means necessary attributes. However, the decision as to whether a particular software system is a DSS is largely a matter of judgment. Overviews of several DSS definition issues are available in the literature [Alter, 1980; Ginzberg and Stohr, 1981; Sprague and Watson, 1989].

DSS classification schemes and frameworks. Another aspect of DSS definitions concerns efforts to classify extant DSS applications. Two efforts will be mentioned here. Alter divides DSS software into seven types depending on the degree to which system outputs could directly determine the decision [Alter, 1977]. Three of these (file drawer, data analysis, and analysis information systems) are data-oriented, while another four (accounting models, representational models, optimization models, and suggestion models) are model-oriented.

Bonczek et al. also differentiate DSS systems on the basis of their data handling and modeling capabilities [Bonczek et al., 1981]. They focus on the nature of the language provided by the DSS to manipulate data and models, and the degree to which these languages are procedural. They define three levels of procedurality:

1. Procedural languages require users to specify how the data is to be obtained or how the model is to process information.
2. At an intermediate level, DSS can provide a means for users to provide parameters to prespecified data retrieval requests or prespecified models.
3. At the highest level of sophistication, nonprocedural languages require users to state only the information that is needed.

The concept of a nonprocedural model manipulation language is relatively unique to DSS, although a similar notion is common in research on systems development [Konsynski, 1986]. The idea is that users should be able to specify whatever they want from a DSS, regardless of whether that information exists in a data bank, must be computed by an existing model, or must be computed by an entirely new model constructed automatically using model components stored in the system. The goal of much research in model management systems (see next section) is to develop this last level of capability.

Along with the basic definitions, the research frameworks of a field provide insights into its worldview and aspirations. We now provide brief overviews of several well-known frameworks but leave a more comprehensive discussion of research frameworks to Chapter 8.

Sprague made an early attempt to extend the concepts of Scott Morton, Keen, and others to build a comprehensive framework for DSS [Sprague, 1980a, 1980b]. The major elements in this framework are technology levels, development approaches, the roles of users and builders of DSS, and performance objectives. Ariav and Ginzberg provide a "systemic" framework for DSS with five main components, as outlined in abbreviated form below [Ariav and Ginzberg, 1985]:

1. Environment
   Task characteristics (structurability, decision phase, operational level, functional area)

Access patterns (interaction mode, user community, relation to other systems)
2. Role
    Levels of support (e.g., retrieve data, run models)
    Decision range (generalized versus particularized)
    Supported process (e.g., cognitive support, learning, coordination, communication)
3. Functional components
    System functions: data, model, and dialogue management
    Division and specialization of labor
4. Arrangement of system components and links to environmental elements
5. System resources
    Hardware
    Software (DSS tools, generators, generalized DSS)
    People
    Data

Silver provides a third framework that concentrates on the effects a DSS has on its users [Silver, 1988]. The framework consists of three "tiers" corresponding to questions commonly asked by DSS users:

- Functionality: What can it do? (It runs an optimization algorithm to support scheduling decisions.)
- User view: What does it look like? (It has "operators" such as LOAD, SOLVE, and DISPLAY, and "navigational aids" such as context-sensitive help features that supply cognitive support to users.)
- Holistic attributes: How will it affect decision making? (For example, it restricts decision making to a fixed process or guides users in their selection of a decision process.)

Several other frameworks that take a systems architecture or systems development viewpoint will be mentioned below.

Model management systems. Database management systems are software tools that help programmers develop data-oriented applications and support ad hoc requests for information. In addition, they provide security functions, help maintain data integrity, and provide data dictionary and other data administration functions. The basic idea of a model management system is similar, as it performs all of the above functions for models plus other functions that are peculiar to models and the modeling process. Automatic model synthesis has already been mentioned [Blanning, 1984, 1987c; Liang, 1988c]. In addition, research has been performed for each of the phases of developing and using models: selection of appropriate models [Athey, 1989], formulation

[Raghunathan, 1987; Murphy and Stohr, 1986], performing sensitivity analyses [Blanning, 1979; Konsynski and Sprague, 1986], and interpreting results [Greenberg, 1987].

The term model management has always had a broad connotation in the sense that it is concerned with the total environment in which models are developed and used. This involves managing the data and user interaction as well as managing models per se. Thus, a framework for a model management software architecture that has been widely adopted consists of three subsystems for user interface management, database management, and model management [Sprague, 1980].

Blanning has developed a relational theory for model management [Blanning 1983]. Other recent developments include the use of techniques derived from the field of artificial intelligence [Dolk and Konsynski, 1984; Elam and Konsynski, 1987; Holsapple and Whinston, 1987b; Dhar, 1989; Krishnan, 1990] and attempts to model the user explicitly to aid in the learning and discovery process associated with DSS [Manheim, 1989].

Blanning provides a comprehensive review of the literature on model management [Blanning, 1990]. Model management was one of the five areas chosen for special study during the ISDP process (see Chapter 6).

DSS and artificial intelligence. The aspirations of artificial intelligence (AI) stand in an interesting relationship to those of DSS. The guiding objective of AI is to emulate human intelligence. For example, in the subfield of AI known as expert systems, the objective is to understand human expertise in some domain and codify it in a computer program [Hayes-Roth et al., 1983]. An expert system is most successful if it completely replaces human decision-makers. The fact that many expert systems support rather than replace decision-makers is an unfortunate fact of life to be explained by the complexity of the problem and our limited capabilities in building such systems. On the other hand, from its inception, DSS has recognized the need to support decision making in unstructured domains. It seeks to provide a helpful environment for exploration of a problem domain but allows its users to draw their own conclusions. Thus, an expert system may use concepts from DSS, and a DSS might contain an expert system component. Depending on the point of view, they are both examples of DSS systems or both examples of expert systems. Turban presents a comprehensive treatment of DSS and expert systems [Turban, 1988]. Henderson explores the relationship between DSS and expert systems research [Henderson, 1987].

Another important contribution of AI to DSS is that it provides sophisticated tools and concepts for building advanced software systems. AI approaches are extensively used in the field of model management (see Chapter 7). One theme suggested in Chapter 7 is a progression from model management to knowledge management in which models in the usual sense are just one of many types of knowledge.

DSS development methodologies. While user involvement is often advocated in other areas of information systems development and implementation, it has been considered of paramount importance to the success of the DSS development process. User involvement is more important in DSS because, by definition, DSS development involves "structuring" or "normative modeling" [Gerrity, 1971] of the decision process. Further, the use of DSS applications has been elective and, historically, focused on the decision processes of individual users. Generally, some form of prototyping or evolutionary development process has been proposed in which developers and users jointly learn the requirements of the model and develop the DSS [Keen, 1980; Moore and Chang, 1980; Sprague 1980].

Carlson and Sprague suggested a detailed DSS development methodology based on a model of users' decision processes [Carlson, 1979; Sprague and Carlson, 1982]. Their approach is intuitively appealing: Decision-makers use conceptualizations of the problem, different decision-making processes, various memory aids, and various conventions for controlling the overall process. Sprague and Carlson's ROMC methodology (ROMC stands for representations, operations, memory, and controls) involves matching each of these four elements with the most appropriate computer representations, processing operations (to support intelligence, design, and choice), automated memory aids, and controls for managing the interaction with the computer.

Stabell proposed an alternative "decision research approach" to DSS design [Stabell, 1983]. This involves the development of both a descriptive model (how the decision is currently made) and a normative model (how the decision should be made). The differences between the two models are then resolved during the design process.

A number of important contributions to DSS thought and practice have come from research into the link between individual or organizational objectives and information systems. While much of this research has been aimed at information systems in general (not just DSS), it has close links to DSS and has had an enormous impact on the field. Important here is the early work by Churchman [Churchman, 1971] on information systems as processes of inquiry and his emphasis on the dialectic approach (evolutionary thesis/counterthesis argumentation) as a method for determining system objectives. Continuing this work, Mason and Mitroff developed methods for "stakeholder analysis" and "assumption surfacing" that have had practical applications and influenced research in this area [Mason and Mitroff, 1981].

One of the most intuitively appealing and popular concepts in DSS design is that of critical success factors (CSFs) [Rockart, 1979b]. CSFs are those few factors on which individuals or organizations must concentrate if they are to achieve their objectives. CSFs differ from situation to situation and change over time. The CSF methodology involves determining the critical factors, choosing suitable measures, and developing information systems to report these measures to management.

The development process and the form of DSS produced by that process are closely linked to the purpose of the DSS. Some authors have asserted that a DSS must support learning [e.g., Keen, 1980], and to some this is the major benefit of a DSS. In any case, there is general agreement that DSS cause changes in decision processes (the alternative is that either they are not used or their results are ignored).

An interesting question arises as to whether designers should try to direct the change in decision processes or should simply provide the DSS as a tool to be used in whatever manner is thought most appropriate by the decision-maker [Stabell, 1983; Silver, 1990]. Most researchers, perhaps taking the middle "S" in DSS literally, seem to have accepted the latter "nondirected" approach. At least this seems to be what is meant by suggesting that DSS interaction should be controlled by the user. Silver presents the cases for both sides of this issue and describes two design strategies—system restrictiveness and decisional guidance—that allow designers to achieve either goal [Silver, 1990].

Ariav and Ginzberg present a framework for understanding and choosing between the different design approaches mentioned above [Ariav and Ginzberg, 1985]. While DSS design and development issues were not singled out as a separate area for research during the ISDP process, they are mentioned at several points in this book. Chapter 6 (on "Technology Environments to Support Decision Processes") has a section devoted to a proposed new design methodology.

User interfaces. Continuing developments in the technology of computer interfaces—such as windowing software, high-resolution screens, interactive graphics, voice recognition, and multimedia systems—have a major impact on the acceptance and effectiveness of DSS applications. A subfield of computer science, human factors, is concerned with the effective design of computer interfaces for a broad range of computer systems including DSS [Shneiderman, 1987]. While obviously relevant to DSS, it is, in general, more microscopic and clinical than DSS research in the area of computer interfaces.

A number of DSS researchers have investigated the effect of computer-generated graphics on management decision making. Much of this research concerns the relative effectiveness of graphical and tabular displays of information. In a comprehensive review of this literature, DeSanctis notes that the research results have been inconclusive [DeSanctis, 1984], with different studies finding advantages for graphical displays [e.g., Benbasat and Schroeder, 1977] or tabular displays [e.g.,

Lucas, 1981], or no significant differences [Dickson et al., 1986]. DeSanctis argues for a more detailed approach that accounts for the task situation, environment, and human information processing strategies (see also [Benbasat and Dexter, 1985; Remus, 1987; Jarvenpaa 1989]).

While the above results on the effectiveness of computer graphics in improving decision making are equivocal, there is evidence showing that graphics is effective as a presentation medium where the objective is either to inform or to persuade [Ives, 1982]. It is also apparent that graphical user interfaces (GUIs) are preferred by many people. Finally, mention should be made of the emerging area of visual interactive modeling (VIM), in which users interact with a graphic image of their problem and immediately see the results of their decisions on the computer screen. VIM applications originated in the area of computer simulation but have had wide application in many other areas. Turban and Carlson provide an overview and give the results of a survey showing that VIM enhances managerial involvement and understanding of the modeling process [Turban and Carlson, 1988].

In Chapter 6, "Technology Environments to Support Decision Processes," one of the ISDP teams takes a broad view of the technical and philosophical issues involved in supporting users as they attempt problem-solving and decision-making tasks. Interface issues—in particular, the close relationship between users and models—also figure prominently in the discussion on model management systems in Chapter 7 and at several other points in the book.

Human information processing and decision aids. Cognitive style research asserts that DSS design should reflect individual differences in the way that decision-makers gather and process information [Benbasat and Taylor, 1978]. For example, a DSS might provide only summary information to a person with a cognitive style that involves "preceptive" information gathering (looking at the whole picture rather than messing with details). Unfortunately, research seeking to show an advantage in matching DSS features to users' cognitive styles has not provided strong prescriptions for DSS design [Huber, 1983].

Although DSS is concerned with supporting decision making, there has been relatively little research by DSS researchers on the decision processes of individuals and the social interaction that takes place as groups make decisions. Apart from the foray mentioned above into cognitive style research, DSS researchers have generally accepted the Simon phases of decision making (intelligence, design, and choice) as providing an adequate model of decision making. Recently, however, there has been a realization that cognitive science and behavioral decision theory in particular have important implications for DSS design and use. Chapter 3 in this book explores these relationships in detail and develops a framework for research that borrows from both prior DSS research and the more process-oriented research of behavioral decision theory.

Generic decision aids (sometimes called cognitive aids) are aimed at improving the decision-making process itself, independent of any particular decision situation. Such decision aids can

- move the boundary between what is structured and unstructured by helping users discover and understand various components of their decision problem,
- suggest a sequence of human information processing steps that should be performed,
- help users manipulate intuitive and judgmental relationships, or
- extend human memory and computational capabilities.

Multiple-criteria decision-making techniques are examples of cognitive aids for situations in which the choice phase of decision making is unstructured because choices have to be made on the basis of multiple conflicting criteria [Keeney and Raiffa, 1976; Zionts and Wallenius, 1978; Saaty, 1980]. Johansen discusses cognitive support for groups [Johansen, 1989]. As another example, a relatively recent stream of DSS research is investigating the possibility of using software to enhance human creativity [Weber, 1986; Elam and Mead, 1990].

Executive information systems. The idea that top executives would use the computer to assist them in their control and decision-making tasks has been slow to be realized. Nowadays, however, executive information systems (EIS) are being introduced at an accelerating rate. The first papers describing EIS appeared in the late 1970s and early 1980s [Rockart, 1979a; Rockart and Treacy, 1982]. Currently, approximately one third of the largest firms in the US have installed EIS systems [Rockart and De Long 1988].

EIS generally obtain status information from the organization's MIS and external information from a number of information utilities that supply stock market data, economic data, and trade information. While EIS is generally considered a part of DSS, EIS systems often serve the same purpose intended for MIS systems. Thus, EIS differ from traditional DSS in that they are primarily used by managers for status reporting, whereas traditional DSS are more often used by analysts for modeling and what-if analysis.

There are probably two reasons for the current interest in EIS. First, modern technology makes these systems both more powerful and more palatable than the paper-based MIS of the 1960s and 1970s. Database and communications technology allows a much more comprehensive and immediate snapshot of the status of the organization and its environment, while the interface technology—pointing devices, high-quality graphics, and navigational aids such as hypertext—provides greater ease of use. The second factor influencing EIS use is the accelerating pace of business and the simultaneous need to make organizations more flexible by reducing layers of management [Huber, 1984a]. In this environment, information technology may play an important role in increasing management's span of control.

Group decision support systems (GDSS). Most DSS focus on a single user or group of users facing a single class of decision problem and support a single mode of decision making (e.g., interacting with a model). Over the last decade, however, there has been growing activity in the field of group DSS, which is concerned with the application of DSS technology to support group decision-making activities. Usually, GDSS are designed to be useful in multiple-decision situations (no specific model) but in a single mode of decision making (e.g., group meetings or computer conferencing).

The GDSS field builds on almost a half century of work by behavioral theorists who have studied small-group dynamics [Cartwright and Zander, 1968; Homans, 1950] and more specifically group decision-making behavior [Kelly and Thibaut, 1969; McGrath and Altman, 1966]. As in other areas of DSS, the presence of computer support obviously changes the nature and limits of unaided group work. GDSS researchers are beginning to focus on these issues [Huber, 1984b]. While the task of supporting group dynamics is obviously extremely complicated and there have been failures, GDSS systems have also had some success in real-world applications.

DeSanctis and Gallupe provide an overview of the field of group DSS. As discussed in their paper [DeSanctis and Gallupe, 1987], information technology can support groups in four different situations:

- meeting at the same time in the same place (e.g., in a decision room with electronic support),
- meeting simultaneously in time but separated in space (e.g., video conferencing),
- communicating over time in a single location (e.g., an office using a local area network), and
- communicating across time and space (e.g., computer conferencing and electronic mail).

The ISDP team that worked in the GDSS area focused on the first of these four areas—that is, on research aimed at supporting the decision processes of groups located in a single meeting room (see Chapter 5).

Computer support for collaborative work (CSCW) is another new label for research that focuses on building tools to help people work together [Olson, 1989]. It has its roots in office automation as well as social science. Obviously, CSCW intersects with GDSS. CSCW focuses on the use of computer-based connectivity to support coordination and collaboration of knowledge workers and to enhance the efficiency and effectiveness of knowledge work processes in general. On the other hand, GDSS tends to focus on processes that lead to management decisions.

Organizational decision support systems (ODSS). This is a relatively new research field. There are two interpretations of ODSS. The first interpretation is that ODSS are a subset of DSS designed to support decisions that are of organization-wide importance. In this view, ODSS consist of a communication infrastructure together with DSS, GDSS, and EIS systems designed to support top management. A broader view, and the one that will be adopted for the most part in this book, is that ODSS is a natural extension of research focus from individuals (traditional DSS), to groups (GDSS), to the organization as a whole.

There are, in turn, two aspects of this broader view of ODSS. The first recognizes the need to provide the technological infrastructure and management control systems to support the development and use of DSS of various types (corporate planning systems, functional area support systems, executive information systems, and GDSS) throughout the organization [Philippakis and Green, 1988]. This has the same flavor as current work in end user computing (EUC), which has as its object the study and support of all forms of computing by end users [Panko, 1988]. The second aspect of the broader view of ODSS is more normative in flavor. In this research, the objective is to link DSS and organizational design [Huber and McDaniel, 1986; Watson, 1990]. Research on intelligent organizations [Huber, 1990] and organizational learning [Argyris and Schon, 1978; Shrivasatave, 1983; Elofson and Konsynski, 1990] is also relevant to this view of DSS. Another view relevant to this discussion likens the modern organization to an "information refinery" [Clippinger and Konsynski, 1989].

The nature of ODSS and some possible research directions were investigated by one of the ISDP teams (see Chapter 4).

Empirical evaluation of DSS performance. There are two related questions. Does the use of a DSS improve the quality of the decisions produced? Are economic or other benefits attributable to the use of DSS? The first question is important because it addresses the explicit goal of DSS (namely, improving decision making) and because in many situations it is difficult to directly observe the economic benefits obtained from DSS use. However, for decision problems that are appropriate for DSS, it is difficult to determine the attributes of quality and probably even more difficult to measure them. (Decision problems that have unequivocal metrics for quality are best considered as structured problems, which by definition removes them from the domain of DSS.)

Early empirical evaluations of DSS emphasized field studies of working DSS [e.g., Alter, 1980]. Subsequent research has emphasized controlled experiments in laboratory settings. Experimental approaches to measuring the effect of DSS on decision quality usually involve a controlled experiment with two groups of subjects—one using the DSS and the other not. The effectiveness of the DSS is determined by "output measures" of the quality of the decisions made by the subjects. These measures are generally based either on the judgments of a panel of experts or on quantitative measures of performance in a computer simulation.

Sharda et al. review laboratory studies of DSS effectiveness based on computer simulations [Sharda et al., 1988]. Dependent variables included decision quality (e.g., higher profits in a game situation), time to make decisions, number of alternatives considered, and confidence in the decisions made. The results of these experiments are mixed but generally support the notion that decision aids can have positive effects on performance. Thus, six of the 12 studies reported in Sharda et al. showed that DSS users had higher profits in the gaming simulation, five studies showed no significant improvements, while only one study showed DSS users having a worse performance. Where reported, the results on other dependent variables were also mixed. Two studies, for example, showed that DSS users took longer to make decisions, and two studies showed no increase in confidence in the quality of the decisions as a result of using a DSS.

Benbasat and Nault review empirical research on managerial support systems (DSS, GDSS, and expert systems) and also report mixed results with regard to DSS effectiveness [Benbasat and Nault, 1990]. They draw attention to the need for theory that provides a better understanding of the relationship between decision support and performance.

Determining the effectiveness of DSS in real-world applications is also a difficult matter. Keen discusses problems with traditional quantitative cost-benefit analysis and recommends an approach based on first determining all of the ways in which a DSS can provide value to an organization, emphasizing qualitative factors such as improved decision making and learning [Keen, 1981]. Continued research on the determinants of DSS success is obviously much needed (see [Ginzberg, 1983]).

DSS in practice. If the number of applications is any indication, then DSS has been a great success. Initially, most DSS software was targeted at the financial area, particularly for corporate planning operations. These systems usually contained forecasting algorithms that helped to project financial statements. Over time, graphics capabilities and optimization subsystems were added. By 1976, it was reported that 73 percent of 1,881 corporations were using corporate planning models [Naylor, 1979]. While research interest in such systems may have faded in recent years, corporate planning and forecasting systems currently constitute about 50 percent of all DSS systems [Hogue and Watson, 1985].

Probably the most important events in the history of DSS applications were the advent of the personal computer in the early 1980s and, almost simultaneously, the introduction of VisiCalc, a new class of DSS generator based on the spreadsheet metaphor. To a large extent, the ensuing computer revolution was powered by the spreadsheet, especially Lotus 1-2-3. For the first time, end users could easily develop their own models, and it was surprising to see how diverse and innovative their applications were. By the end of the decade, there were 20 million PCs in daily use and untold numbers of DSS applications.

Eom and Lee survey DSS applications reported in scholarly journals from 1971 to 1988 [Eom and Lee, 1990]. The authors accepted papers as describing DSS applications if they included descriptions of the semistructured or unstructured decision supported, the data-dialogue model system, the human-computer interface, and the nature of the computer-based support for human judgment and intuitions. Using the ABI/INFORM database, they found 203 articles on DSS applications. They report, among other things, that most (past and current) applications are in the marketing, transportation, and logistics area, and that a very wide range of management science and statistical tools are imbedded in DSS. The articles in the survey are probably only representative of "leading edge" DSS (systems interesting enough to be accepted for publication). Nevertheless, they clearly demonstrate a very broad range of DSS types and applications.

Finally, as discussed above, over the last couple of years group decision rooms have come out of the laboratory and are now being built and used successfully by a number of organizations (see Chapter 5 for more details).

DSS: The need for new directions

Evaluation of the DSS field. The DSS movement has served to define an important area of research related to organizations and managerial decision making. The information technology revolution implicitly assumes that technology can benefit humans in organizations. With its focus on individual, group, and organizational decision-making processes, DSS should play a central role in this regard.

A second benefit has been that DSS research has attracted researchers from other disciplines such as management science, artificial intelligence, human factors, cognitive science, and organization theory. Each of these disciplines has something to say that is important to an understanding of the real and potential role of DSS in the enterprise. Conversely, DSS can serve as a focal point for multidisciplinary research on how information technology can be used to improve organizational processes.

In our opinion, DSS has made and will continue to make valuable research contributions. In any field, there are false starts as promising ideas turn out to be unimportant and hitherto neglected areas surface in their place. This is naturally true of DSS, which has both a difficult mission and is subject to enormous changes—from progress in technology and from changes in the environment of organizations.

Among the established DSS research areas outlined in the previous section, probably the most significant, distinctly DSS contributions have come from work in the following three areas: DSS design methodologies, model management, and group DSS. The first area, design methodologies, has given us new insights on how to align DSS with individual and organizational objectives and how to go about the implementation process. The philosophical debates and methodologies developed here have had a major impact on the broader arena of information systems thought and practice. The second area, model management, gives promise of a new class of software to support work processes in general (not just DSS). The third area, group DSS, involves the development of new technologies and the study of their impact on social processes within organizations—a direction that may have considerable importance for the future.

Need for a fresh approach to DSS. We began the section on the origins of DSS with Little's observation that managers rarely use management science models. This is certainly not true for DSS applications. Indeed, at least in the end user computing area, there are concerns that there may be too much indiscriminate and ill-informed use of decision models. We also believe that past DSS research has made some significant contributions. However, it is time for a new impetus in DSS. Technological advances make ever more sophisticated forms of computer support possible, while on the demand side the faster speed of business, internationalization, and competitive pressures are forcing a restructuring of markets and organizations that is entirely dependent on the successful use of computer and communication technologies.

To find new directions, it is often useful to look at the past. To date, DSS research and application have focused primarily on the following:

- The choice phase of decision making: There has been less research on developing systems to help in the intelligence or design phases.
- The DSS system and model rather than the processes actually used in organizations to make decisions.
- Support for individual decision making: Systems to support groups are a relatively recent phenomenon.
- Modeling and data analysis: The effort has been in trying to structure as much as possible of the decision problem. The unstructurable part

has been left unsupported. General problem-solving abilities (analogy, intuition, problem redefinition, and so on) have been largely neglected.
- "Hard" quantifiable information rather than "soft" qualitative information.

Running through the discussion at the ISDP workshop, and also much of the DSS criticism in the literature, is the feeling that the "decision focus" of DSS is too limiting. We believe that these researchers are finding fault with the "system is all" focus of much DSS research: the attempt to build a logical entity that, given inputs, will produce correct outputs, and through a process of sensitivity analysis, give valuable advice to managers.

In what ways is this limiting? First, these critics assert the importance of the user in the DSS dialogue. They call for models of the user that take into account intuition, motivation, cognitive limitations, and cognitive styles. Second, they point out the need to look at the DSS in its organizational context, emphasizing political and cultural issues that affect the success of the DSS in changing decision-making behavior and influencing the actions taken by the firm. Third, they point out that many decisions made by organizations may not be explained well by a "rational" model in which choices are made to maximize the likelihood of obtaining stated objectives. Rather, the actions taken by organizations can be the result of inertia or of fixed patterns of response that do not correspond to a rational analysis of payoffs in the usual sense. Alternatively, the actions taken by organizations can be the result of political processes—of bargaining between individuals and groups who are trying to maximize their own welfare rather than that of the organization as a whole. (Allison provides a fascinating analysis of the Cuban missile crisis from these three points of view: rational, organizational process, and political [Allison, 1971].) Finally, as if this list was not already long enough, the critics point out that actual decision processes involve many people over long periods of time and that decision making (choice) is only a small part of their total activities. These other activities include information gathering, communicating, coordinating, and the use of "soft" information such as rumors, legal opinions, trade reports, and news items. These activities are not well supported by traditional DSS.

The previous work in DSS with its emphasis on models and supporting individual managers and groups is still valid—but too limiting. The problem, we believe, is that this is a bottom-up approach. To respond to the above criticisms, we need a top-down approach so that the performance of the organization as a whole can be improved. To develop this new approach, we must break a mind-set that has been pervasive in DSS research and practice, and was implicit even in the work of Gorry and Scott Morton, John Little, and other pioneers of the DSS field. This is the focus on single DSS or single modes of decision making, rather than on multiple systems and multiple modes of decision making.

The single DSS paradigm is as follows:

1. Discover an important decision or class of decisions.
2. Determine the information needs of the decision-makers.
3. Construct a DSS model to support the decision-making process.

There is nothing inherently wrong with this approach; nor should it be abandoned. It is simply myopic. What we advocate is that it be seen as only one part of a much more integrating form of decision analysis. Decision processes in organizations are rarely susceptible to viewing through a single window (i.e., the model). Rather there may be several organizational processes involved, and many different forms of information needed by different individuals and groups over an extended period of time. There is the need for coordination and learning, for preparing for the decision-making process, for negotiation, and for following through in an implementation phase. In general, the single-model paradigm is less effective, the more strategic the decision, the more it affects many different people, and the more complex it is. In these situations, many forms of evidence, both "soft" and "hard," are likely to be gathered to help make (or justify) the decision.

Similar statements can be made about the preoccupation of much DSS research with a single mode of decision making. Most existing DSS focus on interaction between a model and one or more users. The implication is that the users will use the model, find a good solution to their problem, and make their decision. Most GDSS research also focuses on a single mode of decision making (a group in a meeting room), as does research in the area of collaborative systems (a group communicating via e-mail, or participating in a computer conference or in a video conference). While these forms of decision making are interesting and useful, there are many decisions that are not made using the above mechanisms, and many decision processes that involve combinations of these mechanisms with other more traditional forms of decision making.

We do not mean by the above that no decisions are made using single models or single modes of decision making. Our major concern is that there are other things going on in real decision processes that are not captured by this approach to DSS and that there are new opportunities to apply information technology, if only we knew what to do and how to go about it.

Why "Information Systems and Decision Processes"? We agree with the above criticisms of DSS. We also believe that we should, as Elam et al. assert in their "visions" paper [Elam et al., 1984], return to the original objectives of DSS with its focus on support of the decision processes of management. Here the important emphasis should be on the processes involved rather than the decision. This means looking realistically at decision processes in organizations and then searching for ways to support those processes most effectively. This is, as we shall explain in detail in the next chapter, much more than just covering all the phases of decision making or taking an inventory of decision-making types and tasks, and setting in motion streams of research and development aimed at supporting those tasks. It means taking a hard look at where management support needs are greatest—working from an organizational perspective. In our view, this does not mean only looking at important problems that are faced by the organization or organizations in general. It means also working on the infrastructure of organizations to change their ability to make decisions and to take actions. Note the parallel here with the current emphasis on redesigning or "reengineering" business processes [Davenport and Short, 1990; Hammer, 1990]. We believe that there is a parallel need to reengineer decision processes.

Chapter 2

Decision Processes: An Organizational View

Benn R. Konsynski and Edward A. Stohr

In this chapter, we present a concept of the decision processing view of the firm. The framework offers an alternative "lens" for understanding and evaluating alternative approaches to the support of decision making. It is important to note that agreement with the thesis of this chapter is not required to understand or appreciate the other ISDP work.

In the decision process view of the firm, the enterprise is viewed as a nexus of decisions. The enterprise exists to make decisions in a business environment, and is defined by its decision opportunities, authorities, responsibilities, and so on. In this view, decisions are the essence of the enterprise and help to define its boundaries, practices, and operations. Note that this view is independent of the nature of the decision-maker—which can be either a computer system or a human. Indeed, a key motivation for this approach is the quest for a paradigm that permits an understanding and explanation of both historical organizations and the new information-intensive organizations that are just now emerging.

A simple analogy may help illustrate our notion of a decision process. In the brain, a single neuron is connected by dendrites to dozens of other neurons. The neuron receives electrochemical signals from the dendrites. If a threshold level of stimulation is exceeded, it "fires," passing its messages to the other neurons to which it is connected. In our analogy, the neurons are decision-makers, the dendrites are information channels in an organization, and the binary choices to fire or not to fire represent decision choices. In our opinion, the decision-making view that has prevailed in DSS has concentrated on the firing or choice aspect and has considered only those incoming information streams that carry relatively structured, cognitive information. Other information sources that carry unstructured or noncognitive ("affective") information have been ignored, as have the consequences of the decision choice: the impacts on the organization and the actions that are taken as the result of the decision.

The decision process view that emerged from the ISDP workshop involves a holistic approach to the support of decision making. An organization consists of a complex man-machine system that reacts with its environment and is dynamically making decisions and performing actions. Not all of these organizational decisions and actions are the result of rational, analytic processes. Some human behavior consists of conditioned reflexes and unconscious acts, and the same is true of organizations. The decision process view is based on the idea that we can, to some extent, design the formal decision processes in an organization and support them using information technology. Furthermore, and perhaps just as importantly, we believe that we can help create an organizational environment and technical infrastructure that will support informal and ad hoc decision processes. This view is not new; it simply needs reassertion and active research. It was part of the original vision of DSS described in the last chapter, and, as discussed below, similar views have been espoused in the literature of management science, organization theory, and DSS itself.

First we review some of the assumptions implicit in much previous DSS research that have served to unduly narrow the field of inquiry. Then we list some alternative assumptions as a way of reinforcing our contention that a more encompassing worldview is necessary. We describe some concepts related to the role of decision processes in organizations that have appeared in previous research. We proceed to define some terms essential to a decision process perspective—decision, process, and decision process—and provide a more detailed discussion of the nature of decision processes. We discuss a number of research and design perspectives that are relevant to the development of research on decision processes. Then we step back from the details to develop a research framework that allows us to see the roles of the many different reference disciplines that are relevant to research on information systems and decision processes. We conclude the chapter with a brief summary and a short description of the contents of the remaining chapters in the book.

Toward a broader view of decision making

In Chapter 1, we discussed some limitations of the dominant DSS paradigm of the last decade. To be fair, many important problems were solved using this paradigm and, as a first approximation, the simple worldview of much previous DSS research is often justified. Nevertheless, there are important situations for which the DSS paradigm is inadequate. Moreover, it has constrained our thinking so that important aspects, perhaps the most important, of organizational life have not seriously been considered as contenders for support by information technology. For example, coordination and control processes are a neglected area of DSS research. These involve "placement" of resources in the proper location in space and time, or making sure that resources (human or otherwise) work together toward a common goal. From our point of view, coordination and control processes are simply a class of decision process that can be analyzed in terms of intelligence, design, and choice phases, as can any other decision process.

In summary, we believe that it is time for a broader view of decision making in organizations that includes the traditional view where appropriate but relaxes many restrictive assumptions and has more general applicability. This broader view is sketched in Table 1.

Scanning down the "Narrow View" column we see a perfectly "rationalist" view of the world. Again, the usefulness of this perspective should not be doubted: Many important real problems fit the rationalist mold, and the techniques of management science and DSS are routinely applied across a broad spectrum of activities with annual savings in many organizations that run into millions of dollars. Our argument is simply that new organizational forms and management practices, as well as emerging new technology capabilities, invite a review of these perceptions and a consideration of some of the factors shown in the right-hand column of the table. We have an opportunity to redesign organizations with a set of decision processes radically different from what would have been considered possible under the previously held assumptions about the nature of decisions.

A model of decision processes in organizations

The idea that decision making has a central role in organizations has its roots in work of the late 1950s and early 1960s [Simon, 1957; March and Simon, 1958; Cyert and March, 1963]. Simon stated the motivation for a decision process view when he observed that decision making in the postindustrial world was likely to be much more complex than in the past and that "decision making processes rather than the processes contributing immediately and directly to the production of the organization's final output will bulk larger and larger as the central activity in which the organization is engaged" [Simon, 1973]. Marshak and Radnor proposed an information economics view of the firm [Marshak and Radnor, 1972]. They placed information structure (who reports what to whom) and information value in decision making in a central role in determining the shape of organizations. More recently, Huber and McDaniel proposed a decision-making paradigm for organizational design [Huber and McDaniel, 1986]. They argued that environmental forces—increased speed, complexity, and turbulence—were placing a premium on the ability of organizations to make effective and timely decisions. Huber and McDaniel then proposed 10 organizational design guidelines based on the decision-making paradigm, some of which will be mentioned below. While we tend to place more emphasis on process aspects and are concerned with the analysis and design of decision processes at a finer level of detail, our decision process view of organizations is similar to the Huber and McDaniel view.

It is important to stress that we look at decision processes primarily as meaningful units of analysis. When we study a portfolio of decision processes and their relationship to organizational purpose and structure, we are at a macro level of analysis that is relevant to questions of organizational design. When we look at decision processes individually, we must consider their relationship to other decision processes in the organization, but we are working at a more micro level. This micro level of analysis extends that used in traditional DSS studies by including a broader range of decision phases, inputs, and outcomes.

Simon's statement at the beginning of this section contains an important distinction. Decision processes are not the same as production processes. This implies that a complete theory of organizational design must simultaneously be concerned with both categories of process. As our focus here is on decision processes, we will necessarily take an incomplete view of the total organizational design problem.

The relationship between decision and production processes constitutes an interesting research question. For our purposes, we will assume that decision processes in an organization exist to guide productive processes at two levels. At the higher level—in strategic analyses, capital budgeting, production planning, and controlling functions—decision processes are used to invent, design, analyze, specify, direct, monitor, and control production processes. At the lower level, decision processes are embedded in production processes, to provide intelligent coordination and control. Decision processes at both levels of analysis are executed either by a single human decision-maker, a computer system, or a complex combination of humans and machines acting within an organizational context involving patterns of communication, policies, standards, and cultural norms. Especially in the latter, multiperson, multimachine case, it is also fruitful to think of decision processes as being embedded recursively in other decision processes, as we will discuss below.

In order to understand the role of decision processes in organizations, we need to define the terms: decision situation, decision, process, and decision process. We will take a morphological view and examine the assumptions associated with each of these terms.

By *decision situation* we mean the occasion to make a *decision*, that is, to recognize choice, understand the situation, analyze options, assess implications of choice, select an action, and implement it. For our purposes, the presence of some or all of these factors is required to profile a decision situation. A *process* is a purposefully directed application of

Table 1. Toward a broader view of decision making.

Narrow View	Broader View
Single decision-maker	Multiple decision-makers
Single decision process	Multiple decision processes separated in place and time influence a single decision
Efficacy of computer models	Multiple influences on decision choice
Reliance on quantifiable information	Importance of qualitative, "soft" information
Reliance on rational factors	Importance of politics, cultural norms, and so on
Optimizing and efficiency as goal	Other criteria such as fairness, legitimacy, human relations, power enhancement
Decision-makers want the same goals as the organization	Sometimes, decision-makers want to further their own ends or are indifferent to organizational goals
Single goal for decision	Multiple conflicting goals
Choice is the major problem	Support is needed for other phases of decision processes such as intelligence, design, implementation
Decision situations are unique	Many decisions are repetitive; the ability to learn from past approaches to structured and unstructured decision situations is important
Decisions are made with some intent in mind	Some decisions are arbitrary, mindless, or capricious
Decision processes always result in decisions	Some decision processes are initiated to prepare for "potentially" needed decisions; others to ratify past decisions
Goals, possible actions, consequences of actions can be determined (the problem is structurable)	Problems are often unstructured

resources over a period of time. A *decision process* may be directed toward the attainment of a decision, it may be a response to a stimulus (e.g., a transaction), or it may be otherwise related to the performance of the business and management processes that characterize the organization. In the term decision process we combine ideas of *action for decision* and *decision for action*; that is, there is a continuity between the preparatory phases of decision making, across the point of choice, to the execution of the actions decided upon during the decision process. Collectively, these actions constitute the behavior of the firm. Thus, one might characterize an organization on the basis of its portfolio of decision processes.

This decision process view of the firm is not the same as the decision-making view of the firm. The decision process view focuses on the decision process as the unit of analysis for research and design rather than the decision or decision situation, as in the decision-making view. The old view of DSS supported and reflected the decision-making view of the firm. To our mind, the decision-making view is characterized by an overemphasis on the choice phase of decision making and an overemphasis on decision-makers and models in isolation from many of the ancillary activities and influences that bear upon decision outcomes in the real world.

Decomposition of tasks and decision processes. The tasks undertaken by an organization represent responses by the organization itself, or by groups and individuals within the organization, to perceived needs for action. These perceived needs arise as a response to external stimuli or come from within the organization as a result of formal or informal organizational objectives or of the political objectives of groups and individuals. The execution of each task involves a decision process life cycle that potentially involves phases of intelligence, design, choice, action, and feedback. The actions that result from decision choices are new tasks that again are associated with decision processes necessary for their execution. Tasks can also be decomposed on the basis of their innate structure. Thus, manufacturing tasks are broken down into job steps, and project-oriented tasks into separate activities. Each such subtask can again be decomposed into separate decision phases, according to its innate structure, and so on. This complex recursion extends into the detailed decision processes that go on inside machines or humans as they solve problems and execute actions.

While we think that this is a reasonable approximation of reality, it is tremendously complex. The analysis of decision processes is therefore carried on at different levels. At an organizational level, tasks are broken down only so far as needed for the allocation of responsibilities and authorities and to achieve coordination and control at a macro level. At the level of the individual decision unit (machine, human group, or individual) we reach a problem orientation, and the analysis may involve the use of the familiar tools of management science and decision support systems.

Decision process life cycle. Adopting decision processes as the objects of study implies an extension and refinement of the intelligence, design, and choice life cycle phases that characterize the decision-making paradigm. A suggested breakdown of life cycle phases is as follows:

- Scanning
- Interpretation and assessment
- Design
- Choice
- Ratification
- Implementation
- Feedback

Decision processes do not necessarily proceed linearly through the above phases but may repeat earlier phases in the light of new information. Note that each phase is potentially a separate decision process having different implications for automated or nonautomated support. The usual intelligence phase of decision making is broken down into the two phases of *scanning* and *interpretation and assessment.* Scanning involves search that may be directed or undirected. The interpretation and assessment phase involves judgment applied to the results of historical analyses, threat assessment studies, and so on.

Having achieved an assessment of the environmental situation in the scanning and interpretation phases, experience and values are applied in the *design* phase to determine possible options and alternatives and to develop criteria for choice.

The *choice* phase involves the selection of the actions to be taken according to some process of argumentation. The process of argumentation may involve modeling, group discussion, or even flipping a coin.

Ratification involves the attainment of consensus or authority in acceptance of the choice.

The *implementation* phase involves the determination of the means and mechanisms for and consequences of implementing selected actions. Implementation also involves execution of the action via a separate decision process that provides a control and coordination function.

The *feedback* phase involves the evaluation of consequences of decisions and the determination of the quality of the process. Evaluation and feedback are common means of attaining continuous improvement in production processes but have been notably absent with respect to decision making—apart from "bottom-line" financial measures that provide feedback on the effectiveness of the totality of decision processes in the organization. One of the implications of a decision process view is that the quality of the decision process itself, as well as the desirability of outcomes, is of interest. Feedback is needed even for unstructured, once-only decision situations, so that successful and unsuccessful strategies for problem solution can be recorded and analyzed for possible use in future situations.

The above list of life cycle phases appears ordered and logical, but in practice, especially in fuzzy, unstructured situations, decision making may best be described as "muddling through." Some of the above phases may be trivial and ignored. The decision process may not proceed sequentially but may involve looping back to previous phases. The life cycle may not be completed—for example, there are many "potential decision" situations that involve preparation for a decision that never has to be made. Alternatively, decision-makers may ignore the initial life cycle phases and use preconceptions of the problem that is to be solved, the actions that are viable, and the criteria to be used in the choice phase.

Classes of decision process. Table 1 indicates the range of decision situations that have and have not been tackled in an organized way by prior research. An alternative list of attributes that can help characterize types of decision process is as follows:

Repetitive	versus	Nonrepetitive
Routine/structured		Nonroutine/unstructured
Potential		Definitely occurring
Organized/formal		Ad hoc/informal
Major importance		Minor importance
Time-critical		Non-time-critical
Efficiency goal		Social/political goal

Other important considerations include the following:
Phase of decision making
Organization, group, or individual centered
Functional area involved
Management task (planning, coordinating, controlling, etc.)

Space does not permit detailed discussion of each of the above dimensions. Suffice it to say that they may all be relevant to the selection of the decision process that should be designed and implemented in a given situation. For example, we know that to handle highly important "bet the business" decisions organizations use decision processes entirely different from those they use for more mundane decisions. We also know that entirely different decision processes are involved when political issues are important. For example, a voting or election process may be used to make the decision, or the issue might be resolved by debate according to Robert's Rules of Order or some other protocol that ensures fairness and due process. Each form of decision process requires information, and some may warrant more computer support than others. Our point is that they should all be part of the portfolio of design issues for ISDP research.

The fact that there are potentially so many different types of decision processes, many of which have not previously been the subject of intensive investigation by information systems researchers, offers many research opportunities. It also represents a challenge. We need to understand these processes better and determine the forms of support that are possible in each case. Alternatively and preferably, it is possible that research will reveal a small number of basic categories of decision processes that can be developed and then adapted or modified for special cases.

There are a number of key questions. How should the organization be designed to handle a given mixture of decision process types? How should each type of decision process be organized? What kind of information technology support can be provided? Some research and design approaches are discussed in the next section.

Decision process research and design perspectives

Too often we focus on tools to improve the decision processes that currently exist in organizations. DSS should be viewed as an opportunity to redesign the business process, not "speed up the mess." Given the information technology that is available today, we have a unique opportunity to restructure and redesign the decision processes in organizations. In this section, we discuss several perspectives on the design of decision processes that we believe are important considerations for research in this area.

Causal mechanisms. Given that decision processes are a useful unit of analysis, there are various ways in which they can be investigated, depending on the purpose of the analysis: description, understanding, design, or evaluation.

In his well-known account of the Cuban missile crisis, Allison showed that organizational decision making can be interpreted from a number of different standpoints [Allison, 1971]. He named three: a rational actor model, an organizational process model, and a political model. In the rational actor model, the behaviors of organizations are seen as purposeful acts that result from the pursuit of explicit goals by individuals or groups. The organizational process model attributes behavior to bureaucratic forces responding to stimuli in terms of patterned responses. The political model views organizational behavior as the result of bargaining or power plays by different groups within the organization, each pursuing its own ends. Each of these explanations of behavior seems plausible.

From the point of view of the design of decision processes, they have very different implications. The rational actor model is familiar ground for most DSS designers. The other two viewpoints offer interesting research challenges. To the extent that these causal mechanisms are valid in general, or in a specific organization, they must be considered in the design of decision processes.

A second perspective on causality involves a debate about whether information technology is a primary determinant of organizational behavior and structure or whether managerial and human considerations shape the technology to fit whatever organizational goals and structure are desired. To resolve this debate, Markus and Robey propose an "emergent view" in which the outcome of information technology introduction in organizations is jointly determined by technological and organizational factors [Markus and Robey, 1988]. This emergent viewpoint seems most relevant to our conception of decision processes as interacting man-machine systems.

Evaluation of decision processes. The design and evaluation perspectives on decision processes are closely linked by the view taken with respect to means and ends. Quinn and Rohrbaugh developed a "spatial model" of organizational effectiveness consisting of three value dimensions [Quinn and Rohrbaugh, 1983]. The first dimension is related to organizational focus—from an internal, micro emphasis on the wellbeing and development of people to a macro emphasis on external measures of organizational performance. The second dimension is related to organizational structure—from an emphasis on stability to an emphasis on flexibility. These two dimensions create four quadrants in a two-dimensional space in which four organizational models can be placed, each of which is associated with a particular set of means and ends (the third dimension). The following is a summary:

Human Resources Model (internal, flexibility emphasis)
    Ends: Human resource development
    Means: Cohesion, morale

Internal Process Model (internal, control emphasis)
    Ends: Stability, control
    Means: Information management, communication

Rational Goal Model (external, control emphasis)
    Ends: Productivity, efficiency
    Means: Planning, goal setting

Human Resources Model (external, flexibility emphasis)
    Ends: Growth, resource acquisition
    Means: Flexibility, readiness

Table 2. Information sources and decision processing technologies.

Information Sources	Decision Processing Technologies
Human contact	Informal meetings
News media	Formal meetings
Library	Votes and elections
Paper files	E-mail
Computer files	Computer conferencing
On-line financial/market data	Video conferencing
Database	Management information systems (MIS)
Model base	Executive information systems (EIS)
Knowledge base	Decision support systems (DSS)
	Group decision support systems (GDSS)
	Groupware (coordination support)
	Management science models
	Statistical tools
	Expert systems

Quinn et al. used these same dimensions to develop a slightly different set of means-ends models for the evaluation of group decision processes and suggested two measurement criteria for each of the four perspectives [Quinn et al., 1985].

No doubt other viewpoints on causal mechanisms and evaluation criteria are possible and insightful. Our point here is that the explicit recognition of competing values and dimensions should be taken into account in research on decision processes.

Assembling the information and processing technologies. In Table 2, we look at the firm as a machine for processing information to produce decisions. The information inputs considered go beyond computerized data and include all sorts of soft information that is usually conveyed by word of mouth or in written text. The various processing technologies available to the firm are shown on the right of the table with their position determined roughly by the kinds of information they process.

Table 2 illustrates the rich range of information types and information processing mechanisms that are available to the firm. A single decision process may make use of many sources of information and many processing technologies in the course of its execution. Rumors at a trade show may trigger the process (intelligence), information may be gathered from the organization's library, a database may be developed, informal meetings may be held to organize the decision process, a model may be built and analyzed, and finally the major decision may be made using a GDSS facility and approved and ratified by senior management.

The design of decision processes in this extended (multi-information source, multiprocessing system) sense has been intuitive and informal in most organizations to date. As technological alternatives proliferate and prove themselves to be of value, we believe that there is a need to investigate how these processing subsystems fit within the organization. Also, there is a need to design organizations to make the processing systems efficient and to understand how they can be combined in a given decision situation so that a phased multidimensional process for developing and executing the decision can be developed.

Information and decision networks. There has been much work in the MIS literature on the design of efficient systems to support the processing activities of the firm. Of course, these processing activities involve decision making—sometimes routine and sometimes, as in systems to support strategic planning, anything but routine. However, there has been relatively little emphasis in the MIS literature on the decision-making process per se, that is, on structuring decisions and providing decision-makers with the information they need when they need it. Furthermore, there has been almost no attention to anything but coded information that can be processed in standard computer files. On the other hand, in the DSS literature, there has been a great deal of work centered around the design of models to support decisions and very little work on the analysis and design of the processes and communication channels that influence the decision and perhaps even make the decision regardless of the advice of the model.

One of the great strengths of the critical success factors idea [Rockart, 1979b] is that it combines both decision and information aspects. It focuses attention on the few critical issues that matter to the executive and directs attention to the information needs for those decisions. However, it has little to say about how supporting processes should be organized and how noncomputerized information aspects should be accounted for.

Hansen et al. proposed an interesting semiautomated approach to the design of decision processing systems [Hansen et al., 1979]. They develop the components of an "information-decision net" for an organizational subsystem by interviewing managers and focusing on their decision needs. They then input a list of decisions and corresponding information elements into a graph-based algorithm that sorts the information and produces a properly sequenced and layered information systems design for later implementation. As an interesting sidelight, they observed that "few managers or staff members were able to specify decisions and information requirements beyond those decisions made by themselves and the immediate information used in those decisions." While this is not surprising in one sense, it does seem curious that more attention is not paid to an integrated view of decision needs in organizations.

Location of decision authorities. Organizations consist of decision-makers linked by formal and informal communication channels to each other and the outside world. These decision-makers (human or otherwise) perform decision processes with varying degrees of authority and responsibility. The emerging information technologies allow us to reconsider where judgment and decision making are located, both within and across organizations. How should managers decide the appropriate locations for decision making? This question was simpler in the past when skilled people were the performers of all cognitive tasks (thinking, judgment, assessment, action selection, etc.). Now, machines can perform some cognitive tasks and empower novices to perform other tasks that hitherto required trained individuals.

In addition to the machine-versus-human dimension, decision authority can be placed at different points on a centralization-versus-decentralization dimension and on a specialization-versus-nonspecialization dimension. According to Huber and McDaniel, decision-making authority should be assigned to the hierarchical level that minimizes the combined costs of lack of information about (a) the problem situation and (b) the organization's overall situation and policies [Huber and McDaniel, 1986]. Further, it is important to foster and retain special expertise in the decision-making domain.

Information and decision processing capacity. Decisions are influenced by information that comes from internal and external sources and by the collective knowledge of individual decision-makers and the organization. According to information-oriented organization design paradigms, managing the information supplied to decision-makers is a key to organization structure. Galbraith suggests guidelines that reduce the need for information (creation of organization slack and design of tasks to reduce coordination requirements) and increase the organization's capacity to process information (vertical information systems and lateral communications) [Galbraith, 1974]. A key concept has also been the need to use information to reduce equivocality (uncertainty) [Weick, 1979; Marshak and Radnor, 1971]. The information systems area has a major responsibility to understand these issues and to address the problems of information overload that plague management by using techniques of information filtering, compression, and text understanding.

Another issue of major concern to the design of decision processes is the question of information sharing, both within decision processes and across decision processes. Networked organizations provide the opportunity for unlimited sharing of information, but little is known about the extent to which such sharing can and should be encouraged. Finally, as information becomes cheap and ubiquitous, knowledge becomes the key resource of organizations. Knowledge representation and transfer (learning) also presents a major opportunity for information systems research.

The role of models. Models, both mental and computerized, constitute an organization's vision of reality and define its capabilities. There is a great need to understand the role of models in organizations. We need to improve our ability to build, manage, and interpret models. Furthermore, we need to know when computer models are appropriate within the various phases of the decision process life cycle. Finally and most importantly, we need to understand how models, when relevant, can be "plugged in" to organizational decision making. Too often, modeling takes place but decision making is unaffected—key decision-makers completely bypass the modeling activity or are unimpressed by it. One of the hopes in changing the focus of DSS analysis and research toward a decision process viewpoint is that models can be seen in better perspective and used more effectively. As suggested by Little, we need to develop a new academic area that might be called "modeling science" [Little, 1986].

Implications of the decision process view. We believe that the decision process view broadens the scope of research and analysis in a way that is relevant to the realities of decision making in organizations. Included in the analysis are

- all the processes in an organization that influence decision outcomes,
- all phases of the decision process life cycle,
- all forms of information from soft to hard,
- all forms of processing from face-to-face meetings to computer models, and
- all kinds of decision processes from essentially rational processes to highly political processes.

Decision and performance (the execution of actions that are derived from decision) define the organizational entity. A decision process view of the firm offers an approach to analysis of strategic, managerial, operational, and administrative activities performed by the organization and its partners and competitors. The paradigm offers a context for the examination of a broad spectrum of issues: social, political, organizational, and technical.

A framework for research on decision processes

In this section, we outline a framework for research on information systems and decision processes. As discussed in Chapter 1, one of the

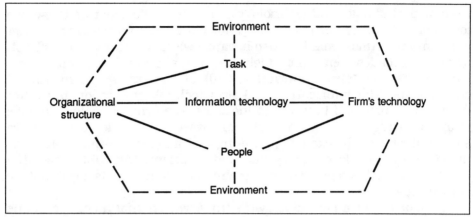

Figure 1. Modified Leavitt model.

key ideas underlying the ISDP research program was to develop multidisciplinary approaches to research. The objective of the research framework developed in this section is to show how the many different disciplines relevant to ISDP can be seen as contributing to a common goal.

The framework is loosely based on two established organizational models. The first of these is Leavitt's depiction of organizational elements and their interconnections [Leavitt, 1964]. Extending and elaborating on this scheme provides us with a static view of the relationships between information technology, its management, and the organization. Further, we identify a number of factors that are important in organizational design and therefore in information systems design. The second established model on which we base our framework is Marshak and Radnor's economics-of-information theory [Marshak and Radnor, 1972] and its extension to agency theory [Jensen and Meckling, 1973; Gurbaxani and Whang, 1991]. This provides a classical decision-theoretic orientation to our framework from which we derive an objective function and some of the dynamic elements of our model.

We use the resulting framework in a loose, nonmathematical manner, to show how various streams of research relate to each other and to the overall objective of information systems design. The framework also helps identify a range of research issues. We stress, however, that the research issues thus generated arise primarily from the *inadequacy* of the formal model in coping with the enormous complexity of real organizations. Looked at in this way, the framework helps articulate many elements required in a comprehensive theory of information systems design. However, more research is needed both on the relationships between the design elements and on the design elements themselves. The suggested research topics are discussed more fully in the final chapters of the book.

In Figure 1, we reproduce the Leavitt framework with an additional "information technology" component shown as a separate entity rather than as part of a general technology component. We separate these two forms of technology partly because information technology is the center of attention in this book, but also because we view information technology in its broadest sense (i.e., including formal and informal communications) as the "glue" that relates all of the other organizational components. The information and firm technology components differ from firm to firm and industry to industry. The firm technology may be manufacturing-based, transportation-based, or service-oriented. In some industries—for example, banking and insurance—the basic technology of the firm is primarily information-oriented, in which case the information technology and firm technology components need not be shown separately.

An important idea behind Leavitt's framework is that a change in one of the five components of the organization, or in the environment of the firm, will necessarily imply changes in the other organizational components.

In Table 3, we further subdivide the components of the model to show a list of factors that are important to decision processes in organizations and that therefore impact the way that information technology can be brought to bear. Note that at least in the long run most of the elements in the list are partially controllable.

The list in Table 3 is not meant to be exhaustive. Nor is the placement of some of the items beyond criticism. One difficulty arises because some items such as roles and responsibilities are better described as attributes of relationships between entities rather than entities in their own right. For example, a person's role and responsibility in an organization are largely the result of an assignment relationship between people and organizational structure. Note that different classification criteria are used within each of the six classes of entity.

The framework so far is primarily static. We know that a change in any one of the six entity classes necessitates a change in the others, but we need descriptive and normative theories to help us describe and prescribe the nature of these interactions. Moreover, we need a framework in which we can provide some guidance for developing these theories. We limit ourselves to the information technology component and its relationships with the other components. However, the organizational structure and information technology components are particularly tightly bound together. At some future point, information systems design will simply be viewed as an integral part of organization design. When this occurs, we will no longer need to talk about the problems of aligning the information architecture and objectives with those of the organization.

The information economics model relates the six elements in the static framework at a high level of abstraction. While the model is usually expressed mathematically, it is preferable here to describe it verbally and to use mathematical symbolism only as a shorthand for expressing the

Table 3. Elaboration of static framework.

Organization Structure
    Formal organization structure (hierarchy, teams)
    Corporate roles, responsibilities
    Corporate goals, strategy, policies
    Informal communication structure, culture
    Formal and informal decision processing mechanisms

People
    Inventory of employees
    Intrinsic factors: Age, education, knowledge, technical skills,
      managerial skills, leadership skills, personality types,
      cognitive styles
    Motivational factors: Personal objectives, utilities
    Interpersonal factors: Corporate political affiliations, friends,
      alliances, influence
    Extrinsic factors: Roles, responsibilities, position in organization

Tasks
    Management categories: Scanning, planning, organizing,
      motivating, monitoring, controlling
    Repetitive activities, nonrepetitive activities
    Individual level: Learning, communicating, deciding, performing

Technology
    Physical asset structure: Land, buildings, plant, and equipment
    Financial asset structure
    Geographic distribution of resources

Information Technology
    Databases, storage devices
    Computational capabilities, software
    Communication capabilities, networks
    Knowledge bases
    Information architecture

Environment
    National and global economy
    Customers, suppliers, competitors
    Products, substitutes
    Technological innovation

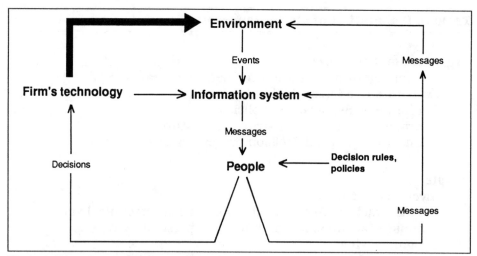

Figure 2. Dynamics of decision processes.

main relationships. We will also extend it beyond a level where it would be tractable either to formulate it or to solve it in any mathematical sense. We are interested only in the general relationships it depicts. Figure 2 shows the dynamics relating the elements of the static framework and will serve to introduce our modified version of the economics-of-information model. Organization structure is not depicted in Figure 2; however, it is embodied in the relationships within and between the other elements.

In the economics-of-information model, the notion of an organization is characterized by the existence of a number of decision-makers, each with different external and internal information sources, computational and communication capabilities, expertise, organizational roles, and decision-making authority. The decision-makers receive information from the environment and communicate information to each other and to the external world. On the basis of this information, the decision-makers make decisions according to decision rules that may or may not be explicit and formally defined. This man-machine decision system operates over time. Events occur, communication actions are performed, and decisions are made. These decisions translate into actions (some of which may be communication actions and others actions in the more traditional sense). In the aggregate and over the course of time, the actions that are taken determine the fate of the firm.

The task of organization (and information systems) design is to

- determine a suitable set of objectives for the organization;
- invest appropriately in human, physical, and technological resources; and

- develop a suitable organizational structure that consists of roles, decision authorities, informal and formal communication channels, information flows, and decision rules.

Thus, the economics-of-information model casts the information system design problem within the context of organizational design. In some trivial cases, Marshak and Radnor were able to formulate and provide optimal solutions for this organizational design problem, showing, for example, how "centralized" and "decentralized" designs compared over a range of cost and uncertainty measures [Marshak and Radnor, 1972].

Symbolically, our version of the information systems design model is as follows:

$$V(d, i) = \sum_{x \in X} u\, (d\, (i\, (x),\, c\, (i,\, x),\, x))\; p\, (x) \tag{1}$$

$$U = \max_{i \in I} W(i) = \max_{d \in D} V\, (d,\, i) \tag{2}$$

For simplicity, we ignore the element of time and do not show any indices reflecting the multiperson nature of the problem.

$V(d,i)$ is the expected utility of information system i, used in conjunction with decision rule d. $W(i)$ is the expected utility of i using the best decision rule for i. U is the expected utility for the firm in which the "organizational design" problem of jointly choosing an information system and a set of decision rules is solved optimally. Note that the problem is decomposed in the sense that the conditionally best decision rule for a given information system can be chosen for each choice of information system. To simplify the model, we have followed the usual convention of identifying actions with decisions.

Our use of this model is quite limited. We want to emphasize that it is mathematically intractable in any but the most trivial situation. Nevertheless, we feel that it can serve as a framework to relate research issues in information systems in general and information systems and decision processes in particular. We support this claim by describing the elements individually and mentioning the research disciplines that have been concerned with each of them. Table 3 and Figures 1 and 2 serve as a frame of reference for the discussion.

X represents the set of all possible "states of the world" x, where each x is sufficiently detailed to determine the consequences that result from a decision. Note that the state of the world includes human, economic, and physical factors both within and outside the organization and potentially extends to a description of any or all of the elements in Table 3. The probability $p(x)$ that x will occur is included in the model to express the uncertainty that pervades real-world situations.

I is the set of all possible information systems *i*, where each *i* represents a specification of actual and potential, formal and informal, information flows to and from each decision-maker. An information system design theoretically covers all the hardware and software elements for the information systems component listed in Table 3, plus a description of who communicates with whom and the rules or protocol for that communication. The content, accuracy, and timing of messages, as well as the computer interfaces provided for the decision-makers, are part of the information systems specification. However, the information *i*(*x*) conveyed in state of the world *x* will usually be subject to uncertainty and distortion. Thus, the message *i*(*x*) delivered by the information may depend only probabilistically (rather than functionally) on *x*.

D is the set of all possible decision rules *d*, where each *d* contains the response of each and every decision-maker or group of decision-makers to the information *i*(*x*) he, she, or they receive from the information system in state of the world *x*. Note that there are components of *d* and *i* for each decision-maker at each point of time. Also, *d* can be partitioned on the basis of the various decision classification schemes shown in Table 3 (i.e., into subsets of components that are routine, nonroutine, etc.).

The cost of information system *i* is denoted by *c*(*i*,*x*) and is assumed to depend on the state of the world that occurs.

The function *u* measures the worth of the information systems design. This depends on the action taken given that a decision is made according to the chosen decision rule, the cost of the information system, and the actual state of the world that occurs. We have shown *u* with no subscripts to indicate the possibility that the organization can devise a single set of objectives to be attained by the information system and can evaluate the alternative designs with respect to this objective. In practice, this is unlikely to be the case. There are likely to be many different sets of objectives that differ from person to person and group to group in the organization. We will return to this point shortly in our discussion of agency theory.

Note that one way of defining "unstructuredness" is to observe that a decision problem is unstructured for a given decision-maker in a given decision-making situation if any one of the components in Equations 1 and 2 cannot be specified fully.

We now indicate three possible extensions of the above model in the interests of greater realism. First, we can include elements of human information processing and organizational implementation by relaxing the assumptions that information translates directly to decisions and that decisions are equivalent to actions. We restate Equation 1 as follows:

$$V(d,\ i,\ a,\ m) = \sum_{x \in X} u\ (a\ (d\ (m\ (i\ (x)),\ x)),\ c\ (i,\ x),\ x) p\ (x) \qquad \textbf{(3)}$$

Here the mental model function m reflects the idea that individuals translate the information signal $i(x)$ into an image of the real-world situation; then, a decision is made on the basis of this image. Next, the action function a maps decisions $d(m(i(x)))$ into actions in the real world; this is a way of stating that the organization may misinterpret or only partially implement decisions.

Second, we should recognize the possibility of learning and adaptation by noting that the information component contains memory in the form of human memory, conventional libraries, and computerized databases and knowledge bases. Specifying components of the decision function d that are aimed at improving these "knowledge" components may be the most effective way of achieving the optimization in Equation 2. Furthermore, some of the most important components of d are concerned with adding new decision components or tasks for execution in later periods.

Finally, we should extend the model to capture motivational and behavioral issues that are not explicit in the model as stated so far. Agency theory [Jensen and Meckling, 1973] attempts this extension. It is assumed that information technology is valuable to the extent that it influences the behavior of decision agents. In Equation 3 this behavior is represented by the term $a(d(m(i(x))))$. However, each decision-maker (or agent) will have his, her, or its own utility function, giving rise to problems of goal congruence. The function u should therefore be modified to reflect a divergence of interests among the decision-makers. Agency theory is concerned with the provision of positive and negative incentives and monitoring systems to motivate the decision agents to operate in a way that is consistent with the overall interests of the firm.

Most information systems (IS) research can be viewed as an attempt to understand the various components of this model and to provide theories, methodologies, and tools that can help organizations improve and organize these components. The relationships between some of the elements in the model and various research streams and subdisciplines involved in ISDP research is sketched in Table 4.

Review and foreword to the rest of the book

In this chapter we have presented our interpretation of the decision process view that emerged from the ISDP workshop. Fundamentally, we accept the basic premise that the processes by which decisions are made, rather than specific decision models or decision situations, are the appropriate unit of analysis. Given that focus, we tried to explore its ramifications. We feel that the emergent decision process view frees the DSS field from several limiting assumptions and opens up rich opportunities for research. It helps relate DSS research to organizational design issues and indicates a broader range of decision activities that might be supported. In the last section, we developed the outlines of a framework

Table 4. Relationship of model components to several IS research streams.

Model Component	Associated Disciplines, Techniques, or Theories
States of the world, $x \in X$	Intelligence activities, forecasting, brainstorming, scenario generation, creativity theory
Probability function, $p(x)$	Forecasting, subjective probability theory, cognitive bias theory
Information systems, $i \in I$	Hardware and software research and development, systems analysis and design, database theory, expert systems, communications
Mental model, $m(i(x))$	Human factors, behavioral decision theory, cognitive science
Decision rules, $d(m)$	Decision theory, optimization theory, simulation, standards, organizational policies, motivation theory
Action function, $a(d)$	Leadership theory, project management and control techniques, MIS reporting
Cost function, $c(i,x)$	Cost-benefit analysis, software metrics, function points, capital budget theory
Utility function, u	Preference theory, stakeholder analyses, critical success factors, agency theory

for ISDP research which attempts to relate the various subfields of information systems research. Whether or not these views of the world have significant advantages over other research approaches remains to be seen. In any case, we hope that they provide some useful background for the remainder of the book, which contains the main output of the ISDP research program.

The next chapter, "Behavioral Decision Theory and DSS," is concerned with the decision processes of individuals. The chapter provides a summary of what is currently known about human decision-making processes and suggests a comprehensive program of interdisciplinary research. Following that, Chapter 4, "Group Decision Support Systems," provides an in-depth discussion of the decision processes of groups when they are supported in meetings by software which helps them perform brainstorming, issue analysis, and other group activities that have hitherto received little or no support from information technology. Chapter 5, "Organizational Decision Support Systems," offers a multifaceted look at the emerging area of systems to support individuals and groups in an organizational context. Essentially, Chapter 5 provides an exploration of some of the organizational issues raised in this chapter. Chapter 6, "Technology Environments to Support Decision Processes," is concerned with the technical and philosophical issues involved in providing an organization-wide infrastructure to support decision processes. The viewpoint developed in that chapter supports an emergent view of the role of technology in organizations in the sense that the support systems environment is seen to be the result of human and social forces as well as technology per se. Chapter 7, "Model Management Systems," addresses another infrastructure question, namely, how model management systems can be developed and extended in capabilities. The chapter describes ways of linking human and machine decision processing more closely through advanced interfaces and artificial intelligence techniques. It also suggests that knowledge management, rather than model management, is a more general goal and that, under this view, models are simply bundles of knowledge of a particular kind.

These chapters contain a wealth of information on the specific topic areas chosen by the teams as well as hundreds of specific research suggestions. Each chapter concludes with a summary of the discussion period and electronic meeting session for each team.

The final two chapters of the book provide our summary and conclusions from the ISDP project. Chapter 8, "Research Challenges," develops the research framework in this chapter in more detail and suggests some major research themes based on the research challenges as we see them. Finally, Chapter 9, "Research Approaches in ISDP," deals with the "how" of a multidisciplinary research program on information systems and decision processes.

Chapter 3

Behavioral Decision Theory and DSS: New Opportunities for Collaborative Research

Joyce J. Elam, Sirkka L. Jarvenpaa, and David A. Schkade

A major goal of decision support systems (DSS) research has been to develop guidelines for designing and implementing systems to support decision making. These research efforts have been strongly influenced by the traditions of management science which hold that, for any decision situation, there is a normative model that prescribes the "best" approach. We know that under a variety of situations individuals do not act in accordance with these models. Thus the goal of a DSS becomes one of moving a decision-maker from his current "nonrational" process toward this normative goal. Embedded in the tradition of management science is the assumption that a properly designed and implemented DSS will lead to positive outcomes: improved insights, better understanding of the problem domain, and better problem-solving strategies. In fact, much of the DSS work has been driven by an almost religious belief that the decision-making situation would be improved with the introduction of computer-based, managerially oriented systems.

However, the validity of this assumption has yet to be proved. Some studies have demonstrated that a DSS leads to increased decision quality; others have shown just the opposite [Sharda et al., 1988]. In order to gain some insights into why these inconsistencies exist, there is increasing interest in DSS researchers to understand the decision-making behavior that unfolds as individuals use a DSS. Such an understanding is needed to move DSS research to a more advanced stage [Todd and Benbasat, 1987].

Thus, a new promising area of DSS research lies in the study of the ways in which individual decision-making behavior affects or is affected by a DSS. It is through an analysis of the user-DSS interaction in decision choice and judgment that we can begin to understand the fundamental cognitive and decision processes at work. This area has also been identified by other researchers as a potentially high-payoff research opportunity [Little, 1986].

The theoretical and methodological foundations for this new research direction come from the psychological study of decision making. Behavioral decision-making (BDM) research will undoubtedly contribute to the successful development of this area, since BDM researchers study or model the processes of decision making. It seems likely that theories of decision making could contribute to or guide the development of DSS. However, there is some interesting decision-making behavior occurring in the workplace that psychologists are not studying. This is the decision-making behavior that occurs as an individual uses a computer-based system to accomplish what previously was done intuitively and without any decision aids. It is very likely that the use of information technology as an intervention into decision processes may well uncover or illuminate important aspects of BDM phenomena already under study or identify new and unstudied BDM phenomena.

For these reasons, the DSS and BDM groups should benefit from the work of each other, and in addition might benefit from collaboration. Since DSS researchers are studying a more constrained set of phenomena, we might expect that the general theories developed by BDM researchers could be improved on. This could mean either modification or adaptation of existing theories, or development of new theories along lines different from those previously developed in behavioral decision making.

The purpose of this chapter is to explore how behavioral decision-making research and research into the effects of DSS on decision-making behavior can be brought closer together. We first briefly recount the distinct histories of BDM and DSS to identify the historical similarities and differences that provide the context in which the proposed collaboration must develop. Second, we propose and describe two broad categories of research that bring these two fields together. Finally, we conclude by illustrating sample programs of research that follow the proposed approaches and by discussing some important issues in carrying out this research.

Background

While the fields of DSS and BDM have some common roots, their paths have seldom crossed. DSS is the younger field (begun in 1971), but BDM is also still relatively young (begun in the 1950s) compared with other branches of psychology and economics.

In order to identify a new research agenda that draws on both fields, we first review the historical development of each field and highlight differences between DSS and BDM research. By understanding these differences, we are in a much better position to identify where the possible synergies between the two fields exist.

Historical development of DSS research. In their seminal book *Decision Support Systems*, Keen and Scott Morton acknowledged that the concept of DSS had evolved from the "behavioral school of management" [Keen and Scott Morton, 1978], that is, from the work of Simon and his colleagues on individual cognitive decision processes such as bounded rationality and human information processing [Cyert and March, 1963; March and Simon, 1958; Simon, 1978, 1979]. Keen and Scott Morton argued that "Decision support requires a behavioral and descriptive grounding. The emphasis is on meshing description—how are decisions made?—and prescription—where can computer technology be applied to improve how they are made?" Their emphasis on supporting the decision-maker called for a general understanding of decision-makers' behavior. This, according to Keen and Scott Morton, was needed to identify the biases and inconsistencies in the process so that the designer knows what kind of support tools to devise to alleviate the problems and deficiencies associated with the limited capacity of human information processing.

After Scott Morton's 1971 work [Scott Morton, 1971], no empirical work evaluating the impact of DSS on the decision processes was, however, published until the late 1980s [e.g., Elam and Mead, 1990; Jarvenpaa, 1989; Todd and Benbasat, 1991]. In the late 1970s and early 1980s, the work on DSS was largely conceptual, but theoretical. A number of architectural models and classification schemes were proposed for decision support systems and decision support applications [e.g., Sprague, 1980; Alter, 1977; Blanning, 1979]. Systems were being built in industry, and case reports of their functionality and usage emerged in the literature [e.g., Carlson et al., 1977; Alter, 1980; Wagner, 1981]. In the 1980s, a small number of field tests [e.g., Edelman, 1981] and laboratory tests of DSS [e.g., Benbasat and Dexter, 1982; McIntyre, 1982; Aldag and Power, 1986; Goslar et al., 1986; Cats-Baril and Huber, 1987; Sharda et al., 1988] were published. According to Benbasat and Nault's review of empirical DSS literature [Benbasat and Nault, 1988], the work fell into three types:

- the impact of the representation format,
- decision making with a DSS versus without one, and
- evaluation of DSS features.

The research slowly improved in its methodological rigor [e.g., Jarvenpaa et al., 1985] and in its theoretical orientation [e.g., Jarvenpaa, 1989]. Some recent research [e.g., Dos Santos and Bariff, 1988] has been aimed at determining optimal DSS design parameters from the human-factors perspective. Still, after 20 years of DSS research, we can only conclude that we still do not have robust design principles for constructing and evaluating decision support systems.

Historical development of behavioral decision-making research. Behavioral decision-making research finds its roots in three distinct yet related streams of research [Kahneman et al., 1982]:

- the comparison of clinical and statistical prediction [Meehl, 1954; Lichtenstein and Slovic, 1971; Dawes and Corrigan, 1974];
- the study of subjective probability in the Bayesian paradigm [Edwards, 1954, 1961; Lichtenstein and Slovic, 1971]; and
- the investigation of cognitive heuristics as adaptations to limited cognitive capacity [Simon, 1957; Newell and Simon, 1972].

The first two streams used models of idealized decision-makers as baselines against which to compare the behavior of human decision-makers, using any systematic deviations as cues to underlying mental processes. The third stream attempted to understand these processes more directly by building models (especially computer models) of the processes as they were observed, rather than through inferences drawn from deviations of idealized models.

BDM research has identified a wide variety of conditions under which decision-makers have been shown to deviate systematically from the behavior prescribed by normative models of rationality [Kahneman et al., 1982; Payne, 1982]. To account for these biases, decision researchers posited heuristics or information processing strategies that allow decision-makers to cope with a complex environment, despite their limited cognitive capacity. The challenge for BDM researchers was to construct a theory of a process that led to biases (e.g., preference reversal) and to see whether the theory generalized to other domains. This emphasis still prevails in BDM research today.

The field of behavioral decision-making theory also attracted several groups of researchers interested primarily in particular applied domains. Social psychologists, for example, studied jury decisions [e.g., Hastie et al., 1983], and auditors and accountants studied audit and lending decisions. Consumer behavior testing of general psychological theories of decision making also gained momentum. Both consumer choice and behavioral accounting researchers differed from decision researchers by restricting themselves to particular contexts—consumers in the first case and largely auditors or loan officers in the second case. Additionally, these two subfields differentiated themselves from behavioral decision-making researchers by emphasizing certain aspects of decision making. Consumer behavior researchers focused on the role of information search, both from external sources such as product labels or from internal human memory, more than decision researchers [Bettman, 1979; Jacoby and Hoyer, 1989]. Behavioral accountants stressed probabilistic judgment rather than choice processes.

In the 1980s, behavioral decision-making researchers at large broadened their research questions from choice behavior to include concerns related to evaluation, decision framing, agenda setting, generation of alternatives, environmental scanning, and so on [e.g., Payne, 1982; Levin et al., 1985]. The emphasis on purely cognitive mechanisms has decreased. Theories now include affective and social factors. For example, study of consumer decision making has found that mood states can have an impact on judgments and choices. More importantly, these states can be altered or influenced by very small changes in the physical environment [Jacoby and Hoyer, 1989]. Consumer researchers have also become concerned with the role of motivation and the decision heuristics used in low- versus high-involvement decisions.

The behavioral decision-making field has also enriched its methodological basis. Several process-tracing methodologies—including verbal protocols [Ericsson and Simon, 1984], eye movement fixations [Russo, 1978], and manual [Payne, 1976] or computer-based information display boards [Johnson and Payne, 1985]—were developed and are heavily used to obtain more detailed and dense data on psychological processes. More and more studies are conducted that use several of these methods. After 20 years of behavioral decision research, the field has demonstrated that individual decision making is much more complex than originally anticipated. Relatively minor subtleties in a decision situation can cause major changes in decision behavior.

Differences in research traditions

As a result of their separate evolutions, the fields of DSS and BDM interpret decision-making ideas differently and consequently pursue different research objectives using different methods. We will next review some of these differences.

Past empirical DSS research (with the few exceptions noted above) has studied the effects of DSS on decision outcomes with little attention to the intervening processes that account for those effects. Hence, the emphasis has been on demonstrating the existence of effects on decision outcomes such as time and profit performance [e.g., Sharda et al., 1988], not on theoretical decision models that can explain the existence of effects. On the other hand, since the mid-1970s behavioral decision researchers have emphasized the psychological explanations of behavior observed. Outcomes of a particular decision have been secondary to understanding the mechanisms leading to the outcome. Also, where DSS has concerned itself with process, it has usually been in terms of executing and actually performing functions [e.g., Elam and Mead,

1990], rather than how a decision-maker structures the process and decides "how to decide" (i.e., meta-decisions) [e.g., Johnson and Payne, 1985].

While DSS researchers have focused relatively uniformly on management or public policy decision making, behavioral decision researchers have studied individual decision behavior in a variety of domains or contexts such as consumer behavior, auditing, medical diagnosis, military tactics, jury decision making, industrial process control, parole decision making, and taxpayer decision making. DSS researchers' limited focus on management and administrative contexts is perhaps related to the desire to address particular external constituencies. Behavioral decision researchers, on the other hand, have generally been more concerned with internal validity than with the external validity demanded by particular external constituencies.

DSS researchers and behavioral decision researchers have differed sharply in the importance attached to individual and task factors in understanding decision behavior. Decision researchers have generally ignored individual differences, while focusing on the task environment and its interactions with characteristics of the human cognitive system that are assumed to be largely invariant across individuals (e.g., limited short-term memory). Psychological theories of decision making have thus put great emphasis on analyzing the specific details of the task environment, especially the structure (e.g., complexity) and representation (e.g., response mode, information presentation format) of the task. This concern for analyzable tasks has led decision researchers to use relatively well-structured settings. Where individual factors have been studied in decision research, they have generally been related to knowledge or expertise rather than personality traits.

DSS researchers, on the other hand, have played lip service to the subtleties of the task environment, while giving considerable attention to individual differences. Zmud stated that "Of the numerous factors believed to influence MIS success, the area of individual differences [especially cognitive style] has by far been the most extensively studied" [Zmud, 1979]. Unfortunately, this research was fraught with conceptual and methodological problems [Huber, 1983]. Jarvenpaa et al. argued that much of DSS research is plagued by poorly defined and analyzed tasks: "Investigators are not able to determine what subjects are actually responding to in the experimental setting... Many results (or alternatively, non-results) are...random error which are 'artifacts' of an experimental exercise" [Jarvenpaa et al., 1985]. Also, DSS researchers have generally used less structured task environments than behavioral decision researchers.

While BDM researchers have emphasized the effects of tasks on decision processes, the emphasis in DSS has been on DSS availability and model features [Benbasat and Nault, 1988]. Unfortunately, this technology focus has not led to common technology paradigms for researchers. First, each DSS researcher has developed his or her own technology environment, which has led to a set of incomparable, noncumulative studies. Second, DSS technology has been a moving target in studies. The readers and reviewers have demanded that the latest DSS technology be used. Rapid technological progress has made a paradigm based on DSS technology impractical to construct, even for those who have attempted to do so [e.g., Jenkins, 1983]. Benbasat and Nault characterized DSS research to date as having attracted much research interest with little result [Benbasat and Nault, 1988]. In contrast, the great concern for differences in experimental results due to the structural characteristics of tasks has led BDM researchers to conduct much more programmatic research than we have seen in the DSS arena.

DSS research has tended to be prescriptive, while BDM research has tended to be descriptive. Although the basis for the design recommendations from DSS research has sometimes included normative considerations (e.g., statistical decision theory, game theory), the emphasis has been on identifying approaches and techniques that are effective in practice. This lack of descriptive studies of actual decision behavior using a DSS is somewhat surprising, given the widely held view that DSS should augment rather than replace a decision-maker. Keen and Scott Morton and Sprague argued explicitly that to design effective decision support systems we need to first understand the process of decision making [Keen and Scott Morton, 1978; Sprague, 1980].

Attempts to develop DSS theories have generally been limited to the testing of theories borrowed from other fields, such as the theory of creativity from social psychology [Elam and Mead, 1990] or the expectancy theory from industrial psychology [DeSanctis, 1983]. BDM researchers first documented interesting patterns of data and then generated explanations or models to account for them [e.g., Kahneman and Tversky, 1979]. Hence, BDM researchers have emphasized theory building, whereas DSS researchers, at best, have tested general psychological or management theories with little concern for building DSS-specific theories.

The two fields also conceptualize "decision support" very differently. For DSS researchers, decision support is a decision support system that is an input to the decision-making process. Decision researchers, on the other hand, conceptualize decision support as an outcome of decision making using a DSS or other aid.

The differences between the DSS and behavioral decision-making fields are summarized in Table 1. Because of these differences, decision researchers and DSS researchers can benefit greatly from considering the alternate perspective. There are also many areas of decision-making activity where interests overlap, and it seems appropriate to ask whether the present separation is in the best interests of the two fields. The next section discusses possible points of contact.

Table 1. Differences between DSS and BDM research.

DSS Research	BDM Research
Input-output	Process
Decision quality	Decision strategy
Concern for realism	Concern for internal validity
Concern for individual	Lack of concern for individual differences
Little concern for task analysis	Great concern for task
Prescriptive	Descriptive
Theory testing	Theory development
DSS is an input to a decision process	DSS is a consequence of using a DSS

Linking DSS and BDM research

What should researchers do to capitalize on the potential synergies between these fields? Both fields are interested in the effects of information technology (IT) on other variables rather than the effects of other variables on IT. Information technology can be thought of as *given* (i.e., prespecified by the environment) or *designed* (i.e., engineered toward a particular goal). These two perspectives direct us to two research approaches that integrate DSS and BDM concerns:

1. The way in which existing IT affects decision behavior.
2. How IT can be designed to improve decision behavior.

Information technology as a cause of decision-making phenomena: IT → DM. Information technology has advanced at a dizzying pace since the invention of the computer some 40 years ago. No sooner has a given technology begun to settle in and gain acceptance (e.g., simple word processors) than a new and more advanced development is offered as a replacement (e.g., desktop publishing). For example, it is hard for most of us to imagine a world without personal computers and associated networks, despite the fact that the first widely available PCs were introduced scarcely 10 years ago as stand-alones (and those models have already joined the dinosaurs as museum pieces). Further, those early PCs, like the workstations and dedicated processors that preceded them, were used primarily by highly educated and technically sophisticated users (e.g., engineers and computer scientists), and were a mere curiosity to the general public.

The market for information technology has changed considerably since then. The test for whether an innovation should be introduced to the public has become a market test, rather than a measure of our understanding of the implications of the introduction. More and more computing capacity is being placed at the disposal of less and less sophisticated users (in a relative sense). Consequently, thousands of undocumented "natural experiments" are being carried out every day by the designers and suppliers of information technology. This first category of opportunities focuses on research that begins by studying and documenting the effects of already existing technologies on decision making.

Although all IT applications were ostensibly developed as solutions to some kind of problem, there are inevitably unforeseen (and unintended) side effects. For example, people now think less carefully before running another complex statistical analysis (e.g., ANOVA) because it is so easy and inexpensive to do. Before computers were available it took weeks of work by an army of research assistants just to calculate one simple ANOVA. Clearly, the advent of mainframes that allow easy execution of ANOVAs has affected decisions about analyzing data. The question might reasonably be raised whether the progress of science is really better off with more ANOVAs that are less carefully thought through than with fewer more carefully considered ANOVAs. Similar arguments have been raised about word processors. For example, since it is now so easy to generate rough drafts that look like finished documents, writers begin concerning themselves with the appearance of a manuscript much earlier in the process. This may well interfere with the creative process.

More generally, the effects of IT could provide a rich source of new and interesting decision-making phenomena. Specifically, from a decision-making perspective, IT can change the structure of a task in significant ways. For example, hypermedia have now made possible quick connections between a variety of things that were only loosely connected before (e.g., sound, text, graphics). How do decision-makers go about deciding which media to use and in what sequence or combination? How does this changed task structure affect behavior? Unfortunately, to date such questions have not been addressed by BDM researchers.

Essentially, this style of research takes IT as it occurs, and attempts to develop models that account for its behavioral consequences. The best information technologies to choose for study are those that are currently (or soon will be) in use in real organizations. These are the information technologies for which descriptions and explanations of their effects are of greatest practical interest. After selecting a technology, a researcher describes the systematic effects of the technology on decision behavior. This involves the identification and documentation of the observable empirical regularities in behavior ("stylized facts") that result from the use of the technology. These facts serve as a simplified characterization of the basic phenomenon that can be used as an input to the theory-building process. A wide variety of both process and performance variables should be included in the search for these facts, to increase the richness and depth of the description. Besides studying the usual measures of task performance, other "outputs" of technology use such as decision time, mental effort, interaction patterns, satisfaction, learning, and transfer of learning should be captured [Payne et al., 1978; Todd and Benbasat, 1987]. For example, in describing the use of Lotus 1-2-3, observations should be obtained on variables such as the average depth and breadth of option use, pattern of keystrokes, and amount of "what-if" processing and hypothesis testing. In a sense this is the exploratory phase of the research program.

Second, theoretical models and explanations that account for the pattern of effects of the technology must be developed. These models have two goals:

1. To improve our understanding of how IT affects behavior (i.e., descriptive theories).
2. To improve our ability to anticipate what behaviors will occur (i.e., predictive theories).

The development of theories and their relationships to previous work is essential to the cumulative advancement of knowledge [Kuhn, 1970]. One way to do this is to use existing decision-making theories as a starting point, and adapt or modify them to account for the stylistic facts of the IT context. However, it should be emphasized that uncritically "borrowing" a general theory and applying it to an IT context is often an inadequate strategy. More powerful theories can be developed that capitalize on the knowledge of DSS researchers about the technology.

The goal of the theoretical models should be to identify and describe the linkages between the IT and the stylized facts. These linkages reflect underlying decision processes that occur during the use of IT. Lave and March provide a general description of this process of developing theories and models from a set of observations in considerable detail, and provide an excellent and accessible tutorial [Lave and March, 1975].

A recent example of the attempt to develop theories for a well-accepted stylized fact in behavioral decision research concerns the phenomenon of preference reversal, which occurs when a decision-maker prefers option A to option B with one type of description, but B to A with a different, but informationally equivalent, description (e.g., choosing directly between two alternatives versus stating how much one would pay for each). While this phenomenon does not involve IT directly, it is a function of how problems are presented, an issue of considerable interest to DSS researchers. Preference reversal was first documented almost 20 years ago [Lichtenstein and Slovic, 1971; Lindman, 1971] and replicated many times [Slovic and Lichtenstein, 1983] before a series of papers developed cognitive explanations for the phenomenon [Goldstein and Einhorn, 1987; Schkade and Johnson, 1989; Tversky et al., 1988].

Third, the theories should be tested. Much previous DSS research has started by "borrowing" theories from other disciplines. The forgoing of the first two steps has often led to the testing of hypotheses that are inadequately suited to the current context, contributing to insignificant results. For example, in their studies of cognitive style, DSS researchers might have been better off to develop a concept of user style or how users behave with computer-based decision aids on their own, rather than to uncritically borrow from psychology research.

Fourth, implications for practice should be developed. Predictive models are the most useful here (especially those that are based on an understanding of the causal mechanism). If a practitioner wants to influence or control the occurrence of a given behavior, a predictive model that embodies a causal mechanism directs the practitioner to variables that should be influenced or controlled. Predictive models derived only from correlational analyses may have high predictive validity in their own context, but generalize poorly to others. To achieve effective prescriptions, a normative model that describes which outcomes are better or worse is also needed (i.e., the theories are oriented toward describing and forecasting events, not evaluating them).

A summary of the steps involved in the IT → DM approach is given below:

1. Choose an IT of interest and document its systematic effects (process and input-output).
2. Develop an explanation or theory to account for these effects.
3. Validate (i.e., test the theory).
4. Develop implications for practice.

Information technology as a solution to decision-making problems: DM → IT. Much of decision research has involved the identification of dysfunctional decision behaviors and the attempt to develop psychological explanations to account for them. Because most of these explanations rely directly or indirectly on how decision-makers process information, the rapidly advancing set of technological options for storing, manipulating, and combining information provides many new possibilities for the development of remedies to these dysfunctions. In this approach, DSS researchers take decision-making phenomena identified previously in the DM literature (e.g., biases due to availability) and attempt to design tools that help to overcome this problem (e.g., force the user to consider a balanced set of information).

This is a well-known and powerful approach used in experimental psychology, in which theory-based manipulations are designed that cause the behaviors to appear or disappear under well-specified conditions. In this case the manipulations are the characteristics of IT. This is more of an engineering approach and is consistent with at least the apparent motivation of many previous empirical DSS studies. That is, the IT is designed specifically to address a given decision-making difficulty or error. However (as noted above), DSS researchers have too often focused primarily on the technology itself, to the detriment of developing a causal understanding of the processes that underlie the phenomenon.

Like the first proposed approach, a research program of this kind also involves several steps. First, a decision-making phenomenon that may be susceptible to the influence of IT must be identified. Since many of the currently identified decision-making phenomena have been addressed using theories of how people process information, there are many possibilities.

Second, an IT intervention designed to alleviate the difficulty is developed. In effect, this is the development and definition of the operationalization of an independent variable. The choice of an intervention should be guided by a theory of the DM phenomenon. For example, if the phenomenon is attributed to faulty memory for facts, then a database might be an appropriate intervention. Alternatively, a new or modified theory that incorporates the special characteristics of the IT can be developed to guide the design of the intervention. For example, if the interface uses only a mouse and pictorially oriented displays with relatively little text or few numbers, it may be necessary to modify or expand on existing theories that emphasize linguistic behavior and processing.

Third, the effects of the intervention should be tested. Hypotheses are more straightforward here than in the first approach, since the DSS was designed explicitly to achieve the effects under study. However, the range of dependent variables should not be limited to those specifically identified in the theory. Like any other IT, there may be unintended side effects that should be documented. These additional effects can provide valuable information about how the theory can be improved or refined. The effects of the DSS should also be tested across the range of likely tasks and contexts to evaluate the generality of the theory and implementation.

Fourth, after the usefulness of the IT has been established, implications for practice should be developed. The DSS can be used either as a component of other systems (e.g., a new dialogue mode) or as a stand-alone aid (e.g., a spreadsheet).

A summary of the DM → IT program is given below:

1. Identify a known decision-making phenomenon to address.
2. Design IT to help (based on decision-making theory or develop own).
3. Validate (test theory).
4. Develop implications for practice.

Building a new research program in DSS/BDM. The two research approaches described in the previous section can result in the creation of a new body of knowledge that documents, explains, and predicts the decision-making behavior that occurs within a computer-supported environment. By redirecting our attention from IT alone to the DM → IT and IT → DM linkages, new and potentially rich areas of research can be pursued.

We are not advocating that in the future the development of all software designed to support information processing activities of individuals be grounded in solid behavioral theory. On the contrary, we see the benefit of experimentation around those technological developments that hold particular promise for increasing the effectiveness of individuals. We are advocating, however, that the developers of technology to support decision making and information processing take into account whatever knowledge currently exists about individual behavior in these areas. Likewise, we are advocating that behavioral researchers in information systems consider the new decision-making environments made possible by technology as exciting laboratories in which to understand possibly new and different types of individual decision-making and information processing behaviors.

These two approaches are obviously intertwined, with each approach producing results that advance the other. IT → DM identifies new decision-making and information processing phenomena that can be specifically studied in the DM → IT research approach. But now the phenomena are embedded within the IT context. DM → IT research creates the new technology which along with experimental, non-behavioral-based technology becomes the independent variable for studies of the IT → DM type.

As mentioned in the previous section, behavioral decision-making research has generated a well-defined set of "stylized facts" that drive much of its research. In order to identify these facts, a review of the behavioral decision theory literature was conducted. In addition, structured interviews were conducted with six leading behavioral decision theory researchers: Professor Robin Hogarth, University of Chicago; Professor John Payne, Duke University; Professor Colin Camerer, Wharton School; Professor Paul Johnson, University of Minnesota; Professor Wayne Hoyer, University of Texas; and Professor Urton Anderson, University of Texas.

The list of "stylized facts" that was uncovered is given in Table 2. Taken together, these facts provide the knowledge base for what is currently known about individual information processing and decision-making behavior. These "stylized facts" provide the starting point for research into decision-making behavior within a computer-based environment. IS researchers are in a position to contribute to the development, refinement, and perhaps replacement of these facts. The challenge for IS researchers is to develop a set of stylized facts that incorporates very explicitly the IT context in which decision making occurs.

Table 2. Behavioral decision research "stylized facts."

Biases

1. Choice and judgment are neither procedurally nor descriptively invariant. It matters how you ask the question and display the information [Payne, 1989].

2. Individuals are likely to overestimate low probabilities and underestimate high probabilities, and be somewhat more conservative estimators than would be expected if they were proper Bayesians [March and Shapira, 1982].

3. Several key judgmental heuristics are often used in choice and judgment that exhibit systematic bias: availability, anchoring, and representativeness [Tversky and Kahneman, 1974].

4. The way in which choices are "framed" impacts which choice is selected, even when the choices are identical from a decision theory perspective [Tversky and Kahneman, 1981].

Strategies

5. Individuals are very good at making decisions one variable at a time but are not very good at pulling together data on multiple dimensions for one evaluation [Hogarth, 1989].

6. Simple strategies have tremendous power, although the impacts of different simple strategies for a particular problem are not well understood [Hogarth, 1989].

7. Incomplete data, incommensurable data dimensions, and multiple alternatives encourage the use of simplifying strategies [Payne, 1976].

Individual Differences

8. Individual differences due to personality type are not important in differentiating different types of decision-making behavior [Hogarth, 1989].

9. Expertise/knowledge is the most important individual difference variable.

Table 2. Behavioral decision research "stylized facts" (continued).

Task Characteristics

10. Decision making is very sensitive to context [Hogarth, 1989].

11. Individuals behave differently in alternative contexts [Jacoby and Hoyer, 1989].

Cognitive Processes

12. Decision-makers process information selectively, and the selection can be influenced by many irrelevant factors.

13. Much of the information that consumers receive is mis-comprehended [Jacoby and Hoyer, 1989].

Outcomes

14. Certain types of feedback ("outcome only" feedback, for example) can actually lead to poorer decision-maker performance [Jacoby and Hoyer, 1989].

Human Information Processing

15. A few, and only a few, gross characteristics of the human information processing system are invariant over task and problem solver. These are (1) the information processing system operates serially, (2) the inputs and outputs of information processing processes are held in a small short-term memory with a capacity of only a few (say, between four and seven) chunks, and (3) the system has access to an essentially unlimited long-term memory [Newell and Simon, 1972].

16. The human information processing system is an adaptive system, capable of modeling its behavior, within wide limits, to the requirements of the task, and capable of modifying its behavior substantially over time by learning [Newell and Simon, 1972].

Developing these facts can only be accomplished through a systematic program of research—something that has been notably absent from the DSS literature. It is very difficult (perhaps indeed it is impossible) to establish reliable empirical regularities and develop new theory, and show direct implications for practice, all in the same study. DSS research should strive to go beyond individual experiments and build models that would explain behavior across many experiments [Little, 1986]. This goal can only be met through separate but integrated studies.

A systematic program of research needs to be based on a common framework or paradigm. Such a framework provides the basis for the generation of research themes that together will pave the way for an accumulated body of knowledge in the DSS/BDM area. The framework that we propose for helping to organize research studies in this area is composed of four factors: the individual, the task, the technology, and the process. By systematically varying and studying different aspects of these factors, we can begin to accumulate knowledge of how these variables interact to affect decision-making behavior. The framework with an initial list of different aspects of each factor is shown in Table 3. Drawing on this framework, we illustrate below some possibilities for future research for both the IT → DM and DM → IT approaches.

Opportunities in the DM → IT approach. There are a number of clear guidelines for IT development that follow directly from the stylized facts given in Table 2. First, issues of the user-computer interface are extremely important. As Payne stated, "It may seem silly, but issues of display and interface really matter." Second, there are breakdowns in process that can be addressed. For example, since individuals are not very good at pulling together data on multiple dimensions, computer-based decision aids are needed to help decision-makers deal with multiple-attribute decisions. Third, since individual differences due to personality type are not very important, fairly generic types of computer-based decision aids can be built. However, since decision making is very sensitive to context, different generic systems may need to be developed for different contexts.

One line of research of the DM → IT type would involve the construction of specific decision aids using these general guidelines, followed by a reexamination of "the facts" revalidated within a computer-based decision-making environment. One specific research question posed by Hogarth concerned the robustness of different simple strategies. He proposed a research project that would involve the development of a computer-based decision aid that presents a decision-maker with a number of simple strategies (i.e., not making a big mistake or focusing on the most important factor in the current decision-making situation) and would then test the robustness of the different strategies by examining the similarity of results produced by them. A related question posed

Table 3. Framework for research in DSS/BDM.

User
> Knowledge levels
> Mental models
> Involvement in decision

Technology (features)
> Off-loading versus supporting a process
> Information presentation
> Interaction mode
> System restrictiveness [Silver, 1990]
> Decisional guidance [Silver, 1990]

Task
> Content area
> Decision type: Common, everyday decisions; repetitive,
>   structured decisions; strategic decisions
> Criticality: Time pressure
> Single- or multipoint

Process
> Information acquisition
> Strategies for choice
> Strategies for judgment
> Editing operations
> Framing
> Setting mental agendas
> Making trade-offs
> Learning

by Payne was, "How adaptive are people in the strategies they employ in different DSS environments?" Research aimed at answering questions such as these would produce new facts on "strategies," as these strategies unfold in a computer-based environment.

Along the same lines, research aimed at understanding how biases in decision making and information processing are either reduced or amplified within a computer-based environment would also be a valuable contribution. Should we show different frames? Should we point out the bias in the frame? Is there a correct frame? In fact, research questions could be posed for each of the categories listed in Table 2.

Another line of research of the DM → IT type can be built around the decision-making phenomena that embody the list of behavioral decision research "stylized facts." To understand this type of research, consider the creative thinking process as the decision-making phenomenon of interest. Creativity is a desirable characteristic in many decision-making situations, but one that is very elusive. We know from the substantial body of research in creativity in cognitive and social psychology that (1) individuals can be taught to be more creative and (2) environments need to be constructed that are conducive to creative thinking. An interesting research question is whether a DSS can be constructed that will provide an environment in which creativity skills can be taught and practiced—and ultimately lead to more creative outcomes.

Some preliminary research has been conducted to answer this question using a "creativity-enhancing" DSS currently under development [Elam and Mead, 1990]. One of the features of this DSS is a set of alternative models that are provided to a user to aid in his or her consideration of a particular problem. A laboratory experiment was designed with one independent variable—decision aid—at three levels: software with model A, software with model B, and no software. Dependent variables were decision process and recommended actions. The study found that the two software treatments produced significantly different outcomes in terms of creativity. Outcomes from the no-software treatment fell between the two software groups. Thus, the hypotheses that the use of this DSS would lead to higher levels of creativity was found not to hold in all cases. Further research is now needed to develop a theory to explain these unexpected results, to modify the software as needed to enable this theory to be tested, and to rerun the original experiment.

Opportunities in the IT → DM approach. Research of this type is driven by a need to understand the effects of information technology that is currently in the field and being used by decision-makers. An example of a research project which is typical of this approach is a study that examined the way that business professionals used Lotus 1-2-3 to address a business-oriented task [Mackay and Elam, 1989]. This study was designed to provide information on how the knowledge that an individual brings to a DSS encounter—both in terms of the technology and the task—affects decision-making behavior and decision outcomes. The task was a preferential choice task. The physical interactions as well as the thought processes underlying the user-DSS interactions were captured. The study found that the lack of expertise in the technology domain inhibited the application of domain-specific knowledge. The behavior and outcomes of the task domain expert/technology domain novice group did not match that of the task domain expert/technology domain expert group. In fact, it matched more closely the other two groups that did not possess task domain knowledge. Expertise may thus play a similar role in a DSS environment for a preferential choice problem as problem complexity was shown to play in non-DSS environments for the same type of problem. Subsequent studies are now needed to test this hypothesis.

For other possible research opportunities, consider executive support systems (ESS). ESS represent a new, emerging technology that is gaining wide acceptance in organizations. There are many questions to be answered concerning what, if any, systematic effects exist on decision-making behaviors and/or decision outcomes when these systems are used. The list of "stylized facts" can help to sort through the many possible effects that might exist.

Consider, for instance, the selective processing fact: Decision-makers process information selectively, and the selection can be influenced by many irrelevant factors. In analyzing usage data for ESS, we can focus our attention on this one aspect. What are the effects on selectivity of information when decision-makers are given an ESS to access, format, and manipulate information? Under what conditions does selectivity seem to become more or less pronounced? What characteristics of the individual, the task, and the technology explain variances found? For example, can we affect certain patterns of information selection through the features we make available in the computer-based tools?

Methodology concerns

Our methodological development in DSS research has not followed the traditional scientific method. Rather, it has proceeded as follows:

1. Testing of hypotheses that have neither been grounded in theory nor drawn from a theory that accurately fits the situation being studied.
2. Polishing the research methodology.
3. Finding theories to ground the hypotheses.
4. Developing and refining constructs.
5. Generating theories using well-defined constructs.
6. Finding out what the problems are in the real world.

The DSS field has not been well served by this development, since it has prevented the development and growth of theory-building research. It must be recognized that not every study must necessarily lead immediately to guidelines for practitioners. On the other hand, researchers doing theory-building research must be able to describe in the long run how their work fits into a program of research that will lead to practical implications.

We must also strive for a more healthy balance between field and laboratory studies. Recently, almost all published DSS studies have been laboratory-bound, often with students as subjects. We must begin to study real people in real settings working on real tasks.

Why collaborative efforts? Collaborative teams composed of DSS and decision researchers are desirable in pursuing either of the two research approaches outlined above. While both groups share an interest in understanding and predicting decision behavior, they also have important comparative advantages that can be a basis for collaboration. DSS researchers bring to the partnership an in-depth knowledge of information technology that is difficult for decision researchers to maintain (especially given the rapid rate of technological change). DSS researchers by their training and experience are well positioned to identify IT options for study that are of current and practical interest. In addition, the IT context used in experimental studies is rarely identical to that observed in practice. Because of their knowledge and experience with the use of IT, DSS researchers are better positioned to translate the theory-based findings into practical implications that are usable by managers in real organizations.

On the other hand, decision researchers bring to the partnership a greater knowledge of a wide range of psychological and decision-making studies and theories. Most previous behavioral decision research has been carried out within a well-established paradigm (experimental psychology). Due in part to this disciplinary tradition, decision researchers have experience in building theories, skills in relating the findings of their research to other theories, and an attitude that important progress in science usually occurs gradually through the cumulative impact of a series of focused but well-connected research efforts.

There are other potential benefits of this collaboration as well. Since a sequence of studies is needed to best pursue these two approaches, teams of researchers are in a better position than individual researchers to run studies in parallel, obtain multiyear funding, and sustain effort and interest over the necessary period of time (probably three to five years). In addition, this kind of interdisciplinary research not only has high potential for substantive impact on the field [Cohen et al., 1983; Little, 1986], but can also facilitate the personal development of the researchers involved as they learn new perspectives.

Acknowledgments

The authors would like to acknowledge the useful comments made by Dick Mason, Charles Stabell, and Steve Kimbrough on an earlier draft of this chapter. We would also like to thank Professors Robin Hogarth, John Payne, Colin Camerer, Paul Johnson, Urton Anderson, and Wayne Hoyer for agreeing to be interviewed and for sharing their knowledge and insights on the topic of this chapter with the authors.

Workshop discussion: Behavioral decision making and DSS

Discussants. The first discussant, Fred Duhl, gave his views as a practicing psychiatrist on some of the issues raised at the workshop. He started by stating that, from his viewpoint, the patterns and issues of problem solving are similar in different fields—they simply need to be interpreted in the appropriate language. Both psychiatry and information systems attempt to bring about change by a process of intervention; in the information systems case, that intervention is made primarily through the technology. In his talk, Duhl focused on the question of how intervention can be successful in bringing about change.

He started by illustrating the importance of social context as a determinant of behavior. Our associative mind functions all the time, picking up cues from sensory inputs and modifying our behavior in ways that we may not be aware of. Our conscious mind functions intermittently. It has the important ability to focus attention on different aspects of the world and to switch its focus from time to time. It is important to command attention and focus it on the right aspects of a problem. This implies that our computer interfaces should be more interesting—we need many sensory inputs to shut out all other data and help us focus only on what really matters. He felt that this was one reason for the success of the iconic interface on the Macintosh computer. The alternative to capturing attention by shutting out extraneous information processing by the associative mind is to understand the latter's existence and influence, and to design our interventions accordingly.

Duhl noted that many children can play video games before they can read—they learn patterns associated with playing the game and this gives them a high degree of proficiency. We should realize that our technology does a similar thing by inducing patterns of problem-solving behavior in users. Sometimes, these patterns (rather than the content of the information exchange or problem-solving process) are important ends in and of themselves. To understand these patterns, it is necessary to observe them over long periods of time, and this is a prerequisite for useful research in this area.

Duhl concluded his talk with an insightful discussion of how we can bring about change in others—something that is of utmost importance if we think of IT as a change agent. Some of the factors useful in bringing about change were the necessity of capturing attention and trust, obtaining a shared vision of the problem, getting people to imagine life after the problem has been solved, providing a sense of safety by designing alternatives when mistakes are made, providing reward, and ensuring that there is an adequate follow-up or maintenance phase.

The second discussant, Dick Mason, complimented the behavioral and normative decision-making team on a very integrated paper. He said that his comments were more in the nature of reflections on the field than comments on the paper itself.

He first stressed the importance of distinguishing between IT and information. It is information that affects us and changes behavior, not the technology per se. He liked Karl Weick's ideas concerning the "equivocality of technology": that technology (in our case information technology) is not a single entity; it is the set of interpretations that we can make from it [Weick, 1979]. These interpretations allow us to understand information and information processing. Referring to the discussion in the paper concerning the results of a DSS experiment that showed that the method of solving the problem was more important than the presence or absence of the information technology, he suggested that the results might be explicable in terms of the patterns of information that were made available in both cases.

In his opinion, the DSS field needed to focus more on the mind as an object of study. Moreover, as Fred Duhl and others at the workshop had pointed out, it is not only the cognitive aspects of mental processes that are important, but also the affective aspects. This is one reason why the multisensory systems (mixing sound, graphics, and text) that are now being introduced might be important in helping us focus attention on the more rational kinds of processes.

Mason also wondered whether we should continue to use the word "decision," which he understood in the sense of making a choice. There is so much more going on in the mind: environmental scanning, pattern recognition, changing conceptual frameworks, preparing for future decisions, and so on. As Mintzberg has pointed out, people do many things besides making decisions (new products are not introduced every day, for example). Taking an opposing viewpoint, we might think of the mind as continuously making millions of tiny conscious and unconscious decisions. Finding the right level of analysis in this sense makes "decision" a difficult concept upon which to develop a theory of support.

Mason then gave some additional examples of cognitive biases that had not been explicitly mentioned in the paper presented by the team. These were

- *conservatism*, whereby decision-makers consistently fail to adjust probabilities as normative Bayesian theory would predict;
- *primacy*, whereby the order in which information is presented affects decisions based on that data; and
- *precommitment*, whereby people tend to use information to reinforce prior opinions.

He felt that it was important for the IS field to focus more on such issues. Finally, citing an experiment from his own experience, he felt that the arguments for "cognitive style" as a determinant of decision behavior had not been disproved, despite reports of ambivalent research results.

In his discussion, Charles Stabell said that he thought the behavioral and normative decision-making team had done an excellent job in raising many important ideas. His remarks would address some more general issues arising out of the paper and the conference as a whole. How we construe the phenomenon of DSS defines what we believe we have learned about the field. He felt that the team had presented an overly constrained description of the DSS field that really did not do it justice. Their paper emphasized a concept of DSS as a physical entity, whereas his concept of the DSS field was that it dealt primarily with issues of support for decision making in a more general sense. He also felt that decision making, properly interpreted, meant more than just choice.

He also disagreed with an underlying theme in the team's paper and presentation that the best way to advance knowledge in the field was to undertake a research program involving detailed research on isolated small phenomena over a long period of time. He felt that the evidence from some 15 years of this type of work was that it was hard to accumulate knowledge this way. In his opinion, it was better to do research at a higher level—at the level of the whole decision process rather than by studying small components of that process.

He felt, however, that persistence was important and that it might be useful to reexamine some of the frameworks from the past to see how well they had withstood the test of time. This was one reason why he thought it important to stick with the decision focus of DSS research; it had been the starting point for the field and had provided a framework for research over a long period of time. Most importantly, the decision perspective has the advantage that it emphasizes the purposeful nature of organizations. While we should be cognizant of other factors going on in the mind, the overall context of the field should be one of purposeful change, which is best captured by maintaining a focus on decisions as the end product of a process of decision making. Finally, contrary to some of the comments that had been made at the conference, he felt that the decision-making focus did, in fact, provide an integrating perspective for the field. This approach had always meant more than simply choosing between alternatives; information aspects and knowledge aspects were both subsumed by the decision process approach.

In conclusion, he felt that it was important to continue the ISDP process by attempting to provide a coherent view of all aspects of decision making and by focusing on decision processes as the frame of reference.

General discussion. The behavioral and normative decision theory team discussion did not use the electronic meeting facilities. The following is a brief summary of the issues raised during the general discussion period.

There was agreement that the behavioral and normative decision-making team had done an excellent job in raising important issues and presenting an integrated program of research in the two fields of DSS and BDM.

Several people commented on what they perceived as a lack of breadth in BDM. To some it appeared too limited in that it considered only cognitive factors and ignored many other mental processes that were important.

There was a debate concerning the usefulness of the concepts of decision and decision making. A number of people thought that the focus on decisions had caused the DSS field to look too narrowly at choice as the main activity of managers. Others thought that "decision making" had been construed too narrowly and that, if broadened in scope, in particular to encompass process aspects, it could still serve as a useful integrating concept for the DSS field.

There was much debate about the usefulness of frameworks as a mechanism for integrating research within an academic discipline. It was generally agreed that it was premature to think of a single overriding framework for ISDP and that multiple frameworks and perspectives were likely to be more useful. Furthermore, since research is colored by the conscious or unconscious framework adopted by the researcher, it was suggested that it would help communication in the field if research papers were more explicit about both the particular framework adopted and the topics in that framework that were being investigated.

Another debate concerned whether or not the field should adopt a primarily design philosophy in which theories would be adapted to develop design principles for testing. It was felt that this might sharpen research efforts and make them more practical. The counterargument held that there was value in research that sought to understand and explain phenomena and that the framework needed for design-oriented research would differ from that for understanding-oriented research.

There were a number of suggestions for research approaches. It was suggested that future multidisciplinary research should have a strong vision of what was to be achieved. One way of conducting multidisciplinary research efforts might be to have people from different research disciplines work on a common case or real-world problem. Another suggestion was that IS researchers should conduct research on themselves as subjects—for example, by designing and building their own support system for cooperative research.

Chapter 4

Group Decision Support Systems

Paul Gray, Steven L. Alter, Gerardine DeSanctis,
Gary W. Dickson, Robert Johansen, Kenneth L. Kraemer,
Lorne Olfman, and Douglas R. Vogel

In most business organizations today, when groups of executives meet, they gather in a room that is little different from the one in which their predecessors met a hundred or more years ago. Technology is evident only in the electric light, the air conditioning, and perhaps a telephone. The information available during the deliberations is combined in a few memoranda or a notebook of financial and other reports. They may receive verbal briefings made with the aid of charts or slides. However, as discussion proceeds around the table and various alternatives are considered, the decision-makers have to rely principally on what is in their heads and what has been told them.

The foregoing description of meetings appeared in 1981 in one of the early papers on group decision support systems [Gray et al., 1981]. Although this description is still accurate in most companies, major changes occurred in the 1980s. The personal computer became ubiquitous in offices as people learned to use spreadsheets, databases, and word processing to enhance their work. Computer literacy is becoming widespread even at senior executive levels [e.g., Palmer, 1988]. The personal computer entered the conference room in a number of experimental group decision support systems built by university research teams who ran controlled experiments in these new environments. As we enter the 1990s, GDSS facilities are starting to appear in major organizations.

Groups, decisions, and GDSS

GDSS is an acronym for *group decision support systems*. The term refers to systems that provide computer and communications support for decision-making meetings in organizations. In its narrowest sense, it is restricted to meetings during which a major organizational choice is to be made. In its broadest sense, it includes the whole spectrum of group meetings in an organization. This section focuses on the nature of groups, the decisions they make, and the role of GDSS in supporting group decision making.

The nature of group meetings. Meetings are a joint activity, engaged in by a group of people of equal or near-equal status. The activity and its outputs are intellectual in nature. The product of the meeting depends in an essential way on the knowledge and judgments contributed by the participants. Differences in opinion may be settled by negotiation, by arbitration, or by fiat by the ranking person present. Negotiation or arbitration usually involves debate and the reaching of a consensus by those present. The results of the meeting are often choices (decisions) that lead to action in the organization.

Purposes of group meetings. The subjects of meetings depend on the level and function in the organization. In engineering, for example, a meeting may center around design decisions; in marketing, the focus may be on advertising choices. At senior managerial levels, the decisions revolve around management of ongoing operations, crisis management, and strategic planning. Table 1 is a partial list of the objectives of group meetings. The list is not an exclusive one; that is, a particular meeting may have several purposes and these purposes will be carried out simultaneously. Furthermore, a particular purpose may not be completed at a single session. Some subjects require a sequence of meetings to reach resolution.

Benefits claimed for GDSS. GDSS involves introducing the computer into the conference room. Like any technological innovation, it can be justified if it provides one or more of the following:

1. Increased efficiency (of group meetings).
2. Improved quality (of meeting discussion and/or decision reached).
3. Leverage (that improves the way meetings are run).

Efficiency gains are achieved, for example, if the meeting requires less time from senior individuals. Improved quality implies such outcomes as increased quality of alternatives examined, greater participation and contribution from people who would otherwise be silent, or decision outcomes judged to be of higher quality.

Leverage implies that the system does not merely speed up the process (that is efficiency), but changes it fundamentally. In other words, leverage is obtained from GDSS if it provides better ways of meeting. One form of leverage has already been found, human parallel processing. This is the

Table 1. Some purposes of group meetings.

- Information sharing among participants.
- Finding a problem or defining it.
- Developing new ideas about a problem.
- Reviewing status, such as in variance analysis on financial results, or schedule and budget adherence for a particular project, or walk-throughs in information systems analysis.
- Reviewing and approving (or disapproving) proposals, such as for capital budgets.
- Making preliminary choices for higher levels in the organization such as a group selecting a list of, say, three preferred candidates for a position.
- Negotiation between organizations (either internal or external).
- Conflict resolution.
- Crisis management.
- Formal selection, say by voting, from among a set of proposed alternatives.
- Planning.

idea that the time of important people can be better used if they provide input simultaneously (i.e., in parallel) rather than sequentially, as implied by Robert's Rules of Order.

All three benefits—efficiency, effectiveness, and leverage—have been claimed for GDSS. Research results exist to support each claim. However, the research results are not clear cut that all of these benefits are provided by the existing combinations of GDSS hardware and software. The research problem faced over the next several years thus includes finding those GDSS that best achieve the claimed benefits.

History of GDSS. Decision rooms where senior executives and boards of directors meet to choose among alternatives exist all over the world. Typically, the higher the level in the organization, the more elegant the furnishings, the deeper the carpets, and the richer the draperies. Technology, however, ends at the door. Whereas the desks outside these rooms are covered with computers, the technology available in these rooms is the telephone; high technology is the speakerphone. Participants in such rooms are typically limited to the information from flip charts, projectors, and briefing books—and what is in their heads.

Churchill's Cabinet War Room, now preserved as a tourist attraction, was a Spartan decision room. It consisted of a rectangle of tables at which sat the men who ran Britain's war effort. The maps on the walls contained its major technology: map tacks showing the location of the war fronts and the convoys. Information was brought into the room by a staff that worked in the surrounding underground labyrinth. Churchill's Cabinet War Room was a forerunner of the crisis management rooms used by the military and by top government officials.

In the 1960s and 1970s, a number of large companies introduced multiple slide projectors into their boardrooms. These projectors, able to fade images in and out, were used for variance review meetings. These systems, developed by Robert Widener, paid attention to human factors by always presenting information as standard graphs so that executives would spot problem areas quickly.

Introducing the computer was the next natural step. In the early 1970s, for example, Stafford Beer and a team of British programmers established a computer-based room in the most unlikely of places, Salvador Allende's Chile [Beer, 1983]. The idea was to try to monitor the Chilean economy on line. Computer screens were built into armchairs much as the coin-operated TV screens in today's airports. The effort was nearly completed when Allende was killed and Beer went home to England. Beer's efforts in Chile were a direct predecessor of the systems being built today by Metapraxis in the United Kingdom (see the later section "Current British systems").

In the United States in the late 1960s, Doug Engelbart, inventor (among other things) of the mouse, instrumented a conference room for his research group at SRI International with a computer terminal in front of each meeting participant [Johansen, 1988]. The CEO of Gould introduced computer terminals in his boardroom. In Texas in the early 1980s, Gerald R. Wagner, CEO of Execucom Systems Corp., a computer software house, built the Planning Laboratory, the forerunner of current US GDSS designs. In Wagner's room, people sat around a U-shaped table. A projection TV system served as a public screen, and terminals connected to a minicomputer were available to participants. The software allowed people to vote, to enter opinions, and to ask what-if questions on a spreadsheet [Wagner, 1981a]. All three of these rooms are now gone. In both the Gould and the Execucom case, they did not long survive their executive sponsor.

Through the 1980s most of the decision rooms in the US were experimental facilities tied to universities or consultancies. Only in the last three years have rooms developed in the universities been replicated in companies.

Current US systems. Table 2 lists some of the current US facilities, and Figure 1 shows the physical layout of typical facilities. In this section we describe the US facilities in broad terms.

The US facilities are divided between two basic philosophies: special purpose and full service. In a special-purpose facility, only one type of

Table 2. Selected group decision support facilities.

University-Based Facilities

University of Arizona	University of Minnesota
Claremont Graduate School	Queens University
University of Georgia	National University of Singapore
Universität Hohenheim	San Diego State University
University of Indiana	State University of New York at Albany
London School of Economics	Western Washington University

Corporate-Based Facilities

Electronic Data Systems	Greyhound Financial Corp.
Execucom Systems Corp.	Bell South
IBM Corp.	Xerox Palo Alto Research Center

Commercial Facility Vendors

IBM Corp.	ICL
Metapraxis	

For-Hire Commercial Systems—Permanent Installations

Decisions & Design, Inc.

For-Hire Commercial Systems—Portable

Applied Future, Inc.	Perceptronics, Inc.
K.R. Hammond	Wilson Learning Systems

decision making is supported, typically voting or the use of multicriteria decision making. In a full-service facility, many different types of problems are supported. In the US, the full-service facilities predominate.

In a typical special-purpose facility, a PC or a terminal connected to a mainframe supports the group. A "chauffeur" operates the equipment and a highly skilled facilitator leads the group through the discussion. The computer is used to record the minutes of the meeting and to solve the mathematical model being developed. Results are projected on a large screen for the group to see. This approach is often referred to as "decision conferencing" [e.g., McCartt and Rohrbaugh, 1989].

People go to a special-purpose facility (located at a university or a consulting firm) or, in some cases, portable equipment is brought to the users' site. The facility is supported by facilitators knowledgeable in the use of the methodology. Such facilities have not had sufficient frequency of use in a single company or government organization to make them economically viable for permanent installation.

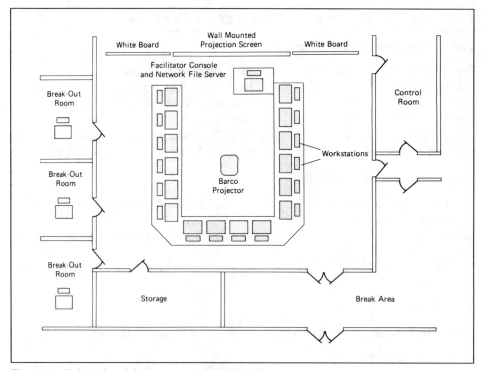

Figure 1a. University of Arizona small GDSS facility.
Sprague/Watson, editors, *Decision Support Systems: Putting Theory Into Practice*, 2/E, © 1989, pp. 284 and 285.
Reprinted by permission of Prentice-Hall, Inc., Englewood Cliffs, NJ.

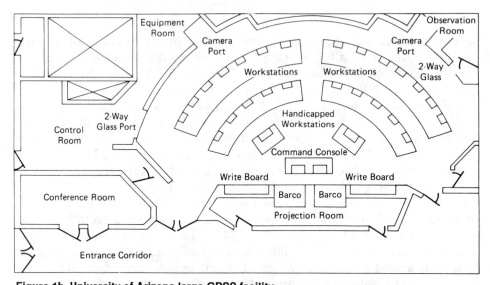

Figure 1b. University of Arizona large GDSS facility.
Sprague/Watson, editors, *Decision Support Systems: Putting Theory Into Practice*, 2/E, © 1989, pp. 284 and 285.
Reprinted by permission of Prentice-Hall, Inc., Englewood Cliffs, NJ.

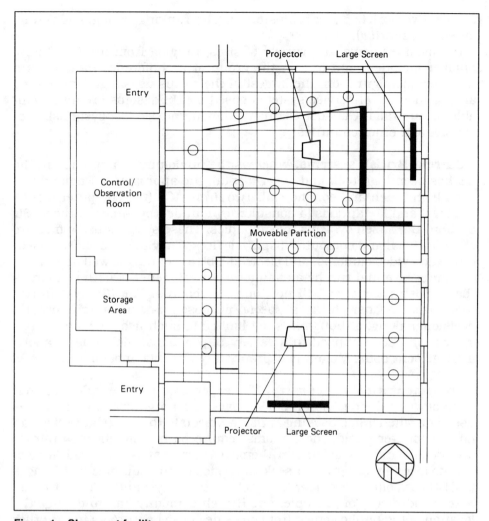

Figure 1c. Claremont facility.

Sprague/Watson, editors, *Decision Support Systems: Putting Theory Into Practice*, 2/E, © 1989, pp. 284 and 285. Reprinted by permission of Prentice-Hall, Inc., Englewood Cliffs, NJ.

In a typical full-service facility, a large number of PCs connected through a local area network are provided so that each individual has computer access. The PC network may also be connected to a mainframe or a minicomputer. Each participant in the meeting has the ability to use the computer for "private work." One or more "public screens" (large monitors or projectors) controlled by a chauffeur provide information seen by the group as a whole. The group is provided with a set of software tools that allow a range of work to be performed. These tools include both the usual software available on networked PCs (e.g., data retrieval, word processing and group editing, electronic mail, spreadsheets, modeling and statistics) and software specific to group decision making and cooperative work (e.g., for brainstorming; for ranking, rating, and voting; for screen sharing).

The facilities come in a variety of sizes, ranging from five to 30 PCs. Smaller facilities tend to seat the group at a conference table or in a U-shaped configuration; the largest of the rooms uses a gallery seating arrangement. Full-service systems based on US designs are also available in Australia, Canada, Germany, Japan, Mexico (six systems), Singapore, and other countries.

Current British systems. Whereas the predominant approach in the US has been high tech and experimental, the approach in England has been high touch and commercial. Two firms, ICL (the computer manufacturer) and Metapraxis (a consultancy founded by, among others, Sir Stafford Beer), sell systems to companies. These systems use a mixture of audiovisual and computer display devices. They include slides, videotape, film, video cameras, and electronic blackboards, as well as a single computer terminal run by a chauffeur. A basic tenet of both vendors is that British executives will not touch keyboards. The ICL system has been used extensively as a special-purpose system for multicriteria decision making, although it is not limited to such use. The Metapraxis system has been applied to a variety of problems, including financial management using Metapraxis' proprietary financial modeling software.

Implementation in industry. The experience to date indicates that technology in the decision room survives in an organization only if it is used and when it has backing at the top. Even in today's relatively cheap microcomputer world, these rooms require both a significant up-front investment and a staff to run them. A room that is not used is soon cannibalized by others who seek the space or the equipment. Changes in CEOs are often accompanied by changes in style and a "not invented here" syndrome. For example, one British company had to change the location of the public screen from one side of the boardroom to the other because a new CEO wanted to put his imprint on it.

The present commercially used systems are mostly the result of transfer of technology from the universities (particularly the University of Arizona). The largest user is IBM. IBM is reported to have 40 systems either in operation or in the planning stage [McGoff, 1990].

Range of current research activities. The principal research activities in the US involve work on full-service facilities. With the facilities being university-based, principally at doctoral granting institutions, the major activities have been

- software development,
- laboratory experiments,

- field studies, and
- hardware and facility development.

Software. Software developed specifically for GDSS has focused on supporting the group process. Although some of the software has built-in modeling assumptions, most of the software has been concerned with supporting group inputs and group voting activities. Where quantitative models are needed, existing software packages such as spreadsheets have been used. The two major university centers of GDSS software development are at the University of Arizona (Electronic Meeting System) and at the University of Minnesota (SAMM). The Arizona software [e.g., Nunamaker et al., 1988] is centrally controlled, with the chauffeur determining what activity is to be performed by the meeting participants and what is seen on the public screen. The Minnesota approach has been democratic, allowing the meeting to run without a chauffeur and with anyone in the room able to change the public screen [e.g., DeSanctis and Gallupe, 1985]. Software is also being developed at Xerox PARC for use in COLAB [Stefik et al., 1987] and at the Naval Postgraduate School [Bui, 1987], and commercially from the many offerings in groupware [e.g., Johansen, 1988]. Consideration is also being given to software that supports groups working cross-culturally [e.g., Gray et al., 1988; George and Nunamaker, 1988].

Laboratory studies. The laboratory studies have tended to be associated with PhD dissertations. Most have followed the social science experimental paradigm, with strong statistical design, the use of randomly selected undergraduates for experimental subjects, and artificial tasks. In these dissertations, comparisons have usually been made between groups performing a task with and without the particular GDSS configuration. The measures of effectiveness examined included efficiency (speed), effectiveness (quality of answer), and satisfaction with the GDSS hardware and software. The results obtained thus far have been mixed, with some, but not all, dissertations finding improvements in one or more of the three measures of effectiveness from the use of a particular GDSS.

Specific laboratory studies have been criticized because

- they use student groups and artificial tasks rather than ongoing groups that have decisions to make that are of importance to the group,
- they usually involve only a single meeting,
- they assume that the particular GDSS and experimental situation used are representative and can be used to draw conclusions about all GDSS,
- they focus on changes in outcomes and individual satisfaction, but not on changes in group process or group dynamics, and

• they differ only slightly, typically in one or two variables being set at different levels, from previous experiments (see the section "Gray, Vogel, and Beauclair assessment typology").

Field studies. With the recent transfer of university technology to industry, field studies of industrial implementations are being undertaken. The first of the field studies are now being published [e.g., Nunamaker et al., 1989b]. Definitive results based on field studies should be available in the 1992 to 1994 period.

Hardware. The hardware used in GDSS research has consisted of sophisticated interconnections of off-the-shelf, commercial computer and display equipment. As the capabilities of personal computers, networks, and (particularly large-screen) displays have improved, these improvements have been incorporated into the research facilities. However, the basic concept has remained the same, and almost all of the equipment used could be obtained from a local computer store. Hardware by itself has not been a subject for formal research, although some attention has been given to human factors aspects of equipment layout and displays. This situation may be starting to change. Work was started in 1989 at the University of Toronto to investigate the suitability of the new video technologies that permit multiple images to be displayed simultaneously.

Facilities. Considerable attention has been paid in design to creating suitable facilities. It was recognized early that since GDSS were intended for use by senior executives in corporations, the physical facilities would have to have an executive look and feel. Such aspects of facility design as seating arrangements, lighting, table shape, noise levels, and colors have been studied [e.g., Mantei, 1989].

Variables in GDSS research. GDSS research is a messy, multidimensional problem because many variables are involved in GDSS design and experimentation. The variables define a very large space, only small portions of which have yet been explored. The variable space provides a basis for defining the directions for future GDSS research. In this section we discuss papers that categorize and define the research variables.

Pinsonneault-Kraemer categorization. Pinsonneault and Kraemer surveyed both the GDSS literature and the social science literature and created a list of 53 variables that are important when studying group decision support systems [Pinsonneault and Kraemer, 1989, 1990]. Figure 2 shows these variables and their interrelation.

Pinsonneault and Kraemer divide the variables into contextual variables (the situations being supported), group process variables (how the

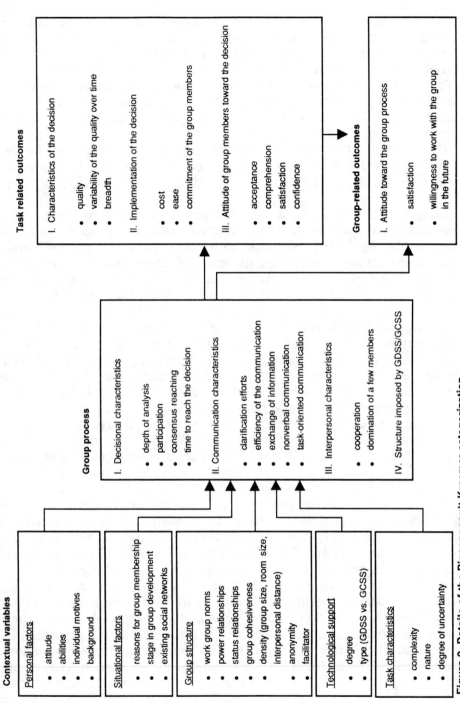

Figure 2. Details of the Pinsonneault-Kraemer categorization.

group works), and outcome variables (with respect to both the task and how the group works). This classification helps researchers think about the many dimensions of GDSS research. A useful way of dividing these variables is to consider those under the control of the experimenter (the contextual variables and some of the process variables) and those which are the outcome of the experiment. The values of the former define the experimental situation, while those of the latter define the set of measurements that need to be taken.

The Pinsonneault-Kraemer categorization is particularly useful because it provides a solid grounding for GDSS research in the social science research paradigm.

Gray, Vogel, and Beauclair assessment typology. Gray, Vogel, and Beauclair carry the Pinsonneault-Kraemer classification one step further [Gray et al., 1990]. They recognize that GDSS experiments can differ from one another in many important dimensions. They present a method for finding which experiments are similar to one another. They use the variables from the Pinsonneault-Kraemer classification which are under the control of the experimenter to classify experimental conditions. The method identifies 20 variables and defines scales for each variable. In some cases, where a variable (e.g., interface design) has a number of components (e.g., response time, type of interface, public screen), indicators are used to help define the variables. Table 3 lists the metavariables, variables, and indicators used, and Table 4 shows representative values for the variables and indicators.

The difference between specific experiments is captured by measuring the average "distance" between variables. Similar experiments, such as those which differ only in the values of one or two variables, will have a small "distance" between them, whereas experiments that are different in many dimensions will be separated by large distances. To make sense out of the data, the multidimensional scaling technique of statistics provides a way of positioning many experiments relative to one another on a two-dimensional graph. Table 5 shows the distances among a group of 11 experiments, and Figure 3 shows the graphical representation obtained from multidimensional scaling for these experiments.

The important point about this approach is that it permits assessing where a proposed experiment lies relative to others that have been done previously. By using these classifications, it is possible for researchers to assess whether a proposed experiment is unique (i.e., explores new ground in GDSS) or whether it is similar to what has been done before. Initial analysis using the Gray, Vogel, and Beauclair assessment scheme shows large replication among experiments, particularly among those performed at the same or similar facilities. That is, many experiments differ only slightly in the value of one or two variables from other experiments performed previously.

Table 3. Metavariables, variables, and indicators.

Metavariable	Variable	Indicator
Personal factors (Group member attitudes, backgrounds)	1. Attitude toward group	
	2. Ability to work in group	
	3. Background of group members	1. Previous group experience.
		2. Education
		3. Average age
		4. Computer ability
Situation (How group came together)	4. Reason for group membership	
	5. Existing social network of group	
	6. Stage of group development	
Group structure (How group is organized)	7. Size of group	
	8. Density	1. No. people/terminal
		2. Terminal separation
	9. Table shape	
Technological support (Characteristics of GDSS)	10. Degree of support (DeSanctis-Gallupe)	
	11. Degree of anonymity	
	12. Chauffeur/facilitator	
	13. Interface	1. Response time
		2. Type of interface
		3. Public screen
Task characteristics	14. Complexity of task	1. Complexity of problem
		2. Complexity of response
	15. Nature of task	1. Urgency
		2. Importance
		3. Routine/creative
		4. Abstractness
	16. Negotiation associated with task	
Group process (How the group works as set up by experimenter)	17. Degree of consensus required	
	18. Communication supported	
	19. Group structure imposed	
	20. Number of meetings to accomplish task	

Table 4. Representative values for variables and indicators.

Metavariable	Variable	Indicator	Value
Personal Factors	1. Attitude toward group (attitude members have toward working in groups and working with the members of the group)		10 Strong dislike 30 Dislike 50 Indifferent 70 Like 90 Strong liking
	2. Ability to work in group		10 Strong Dislike 30 Dislike 50 Indifferent 70 Like 90 Strong liking
	3. Background of group members	Previous experience in working with groups	10 None 30 Experimental groups only 50 Some business experience 70 Middle management 90 Top executives
		Education	20 No college 40 Undergraduate student 60 Undergraduate degree 80 Graduate degree
		Average age	-20 + 2*age for ages <60 100 for average age > = 60
		Computer ability	0 No experience 10 Novice 50 Experienced user 90 Expert programmer
Situation	4. Reason for group membership		10 Required for class grade 30 Paid volunteer or cash prize 50 Paid volunteer and cash prize 90 Regular work activity
	5. Existing social network of group (which has a direct impact on communication and interpersonal dimensions of the group process)		10 Randomly chosen subjects who do not know one another 30 Attended courses together 50 Coworkers (less than a year) 70 Coworkers (less than 5 years) 90 Coworkers (over 5 years)

Table 5. Distances among experiments.

Experiment	1	2	3	4	5	6	7	8	9	10	11
Easton, A. (1988)	-	12	24	24	24	18	17	18	17	19	26
Easton, G. (1988)		-	22	22	22	19	20	19	19	20	20
Connolly (1989)			-	1	1	12	11	12	11	9	27
Valacich (1989)				-	2	12	11	12	11	10	26
Jessup (1988)					-	12	11	12	11	10	28
Zigurs (1987)						-	4	1	1	6	23
Lewis (1982)							-	4	3	8	26
Watson (1987)								-	1	6	24
Gallupe (1985)									-	6	24
Beauclair (1987)										-	25
Heminger (1988)											-

Note: References are given in Bibliography

Distinctions among GDSS, DSS, OA, EIS, CSCW, groupware, and computer conferencing. Group decision support systems are closely related to a number of other current developments. The differences between GDSS and these developments are as follows:

- DSS: Decision support systems, as developed over the last 20 years, have focused on individual decision-makers. The paradigm that a DSS includes a model base, a database, and a dialogue base [Sprague, 1980] has proved useful over time. DSS is a subset of GDSS; that is, GDSS incorporate one or more DSS within them. GDSS adds a communications base and requires greater system reliability, because if a system failure occurs the entire group, rather than just an individual, is affected.
- OA: Office automation is concerned with improving the functioning of the office, particularly the clerical functions in the office. Many office

automation technologies, such as word processing and local area networks, are used in GDSS.

- EIS: Executive information systems provide sophisticated software for data retrieval and for display. As such, they provide advanced database and dialogue base capabilities. Typically, they are weak in model base. Existing EIS systems usually provide a seamless communications interface with the mainframe and have hypertext-like capabilities. As a result, EIS can be adapted for use as a component of GDSS.
- CSCW: A major stream of research has emerged in the last several years around computer-supported cooperative work [e.g., CSCW, 1986; CSCW, 1988]. Like GDSS, CSCW has focused on groups of people working together. The emphasis in major efforts, such as COLAB at Xerox PARC, has been on designers or other professionals working together on a creative rather than on a decision task. One way of looking at CSCW is that it embraces all aspects of work from problem finding to decision making, and hence that GDSS represents one end of the spectrum of CSCW activities. Physically, much of the software and hardware used in GDSS can be used in CSCW and vice versa.
- Groupware: This term, popularized by Robert Johansen of the Institute for the Future [Johansen, 1989], deals with all software and hardware designed to help groups of people working together. GDSS facilities and software are one form of groupware.
- Computer conferencing: Computer conferencing involves groups of people separated in time and space communicating with one another through a common computer file. Although software exists for helping computer conferencing groups reach decisions (e.g., Co-op [Bui, 1987]), computer conferencing has served more as an aid to discussion than to decision making.

In reviewing these descriptions, it is evident that considerable overlap exists among these developments. They share many of the same technologies. Developments in any one of them will rapidly move to many of the others. Over time, it can be expected that these distinctions will blur further.

Collocation in space and time. Electronically supported meetings can be either collocated or separated both in space and in time. Figure 4 shows the four GDSS arrangements according to DeSanctis and Gallupe [DeSanctis and Gallupe, 1985] and gives examples of each. As Robert Johansen points out in his book *Groupware* [Johansen, 1988], software and hardware developments are under way in all four areas.

Limitation of this chapter to "full-service room" environments and decision-making tasks. In this chapter, we focus on people working in

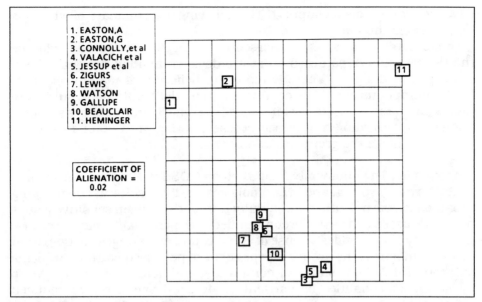

Figure 3. Map of experiments [Gray et al., 1990].
Reprinted with permission from *European Journal of Operations Research,* Vol. 45, 1990. © 1990, Elsevier Science Publishers B.V., Academic Publishing Division.

a single-room environment concerned with tasks involved in decision making. That is, we limit our discussion primarily to people collocated in space and time (top left square in Figure 4). We believe that the existing research infrastructure is best able to support work in this square and that much of what is learned in these situations will carry over to the other squares of Figure 4. From time to time, we will point out opportunities to branch to other squares, such as bringing people into a meeting from remote locations via video conferencing. We will also assume that the research program to be discussed will be carried out in full-service facilities such as were described earlier.

Major research problems

The focus in this chapter is on what we know and what we do not know. The implicit assumption is that what we do not know defines the needs for research.

What we know. This section, paraphrased from Gray and Nunamaker, presents the conventional wisdom on GDSS [Gray and Nunamaker, 1989]. The experimentation with the use of decision rooms is still in its early stages. A number of papers have appeared which report observations, field research, action research, and laboratory experiments. These papers indicate the high potential for the contribution of computer and communication-based mediation, facilitation, and support in creating effective group decision support. The following is a summary of what has been learned thus far.

The research results have underscored the need to review and examine the theories and hypotheses on group decision making that have been developed in the past. There is reason to believe that many previously held assumptions about the conduct of group deliberation are subject to review in the new electronically based forum. Factors such as speed, anonymity, recording of group processes, voting, and other facilitated activities change the group environment significantly.

Anonymity. The anonymity facilitated by GDSS in the use of electronic brainstorming, voting, and other tools is a positive factor in encouraging broad-based participation. Anonymity is important when sensitive issues being discussed can easily be confounded with personalities in the group. Anonymity also provides a sense of equality and encourages participation by all members in the group, independent of perceived status. Problems of "group think," pressures for conformity, and dominance of the group by strong personalities or particularly forceful speakers are reduced substantially, even though the participants are face-to-face. Group members can contribute without the personal attention and anxiety associated with gaining the floor and being the focus of a particular comment or issue.

Anonymity does tend to heighten conflict within the group because members tend to become more blunt and assertive in their comments and often are not as polite as when speaking face-to-face.* Further, as in any written medium, the richness of voice inflections and facial expressions is lost, which can lead to misunderstanding. Occasional face-to-face discussions as well as breaks and social time are important as issues become more sensitive or politically charged.

Facility design. The lighting and physical organization of the facility affect outcomes. Better results are obtained when the facility has aesthetic appeal and provides a comfortable, familiar setting. Carpeting, wall coverings, executive style furniture, and quality acoustics provide an atmosphere well suited to long sessions over a number of days. The facility should be full service and be able to meet the needs of groups that differ in size and task. It should be designed to accommodate a range of group sizes and be able to support tasks that range from passive to active. Breakout rooms (located adjacent to the decision room) that provide computer-based support make it possible to divide a large group into smaller working groups and are useful for changing the environment

---

* Although the flaming phenomenon has been observed in the extreme in computer conferences involving computer science undergraduates [e.g., Kiesler et al., 1984], other more recent evidence [Hiltz et al., 1989] indicates that the problem decreases as the maturity and organizational responsibilities of participants increase.

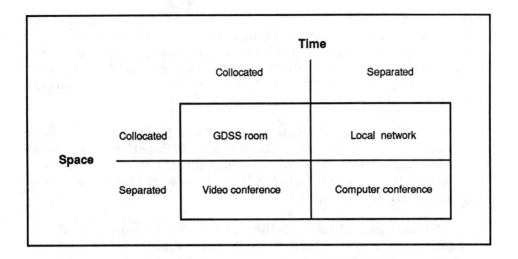

Figure 4. DeSanctis-Gallupe classification of group decision support system arrangements.

during a meeting. Inadequate lighting control and arrangement of lights result in poor legibility of screens both on the public screen and at the individual workstations. For example, front screen projector images are "washed out" by fluorescent lighting, which can reduce the effectiveness of a meeting. Means should be provided to vary light levels during a meeting to match different activities.

Multiple public screens. Using more than one public screen increases group productivity. Not all information can be displayed adequately in the standard format of current computer screens (25 lines by 80 characters). Windowing on a single screen allows presentation of multiple sets of data but reduces the amount of information that is shown about individual items. In a multiple-screen setup, the group can view both the current information being discussed and reference information (e.g., sales trends, financials) at the same time. They can see the existing version and the proposed alternative side by side. In rank ordering, they can see the unordered and ordered items simultaneously.

Knowledge bases and databases. The documentation of meeting activities, the creation of working papers, and the recording of decisions and commitments are particularly useful by-products of GDSS. These outputs are provided without detracting from meeting activities. File servers handle the knowledge bases and databases, facilitate coordination and management of input from individual decision-makers, and serve as "organizational memory" from session to session. The file server functions as a knowledge base repository and provides access to organizational data that is relevant to a particular meeting. A key to effective use of GDSS in supporting planning is the continuity from planning session to planning session provided by an ongoing, expanding knowledge base, which is integrated through the output from software tools. This continuity and integration provide the opportunity for analysis from multiple perspectives.

Communication network speed. Users become impatient if they must wait more than one or two seconds for a screen. Experience has shown that users expect to receive subsecond response for all activities. A wide-bandwidth local area network (LAN) is needed to maintain these high levels of network response.

Fixed versus customized tools. In planning, groups usually start with idea generation, followed by the development of alternatives, and they conclude by converging on a course of action through forming a consensus. A group can go through this process in either of two modes:

- it can create a customized methodology from the set of available tools, or
- it can follow a standard sequence for using the tools.

Some groups prefer to adopt a standard methodology, whereas others feel that their needs are very different from anyone else's and therefore prefer to generate the sequence. Both approaches have given excellent results.

Software design: Ease of use and user friendly. The best GDSS software helps rather than frustrates individual users. It supports a continuum of modes of working ranging from electronically based, self-directed participation to facilitator-directed discussion. However, a minimum amount of instruction and direction is still required. In the system designed by the University of Arizona, for example, it takes less than five minutes to explain how to use each software tool. Efforts to increase software ease of use are particularly worthwhile. Techniques that use color, overlays, windowing, consistent interfaces, and on-demand help screens all help the user (particularly the novice and the computerphobic user) master the software. One or two group members who have difficulty with the software can affect the productivity of the entire group.

Consistency in the dialogue interface protocols permits effective dialogue management, ease of introduction of participants to new support tools, and ease of tool building. Common keystroke assignments, window layouts, use of color, messaging, and icon semantics facilitate this dialogue management.

Screen sharing across and among participants opens new opportunities for particular decision tasks. Activities such as local editing of shared screens, help and monitoring activities, and personal messaging create alternative forms of communication. Using the keyboard as an input device has proved to be much less an inhibitor of active participation than initially had been hypothesized.

Group size and composition. Groups numbering from three to 20 or more of differing composition have used GDSS facilities to accomplish a variety of tasks. One finding is clear: Individual satisfaction increases with the size of the group. Computer support assists groups in building toward a consensus. Larger groups appreciate the inherent structuring that keeps the group from becoming bogged down or subject to domination by personalities. Small groups find that the fixed overhead associated with using the computer-based systems eats up the gains from using the system. Small groups are less likely than large groups to conclude that the computer-aided support is more effective or efficient than an unstructured face-to-face meeting. The various electronic brainstorming approaches do not work effectively with groups of less than four. Such techniques are more effective for groups of eight or more people. Many other techniques, such as stakeholder identification and assumption surfacing, also increase in satisfaction with group size.

The increase in satisfaction with group size is due, in part, to "human parallel processing." That is, in many situations, participants are entering information into the computer simultaneously. They are functioning in parallel rather than in sequence. In a typical meeting that follows, say, Robert's Rules of Order, verbal input is sequential. As a result, if a group of 10 meets for an hour, each participant has the floor for only six minutes on the average. In parallel processing, the group can finish in 20 minutes, and each individual (even a slow typist) makes a larger individual contribution.

Satisfaction. Individual satisfaction is reflected in user reports on the positive aspects of the group decision-making process in a computer-based support environment. Group participants conclude that they are not blocked out of the group and, as a result, they support the group solution with increased confidence.

What we need to know. Although, as was shown in the previous section, we know quite a bit about the nature of GDSS, there is still much to be learned. Some of what we need to know is fundamental data about the nature of groups and their information needs. In addition to understanding what groups do, we need to examine the effect that GDSS has on the way people work in organizations. To do so, we need multiple perspectives:

- effect on the performance of the individual working in the group,
- effect on the performance of the group,
- effect on how organizations work, and
- effect on organizational relationships.

GDSS changes as software and hardware inventions are incorporated in it. Some needed hardware and software innovations can be defined. In addition, we need to know the extent to which hardware and software capabilities affect GDSS performance.

As GDSS moves from the universities to industry, we will need to understand more about implementing these systems. Two areas of importance are cost-benefit studies and critical success factors for implementation.

Information needs of groups. As indicated earlier, group meetings are a joint intellectual activity engaged in by a group of people of equal or near-equal status. Since the objective of GDSS is to support this intellectual activity with information, the role of information in groups is a prime subject for research. In terms of information, Huber pointed out that groups [Huber, 1984b]

- retrieve (or generate) information,
- share information among members, and
- use information to reach consensus or decision.

If effective GDSS are to be built, they must support what groups do. Within the GDSS research community, the knowledge of what real groups do, particularly executive groups, is to a large extent impressionistic or obtained from secondary sources such as research in psychology or management. Some of the impressionistic knowledge comes from the experiences of individual researchers who have worked in organizations and from discussions with practitioners. The secondary sources include streams of field research such as studies in which researchers record and analyze managerial activities during the workday [e.g., Mintzberg, 1971].

Two approaches are needed:

1. Better understanding of what business groups now do and which of these activities and procedures can be and should be supported by GDSS.
2. Creation and test of new ways that groups can function because they have group decision support.

In the first approach, the objective is to obtain baseline data that will allow GDSS to be used to improve the efficiency of existing group

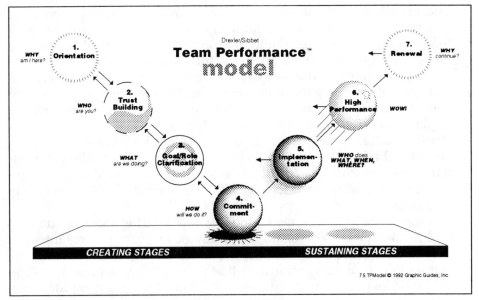

Figure 5. Team performance model [Johansen, 1989].
Reprinted with permission from Graphic Guides, Inc., for Allan Drexler and David Sibbet. *The Drexler/Sibbet Team Performance Model™ 7.5* copyright © 1992.

activities. In the second approach, the research involves not only test but also invention. We can anticipate that GDSS will be used in innovative ways (e.g., human parallel processing) just as, for example, nominal group technique [Delbecq et al., 1975] and Delphi [Dalkey and Helmer, 1963] were innovative, creative ways of obtaining participation in unsupported groups. Experimental tests of the new procedures and structures will indicate whether they offer advantages over current ways of working.

The Drexler and Sibbet team performance model [Johansen, 1989] shown in Figure 5 effectively summarizes the basic dynamics of business teams. It serves as a basis for articulating group activities.

The information needs of groups cover a broad spectrum. The following list outlines the range of information that groups use. In most cases, very little research has been done on how best to support these information uses with GDSS:

• Database access: One of the advantages offered by GDSS is access during a meeting to databases resident on an organization's computer, available from an on-line service such as Dow Jones, or stored in CD-ROM form. The ability to access a variety of data sources on line has been developed extensively by executive information system (EIS) vendors but has not been studied extensively in the GDSS environment. Yet database access is a key element in information retrieval and sharing in a group meeting.

- Information creation: In addition to decisions, the output of a meeting is new information. Most organizations do little to capture such information beyond the creation of memos for the record or minutes of the meeting. In GDSS, all input into the computer can be (and usually is) captured. In some cases, one person in a GDSS meeting is charged with keeping minutes electronically. Although we know that valuable knowledge bases result, we do not know the organizational implications of creating these knowledge bases.
- Dissemination of information, decisions, and responsibilities: An often-cited advantage of GDSS is that the records kept allow participants to know what new information was created, what decisions were reached, and who is responsible for follow-up or for implementing decisions.
- On-line modeling: The next step beyond sharing existing data is on-line modeling. For example, a financial plan is presented in spreadsheet form for a new capital item. Each participant, having computer access, can perform on-line what-if analysis or even on-line modeling as private work and then, if he or she has a good idea, can present the result to the group via a public screen. Exploratory studies have been run in which on-line modeling capabilities were provided to subjects [e.g., Aronson et al., 1987] but this avenue has not been explored systematically.
- Visual decision making: Some decisions involve visuals rather than words or numbers. Organizations decide on advertising, packaging, logos, product designs, and floor layouts, to name just a few examples. At present, if a group reviewing plans for visuals wants to see new alternatives, extensive rework and typically a new meeting are required. Through the use of CAD software, GDSS can be used to provide visuals on line, and shapes, sizes, colors, and so on can be varied as what-if's.
- Idea generation: A variety of idea generation packages for GDSS use exist. There is no consensus as to which are the best packages or implementations.
- Voting: Almost all GDSS provide the ability to vote, rank, or rate. Although easy to implement and widely used in GDSS research, we do not know the extent to which voting is appropriate in real organizational settings.

Effect on individuals. The effect of GDSS on the individual has been a central thrust of research in the US. The focus has been on whether the individual performs better and/or feels better (i.e., is more satisfied) with a particular GDSS than without it. The underlying assumption is that if individuals perform more poorly or are dissatisfied, that GDSS will not be used. However, over time and perhaps because of the US culture's focus on the individual, personal productivity and satisfaction have implicitly become the prime performance measures for GDSS in the US. As indicated below, group output measures may be equally or more important.

The foregoing is not intended to imply that study of the effects of GDSS on individual productivity and job satisfaction should be discontinued. This line of research is, of course, an ongoing one that will need to be repeated for each new system or configuration. Most laboratory experimentation has involved people who are first-time users of a GDSS. The research thus far has focused on groups meeting once (i.e., they have no history and no future) and on comparisons between groups using a GDSS and those without (see the section "Baseline studies"). As a result, learning curve effects and changes in attitude and acceptance from repeated use have not been studied. (An exception is work which followed business school groups using the same GDSS over time.) In the future, studies of individuals will also need to evaluate individual effects for new GDSS against those for the best existing GDSS (see the section "Comparison of alternate GDSS").

Effect on how groups work. A considerable body of work, done mostly in the 1950s and 1960s at Tavistock in England, studied the effects of group process on group outcomes. This literature is little known in the US. Yet the prime measure of effectiveness for an organization is whether the investment in GDSS pays off in improving the performance of the group and the company as a whole.

The British literature, particularly the work at Tavistock, needs to be obtained in the US and reviewed. Experimentation that focuses on the individual within the group needs to be broadened so that it measures group changes as well.

The following list suggests the range of issues in the study of group process:

- Group size: Preliminary results indicate that current GDSS are better suited for large rather than small groups. Two lines of research immediately suggest themselves: (1) Evaluating the optimal group sizes for different GDSS software and systems, and (2) devising GDSS software optimized for small groups (e.g., two, three, or four people).
- Group structure and protocol: Currently available software packages have different group structures and protocols built into their design or into their use. For example, the Arizona Electronic Meeting System [Nunamaker et al., 1988] uses a centralized structure in which there is great flexibility in the order in which tools are used but only the tool currently selected by the chauffeur can be used. In the Minnesota SAMM system [DeSanctis and Gallupe, 1985], the approach is democratic in that any participant can take control of the system and move to any portion of the sequence of steps, but the steps to be performed

are defined. The effects of the assumptions about group structure and meeting protocol are not yet known.

- Number of people per screen: Anecdotal evidence indicates that putting two or three people at a single workstation improves performance because they share ideas and divide the typing load. The idea sharing results in synergy. Whether this impression is correct and whether sharing improves group performance are not known.

Effect on how organizations work. This issue is only now starting to be researched as systems are installed in organizations. Most questions are still open because only a few systems exist in organizations. We have no experience base, merely conjecture and hope. As we head into the 1990s with GDSS being installed in major firms such as IBM, an opportunity exists for field studies to complement laboratory studies.

Organizational effects can occur in three ways:

1. Changes in the way organizations accomplish their work (discussed in this section).
2. Changes in the relationships within organizations (discussed in the next section).
3. The use of GDSS to support organizational decisions (see Chapter 5).

The support of organizational decisions is the subject of the ISDP study of organizational DSS presented in Chapter 5. The focus of that work is on supporting decisions that involve the organization as a whole rather than a single manager or a team. A DSS or a GDSS may be used to support organizational decision making.

In this section we focus on how organizations accomplish their work. Drucker [Drucker, 1988] and others have noted the trend toward the use of team problem solving in organizations. The need to coordinate teams has led to an increase in the number of group meetings. GDSS offers one avenue toward making these meetings more efficient and more effective.

In thinking about the use of GDSS to support team meetings, some researchable questions naturally come to mind:

- Does GDSS simply provide a more cost-effective way of running meetings than previously?
- Are new types of meetings being held because of the capabilities available from GDSS?
- Are some existing meetings being eliminated or the number of meetings required to resolve an issue being changed?
- If time to closure on an issue decreases from the use of GDSS, is the organization losing concepts, ideas, and understanding that comes from longer gestation periods?

- Are the tangible outputs of GDSS (e.g., knowledge bases; recording of minutes, ideas, and assignments) being used to improve the quality of team performance?
- Since GDSS provides a technological environment to support problem solving, are GDSS facilities and groupware being used for computer-supported cooperative work (CSCW) as well as decision making?
- Are there new, innovative ways of using GDSS that change the way an organization does its work?

Effect on organizational relationships. The concept of departmentalizing results in organizational units working mostly on their own, within their area of specialization and technical expertise. Of course, each unit receives input from and provides output to other units. When resource, technical, or political mismatches exist between units, they must be resolved either on a one-to-one basis or through meetings. Meetings provide a forum for negotiation and conflict resolution.

Introducing GDSS can change organizational relationships. For example, in a GDSS environment, all groups can have access to common models and data, and individual groups can come in with their own data and models. Skill in using the models and preparation of data can give one group an advantage (and perhaps power) over another. The use of anonymity for some group processes such as electronic discussions and voting allows people to give their true opinion rather than being bound by parochial group loyalties. Although the possibilities for these phenomena exist, we do not know whether they do in fact exist. Furthermore, we have no basis as yet for judging whether these effects are desirable or not.

GDSS appears to provide one of the enabling mechanisms that will help organizations move from traditional line-staff relations to project teams. This transition is well under way [Drucker, 1988]. However, many staff functions will still have to be performed. For example, staffs prepare long-range plans and capital budgets that are reviewed in group meetings. How will GDSS change the relations in the organization for these functions?

Hardware effects. The computer hardware for most existing GDSS is equipment that can be ordered from a local computer store. As hardware improvements have come on the market, they have been incorporated. Thus, research results obtained at the same facility at different times may represent very different hardware capabilities. Hardware can make a difference in response time, storage capacity, interface quality, database size, and software packages that can be handled. For example, we know that executives require very quick response times if they are to accept use of these systems.

Hardware costs are high and directly correlated with capability. In the case of GDSS, improving hardware capabilities at individual workstations requires replication at each workstation. Thus, an investment of an additional $5,000 at a workstation results in an investment of $50,000 for a system with 10 stations and $100,000 with 20 stations.

Hardware can both facilitate and inhibit GDSS. The use of networks, the ability to retrieve and manipulate data quickly, the availability of high-resolution personal and public displays, and nearly seamless interfaces between personal computers and mainframes are among the technologies that have made GDSS viable. GDSS designers and users are continually clamoring for more and more computer and display capability. It is not clear, however, in which situations hardware (rather than software or people) is the limiting factor in performance, nor what the marginal benefits are of applying specific technologies to GDSS. Some questions are the following:

- How much does touch screen or mouse or voice input improve a GDSS over a system with keyboard entry only?
- What is the value of WYSIWIS (what you see is what I see) technology such as in COLAB [Stefik et al., 1987]?
- How much does additional color resolution (such as VGA rather than CGA) contribute?

The 1990s promise to bring us more economic versions of technologies such as voice input, video conferencing, and multiple screen images. Although studies exist of the productivity benefits associated with specific technologies for individual users, we know of none that looks specifically at the effects of hardware or hardware enhancements on the performance of groups and of GDSS. Research needs to be conducted at three levels: the systems level, the component level, and the interaction among hardware, software, and people.

For hardware, as for software, there is great room for innovation and invention. We anticipate that GDSS will continue to adapt technologies that come on the market rather than create them.

Facility effects. Some facility design research for GDSS has been undertaken [e.g., Mantei, 1989; Seward, 1988], and some conventional wisdom exists (see the earlier section "What we know"). Most facilities design has relied on good practice (control noise and heat, provide executive look and feel) and on architects and designers experienced in conference room work. Most facilities have been installed in existing buildings where the dimensions of the room and many of its characteristics were fixed by previous uses. A major two-cultures communication problem exists between GDSS designers and architects. Conference room design research, even in a noncomputer environment, is not a topic of concern for architects. Although a number of rooms have now been built, we do not yet know what the best shape for a room is, how much table space should be provided for each participant, or how close participants should be to one another. There are no standards for light, heat, or sound levels; or for the number, location, and brightness of the public screens. Opportunities exist for creative interdisciplinary research in this area.

Software effects. In addition to using off-the-shelf commercial packages such as spreadsheets, existing GDSS facilities usually have software designed specifically for group activities, such as navigating through a meeting, voting, or brainstorming. Software selection and development have generally been a creative design choice to solve specific problems or specific notions of how meetings work. In comparing experimental results achieved at different sites, for example, it is difficult to determine how much the observed differences are due to differences in software (or hardware, for that matter). The widespread use of the Electronic Meeting System software package from the University of Arizona [Nunamaker et al., 1988] has started to bring some order to GDSS software.

Like hardware, software can enhance or inhibit. For example, an unenhanced Unix operating system limits the graphical interface that can be presented to users. On the other hand, software solutions can sometimes overcome hardware limitations. The conventional wisdom, untested by research, is that GDSS must provide quick response, simple interfaces, and the ability to view any data, anytime, in any form requested.

Software in GDSS needs to be considered in two dimensions: the quality of the interface and the specific software required. With a decision support system, we know that to the user the system is the interface [Bennett, 1983]. The design problem involves answering three questions:

1. What does the user see?
2. What does the user have to understand about what is shown?
3. What can the user do about what is shown?

In GDSS design, the interface problem is exacerbated by the need for short training times. Since the software is used by everyone in a meeting, the interfaces have to be crystal clear. Furthermore, the public and private screens have to be compatible so that users can move easily from one to the other. We do not know how much GDSS results on individual performance, individual satisfaction, or group performance are affected by the particular interface provided.

The software required for a particular problem is, of course, situational. Most GDSS facilities try to provide a set of software tools that they believe allows solving a representative set of problems. Such fundamental questions as the following are largely unanswered:

• How much and what kind of software should be provided?

- What are the relative merits of existing GDSS packages?
- What are the specifications of additional software tools that should be created?

For example, we know of no one who has been assessing, or for that matter even tracking, GDSS packages. Existing GDSS packages work in different environments (e.g., DOS, Unix), do different things, and have different effects. We need to know what each package does, how good it is, and how easy it is to implement.

Artificial intelligence. Artificial intelligence (AI) represents a special category of software. Johansen, in the most complex of his 17 groupware scenarios, posits a GDSS in which an AI system is the $(n+1)$st person in the meeting [Johansen, 1988]. We know that a GDSS can be used to elicit expert opinion [Fellers et al., 1988]. We do not yet know whether or how an AI system can be used to support group decision making. An AI-based GDSS represents a new class of system, one that must first be designed and then tested.

Direct and indirect costs of using GDSS. For simplicity, we define direct costs of GDSS as including all those costs incurred in setting up and running the facility and indirect costs as those borne by the people who use the facility. We also limit our discussion to actual outlays:

- Direct costs: GDSS does not come for free. As indicated earlier, full-service facilities are required if GDSS is to survive in an organization. GDSS therefore requires considerable up-front investment in hardware, software, space, and furnishings (250,000 1990 dollars is a typical order of magnitude at commercial prices for a system built from scratch*) as well as investment in people to run the facility after it is built. Ongoing operating costs include people to support the facility, hardware maintenance and updating, software enhancement, and training.
- Indirect costs: Although we implicitly assume that GDSS will lead to more efficient meetings and hence reductions in time spent in meetings, the existence of GDSS may also result in users increasing the time they spend preparing for meetings and the time spent in meeting follow-up. For example, since GDSS offers on-line data retrieval and modeling, preparation now involves creating the databases, spreadsheets, and so on needed to be able to run the assumptions

---

* For example, a room with 10 386-level workstations, a chauffeur/server station, and a VGA public screen will involve $100,000 in computers and electronics, $100,000 in software, and $50,000 in facility costs for custom furnishings, carpeting, lighting, drapes, raised floors, and so on.

being discussed through the models. An analysis is required of the indirect costs of GDSS, that is, the costs generated because GDSS is present.

- Cost analysis: Major capital investments must be justified through cost-benefit analysis. We do not yet have good quantitative models for assessing either the benefits or the costs of GDSS. Most research has focused on finding the benefits associated with GDSS. Determining direct costs appears to be relatively straightforward. Analysis of indirect costs will require a deeper, more sophisticated analysis. If GDSS are to be implemented in organizations, then their costs will have to be justified. A sound cost analysis methodology will help in achieving implementations.

Critical success factors for implementation. In a seminal conceptual paper, Huber defined a number of factors that he believed were critical for GDSS survival in organizations [Huber, 1984b]. For example, Huber argued that GDSS requires much higher equipment "up time" than DSS since a system failure inconveniences not just one person, but a group of important, highly paid people. As GDSS facilities come on line in organizations over the next several years, implementation research such as was done for DSS [e.g., Alter, 1980] needs to be repeated for GDSS. This research involves analyzing experiences with field installations to find the critical success factors [Rockart, 1979] and the critical failure factors. It can be anticipated that the factors found necessary for DSS survival (e.g., early success, infrastructure for support, corporate champion) will also be found for GDSS.

Range of studies needed. In the section "What we need to know," we examined the needs for GDSS research in terms of the gaps in knowledge. In this section, we examine GDSS research in terms of the types of studies that are needed. One way of dividing studies is according to the research methodology:

- laboratory studies,
- case studies, and
- field studies.

In the case of GDSS, all three methodologies are applicable. These studies, in turn, can be divided into

- small-group research and large-group research,
- groups involved in a single session and ongoing groups over many sessions, and
- the range of tasks from simple, artificial tasks to complex, real tasks.

These distinctions were included in the definition of variables given in Table 3. In this section, we look at the range of studies from the perspective of which GDSS is considered and the robustness of the results.

Baseline studies (GDSS versus no GDSS). Almost all GDSS studies reported in the literature are baseline studies. In these studies, the same task is given to groups using a particular GDSS and to similar or matched groups without that GDSS. The usual research hypothesis is that the groups using the GDSS have better individual and/or group performance than those that do not. Baseline studies will continue to be performed for each new GDSS configuration to prove the design.

Comparison of alternate GDSS. Present GDSS environments (hardware, software, physical facilities) are not standardized. Many research papers, however, try to generalize their conclusions from the particular GDSS used in an experiment to all GDSS [e.g., Watson et al., 1988]. Such generalization is premature. Experiments are required that compare alternate GDSS designs with one another. One approach is to replicate experiments in various research environments to see which effects are robust and which are dependent on the environment (see the next section).

We can also anticipate that new GDSS environments—involving improved hardware, software, and facilities—will be developed over the years. In addition to requiring baseline comparisons, there will be a need to repeat previous experiments to measure the extent of the improvements over existing systems actually being achieved.

Robustness of experimental results. Research results thus far have been obtained in individual experiments. Each experiment has been run independently. Where a series of experiments has been run at a particular facility, the experiments have looked at variations in one or two parameters from a base case. Relatively little has been done to determine the robustness of results. By robustness we mean results that apply not just under the conditions of one experiment, but apply to whole classes of GDSS situations. Robustness can be defined across facilities, software, tasks, types of GDSS, group sizes, cultures, and so on.

Some idea of robustness can be obtained by analyzing reported experimental results obtained under different conditions. The survey papers by Kraemer and King [Kraemer and King, 1988] and Pinsonneault and Kraemer [Pinsonneault and Kraemer, 1989, 1990] are first attempts to do so. Techniques such as multidimensional scaling (see Figure 3) can be used to define similar and different situations [Gray et al., 1990]. All these approaches are forms of secondary research. It will probably be difficult to obtain strong results in this way because the research designs of the individual studies were not set up to look for robustness.

What is needed is the replication of experiments under a variety of conditions to determine how robust the observed results are. This type of research is called for particularly when new or unexpected phenomena are observed. By repeating experiments—for example, at different facilities, with different types of groups, and with different technological support—it is possible to see whether the phenomena identified are universal or parochial to the original situation. To accomplish such replication will require cooperation among research groups at different locations. In the past, little credit was given for replication; however, if replication is included in the original paper and papers are joint authored, the institutional barrier to replication should be eliminated. Being a new field with a finite number of facilities where the main researchers know one another, GDSS offers a unique opportunity for replicating research. This opportunity should not be wasted.

Robustness across cultures. A particularly important form of robustness is across cultures. GDSS facilities are now being installed worldwide: in the United States, Canada, Singapore, Australia, and Europe. Most of the research has been done in the United States and carries with it the assumptions of American culture. Preliminary analyses and experiments [e.g., Gray et al., 1988; Park, 1990; George and Nunamaker, 1988] have examined the implications of culture on GDSS for situations that involve other cultures uniquely or deal with intercultural uses such as in international negotiation. It can be anticipated that GDSS designs and payoffs will vary with culture. In GDSS use for international negotiations, translation and cross-cultural data will have to be provided to each party. This work is just in its beginnings but is an important direction for research.

Findings and recommended priorities

Group decision support systems are both a technological and a social invention. Although many studies of GDSS are grounded in the methods and approaches of social science research, GDSS research also involves the interaction between social science and engineering development. In most social science research, the objective is to examine what exists societally. It deals with phenomena that are relatively static. GDSS, however, is a dynamic field that is being invented at the same time it is being studied. Thus, GDSS research involves

• experiments, case studies, and field studies on existing systems;

- finding new ways in which existing functions can be better performed, that is, improved efficiency; and
- finding new functions that can and should be performed given the existence of GDSS, that is, leverage.

In GDSS research there is continual feedback between experimentation and invention of equipment, software, and process. The laboratory research to date has focused principally on the behavioral aspects of GDSS and has been tied to the particular characteristics of individual prototype systems. Although this research has led to valuable insights, it is limited in its generality because much of it may apply only to the characteristics of the particular systems studied.

The next section summarizes the research needs found in the group decision support systems portion of the ISDP project. These findings are supplemented in the appendix to this chapter, which lists the major ideas and research topics developed during the study. Since these needs lead to a potentially very large research program, we prioritize the recommended research in the section "Recommended priorities."

Summary of findings. GDSS moved a long way during the 1980s from being a concept to being a field of intense information systems research. Although much has been learned, much still remains to be learned. In this section, we summarize the areas requiring further research in the following order:

> What groups do
> Effects of GDSS on group work
> Effects of GDSS on organizations
> Effects of hardware on GDSS performance
> Effects of software on GDSS performance
> Cultural effects in GDSS
> Training people to use GDSS
> Cost-benefit analysis for GDSS
> Critical success factors
> Robustness of results
> Innovative uses of GDSS
> Underlying theory
> Barriers to research

Each of these areas represents a major, multiyear, multiperson research program in itself. It is certainly not possible for one individual or even one major institution to accomplish this entire agenda. However, work must begin somewhere. We hope that the following long list will inspire graduate students, particularly PhD candidates, and faculty to begin working in areas that are new to them and in which major advances are needed.

What groups do. Since the objective of group decision support systems is to help groups accomplish their work, knowledge of what groups in organizations really do is fundamental. Much laboratory research on groups and group behavior has been done over the years, but most of it has centered on finding general phenomena and has used student populations as subjects. Knowledge of what business groups do that GDSS can help with is to a large extent impressionistic. Research is required to

- analyze the functions business groups perform,
- examine the processes being used by business groups to carry out these functions,
- determine what makes group meetings effective and what makes them ineffective,
- determine which meeting activities could and should be supported by GDSS and which should not, and
- invent new processes for use in meetings.

As was indicated in Table 1, group functions range from coordination among cooperating workers to hierarchical information passing to attempts at conflict resolution among competing parties. All of these functions may be present simultaneously at the same meeting. The extent of the various functions in a particular meeting is a function of the subject matter of the meeting and the stage in the deliberation on a particular issue.

The foregoing implies that merely going into a number of meetings and, say, video recording what happens cannot be expected to provide the insights needed. Rather, a first step is a conceptual study to define the data that should be gathered—that is, to create a vocabulary by which the functions can be studied.

How the functions play out in a meeting is determined to a certain extent by the process used. Just because a process is currently used does not mean that it is appropriate or optimum.

Analysis of current processes, like the study of current functions, provides baseline data. It also provides the information needed to make assessments of which activities can be supported and, perhaps more important, which *should* be supported. In thinking about how GDSS can contribute, we have to recognize that GDSS technology can be intrusive as well as helpful.

The techniques available to groups in the paper-and-pencil world expanded over the years, for example, nominal group technique and Delphi. As we develop an electronic world for meetings, we have the opportunity to create new ways for groups to work. Some of these inventions may be generic, whereas others may be quite situation specific. Much of this work is not research on GDSS per se. It is nonetheless critical to all that follows.

Effect of GDSS on group work. Existing GDSS studies provide data about the impact of specific systems on both individuals and groups. The data points are quite scattered. A central question that needs to be addressed in GDSS research is, What systems result in what impacts under what conditions? If we can answer this question, we will be at the point of being able to recommend how best to use GDSS for specific problems. Although simple to state, this goal is difficult to achieve.

The breakdown of variables given in Table 3 is a beginning step toward defining conditions. The research questions listed in this section deal with the impacts of GDSS on group work:

- Effect on individuals: This research has two dimensions: performance and satisfaction. Studying the effect on individuals is an ongoing task that needs to be repeated for each new system developed. The underlying assumptions that improving individual performance and satisfaction will result in improved group performance require validation. Much of the research to date has been based on "one-shot" use of facilities. Longitudinal studies involving individuals who use the facility repeatedly (both for multiple sessions involving a single problem and for multiple problems) are needed to determine learning effects.
- Effect on group outcome: Improving individual performance, although desirable, is not the bottom line. It is group outcome. Extensive experimental work on group performance has been done in England, particularly at Tavistock. This work needs to be examined and in some cases repeated in GDSS environments.
- Baseline studies and comparative studies: Baseline studies compare a particular GDSS against the case of no support. Most studies to date have been of this variety. Positive results in a baseline study are necessary but not a sufficient condition. As we gain experience with GDSS and new systems come on line, it will be appropriate to compare their new designs with existing designs to determine whether they offer additional benefits.
- Predicting impacts: The preceding has implicitly assumed a research strategy in which there is a seemingly unending cycle of design and test, analogous to the trial and error that Edison used in inventing the light bulb. We will probably have to follow this strategy in the short term. A more appropriate long-term strategy is to focus on developing an understanding of the underlying processes in group meetings (see the previous section) and then studying how GDSS affect these

processes. Thus, the research objective is to determine not just whether there is an impact but how that impact arises. Once we reach that level of understanding, we will have a model that can be used to predict impacts and guide the evolution toward new systems.

Effect of GDSS on organizations. The effect of GDSS on organizations is a new research dimension for the 1990s. Until now, most GDSS work has involved laboratory research because systems were not in place in organizations. As systems are installed in organizations, field research and case studies become feasible. As GDSS are used in organizations, we can expect that organizational relationships and even organizational structures will change. To understand these changes, both conceptual and field studies are recommended. The conceptual studies should examine the implications of changing the information relationships in organization made possible by GDSS. The field and case studies should look for both the changes postulated theoretically and the changes that actually occur.

Effect of hardware on GDSS performance. Just as GDSS can be liberating by providing new capabilities, it can also be constraining. For example, human parallel processing, a GDSS invention, implies that many people are trying to enter data through the network simultaneously. Yet networks slow down when loads go up, and GDSS procedures create impulse loads on networks. Examination of hardware constraints in terms of GDSS applications should lead to defining requirements for new hardware developments and innovations.

Much new technology is on the horizon, particularly massive computing power at the desk; brilliant, high-resolution video and display technologies; and mass storage such as CDs with write as well as read capabilities. As new hardware comes on line, which should be adopted to support groups? Adoption should be based on what its introduction does to improve meeting outcomes not its technical excellence. Thus, in this area, continuing research should focus on the value added by the new technologies.

Effect of software on GDSS performance. The same issues and hence the same research needs exist for software as for hardware. Thus we can say that

- software and software response can be limiting,
- new software should be adopted if it improves meeting outcomes, and
- the objective of software development should be value added.

In the case of software, developments for GDSS have been generic and have focused more on text than on models or graphics. Much effort has gone into supporting problem formulation and alternative generation (for example, the extensive availability of brainstorming software). Less has been done to support modeling and decision making. For example, advances in decision making such as analytic hierarchy process, influence diagrams, and attitudes toward risk are not yet available in GDSS. Software development is also a natural follow-on to the studies of what groups do and how GDSS affects group work.

In thinking about software, it is important to keep in mind that software and hardware interact and, to a certain extent, trade off. Furthermore, while in a given facility the hardware configuration tends to be fixed for considerable periods of time, it is the software which allows a multiplicity of applications to be undertaken. The implication for research is that a major service to the field would be performed if one of the GDSS research facilities undertakes a systematic program of evaluating GDSS software.

Cultural effects in GDSS. GDSS has been developed principally in the United States and has strong US cultural biases built into it. How groups work differs among cultures. A fertile field for research, currently in its infancy, is study of the interactions of culture and GDSS. One line of research, call it monocultural research, involves examining the changes in facilities and procedures implied when moving to another culture. A second line of research involves multicultural settings such as meetings in multinational organizations or in transnational negotiations.

Training people to use GDSS. Studies of the implementation of information systems consistently show that training people to use the system is a critical success factor. Yet training has not been a major information systems research thrust. In the case of GDSS, the usual approach has been to develop software tools that require a minimum of training (usually a few minutes of explanation). To make more complex systems work, a facilitator (usually highly skilled) and/or a technology chauffeur has been introduced. This approach has eliminated the need for formal training. However, the approach has its limits. Tools will inevitably become more complex as GDSS are applied to more sophisticated problems. Facilitators are scarce and expensive. In the long run, user groups will have to know how to use GDSS by themselves.

The training problem is complicated by the nature of the GDSS audience. The user population includes many senior executives, the very people who are busiest and who are, on the average, least computer literate and least patient with systems. Furthermore, we are still in the early stages of GDSS implementation where practice is not standardized and where we do not yet know the best way to use these systems. As a result, developing and testing training methods for GDSS is a major research need and opportunity.

Cost-benefit analysis for GDSS. The implementation of GDSS in organizations requires major, up-front capital investment. In today's "lean and mean" business world, such costs have to be justified. To aid planners, a cost-benefit methodology for GDSS needs to be developed. This methodology would, most likely, build on conventional practice.

Direct, indirect, and opportunity costs associated with GDSS will have to be considered. As is the case for most social innovations, benefits resulting from increased efficiency will be easier to define than those resulting from effectiveness or leverage. We need to find the value added by GDSS that makes them economically viable and will result in moving them out of the universities and into practice.

Critical success factors for implementation. If GDSS are to survive in organizations over extended periods, we will have to understand the critical factors that lead to success. Field and case studies of implementations need to be undertaken. These studies should pay special attention to why successes were achieved and how these successes can be generalized.

Robustness of experimental results. The existing body of GDSS experimental research, like much social science research, consists of individual studies done under very specific conditions. This approach makes it difficult to use the results to generalize and predict. Given the newness of the field and the existence of a network of facilities, an opportunity exists for replicating experiments to determine which results are robust and which are situation specific.

We recognize that there is little payoff in the research reward structure for repeating someone else's previous experiment. Replication can, however, become part of the initial experimental design. For example, a PhD candidate writing an experimental dissertation can replicate his or her experiment at several facilities. Joint, multiauthor publication should solve the reward structure problem.

Innovative uses of GDSS. Like most technology innovations, the initial uses of GDSS focused on gaining efficiency in performing existing tasks such as recording meeting outcomes, brainstorming, planning, or capital budgeting. The potential exists for a much broader range of applications. Artificial intelligence concepts, such as expert system models, can introduce a nonhuman "participant" to aid the group in its deliberations. Meetings with strong visual components (e.g., package design, corporate logo selection, product design, software walk-throughs) can make use of the interactive graphics capabilities in GDSS. Other possible applications are

- supporting issue-oriented deliberations,
- supporting crisis resolution,

- making personnel decisions,
- video (and/or audio and/or computer) conferencing to bring experts into the meeting for the specific time they are needed, and
- providing a group process adviser.

Theoretical foundations for GDSS. GDSS research has focused on technological innovation and laboratory experimentation. It has relied on the brilliance and insights of very inventive people. It has little theoretical base. Yet theory is needed if we are to reach the goal of predicting what systems result in what impacts under what conditions. A first step in this direction may well be to develop better models of how people work together and of how the introduction of technology affects group work.

Barriers to research. It is axiomatic that it is much easier to write prescriptions for research than to actually perform it. In real life, many obstacles arise which limit what can be achieved. We believe the following are among the major barriers to quality research in GDSS:

- the entry and operating costs,
- the need for large numbers of subjects, particularly subjects representative of real-world groups,
- the lack of standards for reporting research designs and measurements,
- instability of funding,
- lack of an entrepreneur,
- lack of a theory,
- instability of software, and
- cost of software.

As we showed in an earlier section, entry and operating costs for GDSS laboratory research are high because a facility that provides a GDSS with hardware, software, and measurement equipment must be established and maintained. Entry costs will be reduced for case and field studies where many of the required facilities will be provided by the group being studied. However, these cost savings will be used up in other costs such as travel, living expenses, and the difficulty of being away for extended periods of time to make observations.

Experimentation also poses the problem of obtaining large numbers of suitable subjects to be able to draw statistically valid inferences. It is almost a series of catch-22 situations. The conventional wisdom is that the larger the group, the more GDSS helps. Yet the larger the group, the more subjects required for each replication. Students are the most easily obtainable subjects, but students are least representative of realistic situations. The larger the number of replications, the more statistically valid the results, but the number of subjects required is linear in the number of replications.

The cost of running a single well-designed experiment can easily run from $5,000 to $10,000. A program of research to answer meaningful questions quickly approaches $200,000 when fully costed for laboratory setups, research assistants, and maintenance. The high cost of creating and operating facilities implies that universities will engage in many extraneous activities to keep the facility going, such as training sessions or rental to private firms for company confidential use. The glamour of just having a facility implies many "show-and-tell" sessions and many nonresearch activities. In short, the research organizations are in a revenue raising trap that diverts time from research.

These extraneous activities are due, in part, to the instability in funding research in universities. GDSS has been favored recently by NSF and some other agencies because it is a new and glamorous field. However, only a few facilities have been blessed with such funds. Given the fickle nature of federal funding, it is unlikely that such funding will endure.

GDSS requires groupware. Although pricing for software that runs on a network does allow some economies of scale as the number of stations increases, GDSS software is groupware and can involve considerable cost. In absolute terms, the cost for multiple stations is always greater than for a single station.

Unlike hardware, which can be bought commercially off the shelf, much GDSS software (particularly new software tools) must be custom created. The field is fortunate that major efforts have been undertaken by several institutions, particularly the University of Arizona and the University of Minnesota. Nonetheless, software presents two major problems. One is that some GDSS software is unstable and subject to bugs. This instability results from much of the new research software being written by graduate students rather than as commercial products. Second, where commercial products are used, costs are high because (1) licenses must be obtained for multiple rather than single stations and (2) much of the software relies on small markets, pushing prices up.

Standards for reporting GDSS research do not exist. To be able to understand what has been done, it is necessary to have documentation on participants, protocols, measures, measurements, threats to validity, and so on. Data are being obtained over a wide range of group situations, group structures, technological support, task characteristics, and group processes. Until standards are established and experiments can be replicated, it will be difficult to generalize from the individual results being obtained.

Recommended priorities. The previous section presented a long list of areas for research in GDSS. When read together with the sections "What we need to know" and "Range of studies needed," a truly massive set of research possibilities is defined. Clearly not everything proposed here can be undertaken simultaneously. Some priorities have to be set. In this section, we focus on what we believe to be the areas of most immediate importance for GDSS research. These areas are

- what groups do,
- finding ways in which GDSS provides leverage,
- standardization of definition of experiments,
- case/field studies of implementation, and
- theory development.

What groups do. Research on what groups do and how they do it is fundamental input to GDSS research. This work requires interaction with researchers from other disciplines including psychology, communications, and management. Consideration needs to be given to the reasons for group meetings, the information needed by the group, the processes used by the groups, and the group outcomes. Both successful and unsuccessful meetings need to be studied.

Leverages from GDSS. Given the high investment of people and money required to install a GDSS in an organization, simply making meetings more efficient is not likely to justify the costs. Leverage (that is, the ability to do things in new ways and to do new things) will be needed. Innovations in the ways group work, in the ways organizations function, and in applications are required.

Although it is not clear cut whether improvements in hardware and software performance and cost represent research or are development, such improvements may, in fact, provide more significant leverage, particularly in encouraging adoption of GDSS by organizations.

Standardization of definition of experiments. The lack of standards in experimentation is a barrier to research. To make experimental results robust will require replication, standards for comparing experiments, and standards for reporting experiments.

Case/field studies and implementation research. For GDSS to gain acceptance in industry, we will need to establish critical success factors for implementation. With systems now moving from development laboratories to user organizations, the opportunity exists for case studies and field studies of implementations.

Field research should focus not only on current uses of GDSS and related technology but also on types of meetings and common problems of those meetings to find the appropriate combination of technology, training, and human communication.

Some final thoughts

The evolution of GDSS as a research area can be characterized chronologically as follows:

1981-83: Initial papers describe group decision support systems. Simple systems built.

1982-85: Survey papers and research agendas.

1982-86: Initial experimentation and experimental results.

1986-90: Advanced research facilities constructed and GDSS-specific software developed and tested.

1988-   : Transfer of GDSS technology and software to industry.

As indicated by the chronology, GDSS has moved from the laboratory stage toward the implementation state. It is not there yet. Unlike the initial stages of DSS, when there was relatively rapid transfer of technology from the campus to industry, GDSS has been gestating in the university environments for nearly a decade. Several causes may have contributed to this time lag, including the following:

- The much higher investment associated with GDSS.
- The relatively rudimentary state of groupware and GDSS software packages until recently.
- The difficulties experienced when DSS were implemented.
- The lack of focus in organizations on team activities.
- The lack of investment in conferencing facilities in general.

Recent events have changed the situation. In particular, the following have all made GDSS more viable for organizational adoption:

- The emphasis on teams and the flattening of organizations.
- The realization that meetings are absorbing ever greater amounts of executive time.
- The growth of capability and availability of groupware and GDSS products.
- The decreasing costs/increasing capabilities of networked systems.

Furthermore, with IBM taking the lead in installing a large number of facilities, the GDSS concept has been legitimized.

The foregoing arguments all point to a large number of implementations in the 1990s. What will these implementations be like? What will they be used for?

Assuming that what happened with previous waves of information systems implementations is indicative, we can expect that typical GDSS implementations will use only a portion of the capabilities potentially available. Simple things, like keeping a record of a meeting, are much more likely to be widespread than the use of advanced, on-line modeling or what-if analysis. Similarly, brainstorming tools would find broader use than, say, stakeholder analysis. Some of the features of GDSS software, such as anonymity, may prove to be less pervasive and less used than suggested by the current research emphasis on them. This lag between research and practice is normal and does not appear fatal.

What is of greater concern is that we have little experience in implementing GDSS and concomitantly little research data about implementation. The history of GDSS facilities in organizations, with their dependence on the continuing presence of a champion, is not encouraging. (One of the members of the ISDP team, for example, argues that the inability of the systems to survive beyond the whims of an individual implies that they did not do anything sufficiently important.) The lack of experience coupled with the proliferation of systems reinforces the argument for making implementation research a priority issue.

The hardware and software systems developed to date have been mostly one of a kind or prototypes. We are starting to see the emergence of firms (for example, as spin-offs of existing university programs) who are making the necessary investments of money, staff, and time to create fully productized systems.

Many of the current GDSS systems rely strongly on facilitation of both the meeting process and the use of the technology. As technology designs improve and as more people are trained to use the technology, the need for technical facilitation will decrease and hopefully disappear. Furthermore, the technology offers the possibility that it can provide major portions of the process facilitation.

For a group trying to resolve a problem, GDSS facilities by themselves neither (1) structure the task nor (2) provide situation-specific help. Yet the basic idea of DSS is that the computer-based system should do both. Existing GDSS software (e.g., Electronic Meeting System or SAMM) creates structure about the process to be followed but does not impose structure into the information itself. Thus, as a natural next step, we can expect the development of situation-specific GDSS packages that integrate existing GDSS and DSS software for specific problems. The results of these developments will, of course, feed back into our understanding of GDSS in general.

We are at an exciting point in the development of GDSS. The future of the field and the research opportunities in it appear bright. A combination of invention and research will move the field forward. However, to realize the potential that is there, GDSS will have to gain broad acceptance. Whether it will or not is still an open question.

Acknowledgments

The research team was aided by the thoughtful comments of Michael J. Ginzberg and Jon A. Turner.

Appendix: Summary of ideas and research topics

The purpose of this appendix is to record the ideas and research topics developed during our study. This compendium contains many specifics that go beyond the information presented in the text. It is hoped that the table will serve to alert both students and experienced researchers to important GDSS research problems.

These ideas and projects listed come from a number of sources:

1. The results of a major GDSS session held at Claremont on December 8, 1988. Attendees were S. Alter, G. Dickson, P. Gray, S. Harris, K. Kraemer, L. Olfman, and D. Vogel. The charge to that group was to develop a research agenda for GDSS over the next several years. The focus was to be on groups involved in decision-making process who are collocated in space and time (i.e., in a decision room) but was not to be limited to such groups.

2. Think pieces and comments on the initial draft prepared for the ISDP meeting at Tucson in October 1989.

3. Comments by M. Ginzberg and J. Turner, who served as discussants at Tucson.

4. Comments in writing by several team members, including S. Alter, P. Gray, and R. Johansen, after the Tucson meeting.

Table A, which begins on the following page, lists the ideas and topics. The topics are organized in the same order as in the section "What we need to know."

Note: This appendix was compiled by L. Olfman and P. Gray. They are responsible for any errors of omission or commission.

Table A. GDSS ideas and research topics.

Ideas	Research Topics
1. What Groups Do	
Information sharing; one way and two way	Define data to be gathered on what groups do
Problem finding and definition	Study existing business teams in a variety of settings to determine functions they perform and processes they use
Status reviews; control	Develop a taxonomy of meetings
Proposal review and approval; resource allocation	Determine, for typical organizations, the fraction of meetings in each category of the taxonomy
Prioritization of alternatives	Identify specific group activities and procedures that can be supported by GDSS
Negotiation within organizations; between organizations	Critical success factors, critical failure factors for group meetings
Focused problem solving	Identify effective cognitive abilities in group context
Conflict resolution	Develop methods for defining and measuring group performance
Crisis management	A taxonomy of nonelectronic group support
Ranking, rating, voting	Survey research on the number and activities of business teams
Project teams	
Planning and evaluation of plans	

Table A. GDSS ideas and research topics (continued).

Ideas	Research Topics
Socializing	
Establishing power and political position	
Establish agenda for meeting	
Clarify issues, disagreements, facts, conclusions	
Ritual meetings	
Teaching new material; training	

2. Effect of GDSS on Group Work

Ideas	Research Topics
Reductions in time of strategic/innovation decisions	Impact of anonymity
New meeting formats	Longitudinal studies of business teams using GDSS
Equality of participation	Comparison of and refinement of group process techniques in decision room settings
Meeting documentation	Develop and evaluate new forms of group work
Group memory	Effectiveness of on-line modeling
Fewer meetings on same subject	Usefulness of meeting records
On-line modeling	Usefulness of knowledge bases generated by ongoing teams
Unintended consequences of GDSS use	Individual productivity
	Group productivity

Table A. GDSS ideas and research topics (continued).

Ideas	Research Topics
	Group outcomes
	Effect of group size
	Group structures
	Protocols
	Number of people per screen
	Form of control (chauffeur versus democratic versus ????)

3. Effect of GDSS on Organizations

Ideas	Research Topics
Changes in way organizations accomplish work	Impact of anonymity on organization
Changes in organizational relationships	Changes in team effectiveness
Use of GDSS to support organizational decisions	Changes in organizational culture
New types of meetings	Relationship of GDSS to CSCW
Change in time spent in meetings	
Improved understanding of assignments and required follow-up	
Changes in staff-line relationships	

4. Effect of Hardware on GDSS Performance

Ideas	Research Topics
Alternatives to keyboards	Optimal combination of public and private screens

Table A. GDSS ideas and research topics (continued).

Ideas	Research Topics
Enhanced displays; flat screen displays	Optimal "look and feel" of facilities
Access to large picture and video databases	Mock-up tests of anticipated technologies
Voice input and voice response	Improvement of LAN performance to handle GDSS activity bursts
Massive computing power; neural networks	Comparison of input devices (keyboard, mouse, touch screen)
High-definition TV	Contribution of color, color resolution
CD with write capabilities	Value added by new technologies
Communication access to GDSS facility (fax, video conferencing, computer conferencing)	Display quality requirements
Electronic blackboards	GDSS room configuration
Personal electronic tablets for input; writing recognition	Seamless multimedia integration
Portable GDSS	
Scanners	

5. Effect of Software on GDSS Performance

Improved software design of interfaces	Develop a taxonomy of information processing tasks in GDSS
Links to databases	Systematic evaluation of existing software packages for GDSS use

Table A. GDSS ideas and research topics (continued).

Ideas	Research Topics
Integrated software tools	Creation of new software tools specifically for GDSS
Speech recognition	Development of problem-specific expert systems to enhance GDSS
AI concepts	Modeling tools for GDSS
Software implementation of advanced decision-making concepts	Decision tools for GDSS
Hypertext	Human factors/human-computer interaction research in the GDSS environment
Pattern recognition	Develop enterprise modeling software for GDSS use
Interfaces; interface consistency	Develop data gatherer that finds pertinent data for current discussion in corporate database and library
	Software for browsing through group memory
	Customized interfaces for individual group members
	Language translation systems
	Object-oriented interfaces for groups
	Integration of executive information systems with GDSS
	Integration of hypertext with GDSS

Table A. GDSS ideas and research topics (continued).

Ideas	Research Topics
	Visual manipulation of input graphics by participants
	Group "play" tools such as mood meters
	Interface consistency requirements

6. Cultural Effects of GDSS

Ideas	Research Topics
Corporate cultures	Replication of experiments in different cultures
Non-US cultures	Provision of information about other cultures to improve performance
International negotiation	Multicultural interface design
Multicultural interfaces	Translation aids
Language translation	Simultaneous versus sequential translation
Computer literacy	Role of chauffeur in multicultural negotiation

7. Training People to Use GDSS

Ideas	Research Topics
Facilitators	Effective training methods
Chauffeurs	Use of testing to improve training
Computer literacy requirements for senior executives	Role of facilitator
Training on multiple applications	Role of chauffeur

Table A. GDSS ideas and research topics (continued).

Ideas	Research Topics
8. Cost-Benefit Analysis for GDSS	
Direct costs of GDSS	Develop costing methodology
Indirect costs of GDSS	Develop efficiency metrics
Efficiency of meetings	Develop effectiveness metrics
Effectiveness of meetings	
Value added by GDSS	
Individual costs, gains from GDSS	
Organizational costs/gains from GDSS	
Management time, travel	
9. Critical Success Factors for Implementation in Industry	
Demonstrated effectiveness of GDSS as a product	"Real" business problems to which GDSS applies
Perceived business value	Nature of resistance to GDSS
Internal corporate sponsor	Field studies of implementations
Software flexibility, hardware capabilities	Case studies of implementations
Telecommunications infrastructure	Market for GDSS
Integration of nonelectronic groupware	How GDSS makes a difference in organizations
Early success	Critical failure factors

Table A. GDSS ideas and research topics (continued).

Ideas	Research Topics
Infrastructure for creating and maintaining GDSS	
Training	
Change image from academic research tool to business tool	
Internal champion	

10. Robustness of Research Results

Ideas	Research Topics
Cooperation among researchers to replicate experiments	Comparison of results from different experiments
Joint publication of results for replicated experiments	Replication of experiments at a number of facilities
Robustness across facilities	Multiple tasks under identical experimental conditions
Robustness across tasks	

11. Innovative Uses of GDSS

Ideas	Research Topics
Real-time, cooperative document or proposal preparation	Construct and test expert systems that act as a group adviser on specific problems
Crisis management	Evaluation of human parallel processing
Negotiation	Develop a group process adviser
Visual decision making; new analytic methods based on diagrams and pictorial representations	Develop a graphical or pictorial stenographer to capture ideas and descriptions of relationships

Table A. GDSS ideas and research topics (continued).

Ideas	Research Topics
Intercultural meetings	
Integration with video and computer conferencing	
Interactive teaching	
New forms of groups	
Issue-oriented DSS	
Personnel decisions	
New, temporary organizations	
Electronic mediated debates	
Empowering of handicapped people	
Hierarchical meetings that can communicate and also convene as a committee as a whole	
Use expert systems to create $(n+1)$st participant	

12. Theoretical Foundations of GDSS

Human parallel processing	Causal models of GDSS
Value added (Huber, Strassman models)	Predicting impacts of new configurations, technologies
Models of group interaction (Bales, Poole)	Models of how people work together
Group memory	Models of impact of new technologies on group effectiveness

Table A. GDSS ideas and research topics (continued).

Ideas	Research Topics
Predicting impacts of GDSS	Models of groups based on information theory and systems theory
Formative assessment	
Models of decision making	
Information theory and systems theory	
Communications models	
Model of leader participation (Vroom and Yetton)	
Theories of power	
DeSanctis/Poole structuration theory	

13. Barriers to Research

Ideas	Research Topics
Emphasis on software development	Cooperation among research groups (both public and private) to obtain funding
High entry cost	Standardization of experiment definition and research reporting
Obtaining funding	
Differentiating process and product	
Limitations of technology	
Accurate dissemination of research methodologies, protocols, and so on	

Table A. GDSS ideas and research topics (continued).

Ideas	Research Topics
Need for large numbers of subjects; particularly subjects who represent real-world groups	
Lack of investment in conferencing facilities in industry and academia	
Applicability of theories from other fields that are not taught in business school curricula	

14. Research Methodologies

Ideas	Research Topics
Content analysis	Determination of research methodologies applicable to GDSS
Field studies	Baseline studies (GDSS versus no GDSS)
Case studies	Comparison of alternate GDSS
Action research	
Laboratory experimentation	
Software engineering	
Information and systems theory	
Persuasion models	
Survey research	
Ethnographic methods	
Market research	

Table A. GDSS ideas and research topics (continued).

Ideas	Research Topics
15. Other Ideas and Research Topics	
GDSS as "CAD" for management	Determine market for GDSS
	Develop scenarios for GDSS use
	Links among preparations before GDSS session(s), the GDSS session, and the actions taken after the session(s)
	Effect of "destructive personality" on GDSS

Workshop discussion: Group decision support systems

Discussants: In his discussion of the work of the GDSS research team, Michael Ginzberg stated that he thought the central question to be answered by GDSS research was, "Which [GDSS] facilities result in what impacts under what conditions?" He felt that this was not a simple question to answer because it requires that we clarify our notions of conditions, facilities, and impacts.

With regard to conditions, he felt that it was critical to be able to identify situations so that, for any study, we can tell what prior findings are relevant to it, and also to which situation(s) the study's results are applicable. The Pinsonneault-Kraemer framework used by the GDSS team provides a way to address this by allowing us to identify a number of individual, group situation, group structure, and task variables that can be used to categorize and differentiate among GDSS situations. How to measure impacts has received less attention. In addition to the focus on individual performance and satisfaction, we need to consider process changes at the group and organizational levels, and costs and unintended effects of GDSS as well as benefits. Perhaps the least attention has been paid to the facilities question. Most studies have made comparisons of performance with and without the presence of the GDSS; there has been little attention to the effects of different attributes of GDSS.

Facilities, impacts, and conditions define what is studied. The research strategy defines how the study will be carried out. One approach is to test each GDSS configuration as it is developed and to build up our understanding of GDSS one situation and one system at a time. Ginzberg felt that this was a weak method in that knowledge would be limited only to those specific configurations and GDSS that were tested. A better approach is to develop an understanding of the basic processes underlying GDSS use. This means a change in research approach from asking if there is an impact to asking how the impact arises. Given this model, we could use it to test the evolution of technology rather than just reacting to it.

In his discussion, Jon Turner asked a basic question: "Who is in the room and what are they doing?" He felt that the GDSS team had demonstrated a technology push perspective. Like Ginzberg, he recommended an alternative perspective that involves a study of the coordination between workers in the group—that is, a study of process rather than objects. The objective of this approach was to understand the deeper structure of group interaction. More specifically, Turner suggested that

- not enough attention was being paid to group process (e.g., the role of the facilitator);

- the focus of GDSS research had concentrated too much on decision making and not on the support of other group functions such as bargaining, negotiating, advocating, and positioning;

- more attention should be paid to possible contributions from AI in building systems that would have a better understanding of the group interaction process;

- much could be learned from a study of the command and control systems used by DOD and NASA;

- there was a need to utilize recent advances in decision-making techniques such as strategy generation tables, decision quality concepts, influence diagrams, clarity tests, and risk-attitude considerations; and

- more attention should be paid to studying the negative effects of GDSS use.

Summary of electronic discussion. The EMS session for the GDSS group used the Topic Commenter software of the PLEXSYS system. The participants commented on a fixed set of topics set by the GDSS team and summarized their work as follows:

Actual and potential innovations from GDSS. It is important to focus on the organizational context. How can GDSS impact organizations? What can we learn about groups and organizations from GDSS research?

Hardware breakthroughs required. Alternative forms of input/output need to be developed for GDSS. Examples are video, audio, animation, feeds from external systems, feeds to external systems.

Software breakthroughs required. There is a need to break the rigidity of current GDSS software. The software should be more adaptable to group needs and give the user control over a wider range of media and tools.

GDSS software should be interoperable with (and usable in) other knowledge work domains. Software is needed to help in summarizing and interpreting group inputs, providing automated indexes, and so on.

Critical success factors for industry. GDSS technologies must assist managers in achieving either tactical or strategic objectives. GDSS must be presented as an arsenal of tools helpful in a variety of task situations. There must be corporate champions to promote GDSS use. GDSS requires adequate (preferably great) corporate support. To be successful, GDSS must come as a complete package, including a plan, a proposal, and effective selling, as well as well-engineered software.

Socialization of the technology. One way that tools get accepted is through playful exploration. We need to understand how organizations and groups transform tools into uses that were not intended by their designers. Technology must eventually be seen as part of everyday life. A critical mass of users is needed.

These factors imply the following design features:

- the GDSS environment and tools must be user modifiable,
- the GDSS should support exploratory learning, and
- the GDSS should support naive as well as sophisticated users.

GDSS is predicated on a rational actor model of behavior. When thinking about adaptation in organizations, we need a richer model. Research methods to discover such a model include field observation, ethnographics, open-ended studies, and longitudinal studies.

Intercultural GDSS. Different cultures exist within organizations, across organizations, across industries, and across nations. We need to identify the cultural dimensions (e.g., what is and what is not polite behavior) that impact the usefulness of the tool. Can GDSS be used to resolve differences across cultures and reinforce similarities? Are current GDSS biased toward a particular cultural viewpoint?

Theory building for GDSS. Theory building is important for GDSS—maybe there will not be one grand theory but a number of minitheories or contingent theories.

Theories are needed for the following:

- Group processes: formation, social development, task accomplishment, and group facilitation.

- The nature of meetings: types, participant roles, and outcomes.

- Organizational learning: development of norms and values, and their propagation.

- Organizational decision making: types, participant roles, and outcomes.

- The link between task structures and problem-solving strategies.

We must look to the management and organizational theory literature for a start in theory building in the above areas.

Applicable research methodologies. We need to study important problems in real organizations and not be driven by the technology just "because it is there." Group processes are ongoing; we need to study what happens both before and after the GDSS meeting to really understand what is going on. Use longitudinal studies and ethnographic approaches. Our research should be grounded in organizational theory and current cognitive theories such as learning theory, potential theory, and schema theory. A broad range of research methodologies is applicable, ranging from conceptual research to empirical research to field research. Both descriptive and prescriptive research is needed. There is a need to triangulate between different studies that use different approaches.

Major research problems and challenges. The following is a list of suggested research objectives and questions that were proposed during the electronic discussion:

Understand GDSS as one of many tools in an organizational context and as part of a broader program of research in technology and group work. Develop theories that will help match the different GDSS tools to the tasks for which they are appropriate.

What kinds of meetings are suitable or unsuitable for GDSS support?

What can be learned from studying individual behavior in the group context rather than the group as a whole?

Can we support meetings convened for other purposes such as sense-making and learning rather than simply decision making?

How can GDSS contribute to organizational learning and intelligence?

What is meant by an "intelligent GDSS"?

What is the potential for dysfunctional consequences from using a GDSS and how can they be avoided?

What are the unimportant research topics?

Chapter 5

Organizational Decision Support Systems (ODSS)

Jay F. Nunamaker, Lynda M. Applegate, Mary J. Culnan,
Jane Fedorowicz, Joey F. George, Barbara Gutek,
John C. Henderson, John L. King, Benn R. Konsynski,
Susan L. Star, E. Burton Swanson, Joseph S. Valacich, and
Robert W. Zmud

When Michael Scott Morton coined the term decision support systems (DSS) in 1964, there were few managerial computer applications. Computers themselves were large, unreliable, and expensive to obtain and maintain. In order for any managerial application to be developed for such systems, it had to have the approval and involvement of senior management and be important enough to utilize one of the more costly organizational resources. A decision important enough to require the support of such a system would extend beyond the needs of a single manager and would in fact affect several organizational units [Lee et al., 1988].

In the years that followed, as computing hardware became less expensive and as more compact personal machines became available, the focus of DSS shifted to individual systems. Recently, however, through the development of information systems to support groups and through advances in telecommunications technology, the focus of DSS has begun to shift from the individual to the group to the entire organization. Like their early counterparts, these DSS also extend beyond a single manager and affect several organizational units.

Technological feasibility is not the only reason ODSS are being developed, however. They are also being developed because organizations are changing as a reaction to changing business environments. The turbulent organizational environments predicted by many writers [e.g., Huber, 1984a] seem to be here. More and better information is required more quickly than ever before. The scope of business has become international, requiring a knowledge of very different systems of business regulations and trade requirements. To cope with the changing environment, organizations have adopted new forms. Many are leaner, with fewer hierarchical levels and fewer middle managers. Others have gone a step further than the matrix structure, where a single employee reported to at least two bosses, to a greater reliance on semiautonomous teams that may disband after their project is completed, leaving reporting relationships unclear at best. ODSS can help support these new organizational forms by filling the gaps left by the departed middle managers or by supporting the autonomous work teams, for example.

It is these new organizational support systems and the organizational changes they have been developed to support that our task force was formed to study. Our dozen members have been organized into six groups of authors, each of which has produced a preliminary position paper on a particular aspect of the ODSS topic. Swanson and Zmud focus on the concepts behind ODSS and offer guidelines for a system architecture. Culnan and Gutek write about why organizations collect and store information and the role of ODSS in that process. Fedorowicz and Konsynski examine the issues related to the intersection of decision processes and ODSS technology in the new organizational forms. Nunamaker, George, and Valacich focus on the information technology necessary for ODSS designed for three specific changes in organization structure. King and Star take a different approach, looking at organizational decision making from more of a sociological perspective. Finally, Applegate and Henderson specifically consider an interacting team perspective in their discussion of ODSS. Each of these six preliminary position papers will be summarized in the following pages.

ODSS concepts and architecture

E. Burton Swanson and Robert W. Zmud

An ODSS is said to focus on "decisions involving many people" with special attention given to "the unique but crucial decisions which will have a major corporate impact" [Lee et al., 1988]. Thus conceived, the concept enlarges (literally) upon the popular notion of group decision support systems (GDSS), where a relatively small number of people are supported in making shared decisions of mutual importance. However, in an ODSS, managerial control over the decision process is a distinguishing feature.

An ODSS should not be thought of as a manager's DSS, but rather it should be viewed as supporting the organization's division of labor in decision making. Traditionally, this division of decision making has tended to be viewed in a hierarchical manner, where decision responsibilities are assumed to reflect an organization's formal authority structure. But some decisions cut across an organization's existing structure, resulting in the assignment of decision processes to *virtual positions*, rather than to individual managers in hierarchical roles [Mackenzie, 1986]. Examples of virtual positions include a multidivisional task force, a standing committee of functional representatives, and a daily teleconference held across multiple locations to coordinate the introduction of a new product.

It takes time for a virtual position to form and support organizational adaptation. With rapid change, organizations can reach the point where virtual positions are being created faster than they are absorbed. As virtual positions accumulate, the interdependence among them sometimes creates needs for additional virtual positions. The consequence is that the organization can gradually lose its ability to respond to change.

Continuing technical developments make it possible today to provide computer- and communication-based support for distributed decision-making contexts associated with both hierarchical and virtual positions. Such ODSS, if implemented, might very well provide another means of organizational adaptation by bringing new communicative capability to hierarchical and virtual positions.

Distributed decision making. Distributed decision making exists where a set of related decisions is distributed among a set of organizational decision-makers so that not all decisions are the province of the same decision-maker(s). The decisions are assumed to be related in the sense that they are consequential for one another; there is thus an incentive for coordination [Malone, 1988]. The decision-makers are related in turn by means of their organizational roles, which give them full or partial authority and responsibility for certain spheres of decision.

Distributed decisions may be tightly or loosely coupled. Distributed decision making may or may not incorporate group decision making. Distributed decision making may occur where decisions are well defined and understood in advance among decision-makers, or it may occur in situations in which there is substantial ambiguity and equivocality [Daft and Weick, 1984], and the forms of the individual decisions are revealed only in the immediate circumstances in which they arise.

Traditional DSS, in practice, are typically applied to assist individuals in fairly well-structured decision-making contexts. The domain of distributed decision support, however, is more likely to be associated with semistructured decision contexts and semidetermined decision criteria. This domain may be viewed as bracketed by the domain of distributed communications, where decision models are unstructured and decision criteria are undetermined, and the domain of distributed computing, where decision models are fully structured and decision criteria are similarly determined. While an increasing number of decision situations exist which might benefit from an ODSS, appropriate support environments are for the most part lacking.

If, as suggested earlier, virtual positions are proliferating and thus adding to organizational complexity, then distributed decision support offers a potentially attractive coping mechanism. However, when distributed decision making arises, an ODSS is designed to support it. We suggest three alternative strategies for support:

1. Decision ordering: Distributed decisions may be ordered such that higher ordered decisions take precedence over lower ordered decisions. The former establish the context for and inform the latter.
2. Information sharing: Decisions are made independently, but decision-makers share relevant information. Sharing may be directed by management in a top-down fashion, or it may arise from a bottom-up approach.
3. Negotiated choice: Distributed decision making often involves conflict as well as cooperation. Some issues may be resolved by negotiation among affected parties. Where decisions are negotiated, they are in effect made jointly.

Architectural guidelines. According to Kotter, successful managers center their efforts on two activities: setting their agendas and network building [Kotter, 1982]. A manager's agenda is that loosely connected set of goals and plans that directs both short-term and long-term behavior. Network building refers to the development and maintenance of cooperative networks of those individuals likely to play a role in facilitating the manager's emerging agenda. Relating these ideas to an ODSS, two critical architectural requirements involve the capability to build and maintain both the agenda and the network associated with a distributed decision situation. The nature of the network component of an ODSS seems quite clear—enabling communication among the set of distributed decision-makers as well as the capability to access relevant information from other sources. Exactly what is meant by the agenda component, however, is not clear.

In a sense, an agenda is derived from a manager's mental models or cognitive maps. A cognitive map consists of the concepts and relations a participant uses to understand organizational situations [Weick and Bougon, 1986]. Cognitive maps are relevant to groups as well as individuals. Thus the agenda component of an ODSS reflects the necessity of developing and maintaining a collective cognitive map of the distributed decision situation.

One suggested ODSS architecture is shown in Figure 1. As with conferencing systems, this architecture would provide a collection of generic and situational functional capabilities to be used in facilitating multiple, concurrent distributed decision-making situations. The archi-

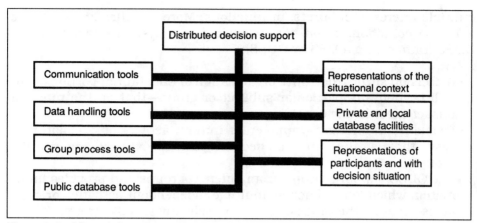

Figure 1. Architectural components.

tecture would incorporate two sets of tools: generic tools made available across all active decision situations, and three situation-specific facilities. The generic tool sets support individual and group communication, data handling, process governance, and public data management. The three situation-specific facilities include a database facility, a participant/task representation facility, and a situation representation facility.

Suggested research directions. Two issues seem particularly important for research. The first concerns the necessity for participants to contribute their time and private knowledge to the ODSS, something that is required for the ODSS to be successful. Many potential barriers exist that are likely to inhibit such contributions. The second issue is the necessity of evolving a common understanding of the situational context among ODSS participants. It is quite likely that participants in a particular decision situation will hold different, possibly incompatible views of the situation. How can components of an ODSS be applied to evolve a common understanding of the decision situation?

Why organizations collect and store information

Mary J. Culnan and Barbara Gutek

Much of the prior research on information use and decision support has focused on problem solving. We believe this view, which characterizes both the DSS and GDSS literature, is overly narrow and overly rational. We view organizations both as coalitions of interests and as goal-oriented adaptable open systems composed of interactive subunits. We view ODSS as organizational-level resources or systems that support multiple interests, subunits, or functions. More specifically, one of the following conditions must be present before a system qualifies as an ODSS (rather than a DSS or GDSS):

- A decision affects the entire organization or substantial portions of it, well beyond any particular subunit or group—that is, the range of impact exceeds any specific group.
- People from different groups enter into an activity or decision process—that is, the range of decision-makers exceeds any specific group.
- The ODSS supports people from different groups and provides information which is used across multiple independent activities or decisions—that is, the range of users exceeds any specific group.

In our paper, we will describe the reasons why organizations want or need information, and then describe the ODSS that support these needs.

Four fundamental activities create opportunities or needs for organizations to gather, store, or use information:

1. Problem solving for a specific task requiring an organizational-level perspective, such as a decision to develop and market a new product which involves research and development, manufacturing, marketing, and so on.
2. Organizations routinely gather or compile information to have a "stock" on hand where information gathering and information use are asynchronous. Information is not gathered to respond to a specific need or to solve a specific problem.
3. Communication across subunits involves the use of information for two purposes: coordination on an ongoing basis and decision implementation.
4. Competing interests, scarce resources, and/or equivocality may give rise to political behavior, accompanied by symbolic or strategic information use.

People may use the same information from the ODSS to support different points of view or different agendas. This use may be "good," as in the case of modeling as a negotiation tool, or "bad," where information is used to distort. Political agendas may also influence organizations to not gather information so that it is not available for use. This may frequently be done when having the information could result in legal liability.

We believe that the ODSS which are likely to be useful in the scenarios we described above will differ from many of the current DSS and GDSS, which are organized around a computer-based information system. While computer technology plays an important role in ODSS, many of these systems take the form of an organizational subunit, as will be shown by the following examples:

- Models and other systems supporting group decision making. These systems most closely resemble the "traditional" DSS or GDSS.
- Scanning units such as a government relations department or a policy analysis unit.
- Libraries, archives, and records management units that collect and organize both external and internal information. Libraries may also serve as scanning units, but are often more passive.
- Public affairs and customer service departments that link the organization to external constituencies.
- Executive support systems that allow a disaggregation of data and provide access to data across organizational functions.
- Bulletin boards and other computer-mediated communication systems.
- Common-access databases, such as personnel records, which "follow" an individual throughout his or her career with the organization, with or without limits to access.

ODSS technology and decision processes

Jane Fedorowicz and Benn R. Konsynski

Many current information technology (IT) initiatives in organizations center around "integration" across traditional application and function boundaries. This quest for integration involves reorganization and coordination of increasingly autonomous agents. Integration initiatives are taking place at a time when many organizations are experimenting with or initiating new multifunctional arrangements involving teams and work groups. These organizations recognize the inadequacy of the traditional functional role assignments and artificial barriers that raise the costs of communications and inhibit information sharing.

Historically, IT research has focused on individual decision making and small-group decision facilitation. Organizational support technologies (computer-based) have existed since the advent of time-sharing and of centralized computing with remote access. For the most part, these technologies have played a passive role in the life of the organization. They include raw computational capacities and passive communications platforms like electronic mail. New organizational information demands and emerging information technologies combine to make company-wide support systems an organizational imperative.

The driving forces of change in business strategy may be derived as responses to external forces or internally driven initiatives. Likewise, technical capabilities are also subject to a sensitivity to external pressures (technology advances, unit economies, production breakthroughs, etc.) as well as the internal design initiatives. It is a continuous challenge for management to monitor the external environment and to coordinate internal proactive and reactive initiatives.

As we design and redesign business relationships and organizational structures, consideration of decision activities that take place across organizational boundaries becomes increasingly critical. We need to address the issue of location of a decision process within and outside the traditional boundaries of the organization. We must include the integrating functions provided by present and future generations of ODSS.

Before proposing an effective ODSS design, it is essential to understand the relationships between the formal and informal decision processes performed by the organization's systems and personnel, and the supporting information technologies that serve to assist those decision processes. The forms of "assistance" range from passive (information access and decision recording) to active (participation in the judgment and decision-making processes).

In this section, we discuss the interplay between the organization, its business and decision processes, and its information technologies. We propose a taxonomy of currently feasible ODSS. We suggest that additional research is needed to fully appreciate the potential of ODSS in furthering the development of new organizational forms and supporting decision processes.

A taxonomy of ODSS. ODSS are information systems that provide an organization-wide platform to enhance, facilitate, and enable the work of the organization members. They provide an information technology infrastructure that establishes an environment for organizational and individual decision making. They are, by their nature, cross-functional. Four patterns of ODSS emerge in contemporary business environments.

Type I. Traditional information systems: Any basic support system within an organization that reinforces traditional norms, often by embedding organization policy in the system's logic. This is the most encompassing, but least distinguishing of the four types. An example would be the standard reporting and control systems, such as general ledger applications. Such environments are *structure enforcing*.

Type II. Organization-wide systems: Information technology used at the organizational level for organization-wide purposes. An example is top management use of an executive information system to access or analyze organization-wide data. Such environments are *structure preserving*.

Type III. Spanning systems: Technology that spans the organization, in that it is used by individuals beyond functional or hierarchical boundaries. These technologies transcend organizational structure, neither requiring nor deliberately defying traditional norms. An example is an electronic mail system used by all members of the organization. These environments are *structure independent*.

Type IV. New organizational structures: Any information technology that changes/enables new organizational structures. An example might be special forms of teleconferencing that permit work teams to be formed independently of geographic or traditional hierarchical relationships. Such environments are *structure transforming*.

The ODSS types decrease in embedded policy, support for static structure, and tight coupling to traditional roles and responsibilities. They increase in flexibility, innovation, and coordination complexity. While Type I exhibits the highest degree of organization policy codified in the application systems, Type IV represents the tolerance of (even anticipation of) change.

There are many instances of overlap among these four types of ODSS. For example, it is entirely possible—and perhaps probable—that many Type III technologies will also enable new organizational structures to be formed (however informally). To illustrate, the electronic mail example has the potential to open up new lines of communication between layers of the organization in a way that was previously taboo.

In many enterprises it will be important to recognize and design for several levels of ODSS that exist in particular business situations. A particular "cluster" of ODSS services is needed for the organization to operate effectively in "normal" business modes. It may be true that yet another cluster of ODSS services is operative in the organization in a "crisis" (or other) mode. Particular changes in linkages, priorities, applications, information resources, technology access, management processes, authorities, responsibilities, status, and knowledge are a part of the organization's contingency plans.

A range of technology application innovations will be a part of the emergence of an organization IT architecture to support decision processes. Examples of potentially fruitful technologies include interorganizational systems, cognitive reapportionment, groupware, computer-supported cooperative work, document-based processing, technology clusters, and information refineries. Each of these technologies offers significant potential in catalyzing changes in organization decision processes. Further research is needed to determine the effect of the technologies on the business processes that may be unique to new organizational forms.

ODSS research challenges. Our preliminary review suggests that an ample number of important research questions exist around all four types of ODSS. It has been our goal to propose research challenges that center around the linkage between the pattern of decision processes and the candidate information technologies that can play a role in the ODSS architecture. The following kinds of questions surface:

Type I. What are the aging and longevity issues associated with these systems? What are effective approaches for development, implementation, operation, and dismantling of Type I environments? In the emerging organization, what is the long-term prognosis for systems of this type? How should the decline and dismantling of these systems be managed? Are there situations in which the rigid codification of organization policies is important in representing the dedication of the organization to an operating philosophy?

Type II. While such systems "scan" the organization, their user community often is a limited subset of the organization. What are the information ownership issues associated with interpretation, sharing, and use? How should cross-organizational information ownership disputes be resolved? Who should set the measurement criteria and performance judgments (information owner or user)? Should the system operate in a voluntary information contribution manner?

Type III. How might we define organization-spanning technology? How might one go about the design, implementation, and assimilation of such spanning environments? To what extent can we "back-in" certain organization norms into the system (e.g., message "channel" protocols for cross-department communications)? How effective are subnet structures, partitions, and boundaries in these environments? How does one enforce the necessary security and integrity constraints in an environment that facilitates open interchange? Can "charging" mechanisms be used to enable the organization to "tolerate" deviation from the existing cultural norms?

Type IV. What are the cultural limits on the change promoted by Type IV environments? What "change" philosophies are supported by alternative information technology architectures? What cultural considerations need to be accounted for in the planning of a Type IV ODSS? What forms of "experimentation" are permitted in alternative Type IV ODSS environments? How can Type IV ODSS foster or facilitate organization transformation through action? Can change initiatives lead to stable structures, Type IV lead to pockets of Type I? What kinds of challenges are made to the organization design, and who gets to make them?

Information technology and ODSS

Jay Nunamaker, Joey F. George, and Joseph S. Valacich

Information technology (IT) and organizational structure have been intertwined since the publication of Leavitt and Whisler's "Management in the 1980's" in 1958 [Leavitt and Whisler, 1958]. In that seminal paper, the authors predicted that there would be dramatic changes in organizational structure due to the influence of IT. There is no question that the typical organizational structure has changed since 1958 [Applegate et al., 1988]. The days of the rigid hierarchical pyramid have passed, giving way to more flexible organizational forms. Perhaps the most notable changes have been in the ranks of middle management: There are fewer middle managers now. And there are fewer hierarchical levels. The extent to which these changes have been the result of IT use in organizations is an open question, but there is no doubt that organizations are using IT as a vital means to cope with the structural changes [Dreyfuss, 1988].

Academics continue to predict structural change in organizations and the role of IT in enabling these changes [Huber, 1984a, 1990; Drucker, 1988; Applegate et al., 1988]. For example, Applegate and her colleagues describe "cluster" organizations, where hierarchies have been replaced with formal and informal communication networks and with project-oriented work groups [Applegate et al., 1988]. IT will allow the widespread sharing of information, shorten the time and distances between workers, identify who in the organization has the needed expertise, provide immediate access to information for managers, and free up workers at all levels for creative work. Drucker describes organizations that resemble orchestras or hospitals, where there are no intervening levels of management [Drucker, 1988]. There are more specialists at operational levels but smaller staffs at headquarters. Most of the work will be done by temporary task forces, whose members can be physically and temporally dispersed, but still work together through IT.

The information systems that will be needed to make these new types of organizational forms function are currently being developed in bits and pieces. For example, since communication via computer networks becomes essential in such organizations, the development of flexible electronic mail and computer conferencing systems is crucial. Similarly, since much of the work in these new organizations will be done by physically and temporally dispersed work groups, systems to support these groups at the same level at which they can be supported today in electronic meeting system decision rooms are vital. And all of these systems must be integrated into organizational decision support systems (ODSS).

Current trends in organizations. Of all the structural changes currently taking place in organizations, the most widely publicized is downsizing. Downsizing describes the practice of reducing both the overall size of the work force and the number of hierarchical levels in the organization [Main, 1988; *The Wall Street Journal*, 1989]. The personnel most likely to be removed in downsizing are in middle management, especially in staff positions.

A second trend that has received attention during the past few years is the movement toward teamwork [*Business Week*, 1989]. The team concept has primarily been applied to manufacturing. Here the organization of work is changed so that what was formerly done by a group of individuals working alone is now done by a group of workers working together. As such, they work as a team. The teamwork concept has not yet been widely applied to the service sector in the US, where 70 percent of the work force is employed. If the types of organizational forms described by Applegate et al. and Drucker come to be, however, most work at the managerial level and in the service sector will be done by teams [Applegate et al., 1988; Drucker, 1988].

Finally, the third trend we are considering is farming out functions formerly handled by the organization itself. Recent examples include IBM's trial contract with Pitney Bowes to run its mail rooms, and Eastman Kodak's decision to hire IBM to run its data processing center and Businessland to run its personal computer operations [Carroll and Wilke, 1989]. In a way, farming out can be seen as another form of downsizing. It reduces the size of the company because all of the personnel who were working in that area no longer work for the organization. (They are often hired by the company that assumes responsibility for the function.)

The current role of IT. Of the three trends in organizations that we have discussed, the one most dependent on IT for support has been downsizing. As was mentioned above, if there are fewer middle managers, but the same amount of work, some means must be developed to deal with that work. The communication functions formerly handled by middle managers must be performed some other way. In the past decade, these functions have been performed to some extent via electronic mail.

Middle managers must also coordinate the work of the people they directly supervise. As the number of hierarchical levels decreases and spans of control increase in size, electronic mail becomes more cumbersome as a coordination tool. To better deal with coordination tasks, managers have turned to electronic calendars and groupware [Dreyfuss, 1988]. As downsizing continues, managers not only have to manage more people, they have to manage more information, and information at a lower level of abstraction. These circumstances have led some managers to demand the development of executive information systems (EIS), which allow them to handle the increased levels of information they now must face [*PC Week*, 1989].

The other two trends we discussed earlier, work group teams and farming out, do not at this point appear to be supported very well by IT. In the case of teams, the IT support may be lacking because most teams are now in manufacturing, which has traditionally used automation to replace workers rather than support them; the teams work in the same place at the same time, eliminating the need for electronic communication; and the emphasis on teams in the American workplace is still very new. However, as the emphasis shifts to teams in the service sector, and as the manufacturing model is abandoned in service organizations, there may be more possibilities to explore for IT.

Farming out is an even more recent phenomenon. It seems clear, however, that coordination will become very important here, but as was pointed out above, it will be coordination between organizations, not within them. The communication role of IT becomes more important, and it is clear that electronic mail as currently constituted will not suffice.

The future role of IT. There are many ODSS technologies that should play a key role in future organizational processes and structures. Organizational objectives to downsize might require technologies that facilitate intraorganizational communication, information filtering, and operational monitoring. Teams also require IT to support communication, but with a focus on intragroup communication, as well as technologies to support coordination and decision making. Organizations opting to farm out activities will require technologies to support interorganizational communication and coordination. Thus, different organizational objectives require different IT and dissimilar implementations of that technology. Many specific technologies can be applied to foster different organizational objectives.

The term *communication technologies* refers to IT designed to foster team, organizational, or interorganizational communication. Common technologies of this class include electronic mail, computer conferencing, and video conferencing. *Coordination technologies* refers to IT used to coordinate resources, facilities, and people. *Filtering technologies* refers to intelligent agents used to filter and summarize information. For example, future implementations of coordination technologies such as electronic mail and computer conferencing can integrate artificial intelligence technologies to sort, prioritize, and automatically respond to an increased volume of electronic messages. *Decision-making technologies* are those designed to improve the effectiveness and efficiency of individual and group decision making. *Electronic meeting systems* (EMS) are computer-based technologies designed to make meetings more productive. *DSS* are individual support environments for the solution of structured and semistructured problems. *Monitoring technologies* refers to IT such as an EIS, which can be used to monitor the status of organizational operations, industry trends, competitors, and other relevant information.

Each of these ODSS technologies is designed to perform general types of activities. However, the application and consequence of each technology may be different, depending upon the situation. For example, teams using an electronic mail system will generally use it to communicate and coordinate activities between specific team members on a project. The electronic mail technology used by the team may reside on a large corporate system or on a local team network. Thus the relative scope for the application of communication technologies for teams may be quite narrow. Yet, for an organization that has farmed out an organizational function to another organization, electronic mail communication may be much more complicated, as multiple systems may need to be bridged for effective, timely, and secure interorganizational electronic communication.

The matrix in Figure 2 relates the ODSS technologies to the organizational design issues described here. The relationship is somewhat arbitrary, yet represents what technologies we feel most strongly support the various organizational objectives described here.

As noted above and displayed in the matrix, organizational downsizing can take advantage of most of the ODSS technologies described here. Key elements of an ODSS for organizational downsizing appear to be communication, filtering, and monitoring technologies. These ODSS subsystems may be part of existing organizational data processing systems or reside "above" them. These key elements must be configured so that upper management is effectively supported with functions previously supplied by middle managers.

The primary ODSS technologies required to support organizational teams include intragroup communication, team member coordination, and decision-making technologies. The key elements required to support the farming out of organizational activities to other organizations will require ODSS systems for interorganizational communication, service coordination, and the monitoring of contractor performance.

Organizational decision process as an open system problem

John L. King and Susan L. Star

The concept of ODSS is simple in principle: Apply the technologies of computers and communication to enhance the organizational decision-making process. In principle, ODSS takes the progress in DSS, group DSS, and group communication support systems to a higher level, much as GDSS expanded the original DSS concept.

ODSS technology	Organizational objective		
	Downsizing	Teams	Farm out
Communication	●	●	●
Coordination	○	●	○
Filtering	●	◉	○
Decision Making	◉	●	○
Monitoring	●	○	◉

● Key requirement

◉ Somewhat needed

○ Little direct benefit

Figure 2. ODSS technology versus organizational objective.

The development of technologies to facilitate decision making at an organizational level must be sensitive to important differences between group decision processes and organizational decision processes. The latter, unlike the former, must accommodate different social worlds where values and outlooks among actors can vary widely. Organizations have developed elaborate and sophisticated means that enable them to "make decisions," but not in the anthropomorphized way that the term "organizational decision making" suggests. Two of these mechanisms are *due process and articulation,* by which inputs to decision processes are regulated, and *boundary objects,* which serve as critical binding and translation devices among participants from different social worlds.

Decision processes. It is clear that groups make decisions in a way different from how individuals do. For one thing, groups need to use protocols for input to the process, means of mediating discussion of inputs, and algorithms for resolution of disagreements and settling on a "group" position. Solicitation of input and mediation of discussion are usually local to the specific group, informed by the personalities, status, and contingencies of its members.

There are some important factors that make group decision making relatively tractable. The most obvious is that it is necessary—without group decision making, organizations would be unimaginable. Therefore, participants are willing to cope with the problems of group interaction in order to arrive at group decisions. Beyond necessity, group decision processes are facilitated by subtle social factors. One is that decision-making groups are made up of people engaged in tasks bound by purposes and objectives. Another is that individuals in groups often work together quite closely outside the group decision-making arena. Perhaps most important, however, is that members of ongoing groups share a common, acquired experience of how the group thinks and works.

The differences between individual decision processes and those of groups are reflected in the technologies designed to support the two processes. Individual DSS are mainly composed of databases and models that help an individual sort out assumptions and options from an array of possibilities. Group decision technologies include greater reliance on communications technology to allow a group to "converse" and methods of group and selective individual displays of information. Also, since the natural tendency in a group is to converse, GDSS applications usually require a human or machine "mediator" to keep the group's focus on making the decision through the device of the technology.

Organization-level decision processes are different from group-level processes. Like group processes, they are necessary in order to accomplish organizational missions. They are the price of organizational power. Also, organization-level decision processes often engage issues of larger consequence and gravity than do group decision processes—issues that galvanize participant attention and care. And organization-level processes usually embody impartiality that divorces "organizational" concerns from the "parochial" concerns of groups, factions, and so on. Unlike group processes, organizational processes do not benefit from the social factors that provide underlying cohesion in groups.

Because members of an organization come from different social worlds, to which they are bound by personal and professional commitments, the milieu of organizational decision making is inevitably an intersection of different social worlds rather than a community in its own right [Strauss, 1978]. Lost in the transition from group to organization are the crucial elements of local memory, cohesion, and tacit knowledge that expedite the discourse of group decision making. Also, the representatives of groups who attend organizational meetings are likely to hold stronger allegiance to their group than to the "organization." These factors virtually ensure that participants in organizational decision processes will be acting in an organizationally suboptimal fashion some or most of the time. The consequences of these circumstances are very important for the designer of ODSS, for they affect everything: the means by which inputs are solicited, the mediation of discussion, and the mechanisms of final decision resolution. It is easy to see that organizational decision processes are very far removed from either individual or group decision processes.

Mechanisms for "organizational decision making." Two mechanisms organizations have developed to enable them to "make decisions" are *due process and articulation,* and *boundary objects.* Due process as found in organizations is the question of whether we can assure that information systems make adequate provision for recognizing, gathering, and weighing evidence from an organization's heterogeneous, conflicting parts. This is an ongoing process, not a one-time event or a single protocol. The work for creating and maintaining due process is articulation. To articulate work in an organization means to coordinate, schedule, recover from errors, assemble resources, and continually redefine the notion of "adequate provision" for pluralism.

The notion of boundary object arose from studies of scientific work [Star, 1990; Star and Griesemer, 1991], where groups of people with very different definitions of the scientific enterprise nevertheless collaborated on research. For example, amateur and professional biologists work together in a natural history museum. For the amateur, a specimen is a thing to be carefully collected and brought to the museum. For the professional biologist, however, a specimen is one indicator among thousands of a complex, abstract evolutionary theory.

The due process component of organizational decision processes consists of means to elicit inputs from all eligible and/or qualified participants. Eligible participants are those who have some formal reason to be present. Due process in many organizational decision processes is embodied in formal protocols of deliberation. The focus of due process is primarily on the protocols of making input to the discussion, and secondarily on the protocols governing expression of dissenting views after the decision is made.

A much heralded effect of technologies to facilitate group decision making is reduction or elimination of social context cues among actors in the process [Sproull and Kiesler, 1986]. To the extent social cues are reduced, several benefits are believed to occur: more equal rates of participation, faster decisions, and better quality decisions. However, if this model is scaled up to the organizational level, there could be problems. Decision-makers at the organizational level do not need technology to make their views heard; they are aggressive enough to do that on their own. Similarly, there is no reason to "flatten" the status differences among decision-makers at that level. In fact, status differences at the organizational level carry important substantive information for other participants, such that eliminating them may be dysfunctional. Further, elimination of social context cues is tantamount to elimination of social context, which strips away the underpinnings of both commitments and qualification on which the whole principle of due process works. ODSS technology, then, would be better used to enhance participants' understanding of their different social worlds.

Protocols in and of themselves do not necessarily enhance decision making. They are often merely containment devices to prevent degradation of the discussion. A principal goal of ODSS must be to go beyond this containment role and produce boundary objects that enhance participant understanding of what views other participants hold and why they hold them. The creation of boundary objects is the most important possible contribution of ODSS to the boundary object aspect of organizational decision processes. But it is also possible that an ODSS would itself become a boundary object in the process. This appears to have happened in the case of other technological interventions in the arena of organizational decision making [Dutton and Kraemer, 1985].

Organizational decision support: An interacting team perspective

Lynda M. Applegate and John C. Henderson

The 1980s have been a decade of change for many organizations. Familiar strategies, rigid hierarchies, and costly, swollen middle management ranks have become the targets of major organizational reform. A number of organization theorists have proposed new organization designs that will enable companies to respond to the challenges of the 1990s. These include network organizations [Eccles and Crane, 1987; Nolan et al., 1988], information-based organizations [Drucker, 1988; Peters, 1989], cluster organizations [Mills, 1990], and fast-cycle organizations [Bower and Hout, 1988]. Although details of these designs vary, they share two unifying themes:

- Teams will play an increasingly important role in accomplishing the work of organizations.
- The effective use of information technology will be critical for success.

This section presents a framework for studying the organizational decision support systems (ODSS) required to support teams in organizations. Research propositions that flow from this framework are also presented.

What does it mean to structure an organization around teams? The concept of organizations as social systems composed of interacting teams can be found in some of the earliest work on organization theory [Barnard, 1938]. Lawrence and Lorsch focus on internal interactions, describing the organization as an "open system in which the behaviors of members are interrelated...and interdependent" [Lawrence and

Lorsch, 1967]. Pfeffer and Salancik extended the concept of organizations as open systems to include the interdependencies and interrelatedness of organizations with other organizations within the environment [Pfeffer and Salancik, 1978].

Hal Leavitt, long a visionary in the field of organizational design, addressed the issue of team-based organization design in a paper entitled, "Suppose We Took Groups Seriously...," in which he discussed the issues that must be considered in shifting the focus of organization design from individuals to teams [Leavitt, 1975]. Leavitt argued that the importance of teams in carrying out the formal and informal work of an organization has been recognized since the time of the Hawthorne studies in the 1920s, and that many organization development and participative management strategies and principles have long focused on teams rather than on individuals. But these teams were always "fitted onto organizations" that were constructed around individuals. Leavitt states (p. 68)

> It was not just the logic of classical organizational theory that concentrated on the individual. The whole entrepreneurial tradition of American society supported it. Individuals were taught achievement motivation. They were taught to seek individual evaluation, to compete, to see the world, organizational or otherwise, as a place in which to strive for individual accomplishment and satisfaction. In those respects the classical design of organizations was consonant with the then existent cultural landscape.

The concept of designing organizations around teams has the potential to provide some distinct advantages, especially in the development of more flexible, adaptive, yet efficient organizations. The literature on small-group dynamics suggests that, as teams assume more control over the design of their work and the management and control of team members, commitment and cohesion should increase [Hackman and Oldham, 1976]. Kanter has emphasized that a necessary condition for organization innovation is the "cross-fertilization of ideas" that occurs when individuals from different disciplines are brought together in interdisciplinary groups and allowed the freedom to create and implement unique solutions to identified problems [Kanter, 1988].

Despite their potential advantages, team-based organization designs present some interesting challenges. Common management activities such as hiring, training, compensating, designing jobs, promoting, and firing all need to be reevaluated. Some, such as designing jobs for teams rather than individuals, seem easy enough to handle, and in fact constitute the basis for the current trend toward quality circles and the work team approach to factory automation. Others, such as evaluating and compensating teams rather than individuals, present some interesting challenges but appear feasible to the extent that the team can ensure that feedback and the subsequent distribution of rewards can be used to motivate and control individual team members. Still others, such as hiring, promoting, and firing teams rather than individuals, present significant difficulties and, more importantly, strike deeply to the core of individualism and entrepreneurial spirit upon which our American society is based. It is clear that simply applying the principles upon which traditional organizations are designed and managed to teams rather than individuals is not the correct approach.

Although a number of companies have introduced self-managing teams into their factories, few organizations have undertaken the difficult task of redesigning their white collar and professional organizations around self-managing teams. The story of GE Canada, which embarked on such a restructuring in 1985, illustrates the challenges and opportunities.* GE Canada elected to meet the challenges of designing its organization around self-managing teams rather than individuals in an attempt to achieve the benefits of flexibility and adaptability, while improving cost-effectiveness and productivity. The effective use of information technology—including communications, information management, and specialized decision support—was a critical enabling factor in the redesign of the GE Canada organization. In the following sections, we develop a model of organization decision support (ODSS) technology that emphasizes the concept of a technology infrastructure for team-based organization designs.

Organizational DSS. Early models of DSS technology [Sprague and Carlson, 1982] defined the components of a DSS as comprising three layers—data, models, and dialogue. The modeling component distinguished a DSS from a traditional transaction processing system. Treacy described an architecture for DSS that consisted of several layers ranging from communications to analytic support [Treacy, 1986]. A key contribution of this framework is the recognition that DSS technology extends from basic enabling tools to value-added applications. The framework proposed in this section for analyzing ODSS builds upon previous DSS and GDSS research (see Figure 3). The model describes ODSS along two dimensions: a technology hierarchy dimension and a functional dimension.

Technology hierarchy dimension. The first dimension of our framework for analyzing ODSS, the technology hierarchy dimension, expands the view of DSS as "layered" technologies that serve both enabling and direct value-added functions. The technology hierarchy dimension is composed of three layers—communications, data, and process—representing a

---

* For an in-depth discussion of GE Canada's restructuring from a traditional hierarchy to a self-managing team structure see L.M. Applegate and J.I. Cash, *GE Canada: Designing a New Organization*, Harvard Business School Publications, Boston, 1989.

		Functional categories		
		Production	Coordination	Policy
Technology hierarchy	Process	Task	Team (intra- & inter-) process support	Process standards/ best practice
	Data	Message	Cooperative/ distributed data management	Data standards/semantics
	Communications	Bit transfer	Conferencing	Communications standards/ connectivity
		Traditional DSS	Group DSS	Organizational DSS

Figure 3. Organizational decision support systems.

continuum ranging from essentially enabling technology (e.g., communications) to direct value-added technology (e.g., process).

The *communications* layer is an enabling technology that permits physical connectivity among individuals within organizations and often even outside formal organization boundaries. This layer forms the foundation for an ODSS, providing the mechanism for individuals to form networks of interacting work teams. The *data management* layer of our model enables the access, storage, and retrieval of data in a manner that safeguards its semantic integrity. This layer of an ODSS converts bit streams into messages. To the extent that these messages conform to a common language and set of standards, they can be used to convey a common understanding among interacting work teams throughout the organization. This reflects a higher level of value added than the communications layer by virtue of engendering a common semantic understanding. The *process layer* reflects the combination of communications and data management technologies with analytic problem-solving technologies to create value-added ODSS applications. It is at this layer that systems to support individual, group, and interacting team activities and decisions are integrated to support business and management processes.

Functional dimension. The functional dimension of our ODSS model reflects the range of functionality provided by the ODSS environment. We define three categories of functionality: production, coordination, and policy. The functional dimension of our framework builds on a model of CASE technology developed by Henderson and Cooprider, who use the term infrastructure to represent a broad range of organizational technology and policy issues that support specific production and coordination technologies [Henderson and Cooprider, 1990].

Production technologies increase the efficiency and effectiveness of specific task execution by a single individual in the organization and thus reflect the traditional role of DSS. From an economic productivity perspective, production technologies enable a higher degree of output for a given level of resource input or, alternatively, the same level of output with less input. We include measures of goal achievement (effectiveness) in our output classification to reflect the decision-making and problem-solving view of DSS.

Coordination technologies increase the efficiency and effectiveness of interdependent task execution among two or more decision-makers. These technologies may be used by a single work team or, in the case of ODSS, extend to multiple interacting work teams. Henderson and Cooprider identify two components of coordination technology: control and cooperative functionality [Henderson and Cooprider, 1990]. Control reflects the need to impose discipline upon the concurrent actions of multiple decision-makers in order to achieve a common goal; it is, in essence, a hierarchical view of coordination. The cooperative functionality is a peer-to-peer view that reflects the ability of each individual to directly influence the action or knowledge of others through information exchange. The process of arriving at consensus and completing an interdependent task usually involves both control and cooperation. In commitment-based organizations, cooperation may dominate control; in compliance-based organizations, control may dominate commitment.

The *policy* perspective becomes critical as one considers the concept of an ODSS. Policy is defined as the procedures, standards, and guidelines that enable a firm to achieve portability of processes, data, and communications across organizational boundaries. It provides the essential guiding principles and common languages and linkages needed by an organization to leverage both individual and group decision support systems across multiple, interacting teams. Without ODSS policies and standards, any individual or group can adopt a communication path, language, and analytic perspective to suit the needs of specific task activities, and thereby markedly diminish the ability to integrate task activities to support organization-wide business and management processes. Support of multiple, interacting teams requires that technologies be shared across organizational boundaries, which, in turn, requires a certain level of standardization.

Just as the modeling component was the distinguishing feature of a DSS, the policy dimension of our model is the critical element that distinguishes an ODSS. A *comprehensive ODSS* integrates process, data and communications technologies and policies across all three functional levels.

Summary and conclusions

The increasing turbulence of the competitive environment has combined with factors such as global competition and customization of local markets to create a need to radically restructure organizations. Important aspects of this restructuring are the increased use of teams and the need to provide information technology designed to support team as well as individual decision processes. An emerging body of research and practice focusing on group decision support and computer-supported cooperative work is addressing this need. Previous research and its application to groupware technologies has taken the team as the unit of analysis and sought to identify how team processes create specialized requirements for information technology support. This chapter expands the focus of earlier work from a single work team to the multiple interacting work teams that make up organizations. (These interacting teams may sometimes include members from outside the organization.) We develop a framework for defining ODSS from the perspective of the organization as composed of many interacting work teams, both stable and ad hoc. This framework describes ODSS along two dimensions: a technology hierarchy and a functional dimension.

Workshop discussion: Organizational decision support systems

Discussants: In his discussion and written comments, Bill King remarked on the diversity of definitions and examples that had been provided by the ODSS team. He felt that the objectives of ODSS, as implicitly defined by the team, had been the overriding goal of the MIS field for decades, and were not greatly different from the original goal of DSS. This superordinate goal of the IS field was now being restated in terms of modern concepts, theories, and technologies and at a time when advances in understanding and technologies give it a greater chance of success.

King feels that to advance we need to avoid the pitfalls of the past. For example, DSS began with a focus on unstructured problems but gradually "slipped" into a focus on structured systems. ODSS should not be too broadly defined such that all systems qualify; otherwise, it will have a very brief life cycle. King urged the development of some useful taxonomies for ODSS and clear definitions for entities such as teams, groups, and committees. A good taxonomy for ODSS will allow researchers to recognize the similarities and differences in systems and to recognize the differences between systems. Good descriptive field research on complex, distributed, multitechnology systems can be guided by the taxonomy, and, in turn, used to refine it. Although some results from GDSS may be useful, ODSS should not be viewed simply as an extension of GDSS. While GDSS concentrates on single work teams, ODSS examines interactions between interteam processes.

King concluded by stating that the codesign of organizations and systems should be the goal of ODSS research. We may well be at a historic point where there is both the enabling technology and the recognized need to restructure organizations: "The decades old goal of the IS field may finally be achievable; we cannot afford to miss the opportunity!"

In his written comments, entitled "The Interplay of Division of Labor, Teams, Rapid Change, and Requirements for Competitive Advantage," Steve Alter pointed out that the ODSS papers were primarily concerned with the need to support organizations (rather than individuals) in an environment characterized by (1) the need to change and respond rapidly, (2) greater reliance on teams rather than hierarchical structures, and (3) downsizing of organizations, especially through reduction in the number of levels.

His experience had led him to be cautious in making generalities about broad categories of systems such as GDSS and ODSS. He felt that research and speculation about ODSS should carefully consider factors that would impact the type of ODSS that might be appropriate. For example, are we talking about (1) support/overhead functions (e.g., corporate finance or core business functions that provide competitive advantage such as manufacturing or selling)? (2) temporary teams of executives, permanent teams of workers, or something in between? (3) something that exists or something that doesn't exist? For example, would we include as an ODSS the structured planning systems and management control systems used by most businesses of any size? If not, what would make them an ODSS?

Alter then suggested that the environment in which ODSS exist can be "positioned" in a two-dimensional framework whose axes are the degree to which the organization is permanent and the degree of stability in the situation (see Figure A):

- Organizational permanence: It is fashionable to predict that organizations of the future will move in the direction of (temporary) teams rather than traditional static organizational hierarchies. Temporary teams are good in novel situations that must be handled in an innovative way. Organizational hierarchies are good in situations where standard procedures can be developed and supported. In Alter's opinion, competitive advantage has usually come from developing better standard ways of handling repetitive situations (i.e., accomplishing a company's mission better than the competitors). It is possible to characterize organizational permanence along the following dimensions: (1) static division of labor usually accomplished through fixed organizational hierarchies, (2) permanent teams such as a work team in a factory or an interdisciplinary team that meets periodically to

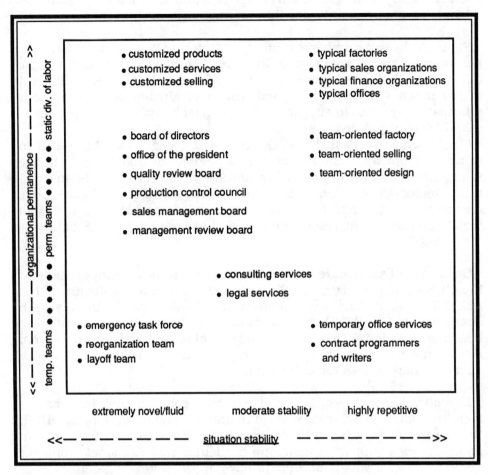

Figure A. Real-world examples of various combinations of organizational permanence and situation stability.

coordinate work or share insights among experts, and (3) temporary teams (project-oriented teams with a short-term mission and predictable life span).

- Situation stability: Situation stability can be viewed along the following dimensions: (1) extremely novel/fluid (problems with no precedent for which there are no existing policies or procedures), (2) moderate stability (there are no fixed procedures outlining what to do and what not to do, but the situation can be dealt with through analogies to or extrapolations from related situations), (3) highly repetitive (the work is done repetitively based on well-understood guidelines and procedures). It is exceptionally difficult to attain long-term competitive advantage by treating situations as though they are novel/fluid. To the contrary, competitive advantage is attained by making situations more and more standard within an organization.

Figure A shows a number of examples of combinations of organizational permanence and situation stability. Alter believes that ODSS for these different types of situations would be so different that it would be difficult to say much about ODSS beyond what has already been said about information systems (management support, technical competence, user-friendliness, rapid response, etc.).

Finally, Alter suggested that the framework might also be useful in thinking about what is really meant by predictions about rapid change in organizations. What kinds of organizational structures exist in organizations today? In which direction (imaginary quadrant in Figure A) are organizations moving? Do certain quadrants represent the forces of inertia and others represent the forces of change? Are ODSS catalysts for change?

Summary of electronic discussion. The electronic meeting session for the ODSS group utilized the Electronic Brainstorming software of the PLEXSYS system. The participants were asked "What are the research challenges in ODSS?" Their responses are collected under a number of headings as follows. To illustrate the general nature of the outputs from a brainstorming session, the comments of the participants are reproduced in more or less verbatim form.

Definition/taxonomy of ODSS. There was concern that the various members of the ODSS team seemed to have several definitions of ODSS: "In one definition it is a support system for the whole organization. In another, it is a support system for a particular organizational problem." Some felt that it was important to have an all-embracing definition in order to clarify research directions. Others felt that it was good to have a diverse set of viewpoints. Still others felt that the field was at an early stage and that definitions were not overly important. There were suggestions to do field observation to provide a basis for the development of a taxonomy and to allow a well-defined set of terms to develop. Finally, there were some suggestions to drop the D out of ODSS and to broaden the concept to include processes that did not necessarily lead to decisions.

The following are three specific comments:

• The purpose of ODSS is to enhance the effectiveness and efficiency of information in distributed decision situations, as well as to support knowledge acquisition, representation, and use in these decentralized and distributed environments.

- Instead of ODSS, how about simply IT/O—information technology in support of organizational processes (which include processes in informal and formal groups, and across formal organizational boundaries)?
- Are we really moving toward *organization* decision support systems? I think we are presently in a strong mode of team-based organizations, with less concern for organization-wide points of view—except at the level of customer links, etc., which are really *inter*organizational decision support systems.

The role of teams. How to support multiple interacting teams is a central issue in ODSS. It was pointed out that there are many kinds of teams: formal or informal, task-specific or more general, transitory or permanent. However, teams are only one form of group in organizations. Group behavior is subject to organizational norms and values which must be taken into account when designing support systems. Research challenges that were suggested follow:

- How do we build systems to support coordination and cooperation both within a team and between teams?
- If organizations are composed of interacting teams, are there new roles for individuals that are created and/or supported by the technology?
- How can ODSS deal with the creation of new teams and the dissolution of old teams that have achieved their goals?
- Saying that teams are replacing hierarchical structures avoids dealing with the tougher issue: What are the relationships between the organizational hierarchy and teams?

ODSS infrastructure. We need to learn how to define highly flexible architectures for ODSS, so that we can put systems into play, observe them in use (or lack of use), and rapidly modify the system to improve it. We need a platform, tool generators, initial tools, user-developable and modifiable tools, and user support delivery systems (training aids, consultants on line, etc.). These architectures should be experimental in nature; formal "architectures" can be confining.

Before we begin to define an architecture, we need to describe the organizational phenomena we are trying to support. At a minimum we are trying to support the exchange of information. If we provide this service, different groups, people, processes, and so on will augment it for their own purposes.

We need to understand the differences between decision-oriented or task-oriented information systems and the development of the technological *infrastructure* necessary to carry on day-to-day business and to support various communication and decision-making processes within an organization.

What exactly should "our" role be in studying the "plumbing" (the technological infrastructure) associated with ODSS? Should we study infrastructure or specific models and databases?

We need to develop a basic platform of technology, a family of tools for building applications tools, and then a large variety of specific tools and tool modifications *in use*.

Representational issues. We need to make a distinction in representation between problem-solving structure and task structure; then we can describe teams in various settings.

Representation is a key issue in ODSS. What information representations are useful to individuals? teams? formal organizational units? Semantic networks are the basic primitives. Note that we are accepting the need to deal with phrases and fragments, not formal documents alone; and estimates and guesses, not simply "accepted" numbers.

Semantic networks are an excellent underlying representation but, like organizations, fully connected semantic nets quickly become too complex and intractable. In our previous research we used a frame representation to help organize complex semantic nets which enabled dynamic structuring—frames on nets is like teams on nets.

General ODSS research issues. How can we assess whether the system is supporting the way the organization does business? What are the dimensions of performance? How do you measure success?

We must realize that people in organizations participate in more than one kind of group. That is, we don't need to build one organizational system, but a variety of systems to accommodate the diversity of groups and tasks (e.g., formal groups, ad hoc teams, task forces). The challenge is to design cooperating ODSS.

How do the characteristics of an ODSS shift the types of problems that individuals and groups "find"? One system that is in use in a company has expanded the realm of managerial work from solving problems to finding opportunities and implementing change.

Rather than shifting problems, how can ODSS shift the organizational forms that can solve existing problems? How do specific policies surrounding the development and use of technologies enable or constrain the organizational processes that span across organizational boundaries (both internal and external)?

We need to understand the motivation for people to participate constructively in organizational information sharing activities. What mechanisms can promote sharing? What classes of information should be shared?

We need research that covers individual cognition (learning, problem solving, problem identification, etc.) in the context of interpersonal interactions in groups. Then, the ODSS context frames alternative degrees of group formality: task-specific versus independent, and so on.

We need to develop a classification of generic organizational problems in terms of identifying (1) the processes to be supported, (2) the communications technology needed, and (3) the problem-solving (inferencing) technology that maps onto these generic problems. The classification scheme should be situational, contextual, or problem dependent. Questions: Do different industries have different problems? Are centralized organizations different from decentralized organizations? Small organizations versus large organizations? Product versus service companies? What is the impact on ODSS of organizational strategy, mission, and purpose? Culture? Geographic scope?

Are there stages in the development of ODSS technology so that the first stage is passive receptivity (e.g., large bulletin boards or information dissemination stations), while later stages involve more active use by organization members?

General comments. The breadth of ODSS may help in thinking about organizational decision making. The framework is not only what happens with a model or a computerized database, but also the e-mail, the gossip, the environmental background information, etc.

It is not the IT itself that is going to produce interesting effects in an organization—it is how the IT, strategy, and structure work together. We need many detailed case studies to begin to understand the extent to which these organizational forces create alignment and subsequent effects.

How much structure are we assuming here? If ODSS, following the DSS philosophy, is ill-structured, why are we pursuing structure? Should we be developing representations and mechanisms for handling lack of structure (or flexibility in structure)?

At this point, there is not a clear distinction (there exist multiple unclear distinctions) between a "group" and an "organization." Is the ISDP a group effort or an organizational effort? What are the important distinguishing characteristics between organizations and groups?

I suggest we accept that an organization is a set of teams. Some are formal and/or permanent; others are task specific; others are temporary and ad hoc, as in an informal grouping to organize a meeting.

Before we can build organizational DSS, we must understand and define the organizational processes that we are attempting to support.

The real benefits of ODSS are probably going to be interorganizational. Existing organizational structures reflect information processing needs within the firm—hopefully, those will decrease as we begin to interconnect with our customers, suppliers, government agencies, etc.

To the extent that we believe that the boundaries among organizations are becoming more porous, it is becoming difficult to define an organization without including the concept of interorganizational alliances.

ODSS should deal with information systems support within and across formal and informal organization boundaries.

Research approaches. We should develop some good case and field studies to better understand the research issues in ODSS. Discover examples and study them intensively using field observation and longitudinal studies.

We (IS academicians and friends) are an organization. Why don't we set up an ODSS to help us? Why is it that our paper reviews take just as long to do as with our friends in disciplines with little understanding of technology?

How do we implement a grounded theory approach—for example, what phenomena do we observe? Any activities or only a specific class of activities? One approach would be to look at what groups do in organizations and how they do it.

Before we do research on ODSS, we need to build a few of them to see what they are and what bear traps exist out there. Let's adopt a prototyping rather than life cycle approach.

Theories are not necessary for acquiring knowledge or making sense (or discovering) phenomena. That is only *half* of the scientific method. Witness, for example, NASA's failure of theories in space exploration—yet NASA acquires a remarkably rich source of data/phenomena to further *be explained* by theory. Sometimes the world is *data* rich but theory poor.

Chapter 6

Technology Environments to Support Decision Processes

Ralph H. Sprague, Jr., Izak Benbasat, Omar El Sawy,
David King, Timothy R. Hill, Henk G. Sol, and Peter A. Todd

As part of the ISDP project to chart new directions for DSS research, our team has been working to define, understand, and explore the concept of information technology support environments. Information technology is intuitively characterized as the set of information and communication technologies evolving from research and development in computer science, telecommunications, and engineering activities. The support environment is more difficult to define.

The word *environment* can be rich in meaning, but like so many generic words, it is overused to the point of being nearly meaningless. Relevant to the context of this chapter, there are organization environments, cultural environments, physical environments, and even operating systems environments. (Are you running in a VM or a Unix environment?) Many of these environments can be considered to "support" people in organizations as they attempt problem-solving and decision-making tasks.

We characterize the *technology environment* as the set of technology capabilities and the manner in which they are used by people in performing these tasks.

The concept of a technology environment for the use of support systems is intuitively comfortable but hard to define rigorously. The differences in the "look and feel" between the icon-oriented, visually rich environment popularized by the Macintosh, and the command-driven, semantic structure of the MS-DOS environment, are quite clear. A rigorous theory or even a definition is much more difficult. Nevertheless, our use of the term technology environment will encompass the human-machine interface or interaction also. The use of the word environment emphasizes the blending or merging of the cognitive and technology processes, instead of focusing on their differentiation.

The contributions from the team members deal with this topic from several directions. They are presented here in abridged form, in the words of each author. The first section starts with the most natural interpretation of the technology environment—the capabilities and functions of the hardware and software. David King presents a summary of the current and expected future capabilities of technology, and an enumeration of the deficiencies and limitations it has. For the latter, he briefly describes the research efforts aimed at overcoming these deficiencies.

Benbasat and Todd argue for a different point of departure. Perhaps, they say, the cognitive characteristics of users form the starting point for developing the technological environment. They examine a set of theories regarding the way people use such systems.

Rather than focus on the technology directly or the cognitive attributes of the users, Sprague and Hill suggest a focus on the kind of work that will be supported by the technology. Richer representations of the work may lead to a better definition of the requirements for the technology environment. They then explore two ways of representing this work—a conceptual approach and a more formal approach based on neural network theory.

Henk Sol reminds us that whatever perspective is chosen, real systems must be designed and developed to provide the improved performance promised by these systems. Looking first at three levels of impact—the micro, meso, and macro—he illustrates the way systems can assist in problem-driven tasks. He then shows how the design of such a system will be dependent on patterns of thinking, modeling, working, and controlling.

The final section, by Omar El Sawy, presents a conceptual model that relates all of these different perspectives into a "research generator." Based on the researcher's perspectives, interests, and skills, an aggregate research program can be represented by exploring the four major components of the generator.

Evolving functionality for the technology environment

David King

This section of the chapter focuses on technological issues. While IS technologies can be used to support a variety of generic applications in an enterprise, this discussion is concerned with the use of IS technology for strategic monitoring, analysis, and decision processes. In the same vein, while IS technologies can include everything from computer hardware to communications technology, the primary emphasis in this discussion is on computer software—in particular, languages and user interfaces—designed to support individuals working alone and in groups on problem-solving and decision-making processes.

Although the emphasis in this section is not on hardware, some discussion of where computer hardware is going in the near future is required to set the stage for current and future developments in software and user interfaces. While they are not currently in widespread use, there is no doubt that workstations will come to dominate the IS world in the near term. Crudely put, a workstation is a computer device that has

- a large internal memory (eight megabytes or more),
- a fast processor (10 MIPS or faster),
- bitmapped, high-resolution graphics display screen (with one million pixels), and
- a large amount of disk storage (either locally or on a server).

The forerunner of the workstation was the PC. In the PC world the emphasis was on the individual user running single, stand-alone applications. The workstation world, however, is a networked environment with a single workstation capable of running multiple applications simultaneously (i.e., multitasking) and accessing multiple sources of data where the applications and/or the data reside either locally or on some other processor/server on the network. This functionality is couched in the phrase, "The network is the computer."

Human-computer communications: Who's in control? A continuum exists between those IS applications where the user is in control and those where the computer is in control. Decision support systems (DSS) fall at one end of the continuum and (the current generation of) expert systems (ES) tend to fall on the other end. Historically, DSS have been designed to assist users with (a limited set of) decision processing tasks. In a DSS it is up to the user to decide what to look at, how to look at it, and how to interpret it. The advent of ES has enabled knowledge engineers to automate many of these same activities. For instance, in an ES designed to do mergers and acquisition analysis, the ES decides what information is needed for the various companies involved, what scenarios are to be run based on this information, and what recommendations to make. Of course, in an ES it is still up to the user to decide which recommendations to enact (if any).

Augmented systems. Between the two extremes of user control and computer control, there exists a rapidly growing body of research and prototypical systems. These systems are the wave of the future. In the DSS literature these systems have been labeled "symbiotic" DSS [Manheim and Isenberg, 1987] and "intelligent decision support systems" [Turban and King, 1986]. In the world of user interface design and artificial intelligence (AI) these systems have been labeled "augmented" systems [Engelbart, 1988]. For science fiction buffs and futurists, the systems can be thought of as "cyborgs"—that is, humans who use technology to enhance their capabilities [Glenn, 1989].

Much of the work on "augmented" systems owes its origin to the work of Doug Engelbart and to the early work done on office automation at Xerox PARC. Engelbart characterized humans and tools in the following way [Engelbart, 1988]:

Human System	Tool System
Organization	Media
Procedures	Portrayal
Customs	Travel and View
Methods	Manipulate
Language	Retrieve
Skills	Compute
Knowledge	Communicate
Training	

In the list, the characteristics are not matched in a one-to-one fashion.

The essential idea was that tool systems should be designed to extend human capabilities in imagined and unimagined ways, to change the basic character of communities, and to make humans and communities more effective.

The desktop metaphor. The first computer system to support this paradigm was the Xerox Star. The Star technology, whose features were later popularized by the Apple Macintosh, was based on a "desktop" metaphor. That is, the screen of the computer was designed to emulate the top of the user's desk with multiple sheets of paper, folders for organizing those papers, and editing tools for creating and modifying those papers in a WYSIWYG fashion. From the standpoint of user interfaces, the import of the system was that it presented the user with a set of virtual objects that were synonymous with objects in the user's "real" world and that could be directly manipulated by the user (through a mouse input device). Initially, the system augmented the user's capabilities by providing a set of tools for "speeding up" the editing, storage, and retrieval processes. It wasn't until the recent advent of "desktop publishing" and "multimedia" systems that these processes were affected in any "qualitative" way—profoundly impacting the nature of the documents that could be produced by the user.

The phenomenal success of products like Apple's Hypercard product (and other clone products) is indicative of the utility of the object-oriented paradigm, visual programming [Shu, 1988], and direct manipulation interfaces. Object-oriented tool kits of this sort will certainly dominate decision and executive support systems in the near future. From the standpoint of strategic planning and decision processing, however, these systems have severe limitations. In particular, the objects they provide

- do not really reflect the world of strategic planning or decision processing,
- are still manipulated in a rather crude and obtrusive fashion, and
- lack the knowledge necessary to "augment" the intelligence of the user.

Limits in current approaches. This section reviews the limitations of the current workstation environments.

Limits in the language. "Desktop" environments are basically designed to support staff analysts with computational and document processing needs. A business plan is typical of the type of output supported by these environments. But strategic planning and decision processing involve much more than analysis and writing. At a higher level, the world of decision processing is made up of goals, plans, opportunities, problems, and the like. It does not consist of spreadsheets, folders, editors, printers, and so on. The point is that even though the "desktop" provides a set of objects that can be directly manipulated, these are not the objects of the decision processing world. The distinction is similar to the distinction between the "data-oriented" approach to information systems modeling and the "behavior-oriented" approach [Olle et al., 1988]. The data-oriented approach focuses on the flow of data objects, while the behavior-oriented approach focuses on events and tasks. There is currently no workstation environment in the corporate arena that supports this higher level world.

In the AI arena, however, research efforts are under way to develop languages and systems to support decision processing at this higher level. The efforts are focused on three interrelated areas:

- AI-based planning: Unlike ES, where the emphasis is on "declarative" knowledge, there is a whole segment of knowledge-based systems aimed at dealing with "procedural" knowledge. This area is labeled AI-based planning [Wilkins, 1988]. In this area the aim is to use the computer to develop (strategic) plans for accomplishing one or more goals. Here, the developer works in a language made up of goals, tasks, plans, preconditions, and so on. While these techniques have not been applied to business enterprises (Dhar's work is an exception [Dhar, 1984]), they are being widely used in military planning tasks (e.g., battlefield management [Lehner, 1989]).
- Cooperative dialogue systems: Increasingly, natural language processing (NLP) is being used to "front-end" database query. The type of

dialogue supported by these NLPs, however, is basically one-sided. In this case, the user poses a question or command, and the computer answers. The computer has virtually no "understanding" of the user. There are NLP systems being developed [Shwartz, 1988], however, that treat human-computer interaction as a two-sided dialogue. For the computer to participate in such a dialogue, it needs to understand the "goals" and "beliefs" of the user.

- Case-based reasoning (CBR): This form of knowledge representation and reasoning is in its infancy [Hammond, 1989]. Basically, in a CBR system historical cases (plans) are stored in the computer's memory. When faced with a particular task, the systems retrieve those cases which "best" match (under a variety of criteria) the current problem and context. The utility of the elected cases for the problem at hand is evaluated a priori by simulating its results and adjusting the plan accordingly. These adjustments are then stored in memory indexed by those features of the problem which the adjustments are designed to address. While this approach has not been used for decision processing in the corporate world, there is an obvious analogy between this mode of reasoning and the case study method used in many business schools.

Limited I/O. Just as there is a mismatch between the objects in the decision processing world and the objects on the "desktop," there is also a mismatch between the way objects are manipulated by (human) decision processors and the way that they are manipulated on the "desktop." Current workstation technology supports input from keyboards and mice, and output of text and graphics to the screen and the printer. In human interaction, however, voice, gestures, handwriting, and (animated) visual images are all crucial elements in communication. Rapid advances are being made in the area of workstation output. Newer multimedia and hypermedia systems permit the integration of text, graphics (both static and animated), images, video, and voice into one or more windows on the screen. Advances in mass storage devices (e.g., optical disks and CD-ROM) are serving to support these advances in output technology. It is the input side that is progressing at a slower pace. Many executives and managers are "keyboard illiterate." While they don't know how to type, they do know how to talk, write, and gesture. Yet voice and handwriting input devices are in their initial stages of development. Finally, there are very few devices that enable computers to understand human (hand) gestures. There are a couple of "gloves" that will soon remedy this problem [Foley, 1988]. However, these devices are designed primarily to manipulate virtual images of physical objects, and they are still fairly obtrusive.

Limited intelligence. A final limitation that characterizes the current generation of workstation environments is the amount of knowledge embedded in the systems. There are a variety of ways in which current and future systems can be "augmented" with "knowledge" in such a way that the user still maintains substantial control of the system. The resulting systems have been labeled "intelligent support systems" [Fischer, 1989] with emphasis on "support." The following categorizes some of the work that is being done on ISS:

- Conversational advisory systems (CAS): These systems were mentioned earlier in the discussion of cooperative dialogue systems. In addition to their knowledge of NLP, CAS also embody expertise in a specific domain application (e.g., knowledge about financial investments). It is this domain expertise that is one of the distinguishing features of a CAS versus an NL front end.
- Intelligent front ends: Basically, an intelligent front end (IFE) is a system that sits in front of a conventional tool (e.g., a DSS) and provides the user with "intelligent" help (a recent book by Shafer illustrates the structure and some possible uses of intelligent front ends [Shafer, 1989]). What distinguishes an IFE from other knowledge-based systems is the type of knowledge embedded in the system. In most knowledge-based systems, the knowledge pertains to a specific application domain. In an intelligent front end, the knowledge details how the conventional tools (that it front-ends) can be or should be used. In a DSS, for example, an IFE could help the user locate data and models, could indicate which analytic procedures to employ, and could help the user interpret the data. IFEs have been developed for assisting users of statistical packages [Gale, 1986] and for embedding expertise in executive support systems (where users have little interest in knowing how to use the underlying DBMS or DSS on which the system is based) [King, 1990b].
- Critics: A critic is a knowledge-based system that "criticizes" the decisions, plans, and so on formulated by the user. In a standard expert system, the system provides recommendations. The system can also explain how the recommendations were reached. In a critic system the user offers a set of recommendations and the system explains why the recommendations are either good or bad based on its knowledge of the problem. Critics have been used in CAD [Fischer and Lemke, 1990], in Lisp programming environments [Fischer and Mastaglio, 1989], in medical diagnosis [Miller, 1984], in recipe planning [Hammond, 1989], and in analyzing simple business decisions [Raghavan and Chand, 1989].
- Agents: An agent is basically a software robot [Kay, 1984] that mimics a "personal assistant." As Stearns suggests, "The agent is autonomous in that it can carry out instructions without user intervention. The agent can also make decisions based on the criteria a user gives it... The kinds of things you would have an agent do are the kinds of things

you would expect a personal assistant to do for you with a workstation" [Stearns, 1989].

In general, agents are designed to perform small-scale (yet tedious and time-consuming) tasks on behalf of the user. For instance, the "information lens" [Malone, 1986] is basically an agent that enables users to employ rules to "intelligently" handle e-mail messages. Another example is the monitor facility in the Paradigm product [King, 1990b]. Here, users can create monitors (i.e., small rule-based scripts) to keep track of data in a spreadsheet and to activate various procedures when certain patterns occur in the data (e.g., if corporate profits are below plan, the system can automatically create a graph and an explanation of the problem).

One of the major limitations of all the efforts to create intelligent support systems is that the user can operate only in a "microworld" [Feurzeig, 1987]—a world that understands only a single domain. Microworlds are very brittle. As users move toward the boundaries of these domains, the systems break down. Efforts to overcome this "brittleness" are proceeding on two fronts. First, there are efforts under way to build systems with a great deal of "commonsense" knowledge [Feigenbaum and Lenat, 1989]. In this way the system can fall back on its common sense when domain expertise is nonexistent or can't be readily applied. Second, there are efforts aimed at teaching computers how to learn [Michie, 1987], especially through analogy. In this way knowledge gained in one area can be applied to other areas.

The computer as a communications device: The antirationalists. All of the developments discussed above view the computer primarily as a computational or analytic device. The assumption is that by providing the computer with (1) an appropriate language, (2) sufficient knowledge, and (3) an "easy-to-use" interface, the analytic, monitoring, and interpretive capabilities of individual decision processors can be substantially "augmented." This approach is not without its critics. Winograd and Flores [Winograd and Flores, 1986] and Suchmann [Suchmann, 1987] are among this group.

From their standpoint, the basic problems are twofold. First, given his experience in the field of AI, Winograd sees the current efforts in ISS as basically futile. It is his opinion that machines can't really be endowed with anything but minimal intelligence in very limited domains. (Note: Winograd was the first researcher to develop an intelligent microworld [Winograd, 1972].) Second, these critics are of the opinion that the whole effort to "augment" the analytic capabilities of human decision processes rests on a fallacious philosophical premise. That is, that human decision making is or can be a "rational" process. In their view, decision processes are situationally determined. They cannot be planned in detail ahead of time. Simply put, while plans may guide our actions, there is a wide disparity between plans and actual actions. In essence, plans are created as they happen. It is only in hindsight that we have a clear picture of the relationship between goals, plans, tasks, and actual actions.

Because of these problems, the critics suggest that the real focus of research in human-computer interaction should be on "augmenting" human-human communication with computers. If Engelbart's discussions are reexamined, it is clear that he had this type of "augmentation" in mind when he suggested that computers could be used to enhance the activities of communities and make them more effective [Engelbart, 1988]. Empirically, the importance of these efforts is reflected in the use of executive support systems for communications purposes. As Rockhart and De Long have shown, e-mail is one of the most often used features of an executive support system [Rockart and De Long, 1988]. Enhancements to e-mail systems may qualitatively change the way in which individuals work. One example of such an enhanced e-mail system is the Coordinator system developed by Winograd and Flores. The Coordinator system enhances the users' abilities to keep track of commitments and obligations that arise in decision processing tasks.

While not necessarily adhering to the antirationalist view, recent efforts on "computer-supported cooperative work" [Grief, 1988] are all basically aimed at improving computers as a communications medium. Some of these efforts—for instance, the information lens noted above—combine the goals of augmenting both individual and group activities. It is clear that the work in this area is being driven by environmental and technological imperatives. On the one hand, the regional and global diversification of business enterprises demands enhanced communication networks that can work around the clock. On the other hand, advances in the networking capabilities of workstations have enabled development of these enhanced systems.

Summary. As originally conceived, decision support systems consisted of three crucial elements—models, data, and the user interface. Recent developments in decision support systems, especially in the area of executive support, have placed a great deal of emphasis on the human-computer interface. The belief is that the "desktop" and direct manipulation go a long way toward removing the "cognitive" barriers between the computer and the user. Norman summarizes the belief in the following way: "When I use a direction manipulation interface—whether for text editing, drawing pictures, or creating and playing games—I do think of myself not as using a computer but as doing a particular task. The computer is, in effect, invisible" [Norman, 1988].

While the "desktop" has its benefits, it has a number of limitations for those involved in decision processing tasks. This section has outlined some of these deficiencies and has briefly described a number of research efforts aimed at overcoming these deficiencies. What these efforts suggest is that there are alternative views of the human-computer interface that may be more appropriate for these tasks. Negroponte expresses the flavor of these alternatives quite colorfully [Negroponte, 1989]:

> Direct manipulation has its place, and in many regards is part of the joys of life: sports, food, sex, and for some, driving. But wouldn't you really prefer to run your home and office with a gaggle of well-trained butlers (to answer the phone), maids (to make the beds), secretaries (to filter the world), accountants or brokers (to manage your money), and on some occasions, cooks, gardeners, and chauffeurs when there were too many guests, weeds or cars on the road?

Theories of DSS use by individual decision-makers*

Izak Benbasat and Peter Todd

In the previous section, David King has given us some insight into the technological environments facing organizations in future years. Undoubtedly these technologies will have an effect on the way we work, communicate, and make decisions in organizations. Taking into account the rapid pace of technological change today, it may seem pointless to try to understand the impact of specific new technologies. Surely, as technology changes, our old assessments become obsolete and we need to begin predicting anew. While this may seem to be a reasonable position and one that has influenced research in the decision support systems (DSS) field, we do not think it is a perspective that permits us to advance our understanding of the use of information technology. Indeed, we believe that it is possible to gain insight into the influence of information technologies independent of their specific characteristics. In essence, we are proposing a technology-independent perspective to understanding the use and effects of DSS.

If we consider decision support technologies as a generic set of tools or techniques that are designed to leverage the decision-maker's cognitive abilities, there are many existing theories that can help us to understand the likely impacts of those technologies. The commonly held assumption is that better decisions will result from DSS use because cognitive capabilities are expanded. As we will discuss later, there are other theories which might assert that DSS will have no impact because decision-makers cannot or do not necessarily wish to make better decisions. Still other theories might predict that organizational norms will influence the way that technology is employed. These different theoretical perspectives will be explored below in order to assess the possible impacts of the technology environment. Keep in mind that the

* This work has been supported by operating grant OGP2421 from the Natural Sciences and Engineering Research Council of Canada.

value of this approach is that we do not need to consider the specific characteristics of the technologies in order to assess their effects. The influence of technology will be determined by how it affects the decision-maker's perceptions and abilities. Thus, by understanding the specific motivations, goals, and abilities of the decision-maker, we can comprehend how the decision-maker will employ the technology.

Taking this perspective allows us to place DSS research into a theoretical context that would increase our ability to predict and understand the reasons for and the effects of DSS use. This section of the chapter attempts to offer some suggestions about theories, mainly dealing with individual decision-makers, that could be used to further research in DSS.

The theories that are examined are grouped into three classes, labeled as bottom-up, top-down, and middle-out, each of which takes a somewhat different perspective on decision-making behavior. These three perspectives are discussed in the next sections of the chapter.

Bottom-up theories. Bottom-up theories are models that describe how decision-makers solve problems at the elementary information processing level. They could also be considered as approaches to decomposing problem solving into its elementary constituents [Todd, 1989]. In a bottom-up approach applied to DSS, the cognitive mechanisms that a decision-maker employs are examined, and then are either supported or replaced by a computer-based aid.

Elementary information processes (EIP) are basic cognitive operations such as reading data values, shifting the focus of attention, or comparing two values. These low-level operators can be used to model a variety of decision strategies since individuals typically employ only a limited number of cognitive operators. These elementary processes could also be defined for the domain of visual information processing. The idea that decision making can be described as a set of EIP is not new. It is not even an entirely novel concept in the DSS domain. Sprague and Carlson's ROMC model (representations, operations, memory aids, control mechanisms) is somewhat similar [Sprague and Carlson, 1982], though the examination and integration of specific EIP identified in the psychology literature provide for a deeper level of analysis of the impact of various decision aids.

The value of the EIP approach centers on providing a sound mechanism to determine the types of decision aids that will be relevant to support a particular decision strategy. To identify the building components of a specific DSS, the strategies that would provide a satisfactory solution to the problem on hand are identified first. To implement each strategy, a number of tasks have to be performed, and each task could be decomposed into a number of EIP. Problems that follow specific decision rules or heuristics could therefore be described as a series of elementary cognitive operations. Modeling decision approaches in this way is useful. It helps to understand precisely how the decision is made. This knowledge, in turn, is an essential input to the design of computer-based decision aids.

While bottom-up models are useful in suggesting approaches based on human information processing for the design and evaluation of decision aids, they assume that the reason for using decision aids would be to improve decision quality and the consequences of use would be such an improvement. However, these models are limited to the extent that they rest on an implicit assumption that augmenting the capabilities of decision-makers would lead to better decision making. In this sense these models ignore the goals and motivations of the decision-makers, and also assume that they have conscious control over and knowledge of the execution of various decision strategies. Thus, while they are useful in developing DSS from a normative perspective, they will not always correctly predict the outcomes of DSS use. Middle-out theories described in the next section are more effective in describing outcomes of DSS use, as they focus on factors that influence the way in which a DSS might be utilized.

Middle-out theories. These perspectives take into account the causes that influence the application of various decision-making strategies, such as the degree of consciousness and control over the decision process, the overall motivation to perform a specific task, or the perceived importance of effort spent in decision making. These factors may mediate the effects of any support tool that is developed based on an EIP approach described in the previous section.

Prospect theory. Prospect theory [Kahneman and Tversky, 1979] argues that, in situations that involve making risky decisions, strategies that are inconsistent with normative models are used. Specifically, there are two classes of aberrations termed the *certainty* effect and the *isolation* effect. The certainty effect results in underweighting outcomes that are probable when compared with those that are certain. The isolation effect causes common attributes of problem solutions that are perceived to be equal to be discarded before a selection is made.

Prospect theory identifies two phases of decision making. The first phase, called *editing*, is concerned with the simplification of the problem space through the use of processing mechanisms such as coding, combination, cancellation, segregation, rounding, and dominance. Editing is influenced by the certainty and isolation effects discussed above. The second phase, *evaluation*, is the selection of an alternative from the remaining, modified solution set. Selection of a solution may be dependent upon the simplification procedures used and on their order of application. The simplified problem space may be very different in character from the original unedited problem. This can lead to errors or biases in decision making.

Prospect simplification (editing) is likely a hardwired approach to the evaluation of alternatives based on a generalized utility model. Change or variance in decision outcomes is attributable to the editing of the initial representation of the problem. The way in which the problem is represented is affected by contextual variables, such as whether the problem is presented in terms of potential gains or losses. The evaluation process is constrained by the basic limitations of the human information processing system and tends to operate "automatically." That is, evaluation is not under the direct, conscious control of the individual.

One way in which prospect theory would explain why decision behavior does not conform to normative theory is the fact that the apparatus being used to support the decision process is not designed for implementation of the normative model. For example, the human perceptual system attends most readily to changes or differences, while the utility or value models require processing in terms of absolute magnitudes. As a result, process differs between the predictions of the normative model and empirical observations.

The implication from prospect theory is that very little progress is likely to be made in terms of aiding or assisting decision making. If individuals do not have conscious control over the mechanisms that they use during problem solving, then no amount of training or assistance will facilitate the improvement of decision making. Decision behavior may be manipulated in this case by a conscious framing of the problem to invoke certain processes from the decision-maker, but, after that point, support tools may be of little use. In this sense, prospect theory might provide an explanation for the lack of significant findings in some of the prior DSS research.

Prospect theory also challenges the relevance of the most commonly examined independent variable: the DSS. The theory posits that a decision-maker might have already applied sufficient structure to the problem prior to using the capabilities provided by the DSS. This editing causes the decision-maker to overlook potential solutions. Thus, studying decision aids that focus on support for design and choice phases of the decision process may have little potential payoff. This suggests that the problem identification phase should be the key concern of DSS designers. DSS studies should focus on evaluating features that support problem formulation and diagnosis. This phase, however, has received the least attention and is the most difficult to support.

Cost-benefit theories. An alternate view of decision making is provided by those who consider strategy to be under the conscious control of the individual. The use of a particular strategy is based on some form of cost-benefit evaluation [Payne, 1982]. Decision-makers presumably compare the amount of cognitive effort required to implement a particular strategy with the expected benefits (decision quality) associated with the implementation of that strategy. The benefits are typically measured as the likelihood of an approach leading to a good decision. Given values for cognitive effort and decision quality, a trade-off is made. In terms of DSS research, the key message of cost-benefit theories is that decision-maker behavior cannot simply be viewed as being solely concerned with decision quality. Thinking is hard, and as a result effort may be an important determinant of DSS use.

The relative importance of each component in the trade-off evaluation will have implications for DSS use. Let us assume that there are two classes of objectives that a decision-maker is likely to have: maximize decision quality subject to an effort constraint, or minimize effort subject to a quality constraint. These two views influence the way a decision-maker approaches problem solving and utilizes decision-aiding technology.

For the decision-maker concerned with maximizing decision quality, we would expect that a DSS which relieves cognitive load and therefore expands the bounds of rationality would lead to improved decision quality. The savings in cognitive load effected by the DSS would be invested into the problem, which in turn could lead to greater information use, more alternatives being examined, and presumably an improved decision process. On the other hand, when a decision aid that reduces cognitive effort is available, the effort-minimizing decision-maker might opt for the least effort route rather than converting the freed resources into extra effort which may lead to better quality decisions. Thus, when using a decision aid, we would expect that this type of decision-maker would follow the strategy which provided an acceptable solution with the smallest possible expenditure of effort. Consequently, in a decision-aided environment, the effort-minimizing decision-maker would not necessarily exhibit higher effectiveness or improved decision quality.

In summary, cost-benefit theory suggests that a decision-maker's motivations and values influence DSS use and that an exclusive focus on decision quality as the dependent variable is inappropriate. This implies that studies that consider the *joint* effects of effort and quality, or control for one while manipulating the other, are more likely to provide consistent and interpretable results.

Expectancy theory. According to expectancy theory, the motivation to perform a specific task will be a function of the expectation that effort will lead to a desired positive outcome. DeSanctis developed a conceptual model of user behavior based on this theory in order to predict DSS use [DeSanctis, 1983]. She hypothesized that DSS use is determined by

- the expectation that high (low) DSS use will lead to decision making of high (low) quality,

- the expectation that decision making of high (low) quality will lead to certain outcomes, and
- the individual's perceptions of the rewards associated with these outcomes.

This theory has obvious face value in that DSS use is associated with expectations of benefiting from such use.

It could be argued that expectancy theory models, by focusing on the perceived performance levels to be attained at different levels of effort (including that of DSS use), measure effort and quality jointly. This could be a way to link them to the cost-benefit theories discussed previously. Also measuring motivation, with all the intrinsic and extrinsic rewards considered, would be better than simply examining the decision quality outcomes. This is particularly relevant in settings where overall expectation of decision quality is low but use is mandated or encouraged by the organization.

To summarize the theories discussed in this section, DSS use does not necessarily result in improved decision quality because decision-makers are not interested in decision quality only (cost-benefit theory), because in some cases they have no control over the decision process (prospect theory), or because their motivation to perform is limited due to the absence of an obvious relationship between system use and some desirable outcome (expectancy theory).

Top-down theories. The theories discussed in this section view the decision-maker as acting not in isolation, but in an organizational or social context. As a result, the goal and motivations of the decision-maker are mediated by organizational realities. Two theories are considered. One views individuals as purposeful, rational actors that combine their own beliefs with those existing in the organization. The second theory takes a political view of organizations as a collection of individual actors, each with separate agendas which may be complementary or conflicting with other members or influence groups in the organization.

Reasoned action theory. The theory of reasoned action [Fishbein and Ajzen, 1975] specifies that there is a relationship between an individual's beliefs, attitudes, and behaviors. According to this theory, actual use of technology will be dependent on the individual's intention to use it. This intention in turn is determined by the individual's *attitude toward use* and his *subjective norm*. Subjective norm is influenced by the belief that use is expected by those in the organization who are important to the individual—for example, a superior—and the individual's motivation to comply with what others expect. Therefore, attitudes toward use, perceptions of others about technology use, and motivation to comply with others are posited as factors influencing intention to use. In order to link intent to use with actual use, other factors such as the availability of technology to the individual will also have to be measured.

Using this model would lead researchers to examine both individual perceptions, such as improved decision making, and organizational factors, such as how others view system use as a symbol of status, power, or competence. These issues are most relevant to DSS implementation; obviously, use is a prerequisite for the DSS to leverage decision quality. In addition, if the weight on the subjective norm is high and the system is used only because of the influence of others, then it is quite likely that use may only be for the sake of appearances and that no real benefits will be derived from the system.

The strength of these models is that they encompass the "success factors" which have been consistently mentioned in the DSS implementation literature. These include top management support (a subjective norm) and factors influencing attitudes, such as felt need, ease of use (compatibility), and prototyping (trialibility). As such, these perspectives are helpful in integrating the elements discovered in the disparate "factor studies" conducted by DSS implementation researchers.

Political actor theory. Viewed from a political actor theory perspective an organization is not a homogeneous unit with a single unified objective, but rather an aggregation of individual actors each with his own agenda. There is no sense of an organization working toward a common goal such as profit maximization. Instead, each individual pursues his own vested interests. When interests correspond, coalitions may be formed. Where interests diverge, confrontation and negotiation may take place in an attempt to reach consensus. In such an environment, each group or coalition will be trying to build its own power base so as to be able to manipulate the agenda of the organization as a whole [Keen and Scott Morton, 1978].

The overall impact of information systems on organizations has also been examined from such a political perspective. The development and use of information systems in this case can simply be regarded as an exercise in the manipulation of others. The goal of a DSS user is not to make the best decision in any normative sense, but rather to ensure that a decision taken and implemented is most closely aligned with his own vested interest. The DSS would simply serve as an additional tool for influencing the way decisions are made in organizations. It would become a decision justifier and ratifier rather than a decision aid.

In terms of identifying the types of tools to be investigated in DSS research, political perspectives may not be highly helpful. From such a perspective the content and quality of systems from an objective viewpoint will be relatively less important. There is no central focus on making a correct decision. In some sense, the design of the system might be tailored to impress, persuade, and potentially mislead others. This may imply that systems could be examined to determine their relative political/persuasive influence, such as the extent to which model assumptions are apparent or transparent to users.

Concluding comments. While the theories proposed in this section might not be the only ones that are worth considering, our view is that they are thought provoking. They make interesting and sometimes contradictory predictions about the effects of DSS use and why individuals would use this technology. Furthermore, each of the theories discussed can be used to study a wide range of technologies. Changes in currently available hardware and software should not affect the way in which we apply and interpret the findings of the studies grounded in these theories. This means that the theories provide a stable base for conducting DSS research in a cumulative fashion.

In selecting the specific theories to be discussed, we adopted what might be considered an ecumenical view that takes into account the contribution of theories from a wide variety of areas. At this stage there is no obvious candidate for a single grand, guiding theory of decision making as it relates to DSS. Consequently, a range of theories that might play a role in guiding DSS researchers is described here. Considering them could provide useful insights into predicting the influence of utilizing DSS and help stimulate new and more fruitful research in the DSS area.

The nature of the work

Ralph H. Sprague, Jr., and Timothy R. Hill

The section "Evolving Functionality for the Technology Environment" examined the capabilities and functionality of the technology as a primary determinant of the technological environment, while the section "Theories of DSS Use by Individual Decision-Makers" considered the cognitive processes that the individual brings to bear in using that technology. Another approach is to examine the characteristics of the task or work rather than the technology or the users. The task undertaken, the problem to be solved, and the objectives to be pursued by the user of the system tell us much about the nature of the required support and the characteristics of the technology environment. In this section we will consider two representations of the work that is to be supported by the technology. The first is an intuitive dichotomy of work, based on several characteristics. The argument is that DSS should be aimed at supporting one of these "kinds" of work and not the other. The second representation is developed to explore the alignment between problem-driven work and neural network technology as a basis for identifying new areas of support potential.

Procedure-driven or problem-driven work. The concept of clerical versus managerial work is intuitively comfortable. These terms are used casually throughout the literature. They seem somewhat related to more carefully described concepts, such as programmed versus non-programmed decision making, or structured versus ill-structured situations.

Several articles have explored a similar intuitive dichotomy which the authors labeled Type I and Type II information activity [Panko and Sprague, 1982, 1984]. These rather sterile labels were designed to neutralize the connotations evoked by words like "clerical" and "managerial." The key characteristics of this dichotomy include

- Transactions: Type I work consists of a large volume of transactions with a relatively low value (or cost) connected with each. Type II work consists of fewer transactions, but each is more costly or valuable.
- Procedure: Type I work is based on well-defined procedures, while Type II work is procedure-independent: A variety of procedures might work, and different people might use different procedures.
- Output: The output from Type I work is more easily measured because it is defined by quantities of procedural iteration. The focus is on performing the necessary process or procedure quickly, efficiently, and usually many times. Type II output is not easily measured because it consists of problem solving and goal attainment. You can assign a Type I task to an information worker by explaining the sequence of steps required to accomplish it. With a Type II task, you must specify the desired outcome. Figuring out the necessary steps in the sequence is part of the job.
- Data: Type I work uses data in relatively well structured form, whereas Type II work deals primarily with concepts that are represented in less well structured form, usually with a great deal of ambiguity.

At first glance this dichotomy looks similar to the "clerical" versus "managerial-professional" breakdown that has been used for many years. Upon closer examination, however, it is clear that clerical personnel, especially secretaries, frequently have procedure-independent tasks defined only by their outcome. Likewise, most managers and professionals have a certain proportion of their work which is procedure-defined. Having avoided connotations by using the sterile Type I and Type II labels, examining the attributes suggests that the best names might be *procedure-driven* and *problem-driven*, where "problem" includes goal, objective, and overall attainment.

It can be argued that the nature of the task, according to this two-way classification, is the most important characteristic in determining what kind of support is required from information systems. It should be clear that most uses of information systems in the past have been for supporting procedure-driven tasks. It is easiest and most natural to use a process engine (computer) to support procedural tasks. It is also clear that the challenge of the future is to use information systems to support problem-driven tasks. The nature of the tasks is different, the mentality required to do it is different, and so the information support must be different from the traditional process approaches.

This representation of work that should be supported by DSS has proved helpful in presentations to DSS users and builders. It is, however, an intuitive construct and soon breaks down under any attempts at formalization to guide construction of the technology environment. A more useful model or representation of the work to be supported by DSS may be evolving from neural network or connectionist constructs.

Aligning problem-driven work with support technology. While the general concept of problem-driven work provides an enlarged focus for DSS, a more specific representation is needed to identify specific implications for research and design. Ideally, such a representation would allow the work to be described in the same terms used to describe technological functionality. It would thus provide a "common ground" for integrating the technology into problem-driven work in a natural way.

While the full achievement of this goal is admittedly improbable, it may be worth exploring the approach, given the emergence of neural-based technologies. Guided by biological models of the brain, neural-based system research is aimed at developing technological capabilities along the lines of human cognition [Rumelhart and McClelland, 1986]. Therefore, by focusing on the way people think about their work or their internal representation, the characteristics of the task and those of this coming technology might be aligned more closely than has previously been possible. This is a particularly worthwhile effort since the current capabilities of neural-based systems suggest great future potential for the high-level support of complex tasks, such as those involved in problem-driven work.

Toward this end, the attributes of an internal representation of problem-driven work are examined and then shown to parallel those of neural network models in an intuitively appealing way. This supports the identification of key characteristics of problem-driven work, to which the potential of neural network technology support may be related directly.

An internal representation of problem-driven work may be characterized in terms that relate directly to basic neural network modeling constructs, identifying key areas of potential support. An example serves to illustrate the approach.

Consider a recently hired vice president at a small company that supports the data processing needs of local financial institutions. Since joining the company, she has recognized programmer turnover as a primary concern. An extremely tight local labor market and chronically poor documentation have combined to exacerbate the problem, and she has placed high priority on bringing it under control. Clearly this is typical of the kinds of problem-driven tasks which managers face, and which provide new challenges for technological support.

Decomposability. One of the key attributes of problem-driven work as characterized by the internal representation is the decomposability of abstract tasks into equivalent sets of less abstract subtasks. (The same idea was applied by Benbasat and Todd in the section "Theories of DSS Use by Individual Decision-Makers" in describing information processes.) The accomplishment of abstractly defined tasks requires decomposition into specific subtasks that can be performed directly. Subtasks such as this exist at the elemental or atomic level, beyond which they are not considered in any greater detail. But between the most abstract level and the elemental (performable) level, there may be many intermediate levels at which it is meaningful to represent subtasks of intermediate abstraction.

This concept can be illustrated by our example of the vice president who faces the abstract task of solving a programmer turnover problem. Clearly she will have to decompose this task into specific doable subtasks. To extend the example, assume that she has determined that, to improve the situation, she must (1) improve programmer morale and foster loyalty, and (2) institute tight controls on documentation and programming practices. Thus the abstract task has been decomposed, and it is meaningful to consider the task at this intermediate level of abstraction. But these subtasks must clearly be considered in more detail. For example, progress on the first subtask may be achievable through (1.a) increasing salaries and (1.b) improving working conditions. Also, achievement of the second subtask may imply that (2.a) an entirely new set of programming standards be defined and (2.b) the programmers be trained and encouraged to adopt them. Again, these subtasks may need to be decomposed if, for example, increasing salaries implies that the home office must be convinced that the increase is warranted (1.a.1), despite the fact that the current salaries are already higher than those for any other corporate location. This view of tasks also suggests that the representation must support "recomposition" in the sense that effects of achieving elemental subtasks may be evaluated at the higher levels of abstraction.

Gradual accomplishment and thresholds. Another attribute of problem-driven work which is key to an internal representation is the concept of *gradual accomplishment and thresholds.* That is, the achievement of problem-driven tasks is often realized over an extended period of time, making it meaningful and necessary to represent the *degree* to which it is accomplished. This is in contrast to the traditional focus of a decision, conceptualized as a discrete event. Typically, little is accomplished in the early stages of a task, while the marginal "return on effort" is low. Later, initial effort investments begin to pay off in higher marginal returns and much progress is made. Later still, the task may be largely accomplished and the marginal return on effort drops again. Over time, then, the degree of achievement often takes on an "S" shape, asymptotically approaching full accomplishment. In the latter stages of accomplishment, the task is often considered to be achieved for all practical purposes. This represents a *threshold* level at which point the subtask is, essentially, contributing its full share toward the accomplishment of the corresponding supertask at the next higher level of abstraction.

Again, consider the example. Assume that the vice president has been working on the turnover problem since she joined the organization three months ago. Initially she may have determined that a drastic 22 percent increase in programmer salaries was needed. Since then, she has been working, through a series of high-level discussions, to convince the home office that the increase is warranted, and she feels she is slowly making progress. This progress corresponds to the partial accomplishment of a subtask (1.a.1), for which the goal is approval of the 22 percent increase. And yet, since no raise has yet been approved, this progress has not yet contributed at all to the overall goal of improving turnover effects. However, if an emergency "stopgap" raise of 12 percent was approved, it would represent greater partial accomplishment of the subtask and would contribute, to a smaller degree, to the achievement of the main goal. Alternatively, if an 18 percent increase were approved, the vice president might consider this task to be accomplished for all practical purposes. She might push for extra increases sooner in the future, but the incremental contribution to the main goal would not warrant the same level of effort. Also, further lobbying at that point might have political costs and result in small gains in the area of turnover, accompanied by large losses in other major thrust areas. Clearly, such trade-offs affect threshold levels and suggest the need to represent interaction between tasks.

Subtask interaction. The complex interaction between subtasks is another attribute of problem-driven tasks which is key to an internal representation. The relationship between the task and each of the subtasks into which it is decomposed may differ between subtasks. For example, the accomplishment of one subtask might contribute less than that of another toward the accomplishment of the "parent" task. Indeed, the partial accomplishment of a strongly contributing subtask might be more valuable to the parent task than the full accomplishment of some other subtask. Furthermore, the accomplishment of one subtask might affect that of more than one parent task. It might contribute strongly to one parent while contributing weakly, or even strongly negatively, to another parent. The degree to which a "grandparent" task is affected would depend also on the grandparent-parent relationships.

The interaction between tasks may also be illustrated by the example. In gaining home office support for the salary increases, the vice president may, at the same time, be negatively affecting other tasks, even those which contribute positively toward the main goal of solving the turnover problem. Recall that one of the subtasks required to improve employee morale and loyalty was to improve working conditions (1.b). A subtask of this might be a major upgrade of equipment, requiring another major concession from the home office. Clearly accomplishment of this subtask will detract from that of the salary increase approval. And the ultimate effect on the turnover problem depends on the relative strengths of the task/subtask relationships in the intermediate levels.

Of course, the approval of equipment upgrades would positively contribute to tasks other than improving employee morale and the turnover problem. The improvement of customer relations might be a task of importance equal to that of solving the turnover problem, and would benefit directly from faster response times and fewer down times. Indeed the accomplishment of this task might contribute more strongly than the solution of the turnover problem to the even more abstract goal of enhancing profitability! Thus, tasks can rarely be considered in isolation but must be viewed as part of a larger framework that accounts for complex interactions.

Simultaneity. A fourth key attribute of problem-driven work is implied by the others—the *simultaneity* of task accomplishment. Since accomplishment of one subtask may contribute to that of many parent tasks, and since tasks are accomplished gradually over time as efforts are shifted from one task to another, problem-driven work may be viewed as the concurrent accomplishment of multiple tasks.

The neural network model. The key attributes of problem-driven work described above align closely with the basic characteristics of neural network models. Some neural networks are modeled as hierarchical layers of interconnected nodes in which the layers correspond to different levels of abstraction of a concept. At the "lowest" layer, nodes represent elementary subconcepts, while upper layers represent more abstract concepts based on collections of lower layer nodes. This aligns well with the concept of decomposability of tasks into elementary subtasks.

The neural-based orientation also lends itself well to representing simultaneous, partial accomplishment, complex interactions, and threshold effects. Typically, a node in a neural network accepts input signals from some nodes and sends output signals, based on some function of the inputs, to other nodes. The incoming signals determine the level of stimulation of a node, which is often a continuous value in a predefined range such as 0 to 1. The signals travel over the internode connections which can vary in type and strength. Connections can be either *excitory*, such that the output signal from a "child" node tends to contribute to the output signal of the "parent" node, or they can be *inhibitory*, so that the child output signal tends to attenuate the parent node output. Furthermore, connection strengths can differ between connections, so that, for example, a strong signal traveling a weakly connected path may have little effect on the parent node. At each node, the output signal is a function of the incoming signals. In neural-based models, a sigmoid or some other S-shaped function is often used to capture the *threshold* effect of neurons by which a node will tend to produce little or no output signal until its incoming stimulus reaches some critical threshold level. Neural network models typically represent the flow of signals as occurring concurrently throughout the network. Thus, the key attributes of problem-driven work which were identified above align well with neural network representations.

Using variations of this basic framework, researchers have had remarkable success in simulating human performance of complex tasks [e.g., Fukushima, 1988]. Neural networks are especially useful for performing ill-defined, "fuzzy" tasks such as those for which the explication of formal logical rules and the application of traditional artificial intelligence methods have proved difficult or impossible.

The parallel between the attributes of problem-driven work and neural network models suggests potential for working toward the ideal of a representation of the work that would allow the direct integration of the technology. At the very least it suggests some new directions for exploring the potential application of this technology in the support of problem-driven work.

For example, one possible form of support is the automation of sub-hierarchies of the internal task representation. Implicitly, this has been the traditional approach to technological support, but the technology has been limiting to this point. Consequently, support systems have generally been limited to performing task subhierarchies of predetermined or largely constrained *structure*. This is appropriate for procedure-driven activities which may be characterized by basic task hierarchy structures that are clearly definable and stable. But for problem-driven activities, task hierarchy structures are difficult to preconceive and may require "force-fitting" to integrate fixed-structure support system subhierarchies. Neural-based systems have self-adaptive qualities that offer potential for more flexible support [e.g., Widrow and Winter, 1988].

Another form of support suggested by the model is extending or enhancing the human capability to evaluate the implications of the task hierarchy relationships. Payne suggested that a cost-benefit contingency is applied in allocating goal-directed effort [Payne, 1982]. In terms of the hierarchical task representation, this implies evaluation of the effort/accomplishment trade-offs linking elemental subtasks to higher level tasks throughout the hierarchy—the effects of applying effort to elemental subtasks must be "filtered up" through the hierarchy to assess the contribution to task accomplishment. This is relatively easy for procedure-driven activities, but the hierarchies representing problem-driven activities are more complex and thus more difficult to evaluate.

While for procedure-driven activities, the strength of intertask connections may be considered to be deterministic, problem-driven tasks are characterized by more loosely coupled, "fuzzy" task/subtask relationships. When accomplishment effects are filtered up through such hierarchies, the impact of connection variability is compounded, making estimation of high-level progress difficult. Evaluation of effort/accomplishment trade-offs is further complicated by the "output" functions that determine task accomplishment level based on total subtask accomplishment. For procedure-driven work, task accomplishment functions are more likely to be simple linear or step functions and consistent throughout the hierarchy. However, problem-driven activities are characterized by more complex and subtle task accomplishment functions, such as S-shaped functions, for which the threshold level is less rigidly defined. Thus, the ability of neural networks to deal with "fuzzy" problems may be useful when addressing these difficult issues with technological support.

A variety of other directions for supporting problem-driven work are suggested by the task hierarchy representation. For example, tracking the progress of tasks over time may be difficult for problem-driven task hierarchies that may include many different types of tasks and may span lengthy periods. The pattern recognition abilities of neural networks may be brought to bear in extending and enhancing environmental scanning capabilities.

In summary, neural-based systems represent a new wave of technological potential for advancing systems support. However, unlike previous technological breakthroughs, neural-based technology represents a fundamentally new orientation based directly on human cognition. In order to fully exploit this technology, a fundamentally new orientation for systems support may be useful. Ideally it will be possible to describe the way people represent problem-driven work so that the technology can be integrated directly to provide support. Toward that end, a reasonable alignment can be drawn between the attributes of problem-driven work and those of neural networks. This alignment suggests the potential of this effort and identifies some new directions for technology support development.

Design perspectives for systems to support decision processes

Henk G. Sol

Additional perspectives on the nature of systems to support decision processes are available by considering issues of design. Systems to support problem-driven tasks go under many names. Included are decision support systems, group support systems, expert support systems, computer-supported collaborative work, executive information systems, and office information systems. These are all information systems supporting decision processes, and all designed to improve the performance of individuals and organizations.

Three levels of support. This approach reveals three system design perspectives [Bots and Sol, 1988; Sol and Van der Ven, 1988; Sol and Stuart, 1988]:

1. From the *micro* perspective, we look at the task improvement of knowledge workers in their workplace. It is at this level that we recognize the focus on human performance.
2. From the *meso* perspective, we are concerned with the coordination of workplaces in an organizational setting. The shift of attention toward organizational decision making demands the design of organizational networks providing the correct balance between tasks and processes and using flexible information architectures for reporting and control.
3. Looking from the *macro* perspective, we extend our scope to information infrastructures between and above several organizations. Here we encounter the use of information technology as a competitive weapon in strategic alliances.

The following examples illustrate these three perspectives:

- A lawyer is working on a case from behind his workstation. He has a text processor at his disposal and an application that supports judicial reasoning. He has access to internal databases on arrests, and he has an external link with the law court, his colleagues, and public domain document collections.
- A farmer oversees from his mobile workstation the condition of his livestock. In a central file the data about the animals are collected and stored. The farmer can analyze this data for individual animals, but he can also make more aggregate analyses. He can use connections with veterinary surgeons and the agricultural institute to react instantly to circumstances that occur. He can also use the external connections to order cattle food from his suppliers.

- A teacher uses his workstation to correct students' exams. He can compare the results with previous results by logging in on the central student database system. By using the electronic mailbox facility he can contact other members of the faculty and staff.
- An unemployment benefit from a social security fund is prepared by a civil servant, who is assisted by an expert-support system. He can consult central financial and historical databases, and he can also check out other security funds.
- An insurance expert has to deal with the damage caused by a collision of two cars. An expert system will advise him. The central information center of his company will provide him the policy information and the financial situation. If needed, an expertise agency can be hired using external communication links. The agency will then report to the insurance company using the same communication channel. The results will be stored in the central information system and the money transfer can be done electronically.

More examples like these can be easily obtained from comparable applications in the medical sector, the travel business, and the transportation sector. All examples show us workers who are supported at their workplace in the fulfilling of their Type I and Type II tasks. Documentary support plays an important role, but so does expert support and the connection with financial and administrative systems.

Knowledge workers on the micro level use communication lines to access the meso level and the macro level. However, the decision on how these lines will be used is not determined by the information technology, but is dependent on the tasks and processes the knowledge worker wants to perform.

Problem-solving processes. Another influence on design is the pattern of problem solving used. We have made several observations on instruments for the description of problem-solving processes. We generalize these observations in the following requirements:

1. The paradigm and the model cycle should be expressible in a system of instruments in order to be able to discuss the implicit premises in a common frame of reference and to delineate the scope of the activities involved. We call this "metatheoretical freedom."
2. A system of instruments may confine the flexibility to construct a conceptual model and an empirical model. As each language has its own expressive power in a context for conceptualization, this context should not be restrictive, but extensible. We call this "conceptualization freedom."
3. The empirical model should support the conceptualization and specification, as well as the solution finding, by iterative analysis

and synthesis. This asks for "modeling freedom," leading to consistent model systems that show a good correspondence. The structure laid down in the model should not be constrained by the way dynamic analysis is to be performed with the model system on a computer. Structuring should not only be strictly hierarchical, but also nested structuring of entities should be possible.

4. "Solution finding freedom" refers to the ability to generate solutions by changing the alternative space and the ways this space can be explored in view of human cognitive constraints.

Methods and tools. Finally, the design and implementation of information systems that support decision processes put specific demands on methodologies and tools. We elaborate these by several aspects of the way of thinking, modeling, working, and controlling.

Way of thinking. In the design of information architectures the process-oriented approach has been replaced by the data-oriented one. In practice this has shown up certain disadvantages because it relies too much on the ability of users and information staff for abstract thinking. The emphasis on the micro and meso design problems shifts the attention back to the area of processes and tasks. The increasing complexity also appears to increase the failure rate of transaction processing and management information systems.

A possible solution to the complexity problem is to define smaller subsystems and work on these under closely defined coordination, the latter being an essential ingredient of the policy.

The increasing interweave of real systems and information systems, especially in heavily information-dependent organizations, requires new policies to take account of time-critical and worldwide distributed applications. Especially in this area, links must be made with often parallel primary processes in an organization, the interdependencies of which need not be obvious at first sight.

Way of modeling. The new policy requires specification methods for descriptive and prescriptive models at the micro, meso, and macro levels, each necessary for answers to *why*, *what*, *how*, and *with what* questions. The emphasis used to be on prescriptive models (*with what* and *how*), but new models will have to have the ability to switch easily between *with what* and *how*, and *what* and *why*.

New descriptive models are based on object specification, combining data and processing aspects. This obviously requires extensive verification and validation facilities [Bots and Sol, 1988; Cohen and Sol, 1988; Dur and Sol, 1989, 1990]. In this context, decisive roles are played by animation and visualization [Wierda and Sol, 1989], gaming [Bots et al., 1989], and object-oriented user interface design [Dur and Versendaal,

1989]. The development of data structures requires a feeling for declarative procedural specification of facts and rules.

Way of working. The development of systems according to the modeling method above includes the following steps:

- generation of task and process descriptions at workplaces,
- transition from descriptive to prescriptive models by simulation,
- freezing of the dynamic models,
- solution of coordination problems between workplaces, and
- transition from design to efficient architectures and dialogue structures.

Simulation is characteristic of this way of working; education and training opportunities may be included, while knowledge systems may be supplied with information during use. Understanding is a prerequisite for construction; adaptation is more important than completeness [e.g., Verbraeck and Sol, 1989].

Way of controlling. Methodologies often overemphasize project control: Checkpoints which are defined for better project control often fail to guarantee the quality of the end product, process efficiency, or user involvement. It is becoming increasingly clear that only the creation of an appropriate organization structure can result in optimal control of existing and new information systems: Control of facilities is gaining in importance.

Keywords coming to mind in this area are participation, consolidation, and "middle out" rather than "top down" or "bottom up."

Summary. Improving the performance of organizations by supporting knowledge workers is not done automatically by drawing on information technology. A design challenge has to be taken up for which an approach has been outlined above.

Research can contribute a great deal in defining new ways of thinking, modeling, working, and controlling. The interactions between concept and empiricism and between theory and practice have already been fruitful—and must remain that way in order to keep the discipline of information systems young and vigorous.

We must not, however, neglect education and training of knowledge workers to handle challenges professionally during the next decades and to design methodically and responsibly in an environment that will be quite different from the one we know today.

Revving up an ISDP research generator for contingent representations of the technology environment

Omar El Sawy

Examining the structure of theorizing. Each of the viewpoints presented above seeks to help chart a research agenda that has at its core an emphasis on better understanding and investigation of the conceptual underpinnings of technology environments. However, each of those viewpoints implies theorizing that has its own underlying causal structure that relates information technology to human performance. The causal structure of theories can be thought of as including three dimensions: causal agency, logical structure, and level of analysis [Markus and Robey, 1988].

Causal agency refers to the theorizer's beliefs about the nature of causal action and the direction of causal influence. For example, the King viewpoint adopts a *technological imperative* in which technological functionality constrains, enables, and largely determines human performance. On the other hand, the Benbasat and Todd viewpoint adopts an *organizational imperative* that assumes unlimited choice of technological capabilities and which generates theories of DSS use that are independent of those technological capabilities. The definition by Sprague and Hill of the technology environment as the blending or merging of the cognitive and technology processes embodied in a human-machine interface implies an *emergent perspective*. In an emergent perspective, the uses and consequences of information technology emerge from complex interactions between the person and the technology. Each of these three perspectives by its very nature illuminates some facets of ISDP theory and research more than others.

The second dimension of theorizing is *logical structure*: Is the theory a process theory or a variance theory? For example, the Sol viewpoint that accentuates the design process implies an emphasis on process theories, while the Sprague and Hill viewpoints on task description and categorization imply mostly a variance theory. Variance theorizing is more likely to help predict levels of outcomes based on levels of predictor variables, while process theorizing is more likely to help us understand how outcomes are developed over time.

Finally, the third dimension of causal structure is the *level of analysis*. Sol's illustration of the various trade-offs in three levels of analysis—micro, meso, and macro—shows that a different level of analysis will illuminate certain facets and not others.

Thus, depending on the selected dimensions of causal structure, different theories and consequently different ISDP research agendas will emerge.

Examining alternative conceptions of the technology environment. However, even with a selected causal structure, there are alternative conceptions and assumptions about the technology environment itself. For example, earlier in this chapter we defined the technology environment as the blending or merging of the cognitive and technology processes embodied in a human-machine interface. It includes hardware and software that present representations to the user and accept actions from the user. This definition brings to mind at least five quite different basic conceptions and images of the technology environment:

- Technology environment as tool kit: Is the technology environment a set of tools that the information worker exists outside of, but blends or merges with when he or she needs to draw on them?
- Technology environment as medium: Is the technology environment a medium in which the information worker continuously exists and through which he or she adapts in order to function effectively? Does this medium change meaning and have symbolic significance?
- Technology environment as intelligent agent: Is the technology environment an embedded component of the information worker's mental capacity likened to a set of intelligent agents such that the information worker can be likened to a cyborg to the external observer?
- Technology environment as link or window: Is the technology environment a link or intelligent window between the information worker and the organizational environment?
- Technology environment as workstation: Is the technology environment a congregation of technological capabilities that in combination offer efficient methods of work for the information worker in a specific geographic location?

Each of these images is plausible. Each has different underlying assumptions. Which one should we choose to develop more carefully and model?

In order to answer this question, we conducted an electronic polling of ISDP workshop attendees in Tucson. We provided and explained the above five alternative models of the technology environment and asked them to respond to this question: Which model of the technology environment would you be most likely to use in your own research? The results are shown in Table 1 and reinforce the notion of equivocality of technology perception with amazing fidelity. Thus, even among a small group of researchers at the same workshop, there is no unitary conception of technology environment. Each of these conceptions is plausible as a basis for ISDP research, and will in all likelihood generate a different ISDP research agenda.

Also, as we begin to examine the different ways to define and describe the information technology environment, it becomes apparent that it

Table 1. Results of ISDP group polling.

Technology Environment Characterization	Highly Likely									Not Likely	N	n	Mean
	10	9	8	7	6	5	4	3	2	1			
Tool kit	2	3	3	3	2	2	1	1	1	3	21	21	6.0
Medium	2	4	2	1	1	3	2	2	2	1	21	20	5.9
Intelligent agent	5	2	1		2	3	2	1		4	21	20	5.9
Link or window	2		3		2	2	2	4	2	2	21	19	4.8
Workstation		3	2		4	1	2	2	1	6	21	21	4.5
Other	3		1		1			2	1		21	8	6.0

might not be possible to do that in a useful and robust theoretical way without placing it within a broader view of the ISDP research context. Similarly, the research issues related to technology environments that will surface will depend on the assumptions we make about the other aspects of DSS and about organizational contexts.

Construing a model of ISDP research. The above examinations suggest that we need to combine the alternative conceptions of technology environments and the various structures of theorizing into a larger model that reconciles them within the broader framework of the other four ISDP research themes: organizational DSS, group DSS, model management, and behavioral decision theories and DSS.

In order to produce research efforts that are cumulative and mutually compatible with the other ISDP research themes, we need to be aware of the assumptions we are making about the aspects that interact with the technology environment in our envisaged theories and models. What that means in mnemonic DSS parlance is that the research issues that surface will not only depend on examining the technology environment defined through the second "S" in DSS, but also examining the influence of defining its interaction with the "D" and the first "S," and the organizational environment. A case in point is the need for Sprague and Hill to introduce the notions of procedure-driven and problem-driven tasks in order to set the ground for defining a model of the technology environment.

Given the multiplicity of alternative assumptions and models that can be construed, are we therefore implicitly rejecting the idea that a unitary theory of decision support exists or can exist? It is apparent that we are. Perhaps we should then explicitly postulate the existence of distinct types of decision support, each of which can be explained by a number of correspondingly different theories which may have different conceptions of the technology environment. These theories may include different variables or they may contain the same variables while positing different relationships between them. In other words, the ISDP domain may be best understood and conquered by the search for a set of contingent theories, rather than a quest for a unitary theory.

In order to systematically consider such contingent theories and alternative models of the technology environment, we introduce what can be termed an "ISDP research generator." Similar to the notion of DSS generators, it can be used to generate specific instances of ISDP research. Similar to the Leavitt diamond, it is broad enough that it can accommodate various conceptual constructions and representations for each of the four sets of variables. Different from the Leavitt diamond, the designer (theorizer/researcher) is included as part of the diamond through the incorporation of preferences and perceptions. The ISDP research generator is depicted in Figure 1.

The way that the ISDP research generator works is as follows: Any change in the definition of any of the four sets of variables will affect the other three, and they will have to be adjusted accordingly to build a plausible theory. Changes in definition can come about by changing such things as assumptions about the variables, the unit of analysis used to describe them, and the degree of granularity of definition.

The process by which this ISDP generator produces instances of theories and research studies can be an ordered deliberate process, but it can often operate in the "garbage can theory" mode where confluences of researcher attention and preferences determine the parameters of the generator.

Illustrating the face validity of the ISDP research generator. In order to illustrate the usefulness of the ISDP research generator, its application to two pretheorizing instances is exposited below. The instances are drawn from two empirical studies whose results were then used as springboards to generate research agendas. In the first instance, the explicit articulation of the parameters of the ISDP generator made it apparent that the conception of the technology environment as intelligent agent was the most appropriate match, and consequently the most useful for generating a fertile and plausible research agenda. In the second instance, the use of the ISDP generator illustrated that the model of the technology environment as medium was the most fruitful for further theorizing.

Illustration 1. Building a theory of DSS for enhancing strategic decision making in turbulent environments. (This example is constructed from El Sherif and El Sawy's work [El Sherif and El Sawy, 1988].)

• Perceptions of Role of Decision Support
  Enhancing the effectiveness of strategic issue identification, structuring and articulation, and conflict resolution.

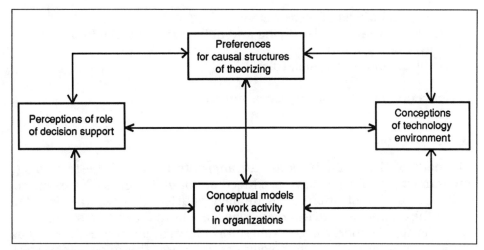

Figure 1. ISDP research generator.

Preferences for Causal Structures of Theorizing
     Causal agency: Organizational imperative
     Logical structure: Process theory
     Level of analysis of work activity/decision support: Group

- Conceptual Model of Work Activity
     Characterization: Scanning, learning/experimenting, team playing
     Unit of analysis: Issue

- Conception of Technology Environment
     Information technology as intelligent agent.

Illustration 2. Building a theory of information technology impact on middle management work. (This example is drawn from work by Nilles et al. [Nilles et al., 1986].)

- Perceptions of Role of Decision Support
     Enhancing the effectiveness of attention to critical tasks and managerial roles.

- Preferences for Causal Structures of Theorizing
     Causal agency: Emergent imperative
     Logical structure: Variance theory
     Level of analysis of work activity: Individual

- Conceptual Model of Work Activity
  Characterization: Identifying and doing critical tasks, using and
     evaluating information
  Unit of analysis: Tasks, roles

- Conception of Technology Environment
  Information technology as medium.

In both of these illustrations, an alternate model of the technology
environment would not have produced as many insights. For example,
in the second illustration, a "technology charisma" effect was detected
where the technology environment was a medium that had a substantial
symbolic significance. Also, a "role schizophrenia" effect was detected as
the level of information technology use rose and the middle managers
could not adapt fast enough to the increasing intensity of the medium
they existed in.

The ISDP generator seems to be a useful addition to our techniques for
building plausible research agendas. In this ISDP context with its five
themes, it serves to appropriately clarify the infrastructural role of
assumptions about and conceptions of technology environments in
shaping the broader ISDP research agenda.

Revving up the ISDP research generator. In a broader and more
creative sense, we can think of many alternative constructions for each
set of variables in the ISDP research generator framework. These contingent combinations will generate research instances, the usefulness of
which needs to be more carefully evaluated on a case-by-case basis with
respect to fertility, plausibility, and feasibility.

Some examples of possibilities are shown below. The choice of different
sets of possibilities will influence what model of the technology environment is sought and developed, and what ISDP research issues surface
in the various themes.

- Perceptions of Role of Decision Support
  Support of work activity
  Enhancing the effectiveness of work activity
  Giving expert advice about work activity
  Helping to change the mix of work activities
  Shaping how work activity is carried out
  Shaping the form of work activity
  . . . . ?

• Preferences for Causal Structures of Theorizing

Causal agency: Organizational imperative
Technological imperative
Emergent perspective
. . . . ?

Logical structure: Process theory
Variance theory
Object-oriented theory
Inductive logic
Deductive logic
Abductive logic
. . . . ?

Level of analysis of work activity:
Individual
Group
Team
Department
Organization
Syndicate of organizations
. . . . ?

• Conceptual Model of Work Activity

Characterization: Decision making
Scanning
Learning/experimenting
Problem solving
Team playing
Negotiating
Identifying and doing critical tasks
. . . . ?

Unit of Analysis: Decision
Decision process with multiple decisions
Task
Problem
Issue
Role
. . . . ?

• Conception of Technology Environment
  Tool kit
  Medium
  Intelligent agent
  Link or window
  Workstation
  . . . . ?

The intelligent use of the ideas generated from the ISDP generator can provide a common ground to help us identify the fertile, plausible, and feasible instances of research that are worth doing. Such an approach seems much more likely to yield an impactful and cumulative ISDP research agenda where there are useful synergy and an empathetic awareness among the various research themes.

Rather than parochially staking out turf and putting up fences before having scouted the whole terrain, perhaps we should adopt an "imagineering" approach [LeBoeuf, 1980]. Imagineering implies letting your imagination soar and then engineering it down to earth. In our ISDP context, this implies generating a broad spectrum of research possibilities and then engineering with explicit self-awareness the ones that have the most promise for impact on the field, cross-fertility between themes, and feasibility. Fellow travelers, let's rev her up...

Workshop discussion: Technology support environment

Discussants. The first discussant, Rudi Hirschheim, noted that the mission of the team was rather unstructured and that he was pleased that they had broadened the concept of information technology support environments beyond purely technical issues. However, it was difficult to provide an integrated vision of technology environment when people with such different backgrounds work together without an agreed framework. He also would have preferred a deeper treatment of some of the issues raised by the teams. Finally, he thought that the work of the teams was too "functionalist" in terms of its research paradigm. (A functionalist believes that the world is ordered rather than chaotic, and objective rather than subjective in nature [Klein and Hirschheim, 1985; Hirschheim and Klein, 1989].) He felt that other alternatives to the functionalist research approach, such as phenomenology [e.g., Boland and Day, 1982] or an anthropological approach [Wynn, 1979], could yield different insights.

In his remarks, Hugh Watson stated that Sprague and Hill had made an important contribution to understanding the mission of IS and DSS in organizations and conceptualizing the types of tasks for which DSS are appropriate. He wondered if El Sawy's research generator might generate many unimportant research tasks and suggested that it might be better to use the framework as a means of classifying existing research rather than generating research ideas. He concluded by mentioning an important topic that had not been discussed by the teams, namely, the necessity for organizational support and the form it should take. According to his experience, the ultimate success of a DSS in an organization depends on how well it is supported. For example, the analyses of decision room design, decision room use, and staffing requirements are important research topics given the recent interest and success of GDSS.

Summary of electronic discussion. As discussed earlier, part of the electronic meeting support session consisted of a vote to determine which conceptualization of the technology environment was considered most useful by the workshop participants. The electronic brainstorming session that followed the information technology environment presentation raised the following issues:

1. The need for a better understanding of the concept of "a technology environment" and of the links between the environment and ODSS, GDSS, DSS, and so on.

2. The need to understand the problems associated with breakdowns in the technology environment.

3. People may view the technology environment as a threat rather than as a benign means of support.

4. How does the technology environment impact possible tendencies for disorder or chaos in organizational systems?

5. Investigate support issues in global systems.

6. Investigate support in different-time, different-place scenarios as well as in the same time and same place.

7. Relating to the Type I/Type II dichotomy of work, how can work performance be measured? Productivity? Quality? Process errors?

8. The need for a more meaningful classification of systems types than is provided by buzzwords such as DSS, GDSS, ODSS, etc.

9. Compare the present work with alternative conceptions of technology environments such as those in the UTOPIA, DEMOS, FLORENCE, and MARS projects and with Thompson's classification of organizational technologies.

10. Political and organizational theories as well as psychological theories provide an important means of understanding the impacts of the technology environment.

11. The need to examine organizational theories as a starting point for defining and developing a theory of technological support environments.

12. The need to study issues relating to organizational support for the development, maintenance, and use of the technology support environment.

13. A number of discussants felt that the Type I/Type II distinction was useful and might serve as an integrating framework.

14. Several discussants thought that the "research generator" provided a good framework for ISDP research.

15. How can we introduce the technological environment over time and yet achieve the critical mass of users necessary for its success?

Chapter 7

Model Management Systems

Robert W. Blanning, Andrew B. Whinston, Ai-Mei Chang, Vasant Dhar, Clyde W. Holsapple, Matthias Jarke, Steven O. Kimbrough, Javier Lerch, and Michael J. Prietula.

The notion of managing decision models by means of a model management system, just as one manages stored data by means of a data management system, was first put forth more than 15 years ago [Will, 1975; Sprague and Watson, 1975]. Much theoretical and empirical work has been done since that time, and the state of the art is approaching maturity. However, much more work needs to be done, especially in relating model management to disciplines that are currently considered peripheral, such as artificial intelligence and cognitive science. It is the purpose of this chapter to examine the evolving discipline of model management and accompanying opportunities for research from this point of view.

The field of model management began with the suggestion that there is a need for software that insulates the users of a decision support system from the physical aspects of the organization and processing of decision models in a fashion similar to the way in which data management systems insulate their users from the physical aspects of the organization and processing of stored data. Most of the early papers drew their inspiration from the CODASYL framework for data management [Konsynski, 1981; Stohr and Tanniru, 1980], but later papers extended this work to include a relational framework similar to that of relational database theory [Blanning, 1983, 1987b]. In relational model management, a model is viewed as a virtual relation whose tuples do not exist in stored form but are generated on demand by a stored algorithm, and the input and output attributes of a virtual relation correspond to the key and content attributes of a stored relation. The principal issues addressed in relational model management are model base organization, the relational completeness of model query languages, and the implementation of joins. A relational join occurs in model management when some of the outputs of one model are among the inputs of another model. However, lossy joins do not occur in model management, since the outputs of a set of models needed to respond to a query may be assumed pairwise disjoint.

There is also a rapidly growing application of artificial intelligence to model management. This area has been called expert modelbase systems, by way of comparison and contrast with expert database systems [Blanning, 1987a]. In large measure, this is an area of research and prototype development; there are only a few available products. The principal research topics are

- the development of expert systems for constructing models,
- the use of heuristic search and logic-based techniques in selecting and integrating the models needed to respond to a user query, and
- the development of intelligent systems for interpreting model outputs and especially for explaining anomalies in the outputs.

The umbrella area of expert modelbase systems appears to offer a useful set of topics for research and practical implementation.

It is not our purpose here to review the state of the art in this dynamic area, but rather to examine promising directions for further research. (Blanning provides a detailed discussion of the state of the art of model management [Blanning, 1989].) We begin with the interface between a model management system and its environment.

The hyperknowledge environment of model management systems

Ai-Mei Chang, Andrew B. Whinston, and Clyde W. Holsapple

Much of the existing research on model management has focused on the internals of these systems and not on the environments in which they will be constructed and used. (A review of this work appears elsewhere [Holsapple and Whinston, 1988b].) We suggest that research should also be directed toward a better understanding of these environments. In broad terms, a decision support system (DSS) serves as an environment within which various kinds of knowledge are managed. These include pieces of descriptive knowledge (i.e., data, information), procedural knowledge (i.e., algorithms), reasoning knowledge (e.g., rules), linguistic knowledge (e.g., problem statement grammars), presentation knowledge (e.g., forms, templates), and so forth [Holsapple and Whinston, 1988a]. By knowledge management, we are referring to the activities of representing and processing pieces of knowledge.

In the case of model management, we are concerned with the treatment of pieces of knowledge called models. The notion of a model is not uniformly defined or applied within the model management literature. An analysis of its usage has shown that "model" may refer to an algorithm, data that are input to an algorithm, or a problem statement invoking an algorithm [Holsapple and Whinston, 1988b]. It follows that procedural, descriptive, and linguistic knowledge are all important to the realization and use of model management systems. Because all three of these, as well as other knowledge types, are admissible in a classic DSS framework, it serves as a starting point for considering the environment of model management in more detail. That is, we need more than a framework for appreciating the environment of model management activities in their three interrelated manifestations. Our investigation and understanding of model management can benefit from a theory of decision support systems.

This DSS theory consists of concepts and principles that define possible structural and dynamic characteristics of the environment within which model management can occur. It offers a precise language for study, evaluation, and discourse concerning the context of model management and its relationship to other basic kinds of knowledge management important to decision-makers. The DSS theory outlined here characterizes what is called a hyperknowledge environment, emphasizing the view that this environment can be regarded as an extension of a decision-maker's own innate knowledge management capabilities. It goes beyond those capabilities, thereby relaxing various cognitive, temporal, and/or economic constraints on the decision-maker.

Basic DSS framework. The basic DSS framework from which the hyperknowledge theory emerges has been selected because it is less limiting than other DSS frameworks [Holsapple and Whinston, 1988b]. Known as the Bonczek, Holsapple, and Whinston (BHW) framework, it views a DSS as having a language system (LS), a knowledge system (KS), and a problem processing system (PPS) [Bonczek et al., 1980]. The first two are systems of representation, while the PPS (often called the problem processor) is a software system. The LS and KS fuel the activities of the PPS. The LS is composed of all requests that the PPS can act on with respect to the current contents of the DSS's knowledge system. The KS comprises knowledge that the PPS can use in generating responses to user requests.

The PPS is able to process a problem statement (i.e., an element of the LS) and, in so doing, work with relevant pieces of knowledge (i.e., elements of the KS) until a solution is achieved. The solution is perhaps an extraction from the KS and reported to the user. Alternatively, the solution may be new knowledge that the PPS manufactures from present KS contents. For instance, a particular request may cause the PPS to select some procedural knowledge from the KS and execute it to analyze some of the descriptive knowledge (i.e., data) held in the KS. This produces some new knowledge that is either presented to the user or used to modify the KS.

What is the nature of such a presentation? This may be determined by the PPS based on presentation knowledge held in the KS. How did the PPS recognize the meaning of the original request? The PPS may ascertain the meaning of an LS element by drawing on linguistic knowledge existing in the KS. How did the PPS go about selecting appropriate procedural and descriptive knowledge? The PPS may have an ability to reason, and exercise that ability with some reasoning knowledge residing in the KS. Implementationally, this means the PPS embodies certain artificial intelligence techniques such as inference mechanisms found in expert systems [Holsapple and Whinston, 1987b].

An extension to the generic BHW framework formalizes its notion of responses as a fourth DSS component: a presentation system (PS) composed of all responses the PPS can make to a user [Dos Santos and Holsapple, 1989]. This extended version of the framework is our starting point for developing a theory about the environment of possibilities for model management. To remain generic in the face of technological advances, it is only reasonable that this framework does not enforce some preconceived limits on what the KS can contain, what knowledge management capabilities the PPS can exercise, or what the elements of the LS and PS can be.

Overview of the hyperknowledge environment. This section summarizes major features of an emerging theory of decision support systems which regards a DSS as a hyperknowledge environment [Holsapple and Whinston, 1987a]. Based on a cognitive metaphor, this theory may stimulate new ways of thinking about decision support in general and model management in particular. We begin by asserting that a decision-maker cognitively possesses many diverse and interrelated pieces of knowledge (i.e., concepts). Some are descriptive, others are procedural in nature, still others are concerned with reasoning, and so forth.

The mind is able to deal with these in a fluid and inclusive manner via controlled focusing of attention. In effect, the decision-maker actively acquires (i.e., recalls, focuses on) desired pieces of knowledge by cognitively navigating among the universe of available concepts. To the extent that a DSS can be conceived and devised as a natural extension of such activity, interacting with it should be relatively "easy," natural, or comfortable for the user. That is, the DSS can be regarded as an extension of the decision-maker's innate knowledge management capabilities.

Treating the foregoing cognitive basics as a guiding metaphor, we might conceive of an ideal DSS as a knowledge-rich environment in which a decision-maker is immersed. In this environment, the decision-maker is allowed to contact and manipulate knowledge embodied in any of a wide range of interrelated concepts. The decision-maker is able to navigate spontaneously through the DSS's concepts in either a direct or an associative fashion, pausing at a concept currently in focus to interact with it or an image of it. The type of interaction that is possible depends on the nature of the concept or its image. A decision support environment ideally is an extension of the user's private cognitive world, pushing back cognitive limits on knowledge representation. Its knowledge processing capabilities augment the user's mental skills, overcoming cognitive limits on the speed and capacity of strictly human knowledge processing. Because of this extensive nature, we refer to the consequent decision support system ideal as a hyperknowledge environment.

Current decision support systems are pragmatic, varied responses to needs sensed by diverse decision-makers. For the most part, they can be viewed as narrow, very specialized, inflexible, and partial renderings of the environment idea. Typically, they manage only one or two types of knowledge (e.g., descriptive and procedural), offer noncustomizable interfaces, and do little to facilitate navigation through concepts. Yet if we were to imagine the domain-independent functionalities of all current decision support systems accessible via the metaphorical interface of a single DSS, then the environment ideal begins to be approached. Problem processor generality and intelligence are essential for faithfully adhering to the cognitive metaphor in devising hyperknowledge environments.

In a hyperknowledge environment, a user freely navigates through and works with diverse concepts. Moreover, the concepts can work with and play upon each other. The conventional view of narrowly specialized software tools (e.g., database managers, spreadsheet systems, expert system shells) vanishes, although each can be regarded as a very constrained rendition of the environment view. Just as the human navigates via a cognitive map of the mental landscape and visits various concepts to bring them into the focal point of attention, so too should a user be able to navigate through a DSS's KS via a concept map that shows the environment's content. Having brought some KS concept into focus, the user should be able to direct the environment's PPS to manipulate that concept in desired ways. For each kind of concept allowed to exist in the KS, the PPS must possess relevant processing abilities.

The environment theory recognizes the possibility of a knowledge system that holds interrelated concepts, relationships, and epistemological shapes and sizes. It admits concept relationships that are structured, in the sense of associations and definitions [Bonczek et al., 1980; Sowa, 1984; Brachman and Schmolze, 1985], and relationships that are dynamic, in the sense of active interconcept communication [Holsapple and Whinston, 1986]. Such a knowledge system might be regarded as a generalization of the notion of hypertext, wherein multiple pieces of text are related by semantic associations rather than physical linearity [Conklin, 1987]. Instead of being restricted to paths connecting textual nodes, a hyperknowledge user is able to navigate through a KS that can represent paths through arbitrary (i.e., textual or nontextual) concepts and allows concepts to actively interact with other concepts.

The theory identifies interface possibilities which may or may not be exploited in this or that DSS. What happens when a hyperknowledge problem processor receives a request for the recall or manufacture of knowledge? The PPS must recognize exactly what problem it is that the user wants to have solved. This is accomplished by exercising its innate linguistic processing knowledge and drawing on domain-specific or user-specific linguistic knowledge held in the KS. In this way, the PPS translates the request into a series of one or more elements on which it can directly act for the purpose of satisfying the request. Conversely, what happens when the PPS has completed its recall or manufacture for a recognized problem? It may simply retain the knowledge in the KS for later use. Alternatively or in addition, the solution may be presented to the user by exercising innate presentation processing knowledge and drawing on domain- specific or user-specific presentations knowledge existing in the KS. Thus, the theory distinguishes between surface requests/responses understood by users and deep requests/responses that a PPS understands quite apart from user interface considerations.

Having briefly introduced the theory's central idea of a hyperknowledge environment, we now turn to an overview of its features, undertaken from two essential and complementary angles. The first angle involves an examination of the interface and functionality duality. The second involves formulation of traits and behaviors that need to be considered in devising a hyperknowledge environment [Chang et al., 1988].

Interface versus functionality. Both requests to and responses from the environment can be regarded as messages. Both will be referred to as surface messages, indicating that they lie at the surface which joins a user to the environment. Let M_{SI} denote the subset of LS, consisting of all surface input messages that a user knows how to send an environment. A particular m_{SI} in M_{SI} is physically realized as a series of keystrokes, a mouse movement, touching the screen, or speaking, or via some other overt user action [Bennett, 1977]. Let M_{SO} denote the subset of PS, consisting of all surface output messages that an environment's PPS knows how to send to a user. A particular m_{SO} in M_{SO} is physically realized as an image on a console display screen, a printed pattern, an audio image, or some other overt computer action. M_{SO} will be regarded as a subset of the user's language system. It is thereby symmetrical with M_{SI}, which is a subset of the environment's language system.

Each m_{SI} maps into exactly one deep input message m_{DI}, which specifies what the PPS is to do in order to satisfy the request expressed in m_{SI}. Taken together, the set of all deep input messages (M_{DI}) and the KS contents (e.g., data, rules, procedures) define what decision support functionality a user can cause a PPS to perform. The surface to deep mapping of input messages can be represented as

$$t(m_{SI}, K_{ling}) = m_{DI}$$

where t denotes the translation part of a PPS's user interface capability and K_{ling} refers to the KS's linguistic knowledge available to the PPS.

It may happen that $t(m, K_{ling})$ is null, meaning that m is not in the LS. In such a case, the PPS's functional processing capabilities cannot be exercised to provide decision support. Instead, another part of its user interface capability is employed to assist the user. This assistance manifests as a message m_{SO} to the user, reflecting the degree of success achieved in interpreting m. Results of applying this assistance function to m, together with presentation knowledge (K_{pres}), are arguments for a presentation function that yields some m_{SO}. This is expressed as

$$p(a(m, K_{ling}), K_{pres}) = m_{so}$$

where p is the presentation function and a is the assistance function. It should be clear that several iterations may be followed before the user succeeds in completely and correctly stating some m_{SI}. Even when or as a particular m_{SI} is specified, this mechanism may be used to provide the user with a record of that m_{SI}.

Once the PPS has identified an element of M_{DI}, the instructions embodied in that m_{DI} are carried out. In general, these instructions can activate any mix of the PPS's knowledge processing capabilities with respect to corresponding knowledge representations held in the KS. For instance, some m_{DI} might cause the PPS to use its inference engine capability to formulate a procedural model and identify appropriate data for analysis, retrieve or derive the data, and then execute the procedure with that data to yield some derived data. The PPS's exercise of such functionalities can be expressed as

$$f(m_{DI}, KS) = m_{DO}$$

where m_{DO} is the deep output (derived knowledge) produced by the PPS. Knowledge derived by f from m_{DI} and KS forms a message that can be used in either or both of two ways, depending on the user's intent specified in m_{DI}. The PPS can store m_{DO} in the KS or present it in a manner conforming to the user's request. This is accomplished by the p function portion of the PPS's user interface:

$$p(m_{DO}, K_{pres}) = m_{so}$$

possibly drawing on presentation knowledge held in the KS.

Effectively tapping an environment's knowledge resources depends on the phenomena of contact and impact [Chang et al., 1988]. In a cognitive environment, the decision-maker must contact a concept of interest before impact can occur. Impact refers to situations wherein the decision-maker is affected by the concept or affects the concept. Similarly, in a hyperknowledge environment, a concept must be contacted before it can be impacted by or have an impact on the user. It follows that M_{SI} includes both contact and impact messages. Similarly, some elements of M_{SO} are concerned with presenting the results of contact activities, while others involve presentation of impact results.

Either implicitly or explicitly, the user must be provided with a concept map as the basis for establishing contacts. This implies the existence of a concept map, indicating what concepts are in the environment and what their interrelationships are. An implicit map is one that is viewed external to the DSS. For instance, it may reside in the user's cognitive environment, akin to Bennett's notion of a "knowledge base" [Bennett, 1977]. However, due to cognitive limits, maintaining and using such an implicit map becomes burdensome or even infeasible for ambitious environments whose KS are large, varied, and frequently changing. Alternatively, we propose that an explicit map be provided by the DSS itself. A significant portion of M_{SO} would be concerned with portraying available concepts and relationships. In addition, corresponding elements of M_{SI} should be devoted to manipulating the map. Chang et al. introduce possible notational conventions for concept maps [Chang et al., 1988].

When a user has established contact with some concept (e.g., a procedure) pertinent to a decision process, the DSS must facilitate interaction with that concept. The nature of the desired interaction is indicated with some m_{SI} submitted by the user. Via M_{SI} elements, the user is able to impact the concept's state and behavior. Conversely, via M_{SO} elements, the concept is able to impact the user's consciousness by conveying some recalled or manufactured knowledge. It may also impact (i.e., interact with) other concepts as a by-product or chain reaction. Chang et al. discuss general terms of impact [Chang et al., 1988].

The fabric of hyperknowledge. The foregoing characterization of dynamics fits the BHW framework. These dynamics involve transformations of messages from the environment's LS to the user's LS (i.e., the environment's PS). The transformations are carried out by the PPS (subject to KS contents), which embodies t, a, f, and p functions. From a user's perspective, the DSS augments personal cognitive concepts with an environment of diverse and interrelated concepts that can be contacted for impacts. An explicit concept map is available to assist the user in navigating through this hyperknowledge space. But what is the nature of this space? What laws govern its constitution? What primitives must exist as a basis for devising a PPS to handle such a KS?

Various propositions have been advanced to begin to formally answer such questions [Chang et al., 1988]. Some central ones are briefly reprised here. Such formalisms can be valuable in several respects. To the extent that they are general and reasonably comprehensive, they give DSS researchers a common ground for detailed study, discourse, and evaluation. They can also offer a stimulative language for uncovering new DSS possibilities (e.g., in the area of model management).

Proposition: There exists a function $\chi(KS) = \{c_1, c_2, ..., c_n\}$, where c_i is a concept tag and $c_i \neq c_j \ \forall i, j \in \{1, ..., n\}$. A KS is composed of concepts, each of which can be referenced by a unique tag or identifier. As part of its functionality f, a PPS is able to apply χ.

Proposition: There exists a function δ such that $\delta(c_i) = DC_i \subset \chi(KS)$, where DC_i is the set of all defining concepts for c_i. They are the concepts that can serve as definitions (i.e., instantiations) of c_i. A concept map of KS must be able to portray the definitional relationship existing between the c_i node and the node for each element of $\delta(c_i)$.

Proposition: There exists a function τ such that $\tau(S_i) = S_j$, where S_i and S_j are sets of concepts and $\forall c_j \in S_j, S_i \subset \delta(c_j)$. Together δ and τ allow the PPS (and therefore a user) to recognize and navigate through an arbitrary KS's definitional relationships.

Proposition: There exists a function α such that $\alpha(c_i) = AC_i \subset \chi(KS)$, where AC_i is the set of all associated concepts for c_i. To be faithful to the cognitive metaphor, a DSS should have an ability to identify every concept associated with a given concept. The concept map must make such associations clear. The AC_i elements can be viewed as qualifying c_i. Conversely, c_i can be viewed as qualifying AC_i elements. Considering an association of two concepts conveys more about each than considering the same two concepts in isolation from each other. In any associative relationships, there is at least one concept that participates as the *agent* and at least one concept that participates as the *object*.

Proposition: Each associative relationship has a tag, differentiating it from other associations in the KS. There exists a function α_A such that

$$\alpha_A(c_i) = AT_i$$

where AT_i is the set $\{A_i, ..., A_k\}$ of tags for all associations in which c_i participates. In a concept map, these association tags connect nodes formed by concept tags.

Proposition: In allowing associative relationships in its KS, an environment possesses functions α_a and α_o such that

$$\alpha_a(c_i) \cup \alpha_o(c_i) = AT_i$$

where $\alpha_a(c_i)$ is that subset of AT_i for which c_i is an agent of each of its elements, and $\alpha_o(c_i) \subset AT_i$ for which c_i is an object of each of its elements.

Proposition: If $A_i \in \alpha_a(c_i)$ and $c_j \in \delta(c_i)$, then $A_1 \in \alpha_a(c_j)$. Similarly, if $A_1 \in \alpha_o(c_i)$ and $c_j \in \delta(c_i)$, then $A_1 \in \alpha_o(c_j)$. This proposition maintains that associations are inherited.

Proposition: Each association belongs to a specific cardinality class. Such a partitioning of associations is useful for purposes of referential integrity and semantic clarity in a concept map.

Definition: A selection set S is the result of applying a function (e.g., χ, δ, τ, α, A_1) that yields a collection of concepts. Very often there is a need to select a particular concept from S. A selection criterion C is a specification that differentiates all elements of S.

Proposition: There is a function σ such that $\sigma(S, C) = c_i$, where $c_i \in S$ and c_i satisfies C. Such a function is the mechanism for focusing on a particular concept from a set of concepts to satisfy a user's contact needs. Variants of the primitive σ, which produce sets of concepts, are of course possible.

The set $\chi(KS)$ is sufficient to characterize what concepts exist in a concept map. The functions δ, τ, α_a, and α_o are sufficient to characterize structural relationships existing among concepts in the map. These same functions, together with σ and the elements of $\alpha_A(c_i)$, $\forall i \in \{1, ..., n\}$, are sufficient to navigate through the concept map for the purpose of contacting any concept in the KS. They allow us to reach any or all concepts related either directly or indirectly, either definitionally or associatively, to an arbitrarily chosen concept.

Proposition: There must be a function μ such that $\mu(c_i) = MI_i \subset M_{DI}$, where $MI_i = \{M_1, ..., M_p\}$ consists of all messages that can be sent to a contacted concept c_i. Each such message designates a valid kind of impact. Different concepts can be subject to different impacts.

Proposition: If $M_1 \in \mu(c_i)$, then $M_1(c_i) \in M_{DO}$ or is equivalent to an element of M_{DO}. The result of impacting a concept is ultimately a deep output message. It can happen that $M_1(c_i)$ causes contact and impact with other concepts as intermediate manifestations of its behavior.

Proposition: For a full-fledged decision support environment, the function f must minimally have the problem processing capabilities inherent in χ, δ, τ, α, α_A, α_a, α_o, $A_1 \in \alpha_A(c_i)$ $\forall i \in \{1, ..., n\}$, σ, μ, and $M_1 \in \mu(c_i)$ $\forall i \in \{1, ..., n\}$. In principle, each m_{DI} is some composite of these function invocations.

Proposition: In the interest of PPS invariance, the actions taken to realize dynamic relationships (i.e., corresponding to elements of MI_i) may not wholly exist within the PSS f function. Instead they are accessible to it. This is made possible by allowing those prescribed actions to exist as concepts in the KS. They may or may not appear in the surface concept map presented to the user, but do exist in the deep concept map available to the PPS.

The foregoing propositions deal with the representation of knowledge in an environment for decision support. Regardless of whether a model is viewed as a procedure, data, or a problem statement, these representation protocols are relevant. The propositions also deal with the basics of processing hyperknowledge, identifying fundamental functionality that must exist in a full-fledged environment. As such, they offer a set of primitives for devising alternative model management dynamics and establishing an interplay with nonmodel concepts.

Related research directions. Traditional model management research is strongly colored by an investigator's conception of what a model is and by the conception of a context in which models exist. For clarity, it is advisable to be precise and explicit about the meaning of "model" and the nature of the chosen contextual framework. As to the former point, it might be best to refer to a problem statement as a problem statement (i.e., an element of an LS), data as data (i.e., descriptive knowledge in a KS), and a procedure as a procedure (i.e., procedural knowledge in a KS). All three could be regarded as facets of modeling. As to the latter point, limitations (if any) imposed by a framework should be carefully scrutinized as potential causes of research blind spots. One research direction of relevance to model management is the investigation or invention of DSS frameworks in the interest of understanding or overcoming limitations.

Some model management research directions are a continuation of past research into the internals of model management systems [Holsapple and Whinston, 1988b]. For instance, there will be endeavors to invent new tools that are more powerful, flexible, efficient, or accessible than today's tools. In a related vein, research is needed into the activity of DSS development. This is concerned with strategies for tool usage in the design, implementation, and evolution of DSS.

Second, there will be research aimed at uncovering new possibilities for analysis dynamics in terms of what happens when

- a problem is being stated,
- data need to be selected or produced,
- procedural modules need to be selected, sequenced, or interfaced,
- an executing module needs some data input, or
- k-problem solution results are to be presented as a response to the user.

Progress in this direction will open the way for tool improvements.

Third, there is a need to better understand the settings in which analysis is relevant. This includes an appreciation of the implications that different multiperson structures of decision making have for support systems [e.g., Watabe et al., 1988; Holsapple, 1989]. It also includes the topic of DSS valuation [Marsden and Pingry, 1989].

An alternative way of looking for model management research opportunities can occur from the platform of the emerging hyperknowledge theory of decision support outlined here. The constructs and principles that it embodies flow from the strong knowledge orientation of the BHW framework. It shifts the focus away from isolated consideration of model management to the more all-encompassing realm of knowledge management. It asks a host of descriptive, normative, and speculative questions that slice across model management boundaries.

What distinct types of knowledge are germane to a decision-making process? Which of these are amenable to computerized management (i.e., representation and processing)? What existing or new techniques for knowledge management are applicable to each type of knowledge? How should concepts of the same or diverse types be definitionally and associatively related to each other in a hyperknowledge KS? What is the mechanism whereby one concept (e.g., a rule set) contacts and impacts another concept (e.g., a procedural module), which in turn contacts and impacts yet another concept (e.g., a piece of data, another procedure, or another rule set)? Can standard M_{SI} and M_{SO} be devised? How can customized M_{SI} and M_{SO} be rapidly developed? Can they evolve based on experiences with users? In what other ways can the environment be self-adapting to better conform to user traits? To what extent can an environment's interface be independent of its functionality? What roles can interactors, constraint maintainers, and event handlers [Holsapple et al., 1988] play in accomplishing such independence? How general can implementations of the t, a, f, and p functions be? Should the same f implementation be able to handle multiple M_{DI} and M_{DO}?

The foregoing are representative of research issues raised by the hyperknowledge theory. They are by no means exhaustive. Such questions furnish an unconventional vantage point for model management researchers. As such, they may stimulate new insights or investigations that are beneficial to decision-makers who state problems and expect to receive presentations based on the procedural analysis of data. The environment's ability to manufacture new knowledge from existing knowledge may be enhanced by imbuing it with its own intelligence. For instance, artificial intelligence techniques can be used to allow the DSS to interpret problem statements, formulate procedures, acquire data inputs for procedures, and explain results of procedure execution [Bonczek et al., 1981].

Conceptual modeling and change propagation

Vasant Dhar and Matthias Jarke

Thus far, we have examined the relationship between model management systems and their environments. We now investigate a more focused subject, the impact of environmental changes on the evolutionary design of decision models and on their maintenance. The central argument made here is that for certain types of problems it is important to capture the process involved in the development of a model in a way that the history can be used subsequently in reasoning about the model itself. By reasoning about the model, we mean making changes to it in response to changes in the situation being modeled.

Clearly, it does not make sense to model the history of the development process for all problems. For example, in developing a model of an oil refinery for determining optimal operating conditions, the central concern of the modeler is to develop the correct model formulation. Once the model is developed, it is unlikely that such a formulation would change significantly over time, even though a lot of effort might be involved in maintaining the correct values of the input coefficients. In effect, when the structure of the problem remains stable, there is little point in concerning oneself with the reasons for it.

In contrast, there are many problems where the structure of the problem is not apparent in a mathematical sense at the outset of the modeling exercise, nor does it remain stable. For example, in planning a space mission, numerous assumptions are likely to be made about materials, manufacturing processes, deliveries from subcontractors, scheduling, and so on. In such a situation, the term "model" has a looser interpretation and derives its meaning from the objects and relationships in the task environment that are made explicit by the modelers [Dhar and Pople, 1987]. Even though such a model might lack a precisely identifiable structure (in fact, because of it), it is important for it to represent the changing reality if it is to be used as a basis for rational decision making.

There are a variety of problems in addition to the type of complex planning problem mentioned above that fall into the latter category, such as problems that bring together several parties in order to design complex artifacts. Prime examples are software engineering problems, where requirements and specifications are usually fuzzy at the outset and keep changing, requiring frequent modifications to the artifact. For such problems, it makes sense to have tools that can support the process of collaboration as well as the process of reasoning with the knowledge that is generated by the collaborative activity. In this section, our central concern is not on the collaborative aspect of decision making but on illustrating how the knowledge involved in formulating a model can be used in reasoning about changes to it. We shall therefore provide only a preliminary discussion of collaborative tools, concentrating instead on the solution design model (which we view as a general case of the decision model) itself.

The remainder of the section is organized as follows. We begin by describing briefly what we mean by modeling process and its importance. This is followed by a discussion of the technology that is needed in order to model decision-making processes. The example used to illustrate the evolution of the solution design model is one involving the formulation of a model used in determining manpower requirements in a manufacturing context. We conclude with a discussion of the pros and cons.

The role of process knowledge in managing models. It is generally recognized that for problems that are not well understood at the outset, modeling goes through several phases such as those described by Simon [Simon, 1960] and Mintzberg et al. [Mintzberg et al., 1976]. The early phases are characterized by information gathering and open-ended discussion among the participants, the purpose of which is in fact to synthesize a reasonable conceptual model of the situation identifying the objects of interest, alternative ways of accomplishing subtasks, and so on. The later phases focus on the use of such a model as a basis for making good choices. Finally, if choices are tentative and must be continually revised—presumably in response to an evolving conceptualization of the problem—decision-makers must have access to the history of the modeling process. In effect, to be able to "manage" models, which we interpret loosely as the process of using and modifying them, it is necessary to have as much access to the formulation history in as organized a manner as possible.

We view the process description above as involving three types of activity: communication, conceptualization, and propagation. Typically, these activities would follow each other in a spiral procedure of model refinement and enhancement, as proposed for general software engineering problems [Boehm, 1986]. In order to understand the nature of each of these activities, consider a project involving the formulation of a mathematical programming model to solve some nontrivial constraint satisfaction problem. Assuming that multiple modelers and users are involved, there is likely to be an initial open-ended discussion aimed at eliciting a rich description of the problem from the users, followed by a discussion among the modeling experts on possible conceptualizations of the problem, generation of notes and sketches, consideration of what possible mathematical structures the problem fits, the effect of simplifying assumptions, and so on. Tools for this phase are referred to as communication or collaboration tools.

The conceptualization process involves the development of a formal model, which typically includes an identification of the objects of interest and the relationships among them, and at a detailed level how these are to be represented. This implies the use of specific modeling techniques. This might involve using formalisms such as a frame-based language, entity-relationship diagrams, and so on to represent the requirements model (with a formal semantics such that inferencing becomes possible), and mathematical programming models to represent the solution design model.

Propagation refers to the assessment of the ramifications of specific decisions in the application area. For example, in the requirements model, integrity constraints might be used to constrain the allowable operations or outputs. Similarly, selecting a design model (e.g., a transportation problem structure) as a solution would imply a certain problem structure and restrict the types of solution algorithms possible. In general terms, propagation relates the outputs to inputs and records the reasons underlying their relationship. Such information is important for assessing the repercussions of changes to an existing model.

The technology needed to capture, represent, and apply process knowledge. The process of model formulation can involve bringing to bear a lot of knowledge, much of which is not maintained explicitly. Elaborating or making modifications to a model often requires access to this knowledge. Usually, we rely on memory for this purpose, but for open-ended problems where the modeling process is not a one-shot exercise, the limitations are obvious. Our objective is to design systems that capture a reasonable subset of the initially generated knowledge and to allow it to be used subsequently to reason about the model. In the remainder of this section, we describe the technology needed to accomplish this objective.

The technology consists of three components: a tool for work group collaboration, a knowledge representation system for conceptual modeling, and a truth maintenance system (TMS) for reasoning about changes to the model. The first two components have been described in detail elsewhere, so we summarize them only briefly. Our main emphasis is on how the truth maintenance module can interact with these other two modules. To have an effective support environment, the three components must be integrated. This is one of the concerns of two ongoing projects, the NSF project REMAP [Dhar and Jarke, 1988], and the ESPRIT project DAIDA [Jarke and DAIDA Team, 1989].

Work group collaboration. One way to support collaboration would be to keep text records of the modeling exercise. However, linear text becomes progressively inaccessible with size. A tool must therefore provide at least a marginal structure such as that enabled by hypertext [Conklin, 1987], geared toward providing easy access to the records.

Several tools for supporting collaborative activity have been proposed in the literature, some based on ad hoc semistructured message types, others on empirically grounded conceptual models of argumentational or action-oriented conversations [Winograd and Flores, 1986]. For example, the gIBIS system developed at MCC [Conklin and Begeman, 1988] is based on a model of design processes proposed by Rittel [Rittel and Weber, 1973], who proposed representing the conversation among participants involved in imposing structure on unstructured problems using nine specific types of primitives. The fundamental primitive around which conversation revolves is an *issue*. An issue has associated *positions* which are alternative ways of resolving the issue; *arguments* support positions. Issues may *specialize* or *generalize* other issues, and may also *question* or *be-suggested-by* other issues, positions, or arguments. Finally, there are two *other* primitives for concepts that do not fit the predefined primitives.

The evolving conversation among participants in gIBIS is represented as a state transition network with nodes being issues, positions, or arguments, connected by various types of links. Currently, the tool is being used as a repository of knowledge generated in the course of a discussion. However, it has no capabilities for doing any inferencing such as assessing the consequences of changes in previous design decisions. For this reason, we feel that formalizing the conceptual conversation model and mapping the gIBIS primitives into a TMS structure should enhance its usefulness considerably. How this can be done will become clear after we describe the TMS.

There are also several other well-known tools for supporting collaborative activity [Greif, 1988]. Here, we are mostly interested in the use of such systems as knowledge acquisition tools for model construction and maintenance.

Conceptual modeling. Conceptually, we view model formulation and management as a process of constructing and maintaining a layered description of (1) the decision problem to be supported, and (2) the set of models available to do so. Therefore, a knowledge representation system for conceptual modeling has to capture at least three aspects. It must [Jarke, 1988]

- model the problem (requirements model),
- model the models (design model), and
- model the mapping and remapping process from requirements to design.

We discuss each of these issues in turn. The example we use is an artificial synthesis from three real-world applications that turned out to provide very different solutions to conceptually the same problem.

For the conceptualization of decision problems, we need a rich representation that is able not only to capture the objects and constraints that denote the problem at an adequate level of abstraction, but also to capture the evolution of these objects and constraints, as well as the evolution of our knowledge about this evolution. In a nutshell, a knowledge representation language for this kind of task needs a clean structure, formal reasoning facilities, and a built-in time calculus. Moreover, it should be easy to derive well-known informal representations such as dataflow diagrams or entity relationship diagrams from it which can serve as an interactive front end to the representation system and thus form the interface to the (collaborative) knowledge acquisition tool. In the DAIDA project, a knowledge representation language called CML/Telos [Koubarakis et al., 1989] has been developed for this purpose. CML integrates predicative rules and integrity constraints as in deductive databases together with an interval-based time calculus into a structurally object-oriented kernel system that can be externally represented as a hypertext-like mixture of network and frame structures.

For example, consider the problem of personnel management in production cells of a flexible manufacturing system. Every morning, cells are assigned certain production tasks and tooling instructions which lead to required qualifications of the team that works on these cells. Each worker also has a qualification profile, which is in turn determined by education, experience, and similar factors. The problem is to assign to each cell a group of workers such that the qualification constraints are met and goals such as satisfaction of workers, training effect of new work, productivity, and working costs (e.g., for overtime) are achieved. Figure 1 shows a conceptual model of this problem, phrased as a CML semantic network.

There are several possible ways of synthesizing formulations and solution methods for the above-mentioned problem. The general strategy in building a DSS (or any software system, for that matter) is that the developer tries to satisfy some of the constraints defined in the problem model "by design," that is, by writing or reusing procedural programs (which one can refer to as problem solvers). Other constraints are usually

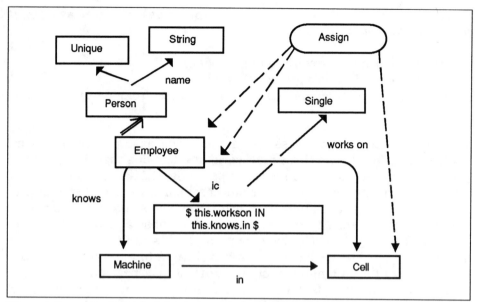

Figure 1. Conceptual model of the personnel management problem.

left completely outside the system (this is why we speak of a decision support system). At best, they are tested by a more passive integrity checker that determines whether the partial solutions proposed by the problem solver lead to violations of the global requirements. Depending on how this is done, the flexibility of the solutions varies markedly. Assuming that a conceptual model of the problem is available, we can envision that the design model of the solver system is embedded in the requirements model in that it explains what subset of the requirements it satisfies and what are the properties of the solution it offers. Figure 2 illustrates this embedding of the system model into the problem world. It also indicates how users of a group tool interact with the multilevel knowledge base.

We discuss three designs that have come up in our collaborators' recent experiences for the kind of problem sketched in Figure 1. The first involves building a transaction-based system, the second is an operations research approach, and the third is an expert-system-style solution. We briefly sketch and compare the features of these solutions from a process viewpoint.

A first solution, discussed in detail elsewhere [Jarke and DAIDA Team, 1989], is to use an advanced software development environment to implement a transaction system which guarantees that no data can be entered which violate the constraints. The required activity of assigning workers to cells is supported by specifying, in an appropriate design language, a transaction that satisfies the constraints if that is possible.

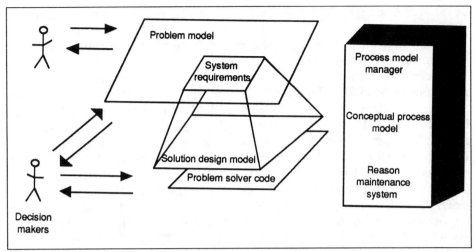

Figure 2. Overview of process-oriented model management.

This specification can then be formally refined into a procedural program that allows a user to interactively propose assignments, and controls whether these assignments satisfy the constraints.

While this approach satisfies the requirements, it leaves most of the work to the user and is thus clearly unacceptable for large-scale applications. Starting from the same conceptual design of the assignment transaction, a more OR-style approach would recognize that part of the constraint structure corresponds to a generalized assignment problem for which a very fast algorithm exists [Buehner and Kleinschmidt, 1988]. Rather than developing software from scratch, the algorithm is selected from a model base, based on its design-level description (see Figure 2). The "implementation" just consists of relating the parameters of this algorithm to the data structures of the conceptual design model (assuming that these data structures can be extracted from an existing database, again described at the design level of Figure 2). All other constraints are left outside the system. In a traditional OR approach, these relationships would not be made explicit.

An expert-system-style solution [Dhar and Ranganathan, 1989] incorporates the constraints of the problem model more directly into a set of heuristic rules, each corresponding to one constraint or a small set of constraints, and rules for making assignments. These rules make assignments from sets of choices, in effect applying the generate-and-test algorithm. A TMS ensures that the assignments do not violate any constraints. Compared with the previous solution, this one will probably be slower because it is not designed to exploit the specific problem structure. On the other hand, it can deal with fairly general constraint satisfaction problems so that even major changes to the problem description would not invalidate the approach.

Generally, design-level specifications of solutions would be maintained in a model base. In the first solution it would probably be called a software database, in the second a model bank, and in the third a rule base—but essentially these terms all refer to specifications of the solution model. It is here where most previous work on model management [e.g., DSS86, 1986] fits in. For example, Blanning chooses a relational or entity-relationship representation [Blanning, 1984]; Dolk and Konsynski, frame-based ones [Dolk and Konsynski, 1984]; still others, Horn logic [Bonczek et al., 1982; Sivasankaran and Jarke, 1985] or aggregation-based graph structures [Geoffrion, 1987]. Only Geoffrion's structured modeling and to some degree PLEXSYS [McIntyre et al., 1986] address the representation of modeling processes, at least in the way of emphasizing a very modular structure of the models. Binbasioglu and Jarkeis made an early attempt to relate knowledge about the models to knowledge about the application domain in which they are embedded [Binbasioglu and Jarke, 1986].

The requirements model and solution design model must be related to each other for various reasons. On the one hand, the relationship between both should be used to determine when an existing solution does not fit the problem description anymore. Conversely, similarity between problem descriptions can also suggest the reuse of the modeling experience and thus adapted versions of the corresponding designs. (In the software development from scratch solution above, changes must be further propagated into the actual coding.) For example, the problem model for the flexible manufacturing system can be adapted to a faculty course assignment model in which part of the developed algorithms can be reused, while different constraint details cause changes or rewriting in others.

It is difficult and often impossible to determine these relationships by just looking at the old and new version of a model. Only knowledge about the decisions that underlie the changes can help explain the transition and give a meaningful picture of the development process. Here we describe one aspect of this providing an appropriate conceptual model for representing these process relationships at various levels of granularity. Another aspect, the use of this process model for inferencing, is the subject of the next section.

Two kinds of process models dominate the software engineering literature: contract-based ones which view system development as a set of commitments, and decision-based ones which view it as a history of executed decisions. For example, the decision-object-tool (DOT) model [Jarke et al., 1989] implemented in Passau's ConceptBase system views model development and maintenance as a process of tool-aided executions of design decisions that transform model versions to other model versions according to constraints set by a decision class (i.e., specification of a development methodology).

The modeling process in large applications, or in large model banks with many different applications, goes through many versions, and versions of the overall DSS have to be configured from versions of component problem solvers, versions of problem submodels, and versions of the mappings between the two. A software process data model can be used to represent the evolution of these relationships over extended periods of time, as well as more local changes. Rose and Jarke discuss the preservation of consistency-in-the-large by conceptual version and configuration management [Rose and Jarke, 1989]. For the rest of the section, we shall concentrate on the handling of smaller subhistories for which large-scale data management is not a problem.

Model evolution and change propagation. To assess the difficulty of adapting the DSS to a change, two cases must be distinguished:

- Changes in the task environment that have not been mapped into the solution model: Such changes can affect the inputs to the model in complex ways. For example, if an employee attends a training course, his qualification profile changes. Accordingly, the input to the solution design model must be modified; that is, the data structure used to represent qualifications must be changed correctly. If such changes occur often, it would be worthwhile incorporating the relationship between training and qualification profiles explicitly in the requirements and solution design models.
- Changes in the task environment that have been mapped into the solution design model: For example, consider the situation where employees may now be assigned to more than one cell during the day (of course, their assignments must now be restricted somehow by their working time). For the OR solution model, this change would lead to a reformulation of the constraints and the need for a new solution algorithm. For the expert system, it is likely that only a few rules will require modification.

In this section we begin by describing the basic features of truth maintenance. We then illustrate how these features can be used to support model evolution.

There are two types of TMS: justification-based [Doyle, 1979] and assumption-based [deKleer, 1986]. The former is designed to maintain one noncontradictory scenario (i.e., where a proposition and its logical negation are not believed simultaneously) at one time, whereas the latter is geared toward exploring multiple, possibly contradictory solutions at the same time. We describe only the former type, since it is the one we envision as capturing design knowledge and using this to maintain a noncontradictory scenario.

Reinfrank provides a survey of truth maintenance systems [Reinfrank, 1988]. We briefly summarize the essential features. In a TMS, every datum has a support status associated with it. A status of IN indicates that the datum is currently believed, whereas an OUT indicates disbelief. The values IN and OUT are computed via justifications associated with the datum. Each justification has two parts, an inlist and an outlist. A justification is considered valid if it evaluates to true, that is, if each datum in its inlist is IN and each datum in its outlist is OUT. Ultimately, all data depend on "ground-level" justifications of two types: premises and assumptions. In a premise justification, the inlist and outlist are both empty. This type of justification is always valid. An assumption justification has a nonempty outlist, which means that it is justified by a lack of belief in some other datum. Such a justification is considered nonmonotonic since its belief depends on a lack of belief in something else. Finally, deductive justifications are those in which the outlist is empty (and the inlist is nonempty). A datum can have more than one justification associated with it. The datum is IN if at least one of its justifications is valid; otherwise it is OUT.

As an illustration, consider the situation where one wishes to determine the most appropriate algorithm to apply in solving an assignment problem like the one described in Figure 1. In the classical assignment problem, where each person is assigned to one machine and each machine is staffed by exactly one person (supply-coefficient and demand-coefficient are both unity), a highly specialized efficient algorithm can be applied to solve the problem. If one generalizes the machine into a manufacturing cell to which more than one person can be assigned (demand-coefficient greater than or equal to one), the problem becomes a little more general. If one further generalizes the problem to one where a person can be assigned to more than one cell (both coefficients greater than or equal to one), the problem becomes a transportation problem. Accordingly, successively more general algorithms must be applied to solve the corresponding linear programming problems. Finally, if the objective function turns out to be nonlinear, an even more general algorithm such as a piecewise-linear approximation or generate-and-test algorithm must be applied.

The situation described above can be represented in terms of the following structures, which constitute a "dependency network" that is maintained by a TMS. For simplicity, we show partial justifications; in a real scenario, the dependency network would be more dense. We also assume that uppercase symbols denote functions, and the lists of lowercase symbols refer to data.

Datum: (apply assignment-problem-algorithm)
Justification: (AND   (INLIST   (supply-coefficient = 1)
                                           (demand-coefficient = 1))
                              (OUTLIST   (nonlinear-problem)))

Datum: (apply manufacturing-cell-problem-algorithm)
Justification: (AND   (INLIST   (supply-coefficient = 1))
                              (OUTLIST   (demand-coefficient = 1)
                                           (nonlinear-problem)))

Datum: (apply transportation-problem-algorithm)
Justification: (AND   (INLIST   ())
                              (OUTLIST   (demand-coefficient = 1)
                                           (supply-coefficient = 1)
                                           (nonlinear-problem)))

Datum: (apply generate-and-test-algorithm)
Justification: (AND   (INLIST   ())
                              (OUTLIST   (apply transportation-
                                               problem-algorithm)
                                           (apply manufacturing-
                                               cell-problem-algorithm)
                                           (apply assignment-
                                               problem-algorithm)))

We assume that the datum (supply-coefficient = 1) is IN, the datum (demand-coefficient = 1) is OUT, and that the datum (nonlinear-problem) is OUT. With such a labeling of the ground-level data, the network corresponding to the above data can be visualized in terms of the graph of Figure 3. Each circle corresponds to a justification, with an arrow pointing to the justified datum, positive arcs connected to the elements of the inlist, and negative arcs connected to the elements of the outlist.

In the network of Figure 3, it should be noted that the algorithms applicable are mutually exclusive. (It could also have been possible to set up the justifications so that this is not the case; that is, the more general algorithm could be made applicable as well, and some external routine could decide which one to actually use.) The particular labeling indicates that the manufacturing-cell-problem-algorithm is the one that should be applied since the problem requirement states that several people can be assigned to a cell (demand coefficient is greater than 1). If the problem description were modified so that a person could also be assigned to several cells simultaneously (supply-coefficient greater than 1), this algorithm would no longer be applicable (the node corresponding to it would go OUT) and the general transportation algorithm would have to be used (it would become IN).

Actually, in reevaluating the status of the data—referred to as reason maintenance—what the TMS does is to execute a constraint satisfaction procedure to ensure that the data as a whole satisfies two properties, namely, consistency and well-foundedness. In a stable state, every datum with at least one valid justification is IN and each one without a valid justification is OUT. A state is well-founded if no set of beliefs is mutually dependent. In terms of a labeled network such as the one in the figure, this means that there is no set of arcs from a node to itself, all of which are labeled positively.

It should be noted that in general there can be several possible ways of labeling the network so that it satisfies the properties of consistency and well-foundedness. The knowledge required to provide *one* meaningful labeling can come from an external routine under which the TMS works, or a user, or both. The network itself is a repository of the knowledge that relates the inputs (problem requirements or description) to the outputs, namely, the structure of the model. In effect, it goes one step further than the conversation networks modeled in collaborative tools like gIBIS by providing an active inferencing capability to reason about past decisions.

The dependency network also illustrates how it is possible to modify the problem structure based on changing requirements that have been expressed formally in some modeling language (such as the conceptual modeling language). In summary, there is an explicit relationship between the structure of the requirements model and that of the solution design model. In the case above, for example, the node specifying that the demand-coefficient is unity is really part of the requirements model (say, an integrity constraint) that is related explicitly to the type of solution procedure required to solve the corresponding problem.

Discussion. In this section, we tried to make a case for using more process knowledge in model management. The use of process knowledge in the problem-solving process may not be the best solution for stable problems but becomes very useful in experimental situations where trying out different alternatives or dealing with a changing environment is crucial. The additional use of process knowledge in the DSS-building process helps in deciding when a once-developed or selected problem solver is still adequate to the problem at hand, when a new solution method should be adopted, and how the experience gained in choosing the solver for the old requirements can be reapplied in choosing a new one. What we finally want is an overall model construction and management architecture that allows the integration of arbitrary problem solvers into a TMS-supported environment, by relating conceptual models of the solvers to the conceptual model of the requirements from which they have been built.

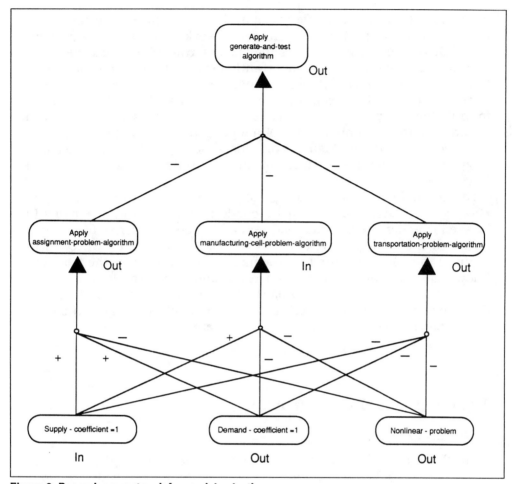

Figure 3. Dependency network for model selection.

At first glance it might appear that the example we have used is contrived: that for structured problems such as manpower planning, once the correct model is in place, few or no changes need to be made to it. While this may to some extent be true, there are two considerations that should not be overlooked.

First, there is ample evidence that even for relatively well structured problems, for which mathematical programming formulations are appropriate, different experts can come up with radically different formulations [Raghunathan, 1988; Orlikowski and Dhar, 1986]. In one study [Raghunathan, 1988], even the structure of the objective functions was different for the same problem description (linear and nonlinear functions), even though they were all judged to be essentially correct. For problems with less structure, one would expect the divergence to be even more radical. Given such differences in the early phases of formulation, it makes sense to provide a collaborative work group support environment where alternative positions may be entertained and recorded.

Second and perhaps more importantly for the alternative positions, it is useful to go a step further and have a system analyze alternative solution models. In effect, by providing a what-if capability during formulation, a system could enable modelers and users to assess in concrete terms the implications of adopting the various positions. The dependency network of Figure 3 did this in superficial terms for a small fragment of one problem, but its usefulness would become realistic on a larger scale.

The ultimate workability of the approach depends on pragmatics. Making knowledge explicit is not a costless exercise, and it remains to be seen whether the benefits modelers and users can derive from it will outweigh the effort involved. The trade-offs involved can be viewed in terms of the following paradox: The more stable a domain, the more the knowledge that can be specified a priori and hence the less the effort required of modelers in specifying the knowledge required to set up the dependency network. However, in such domains, the lesser is the need for supporting model evolution—and vice versa.

Modeling model management

Steven O. Kimbrough

There are broadly two classes of reasons that can be given in favor of having a model management system. The first may be called *reasons of convenience*, the second *reasons of chestnuts*. Reasons of convenience motivated the original concepts of and research on model management. Here, a model management system was seen as "a structured milieu for storing, manipulating, and retrieving models" [Dolk and Konsynski, 1984]. Such reasons for model management systems are ample. If there are to be large-scale DSS in which large numbers of models, particularly sizable models, are to be available to and used by particular DSS applications, then there needs to be system-level, systematic support for storing (and inspecting) models, for retrieving models, for composing large models out of smaller models, for handling various versions of a model, for modifying models, for executing models, and so on. Much of this work was quite properly motivated by analogy with database systems. In both cases—data and models—convenience and sound management indicate that appropriate management systems be developed for the routine processing associated with, respectively, data and models.

The second class of reasons—reasons of chestnuts—for wanting a model management system* gets its name from the following fact. It is an old chestnut that the purpose of modeling is to gain insight into the system being modeled. This truth, however tired, remains true and applies as well to model management systems. A main purpose of a model management system is to provide information automatically that is materially useful for gaining insight into the system being modeled. Indeed, much of the most interesting recent research in model management is exciting just because progress is being made in this regard. Significant progress has been reported in developing systems that can automatically analyze, report on, and in other ways usefully exploit models of interest in management science [e.g., Abelson et al., 1989; Balakrishnan and Whinston, 1991; Bhargava et al., 1988; Bhargava and Kimbrough, 1990; Bhargava et al., 1989; Bradley and Clemence, 1988; Chinneck, forthcoming; Chinneck, 1989; Chinneck and Dravnieks, 1989; Fourer, 1983; Geoffrion, 1987; Greenberg, 1983; Greenberg and Murphy, 1989; Krishan, 1990; Meeraus, 1983; Welch, 1987].

As important and exciting as it is, research in model management that is motivated by reasons of chestnuts has been limited in its outlook. This work has aimed to provide useful information to the system user—information about the models at hand. The strategy, and it is a good one, has been to provide insight-producing information about the system being modeled by producing information about the models of the system. The suggestion we pursue in this section is that for reasons of chestnuts— that is, for the purpose of conveying insight into the system being modeled—model management systems could also provide and exploit information about the user of the DSS. We claim—rather, we speculate— that not only is this desirable, but that it is doable and that it is, with additional research, practicable. In what follows we aim to elaborate and support this speculation. Space, unfortunately, is here much limited, so the support and elaboration actually presented is necessarily but adumbrated. (Further details are available elsewhere [Kimbrough, 1990].)

Theoretical background. In a nutshell, cognitive science may be said to be aimed at developing causal theories of how the mind works, particularly theories of how the "higher" mental functions, associated with reasoning and intelligence, work. The language of thought (LoT) hypothesis is a fundamental or philosophical stance on the nature of how the mind works. The hypothesis may be summarized in the following sloganish way: "Thought consists of the manipulation of sentences in the language of thought" [Pollock, 1986, p. 163]. Fodor, the foremost philosophical exponent of the LoT hypothesis, has recently expressed the idea

---

* These reasons apply as well to data management [Bhargava et al., 1989], but that is a subject beyond the scope of this section.

as follows: "If we wanted to be slightly more precise, we could say that the LOT story amounts to the claims that (1) (some) mental formulas have mental formulas as parts; and (2) the parts are 'trans-portable': the same parts can appear in *lots* of mental formulas," where mental formulas are physical tokens, and are "things that have a syntactic structure" [Fodor, 1987, p. 137].

There is, of course, much more to the story, and much more of the story is, we believe, ultimately relevant to model management, but space limitations free us (temporarily) from having to make good on this claim. Briefly, however, scientific-philosophical theories of the mind are either *representational* or *syntactic* [Stitch, 1983]. There is a lively scientific-philosophical debate concerning what sort of theory is correct, and the LoT hypothesis bears importantly on this debate. Further, a serious possible alternative to the LoT hypothesis has arisen, called *connectionism*. Space does not permit a discussion of the details of the differences in these approaches. Suffice it to say, however, that the differences are real and significant and that application work—such as work on model management—can plausibly yield information that will help decide among these various sorts of approaches to the study of the mind.

Assuming, for the present, the LoT hypothesis, one's theorizing has only begun. There remain, among others, the problems of determining what the sentences in the language of thought look like and what the cognitive manipulations on those sentences are. (Here and elsewhere, we speak of the language of thought only out of convenience. There may be many such languages.) Cognitive scientists have originated several theories that aim to answer these questions. There are three that seem to be quite promising and worth investigating: scripts (associated with Schank and Abelson; related to Minsky's idea of frames [Abelson, 1981; Anderson, 1985; Rumelhart and Ortony, 1977; Schank and Abelson, 1977]), ACT* and PUPS (associated with John Anderson [Anderson, 1983, 1989]), and mental models (associated with Johnson-Laird [Johnson-Laird, 1983, 1988]). Interestingly, although the issue has not been explored in detail, each of these theories is able to give a principled account of intentionality and propositional attitudes, and each is consistent with the spirit of folk psychology.

In addition to these LoT-style theoretical approaches and the direct evidence for them that their proponents have adduced, there are two very interesting independent sources of evidence—pertaining to model management—that tend to support one or another of these (LoT-style) theoretical approaches. First, there is experimental evidence regarding how subjects reason with mathematical models from physics [e.g., Larkin, 1981; Stillings et al., 1987], the upshot of which is that subjects reason with repeatable sorts of errors, all of which lends itself to representation in software and, one can hope, automated remediation. Second, there is emerging work in the history and philosophy of science [e.g., Holyoak and Thagard, 1989; Thagard, 1988a, 1988b, 1989] that uses LoT-style theories for representing scientific theories and theory changes. Intriguing results have been obtained, which suggest that LoT-style theories may indeed adequately represent theories in science and may yield important insights into how scientists reason with and about them. There is no reason to think that these insights—from physics and from the history of science—cannot be extended to the realm of models in management science, but substantial research will have to be conducted if the promise of this extension is to be realized.

Embedded languages. To summarize so far, we have the idea of taking theories in cognitive science seriously in order to model in software how people think about and with mathematical models. We then have the fundamental idea of the language of thought hypothesis. And we have three distinct, established, and causal LoT-style theories that we may use for investigations in the context of model management.

Our aim now is to provide some general comments on how we might (and can) represent mathematical models—the models of a model management system—in software. If we hope to use LoT-style theories to model (mimic) how we represent mathematical models in our heads, then pretty clearly the software representation will be a formal language of some type. This motivation for representing mathematical models in a formal language jibes well with the various *executable modeling language* or EML approaches to model management [e.g., Bisschop and Meeraus, 1982; Bradley, 1989; Bradley and Clemence, 1988; Fourer, 1983; Fourer et al., 1990; Geoffrion, 1987, 1988; Meeraus, 1983; Rayna, 1987; Wolfram, 1988]. We have, in brief, ample motivation for developing a representation language for models in a model management system. This immediately raises the question of what the language should be. Happily, we do not really need to answer this question. Instead, we can—via the technique of embedded languages—usefully exploit many different model representation languages in a single system. Broadly, we can do so by embedding them in a more general language and by declaring information about expressions in the particular embedded languages, including, for example, how to translate from one to another. (Further, we believe that the embedded language approach is useful even when only one language is embedded in the system.) In what follows, we do not hope to provide conclusive support for these claims. Instead, we intend to indicate what we mean by embedding a language, although the details must be left out [Bhargava and Kimbrough, 1990]. A few more comments before we begin on this.

There are at least two criteria for assessing a representation scheme for models in a model management software system. First, the representation scheme should be rich enough to be capable of expressing whatever it is we want to say with or about models. The scheme must have adequate expressive power. Second, particular representations should be transformable at low cost to the forms that are directly needed for the purposes at hand. In a model management system we may need to execute a model, differentiate a model, rearrange a model, display a model, get input for a model, and so on. If our position above—our speculation—is correct, we will also need to represent models as our users represent them. Each of these requirements may have a most appropriate model representation. For example, TEX format is good for displaying a model and perhaps not so good for executing it. A principal motivation for the embedded languages approach is the hope of efficiently allowing multiple representations of use in model management to coexist (and be interchangeable) in a single model management system.

The focus here is on a particular model representation technique called *embedded languages*. The technique has been developed and implemented in a working, delivered model management system [Bhargava et al., 1991; Bhargava and Kimbrough, 1990; Bieber and Kimbrough, 1990, 1992; Bhargava et al., 1989]. What we have to say here presents an argument for the expressive power of the technique. Further, although the practicality of the technique is still to be determined conclusively, the fact that an existing system has been built using it is certainly encouraging.

Here, in an itemized nutshell, is what we want to claim about embedded languages for model management:

- A clear, rigorous, and computational sense can be given to the notion of "taking the LoT hypothesis seriously" in a computer application. We would do this through a modeling and programming technique we called *embedded languages* [Bhargava and Kimbrough, 1990].
- Taking the embedded languages point of view on model management yields a representational technique that both has great expressive power and is natural, given the sorts of things we want to say and infer in a model management system.
- Taking the embedded languages point of view on model management is also practical. Useful model management systems can be built from it. We refer the reader to papers that describe TEFA, an implemented, delivered, and used (but hardly complete) model management system that was designed and built using embedded languages [Bhargava et al., 1988; Bhargava and Kimbrough, 1990; Bieber and Kimbrough, 1989, 1990; Bhargava et al., 1989].

All this, if true, would nicely contribute a morsel of support to the LoT hypothesis, but we already told that story sufficiently for present purposes. To some details, briefly.

There is something paradoxical about the idea of embedding one language, call it $L_{\downarrow}$, within another language, call it $L^{\uparrow}$. It is our intention that formulas—either in $L_\downarrow$ or in $L^\uparrow$—are to be interpreted propositionally. These formulas have truth values. It is also our intention that the $L^\uparrow$ be a language of first-order logic (FOL). Yet in any straightforward view, first-order logic does not permit predication applied to truth-bearing formulas. For example, $F(a)$, where $a =$ Bob and $F(x) = x$ is tall, is a well-formed formula in FOL, with a an individual constant and F a predicate of arity 1. But $G(F(a))$, where G is any predicate at all, is not a legal expression in FOL. How then is this sort of embedding to be done? The purpose of this section is to indicate briefly the answer to this question [Bhargava and Kimbrough, 1990].

To begin, we need to consider three languages: $L^\uparrow$, the embedding language; $L_\downarrow$, the embedded language; and $L^*_\downarrow$, the language—called the target language—modeled by the embedding. Here, $L^*_\downarrow$ will be sentence logic, $L^\uparrow$ an FOL language—and $L_\downarrow$ will have a dual interpretation, to be explained shortly. First, however, it is important to note two things: (1) Although $L^*_\downarrow$ may be a formal language itself, the embedded languages technique does not require that target languages be formalized; (2) it is quite possible to embed several languages in $L^\uparrow$, that is, to have several distinct $L_\downarrow$ languages in a single system. Such a situation would allow, for example, translation rules between $L_\downarrow$ languages to be stated in $L^\uparrow$, and in fact this is done. In the present context, we can envision one $L_\downarrow$ language representing a model mathematically and another $L_\downarrow$ language representing the same model as a user represents it, that is, in one of the LoT-style theories discussed above. The role of $L^\uparrow$ is, at least in part, to exploit the two complementary representations in favor of conveying effectively insight-provoking information to the user.

A simple framework is useful in explaining the basic notions. Consider three related languages, called $L^*_\downarrow$, $L_\downarrow$, and $L^\uparrow$. $L^\uparrow$ is the embedding language; it is completely formalized. (TEFA—the model management language mentioned above—is an example of a particular embedding language.) $L_\downarrow$ is the embedded language. It, too, is completely formalized and has a full interpretation as an independent (of $L^\uparrow$) language. The purpose of an $L_\downarrow$ language is (normally) to *partially* formalize and represent the target language. $L^*_\downarrow$ may or may not be formalized, is normally some variety of natural language, may be formalized in part, and is usually quite complex. In the context of model management, $L^*_\downarrow$ is the (natural and man-made) language we use to represent, discuss, and reason about mathematical models. The idea behind the (standard) EML approach is to develop an appropriate $L_\downarrow$. The motivating idea behind the embedded languages approach is to embed one or more $L_\downarrow$ languages in an $L^\uparrow$ language, which is itself an EML. Further, $L^\uparrow$ can be used to represent information about expressions (formulas and terms) in an $L_\downarrow$ language, including, for example, rules for translating one embedded ($L_\downarrow$) EML into another.

From a logical point of view, a simple idea underlies the entire approach: Specify an alphabet and rules of formulation such that the resulting expressions can be interpreted both in $L^\uparrow$ and in $L_\downarrow$, and such that precise translation rules can be given between $L_\downarrow$ and $L^*_\downarrow$, and between $L_\downarrow$ and $L^\uparrow$.

For example, consider the embedding of a sentence logic language ($L_\downarrow$) in a predicate logic language ($L^\uparrow$) [Bhargava and Kimbrough, 1990]. The well-formed expressions can be interpreted as well-formed *formulas* in $L_\downarrow$ (sentence logic) and as well-formed *terms* in $L^\uparrow$ (predicate logic). Formulas have truth values and terms do not; they refer while formulas do not. Yet a single well-formed expression can be interpreted either way. As an $L_\downarrow$ expression it is a formula, while as an $L^\uparrow$ expression it is a term. The entire scheme rests upon an elaborate, and we think elegant, pun. Our suggestion, which we cannot further substantiate here for lack of space, is that this approach is expressively and computationally powerful enough to represent essentially anything that needs to be said about models, including, for example, what their mathematical structures are, how users conceive of them, and how these two representations are related.

Discussion. Not everything we want from a model management system requires intelligence. Formatting data for input to a particular solver, calling the appropriate routines to get a series of models executed, and many other required functions are quite properly seen as the sort of low-level, bookkeeping activities at which standard computers excel using standard programming techniques. By exploiting procedural attachment and the possibility for fine-grained representation in an embedded language, we believe there need be no undue computational burden due to undertaking a LoT/embedded language point of view. And there is much promise of significant benefit, especially, we conjecture, in the area of modeling users' mental models of problems and models of those problems.

Model management is aimed at providing automated support to modelers and model users throughout all the major modeling life cycle phases. These phases include the following:

1. Identification of the problem.
2. Formulation and specification of the model in some appropriate formalism (e.g., an algebraic statement).
3. Implementation of the model.
4. Validation of the model.
5. Data collection and analysis, pertinent to the particular problem at hand; determination of parameter values.
6. Model solution.
7. Interpretation and analysis of the solution.
8. Evaluation and modification of the model.

Although space does not permit a detailed discussion of these phases and their roles in model management, we believe that what can be achieved with a model management system must rely on proper representation of both models and information about them—particularly information about how users represent and think about models—that is required to perform the above functions. As argued above, this certainly suggests use of some sort of modeling language, especially if the LoT hypothesis is correct. Existing modeling languages, however, focus primarily on translation to and from one or more solvers [e.g., Fourer et al., 1987]. Essentially, they provide a formal representation for the models, but little or no information about the models. It is information of this latter sort that we believe is key to developing advanced, intelligent, general-purpose model management systems. And it is information of this latter sort that is quite naturally expressed in the context of an embedded language.

With the possible exception of phase 6 above (model solution), it is easy to conceive of useful features that could exploit knowledge of how users represent and think about models. The challenge—of conceiving and cataloging such features, of organizing them into a proper framework, of figuring out a theory for how to implement them, and of engaging in the relevant investigative programming and experimentation—can surely keep a lot of us busy for a long time. Such work, at least when based on the LoT hypothesis and the embedded languages stance, promises to have something significant to offer with respect to cognitive science, artificial intelligence, and the philosophy of the mind, not to mention the employment of models on problems in management science. That fact can surely provide the motivation and sustaining excitement for such an extended effort.

Designing DSS interfaces

Javier Lerch and Michael J. Prietula

Computer-based decision models, no matter how well constructed, must be easy to understand, to use, and to modify. This requires that the user interface is designed by taking into account our present knowledge of human problem-solving capabilities. This chapter briefly describes a theoretical foundation on how humans interact with intelligent machines in complex problem-solving situations—but not on *how to design* interfaces for specific situations. In this chapter we propose a cognitive view of DSS human-computer interaction that offers a unified perspective. By "unified" we mean that the view can (and should) be applied to DSS interface design across all types of tasks or applications.

The perspective taken is that one of the primary objectives of a DSS, such as a model management system, is to deliver a tool (or set of tools) that supports humans in decision-making tasks by facilitating the manipulation of task-specific knowledge. Much of the effort in this direction has been exerted by researchers proposing and building such systems using a variety of techniques [Blanning, 1987; Bonczek et al., 1981; Elam and Konsynski, 1987; Holsapple, 1987; Sprague and Watson, 1975]. The rationale behind these systems is that in order to truly support decision making, computer systems need to engage task-specific knowledge as represented by "models." Our perspective characterizes computer models as knowledge structures that can be translated into humanlike knowledge so that interaction can be facilitated.

There are two implications in this perspective. First, the cognitive mechanisms used to explain the events and representations occurring in decision support activities must be equivalent to those underlying general cognition. Second, these cognitive mechanisms must account for phenomena that arise from using model management systems over extended periods of time—including learning and error behavior. Although interesting attempts at viewing the psychological perspectives of model management systems have appeared [Liang, 1988a, 1988b], such approaches have not brought to bear a strong view of cognition and thus have not articulated a perspective that is sufficiently robust to explain and predict human behavior across model management implementations or tasks.

Research in human-computer interaction has established that the design of any interface requires decisions at four levels of analysis: the conceptual, semantic, syntactic and lexical levels [Foley and Van Dam, 1982; Moran, 1981]. At the conceptual level the designer selects objects, their properties, and the operations of these objects. For example, the designer of a text editor explicitly or implicitly selects a set of operations such as *delete*, *insert*, and *transpose* that will act on a predefined set of text editing objects, such as a paragraph or a word, that are bounded by a set of properties. Obviously the selection of object, properties, and operations has a major impact on the decisions to be made at the other three levels. The semantic level defines the meanings to be conveyed between the operator and the application software, while the syntactic level addresses the structure of input and output and displayed information. In our text editing example, the meanings of the specific commands needed to implement the set of operations and their priority are defined at the semantic level, while the structure of the language (e.g., commands may be implemented as operation-object versus object-operation pairs) is addressed at the syntactic level. Another important decision at the syntactic level is how objects, such as a paragraph or a formatting command, will be displayed. Finally, the lexical level involves the design and choice of hardware and software features to implement the capabilities defined at the syntactic level.

In this section we will restrict ourselves to the discussion of the design of DSS interfaces at the conceptual level.* This isolates us from particular technologies and from the recurrent claims that advances in interface technology (both software and hardware) will solve or overcome the general problems of interacting with computer systems. For example, high-resolution bitmapped screens and direct manipulation capabilities were (once) announced as the solution to interaction problems. Similar expectations were harbored for built-in help systems and explanation capabilities. Unfortunately, complex support systems continue to be difficult to learn and confusing to users.

In our proposed approach, the design of the user interface requires an explicit conceptualization of the users and their tasks. Both the machine and the user are viewed as intelligent agents with well-defined architectural characteristics. The interaction between human and machine is characterized as the communication and coordination of knowledge between two intelligent agents.

Conceptualizing the user and the task. The conceptualization of the user and the task is accomplished by first realizing the flexibility of the user's computational mechanism—the mind. For many years, the study of how humans solved problems was based on the removal of knowledge from experimental tasks as a "nuisance" variable that had to be controlled out in order to find the true, unvarying mechanisms of human cognition. However, experimental work in both psychology and computer science provided both data and theory that supported the view that the human mind was extremely flexible and malleable. Furthermore, it was concluded that the role knowledge played in task performance was not peripheral, but essential. Explicit studies of expertise then evolved, focusing exclusively on the acquisition and refinement of knowledge in complex problem solving, which cast knowledge into the central role in interpreting the results and implications of experiments.

Perspectives of human-computer interaction understandably paralleled these developments. For many years, these perspectives were based on the view of the "common man" in which averages and ranges of psychophysical properties were extensively investigated. Data on the effects of such stimuli as flicker rates, screen colorings, and data presentation alternatives on thousands of subjects were accumulated and much was learned about specific aspects of perception, memory, and reasoning. However, the interesting conclusions drawn were insufficient in effectively guiding all of the considerations required for acceptable interfaces. What soon became apparent was the dominant role that

---

* Design decisions at the other three levels are common to all computer-based systems and are presently the subject of ongoing research [Bonczek et al., 1981; Gardner and Christie, 1987; Hartson, 1985; Hartson and Hix, 1988; Helander, 1988].

knowledge would play. Therefore, two general perspectives of interface engineering were thus called for:

- *Human engineering* addresses the species-specific properties of the user, in terms of psychophysical (e.g., screen color), psychomotor (e.g., mouse devices), or psychocognitive (e.g., short-term memory span) considerations.
- *Cognitive engineering* addresses the task-specific aspects of the situation considering the knowledge of the user and the task itself, as well as the underlying behavior of the cognitive architecture at what Newell and Simon refer to as the "knowledge level" [Simon, 1978].

It is this latter effort to which we direct our discussion.

One may initially wonder if the recent advent of sophisticated model management invalidates the design issues of interfaces; that is, the important considerations are either moot ("this interface problem has been solved") or inconsequential ("this interface problem is different"). We do not believe this to be the case; rather, we believe it adds new difficulties to the design. This is especially true with the more ambitious decision support proposals such as the hyperknowledge environment presented in the section "The Hyperknowledge Environment of Model Management Systems." In such an environment the decision support system is "regarded as an extension of a decision-maker's own innate knowledge management capabilities." The user navigates through the knowledge in the system in order to solve a problem (i.e., to make a decision). The system was characterized as being a general problem processor that exploits the particularities of the knowledge in each specific task with the help of the user. Therefore, we may conclude that an intimate understanding of the problem-solving process is required. A similar characterization of the computer system is presented. We call it the machine processor, and it is composed of the problem processing system (PPS) and the knowledge system (KS), as described in the hyperknowledge environment. In this chapter we extend the perspective by including the user (the human processor) as part of the problem-solving architecture and by characterizing the interaction between human and machine as the communication and coordination of two intelligent general problem-solving agents. (A similar perspective derives from the work of Runciman and Hammond [Runciman and Hammond, 1986], who argue that the software engineer—while building the program that runs in the computer—is at the same time implicitly specifying the user program.)

The view we propose also addresses the importance of learning (the accumulation and organization of knowledge) by the two agents in the design of the interface. Our perspective is based on a large research effort jointly involving Carnegie Mellon University, the University of Southern

California, and the University of Michigan. In particular, this project is exploring the specification of a problem space computational model capable of exhibiting general intelligence [Laird et al., 1984, 1987]. Based on this general problem-solving architecture, we propose that the interaction between the human processor and the machine processor during the decision-making process can be described as the communication of knowledge components as defined by the architecture and the coordination of problem-solving activities between the two agents.

The framework upon which the intelligent agent is constructed is a computational mechanism capable of manipulating symbolic structures in a manner that is consistent with the requirements called for, as we have noted, in Newell and Simon's physical symbol system hypothesis [Newell and Simon, 1975]. In particular, it relies on three main concepts: task environment, problem space, and search control.

A task environment refers to "an environment coupled with a goal, problem, or task—one for which the motivation of the subject is assumed" [Newell and Simon, 1972, p. 55]. It is the problem as presented to the problem solver and viewed by an "omniscient observer" [Simon, 1978]. In order to attempt to solve a problem, the problem solver must create an internalized representation of the task environment—problem spaces. A problem space can be envisioned (abstractly) as a set of nodes representing various attainable knowledge states with one or more distinguished states representing the solution to the problem—the goal. Problems are solved by search in the spaces; furthermore, this search is accomplished by a set of procedures comprising search control mechanisms. These search control mechanisms (i.e., search control knowledge) engage and monitor problem spaces, states, and operators.

Learning, the acquisition of skill in cognitive tasks, involves increasingly appropriate adaptations of the cognitive mechanism to perform those tasks [Prietula and Feltovich, 1990; Simon, 1978]. In particular, three adaptations appear to be quite important: the formation of the appropriate problem space(s), search control knowledge, and operators.

When little is known about a particular (and complex) problem, then neither the problem spaces configured nor the search control knowledge available afford much power for solving the problem. General (i.e., less task-specific) methods must then be invoked for representing and searching the problem space—these are the weak methods described by Newell [Newell, 1969], such as generate and test, progressive deepening, iterative deepening, best-first search, exhaustive maximization, analogy by implicit generalization, and hill climbing. Knowledge-lean problem-solving situations are those in which weak methods may be the initial (and perhaps only) ones brought to bear. These methods produce behaviors that are correspondingly simple, as little task-relevant knowledge is available to exploit aspects of the task environment to reduce the problem-solving effort.

The acquisition of knowledge regarding tasks within a particular domain leads to the modification of both the problem space and the search control knowledge, which allows more effective and efficient search (i.e., problem solving). These strong methods are based on components reflecting adaptation to the task in such a manner as to incorporate forms that improve the level of problem-solving ability. By exploiting regularities in the task environment, such methods produce behavior that is more specialized, but more appropriate for solving the types of problems at hand.

The mechanism for learning proposed in this model is based on the concept of chunking [Laird et al., 1984]. Achieving a goal in a particular problem space is dependent upon the selection of the appropriate operator sequence which, when applied, generates a state that satisfies the termination criteria. Figure 4 shows the basic problem-solving mechanism. However, problem solving is not always straightforward; rather, difficulties occur within the problem space mechanism. Collectively, these difficulties are referred to as impasses. When impasses occur, goals are established to resolve the impasse. Impasses may arise, for example, when selection among operators is inconclusive, because either no operators are distinguished (i.e., through explicit rejection or non-proposal) or multiple operators are distinguished and perhaps are even in conflict. A new (different) problem space is then defined to resolve the new subgoal resulting from the impasse. If difficulties occur in this problem space, another subgoal would be created, and so forth. Once a subgoal has been achieved, the impasse in the superspace (i.e., the problem-solving context in which the subgoal was defined) is resolved and problem-solving behavior in the superspace can continue.

The deliberation which eventually achieved the subgoal, however, is not wasted. When the problem solver again encounters the initial conditions that generated the impasse, an impasse does not occur because search control knowledge has been added to the particular problem space which detects the initial conditions and immediately engages the (previously deliberated) knowledge—that is, it has formed a chunk. Figure 5 depicts the impasse-subgoal-chunking sequence in problem spaces. Though a basically simple learning mechanism, chunking is a sufficient learning mechanism to account for the development of strong methods and, consequently, all deliberate (and derivative automatic) cognition [Laird et al., 1984, 1987].

One can view the underlying form of knowledge representation for all aspects of the framework as that of a production system. All knowledge of a task—goals, operators, and so forth—is cast as production rules.*

---

* The problem space computational model is, in fact, partially instantiated in a system called Soar based on the production rule formalism. Soar has demonstrated that the proposed architecture exhibits general intelligence in a variety of domains [Rosenbloom et al., 1989].

1. Select a problem space, P, and initialize it.

2. Select an initial state for P.

3. While no goal-test is statisfied

    3.1 Propose operators to apply to the current state;
    3.2 Select a single operator as better than the rest
    3.3 Apply the operator to the state.

Figure 4. Basic problem-solving mechanism.

As a particular impasse is resolved, several chunks (as productions) are produced, where the antecedent conditions identify relevant aspects of the situation (i.e., elements in working memory) which held prior to the impasse condition and are relevant to the resolution. The consequent part of the produced chunks reflects elements to be retrieved from long-term memory that reflect the resultant of the application of the production—the augmentation of the state and new working memory elements [Laird et al., 1986; Rosenbloom and Newell, 1986].

Finally, an important implication of this perspective is the problem space hypothesis: All symbolic goal-oriented behavior occurs as search in problem spaces [Newell and Rosenbloom, 1981]. What this means is

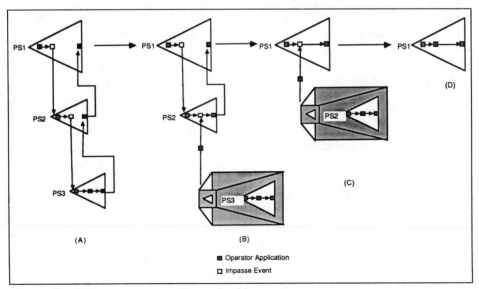

Figure 5. Depiction of impasse-subgoal-chunking sequence.

that deliberation of any kind can be cast in terms of the architecture described. Therefore, tasks such as "reasoning," "judgment," and "decision making" are all addressed with the same cognitive devices: goals, problem spaces, search control, operators, impasses, subgoaling, and chunking. Furthermore, this approach embodies verbal, auditory, tactile, and visual events. The consequence of this view is pivotal for DSS. It implies that the mechanisms for describing problem-solving behavior are sufficient for describing *all* types of interaction with *all* types of decision support systems, including model management systems, whether they are verbal or graphical or whatever. The perceptual encoding of a screenful of objects (e.g., an icon-driven model construction environment) or a screenful of words (e.g., a verbally expressed modeling language) defines different problem spaces, but they are handled by the same underlying mechanisms. Differences found in behavior or performance are thus based on differences in the available knowledge to be brought to bear on problem solving as defined by the relevant problem spaces and search control. An "apparently simple" manipulation of moving from icons to words, or from tables to graphs, is a significant change in the task environment and, consequently, in the problem spaces available to contribute.

As Allen Newell often points out, facts must come from the theory, not the theorist. As such, the theoretical foundations to drive research and development in DSS have been forged.

A problem-solving view of DSS interaction. The two problem-solving agents (human and machine) are viewed as having a similar problem-solving architecture (as described above) realized as a collection of potentially interacting problem spaces, although the characteristics of their architectural components are obviously different. The interaction at the conceptual level between the two agents can be discussed as consisting of two different tasks: communication and coordination. (An elaboration of this section in terms of group decision support systems can be found elsewhere [Prietula et al., 1990].) By considering each of the constructs of the problem-solving architecture in terms of its possible function in both communication and coordination, we can begin to describe the generic components of interaction to which attention should be paid.

Communication between agents. There are three major forms of communication which occur between the two agents: goals, results, and knowledge. The communication of goals can be either the result of explicit task assignment or the result of an impasse. All goals are computationally the result of impasses. For example, the initial goal make-a-decision (regarding some issue or task) results from the incapability of the human agent to make an immediate decision after facing a decision-making situation. The next step may be to select a problem space; for example, the decision-maker may need to select between the problem space characterize-decision or select-mathematical-tool, or may decide to communicate the goal to the other agent and wait for the result. When a goal is received, the problem-solving apparatus of the agent is activated in order to solve the particular problem. If the knowledge is available to directly achieve that goal, then the result of the resolution is communicated back to the sender.

Goals and results are two objects that are commonly communicated in standard interfaces: One agent states a goal and the other agent responds with the result as a consequence of that communication. Of course, this direct interaction is possible only if all the knowledge for achieving the goal is available to the processing agent. This is *not* the general case in complex decision-making situations; therefore, impasses occur. However, if each agent is intelligent, there is an additional class of objects that can be communicated—knowledge.

Knowledge as we refer to it includes knowledge in defining problem spaces and/or operators, search control knowledge, and structures produced by previous impasse resolutions (i.e., problem spaces, operators, search control knowledge, etc.). Consequently, when an impasse occurs, the interface mechanism should allow and encourage the two agents to exchange objects that may resolve the present impasse by setting up a new problem space. A similar approach is suggested by Dos Santos and Holsapple [Dos Santos and Holsapple, 1989]: The exchange of goals and results is called support-oriented interaction, while the exchange of knowledge is labeled problem-oriented interaction. Again, the advantage of our perspective is that both types of communication occur within a unified view of the problem-solving process under a single mechanism—search through problem spaces, universal subgoaling, and chunking.

Coordination between agents. The second task in the interaction is for the two agents to decide how to coordinate their activities—how to assign tasks. Coordination can be seen as another problem-solving task in which its problem space has information about strategies for coordination, knowledge about the domain-specific tasks, and knowledge about the knowledge possessed by the two agents. Obviously the coordination problem can only be solved through the same mechanisms available for other problem-solving tasks: specification of problem spaces, selection and application of operators, chunking, and so forth. Through chunking we expect the two agents to exhibit learning about how to coordinate their activities by accumulating knowledge about each other, knowledge about their own domain-specific knowledge, and knowledge about successful coordination strategies. Chunking should account for the initial rapid learning so characteristic in humans when interacting with software systems. If this mechanism can be embedded (at least partially) in the machine, then adaptive interfaces can be realized in knowledge-intensive tasks such as those intended to be supported by DSS.

Implications for DSS interfaces. Up to this point, we have assumed that the human and machine agents are architecturally identical. This is obviously not the case since they differ in the parameters of their architectural components. For example, human processors have a limited capacity for storing dynamic information. Working memory capacity is usually estimated to be about three or four "slots" [Baddeley, 1981], while the machine processor capacity for storing dynamic information may be considered infinite for any practical purposes. Besides architectural differences, there are important knowledge differences. For example, human processors are currently more proficient in the processing of natural language given their sophisticated organization of linguistic knowledge, which has not been fully reproduced in machine processors. Coordination strategies that exploit architectural and knowledge differences between the two agents should be considered the most promising. For example, keeping track of the problem spaces, states, and operators already used or visited (the problem-solving trace) should be assigned to the machine agent. On the other hand, the initial formulation of the decision-making problem is very likely to be assigned to the human agent because of its heavy requirements on language understanding and world knowledge. Of course, it is possible that this last assignment may be more problematic in the far future if machines can gain proficiency in the acquisition and utilization of this knowledge. Research is under way to provide natural language capabilities to the instantiation of the problem space computational model [Lewis et al., 1989; Rosenbloom et al., 1989]. One might envision an instantiation would be that of a personalized "digital caricature" which resides on your machine and serves as an ombudsman that can be tuned to your personality and your skills. All interactions are made to (through) the caricature, and it learns to anticipate and monitor these interactions.

It is important to note that we do not expect the machine to execute all problem-solving tasks using only the general mechanism described above (search through problem spaces). But we do expect that its interface component will be able to translate any problem-solving behavior into a trace of a search in a problem space. Through this translation, the machine processor can explain results by having an explicit representation of problem-solving strategies [Swartout, 1983]. This, of course, facilitates communication by affording explanation capabilities; but more importantly, it develops the necessary self-knowledge (metacognition) needed for improving coordination.

Our cognitive perspective for DSS interaction calls for two complementary developments needed for a systematic design of DSS interfaces at the conceptual level: (1) to build models of the use, and (2) to build an interface for the machine processor that describes problem solving and learning as search in problem spaces. The first development is very much in line with the tradition in human-computer interaction of building predictive user models. An early example is "cognitive complexity theory" presented by Kieras and Polson [Kieras and Polson, 1985]. Their emphasis was on modeling users' learning and executing procedures such as text editing. A more recent example that uses the same problem-solving architecture presented here is by Young, Green, and Simon [Young et al., 1989]. Their focus is primarily on building user models for knowledge-intensive tasks. Their emphasis is on helping the designer to conceptualize how the user interacts with the system [p. 17]:

> Interface designers are frequently urged to "consider the interface from the user's viewpoint," or some such recommendation. While that is good advice, and may well be accepted as such by the designer, it falls short of helping the designer know what actually to do. But to pose the question "What instructions must we give in order for someone to know how to use the interface?" provides the designer with concrete and practical means of mentally stepping into the user's shoes.

They call their approach programmable user models. Their project aims to force the designer to specify explicitly the knowledge and capabilities required in a user who intends to interact with a given system.

To our knowledge, there are no examples of the second type of development for model management (or DSS in general). This is not surprising since model management systems themselves have only been recently explored. But as stated at the beginning of this chapter, the success of these systems in managing and organizing knowledge does not assure us that they can actually be used by their intended users. Besides all the traditional difficulties in interfacing with computers, model management systems require communication of knowledge between the human and machine processors and demand that the two agents coordinate their activities effectively by acquiring knowledge about themselves and each other. We believe that having a unifying view of their problem-solving activities should stimulate the creation of interfaces that support the communication and coordination needed for effective decision support.

Conclusion

Model management is a subdiscipline of decision support systems and like its parent discipline, it is undergoing a metamorphosis in response to two stimuli. The first stimulus is the increasing power of the technology on which it is based—that is, the technology of information processing and communication—and the second is its successes in solving interesting problems and the consequent appearance of fresh unsolved problems. One of these problems is implementation. With a few recent exceptions, most work on model management has been theoretical and has focused on the representation and manipulation of causal relationships, and not on the implementation of theory and the consequent need to consider questions of computational feasibility and economic trade-off. Although interesting topics in model management theory continue to be investigated, more thought is now being given to questions of implementation.

More thought is also being given to the scope of model management and its relation to its parent discipline. In the past, it has been possible to arrive at interesting theoretical results in model management by concentrating on the representation and manipulation of one type of information—causal relationships—without giving explicit consideration to the management of other types of information used for decision support. These other information types—formatted data, text, voice, visual images, and expert knowledge—have been explored by a variety of specialists, each of whom has found it useful to direct his attention to a single information source and largely to exclude the others. We expect this to stop, not because there is no more progress to be made in any of these areas, but because we have reached the point at which interesting problems are beginning to appear at the boundaries. An example is the integration of formatted data and expert knowledge, which is being explored by workers in the growing area of expert database systems. A similar field of expert modelbase systems (for constructing, integrating, validating, maintaining, and interpreting models) is beginning to appear and will probably be a major area of research in this decade [Blanning, 1987b].

We expect that a salient component of this area will be experience-based problem solving, in which a decision-maker "solves new problems by adapting solutions that were used to solve old problems" [Riesbeck and Schank, 1989]. With regard to model management and information management more generally, the problem of interest is the identification and integration of models and other information types to solve nonroutine problems—for example, to respond to emergencies or crises and to exploit unanticipated opportunities. People solve these problems in part by deduction from first principles (i.e., from a knowledge of the problem domain coupled with simple logical rules and heuristics) but largely by recalling and making productive use of previous problem-solving experiences. This would require that model management systems maintain libraries of successful and unsuccessful problem-solving efforts and present interface procedures for identifying appropriate analogies in the form of models and other sources of information relevant to a particular problem.

Finally, of the many advances in information processing technology that may have an impact on model management, we note four. First, the continually increasing power/cost ratio of hardware will lead to an increase in the development of interactive models having the complexity now reserved for batch processing. This in turn will transform the current "black box" view of models into a "translucent box" view, in which a greater emphasis will be placed on the assembly of model components by end users. Second, distributed model management systems will not only make possible cost savings, as is now the case with distributed database systems, but will allow multiple versions of the same generic model to be adapted to the needs of separate users. Third, CASE tools will be developed to aid in the construction of large-scale models from higher level code and from reusable modules such as data objects. Fourth, the trend to custom chips may give rise to the availability of model-specific chips (e.g., chips for linear programming, rule-based backward chaining, and, of course, neural networks) and thus to adaptive hardware architectures for model management.

Workshop discussion: Model management systems

Discussants: In his comments at the workshop, Gadi Ariav suggested that the model management area needed a framework. He felt that the team had emphasized some important themes:

- a more general concept of the nature of models,
- an understanding of how models evolve,
- the need for an understanding of the modeling process, and
- the recursive nature of models—we need models of models, and so on.

Some important issues that were not covered by the teams include

- a comparative analysis of different approaches to model management,
- a recognition of the temporal aspects of models, and
- retrospective analysis of past judgments.

The second discussant, Marvin Manheim, said that there was an urgent need for a research agenda in the model management field. He felt that there was a tension between a rational model perspective (that models are simply logical entities) and an alternative perspective in which both the machine and the human processor operate on and communicate images of the real-world problem. What is needed is to understand the set of operators needed to change these images and to develop the control logic to manage the interaction. He thought that software such as Lotus Agenda that contained semi-intelligent agents (agents with fixed rules) provided a start for such a semantic network. What was really necessary was to develop intelligent agents that are able to learn about the symbiotic environment between users and the DSS system. Finally, he suggested that "image management" was a better name for the field than model management.

In his discussion of the model management presentations, Nick Vitilari distinguished four categories of models:

- models that define real-world systems,
- models in the mind of the decision-maker,
- models that coordinate the intersection between the decision-maker and the system, and
- metamodels of the models in the DSS and about the organizational environment.

Remarking that the research agenda in model management is complex, dynamic, and at an exploratory stage of development, he saw a need to research a number of different approaches using multiple paradigms. The first research challenge was to cope with the complexity of such systems which comes from three sources:

- the difficulty of model specification and validation,
- the need to understand and coordinate both the model of the real system and the mental processing models of users, and
- the need to incorporate multiple levels of distributed human and artificial decision-makers and the difficulty of predicting the behavior of such a distributed system.

The second research challenge was to manage invention and diversity. Noting that models are arbitrary artifacts of individual modelers, he foresaw a proliferation of models and concomitant difficulties in managing them and understanding good modeling practice. He saw a need for empirical research on how models are used and evolve over time.

Summary of electronic meeting session. The electronic brainstorming session that followed the model management presentation raised the following issues and questions:

1. The need for the intelligent support system to have an understanding of both the human users and the organizational environment.

2. The need for better definitions of model management concepts and for frameworks that could relate model management to the other ISDP areas.

3. The need for reliable models of human cognition—"to know how humans think before we understand how to help them do it."

4. The need to understand complex multiperson decision processes in the real world.

5. The need to understand structure: task structure, problem-solving structure, and the structure of interactions in multiperson decision making.

6. The need to understand how organizational culture shapes models and is in turn shaped by models.

Some researchers expressed surprise at the scope of model management and saw it as a foundation for decision support systems, while others professed a lack of understanding and uncertainty concerning the area. Some other issues over which there were differences of opinion are stated as questions below:

1. Is our knowledge of the cognitive processes of individuals useful when it comes to understanding group processes?

2. Is good research an end in itself or must it have practical utility?

3. Is too much fuss being made over the need for definitions and frameworks at this stage of our knowledge?

Chapter 8

Research Challenges

Benn R. Konsynski and Edward A. Stohr

The preceding chapters provide a diverse set of views on the role of information systems in supporting decision processes. These views differ in the themes chosen by the teams and on matters of research approach and philosophy. Again, we emphasize that the ISDP teams took deep vertical slices of the total subject matter. A number of important topics (such as system implementation and collaborative work) were not treated at all or only in passing. Nevertheless, the previous chapters contain a rich variety of ideas that appear to be fertile avenues for future research, together with a large number of specific research suggestions. In this chapter, we identify several major themes and research challenges that emerge from the work of the teams and the sometimes lively discussion at the workshop. To avoid the confusion between ends and means that often creeps into discussions of research, we will discuss only research questions and directions in this chapter. The final chapter of the book will contain some suggestions on research methodologies and approaches.

As Kuhn has pointed out, progress in science is often marked by a paradigm shift followed by a period in which scientists engage in "normal science" making research contributions that fit the mode and directions indicated as important by the newly accepted paradigm [Kuhn, 1970]. Progress is made, but after the paradigm has been explored for some time it is time for a new direction. A strong sentiment from the ISDP workshop was that the DSS paradigm needed to be replaced by a new paradigm that would provide new directions and methodologies for research. In this section, we list, without comment, several trend-breaking and trend-setting ideas from the workshop. Only time will tell whether or not these provide the basis for a new research paradigm for the DSS field. In the remainder of the book, we fill in the details and attempt a synthesis of these direction-setting ideas around the concepts of decision processes that were introduced in Chapter 2.

To our mind, these were among the more important ideas for reassessing the DSS field that emerged from the workshop:

- Enlarge the decision-making paradigm of previous DSS research to encompass a broader array of decision activities in organizations and to break with the exclusive focus on decision choice models that characterizes much previous DSS research.
- Focus on understanding the underlying processes used by individuals, groups, and organizations to make decisions and carry out their business activities. That is, rather than simply catalog the results of technology interventions, try to determine why those results should be expected.
- Consider the total man-machine system in its context rather than focus only on hardware and software functionality. Subjective and objective factors jointly determine the effectiveness of IT.
- Broaden the scope of DSS research to include all the determinants of decisions, all forms of support for decisions, and both hard and soft information.
- Consciously use multiple philosophical views of the world as a way of increasing understanding. For example, compare and contrast conclusions that might result from adopting rationalist, bureaucratic, or political theories of organizations—or from logical positivist versus interpretivist research paradigms.
- Establish consensus on imaginative and challenging goals for research that will clearly demonstrate significant contributions to both research and practice.
- Develop interdisciplinary long-term programs of research around agreed-upon research themes in order to accumulate usable research knowledge.

The remainder of the chapter is organized as follows. In the next section, we provide a brief overview of the work of the five research teams and attempt to pull together some important research themes from the output of the teams and the workshop discussion. Then we build on parts of the research framework of Chapter 2 to build a more comprehensive framework that seems to capture many of the issues raised during the ISDP process. Neither the framework in Chapter 2 nor the framework outlined here should be considered definitive. One of the major conclusions from the discussions at the workshop was that, at least for a time, the field would probably be best served by a number of different frameworks. In fact, some alternative frameworks are contained in the previous chapters. We devote the final section to a discussion of the major directions and conclusions from the various projects and the research framework. We have avoided the temptation to provide a long laundry list of specific research questions. For these, the reader is referred to the chapters themselves and to their summaries of workshop discussions.

Overview of ISDP research

In this section, we revisit Chapters 3 through 7, summarizing the major issues addressed by the teams and the discussion sessions. We conclude each section with some suggestions for research directions. The final section of this chapter will draw together the common themes and discuss areas that we feel need further attention.

Behavioral decision theory and DSS. In Chapter 3, Elam, Jarvenpaa, and Schkade develop a tightly reasoned approach to interdisciplinary research involving DSS and behavioral decision making (BDM). The focus of the research program is on understanding the decision-making behavior that occurs as an individual uses a computer-based system as an aid in decision making. The objectives are both to build knowledge and to improve DSS design.

The authors first provide a brief history of DSS and BDM research and describe the differences in the approaches used by the two fields. Empirical DSS researchers have been primarily concerned with the impacts of DSS in general, and of specific DSS features such as presentation formats, on decision-making performance. Thus, their work has generally been prescriptive and focused on performance (output-oriented). In addition, until recently at least, DSS work has not been strongly grounded in theory. As a result, we still do not have robust design principles for designing DSS. On the other hand, BDM research explicitly seeks to understand the processes used by humans when performing cognitive tasks such as prediction, making probability estimates, and heuristic problem solving. Theories of cognition have been developed by observing deviations of human decision making from theoretical norms, or by building computer models of heuristic problem-solving behavior. More recently, BDM research has begun to consider noncognitive factors such as mood and motivation on decision behavior. Thus, BDM research has been oriented toward understanding decision processes and building theory; that is, it is descriptive and process-oriented. In contrast, DSS research has been prescriptive and output-oriented. While the two fields are different in motivation and style, they can benefit greatly from an active collaboration. DSS technology provides opportunities for BDM researchers, and DSS researchers can draw on the methods and knowledge that have been accumulated by BDM research.

Elam et al. advocate an interdisciplinary program of research involving two different research perspectives: (1) how existing IT affects decision-making behavior (IT → DM), and (2) how knowledge of decision-making behavior can be used to help design DSS (DM → IT). These two approaches are obviously intertwined with one approach feeding the other. Under the first approach, IT (DSS) already implemented in organizations can be studied to establish outcome-oriented measures of success and empirical facts ("stylized facts") about the effect of the DSS on such attributes of decision processes as decision time, learning achieved, and satisfaction of the decision-makers. Next, to aid generalization from this knowledge, this exploratory research should be followed by the development of theory to explain the observed effects. Under the second approach, the stylized facts and theories that have been accumulated about human decision-making behavior (especially dysfunctional behavior) are used to design DSS to improve human decision making (e.g., to eliminate or correct for known cognitive processing biases). The DSS constructed using this approach are then tested to confirm the knowledge and gain other insights. The authors include a list of established stylized facts that provide interesting possibilities for research. A number of important research opportunities are then listed under both the IT → DM and DM → IT perspectives.

Chapter 3 concludes with some interesting recommendations on how an interdisciplinary program of research in individual decision making and DSS should be conducted. Among other things, the team suggests that strong methodologies be developed along with both field and laboratory studies using real people. The collaborative effort suggested will help both BDM and DSS as the partners bring to the research a wide range of knowledge.

Group decision support systems. In Chapter 4, the GDSS group begins by providing a brief summary of the GDSS field including its objectives, history, current systems, and research efforts to date. Groups and meetings are pervasive in organizations, and groups meet for many purposes including socialization, information sharing, decision making, and conflict resolution. GDSS involves introducing the computer into the meeting room with one or more of the following objectives: (1) increasing the efficiency of the group meeting, (2) improving the quality of the discussion or outcome reached, (3) leverage—not only improving efficiency or outcomes, but using the IT intervention to fundamentally change the way that the meeting process operates. One form of leverage is obtained through parallelism of input and another through anonymity of the participants.

It should be noted that GDSS in this narrow sense constitutes only one area of the emerging field of group support. In the 2×2 table of Chapter 4, Figure 4, GDSS occupies only the "same-time, same-place" quadrant. Other technologies such as electronic mail systems, computer conferencing, and systems to support collaborative work occupy the other quadrants and are currently being researched and developed.

Specially designed "decision rooms" play an essential role in the GDSS field. The use of IT in these rooms is a comparatively recent development and comes in two forms. In a special-purpose facility, a single computer connected to a mainframe supports the group with the aid of large-screen displays. The technology is used mainly for information sharing. In a full-service facility, a number of networked PCs, from five to 20 or more, are made available for use by meeting participants. In addition to large-screen information sharing as in the special-purpose facilities, participants can access spreadsheet and database software (individual DSS), and, most importantly, they are linked electronically through GDSS software to each other and to a shared database. GDSS software supports group work by providing functions such as "electronic brainstorming" and automated voting. The GDSS concept is mainly a product of university research groups and has been tested primarily by means of laboratory experiments. The GDSS decision room concept is now being adopted by business, allowing more opportunities for field research and development.

Research to date in GDSS has involved software development, laboratory experiments, field studies, and hardware and facility development. As discussed in the chapter, Gray, Vogel, and Beauclair used the classification scheme of DSS variables proposed by Pinsonneault and Kraemer to define a set of variables to classify GDSS experimental conditions (see Table 5).

Next, the chapter discusses the major research problems in the GDSS field. It begins with a survey of what has been discovered to date from GDSS research. Interesting findings include the generally positive impacts of parallelism on group efficiency, of anonymity in increasing group participation, of good facility design on overall outcomes and satisfaction, of information sharing on performance, and so on. However, as pointed out in this section, these factors (and the many others discussed) may also have negative effects, leaving much room for research to give a better understanding of GDSS requirements and to guide application development. Major research problems include the need to get a better understanding of the information needs of groups; the effect of GDSS at the individual, group, and organizational levels; cross-cultural effects; hardware and software requirements; direct and indirect costs of using GDSS; and the critical success factors that need to be addressed for the successful implementation of GDSS in industry.

The chapter includes a section summarizing the findings of the GDSS team and gives specific recommendations and priorities for future work. The authors' recommended research priorities are (1) determine what groups actually do, (2) find ways in which leverage can be obtained, (3) standardize definitions of experiments, (4) conduct case/field studies of implementation, and (5) develop theory. Finally, the Appendix of Chapter 4 contains a list of research questions that summarize the team's thoughts on how GDSS research should proceed.

In our view, GDSS is an exciting extension of traditional DSS. An important research goal is to link GDSS to other group decision-making technologies and to other information system components. From a decision process viewpoint, GDSS is just one of a number of new management support tools that need to be integrated into the organizational decision support system.

Organizational decision support systems. Unlike individual and group DSS, organizational decision support systems (ODSS) is an emerging area of study that has not been clearly delineated by a large body of research. In Chapter 5, the ODSS team provides six different perspectives on ODSS that contribute to our understanding of what is involved. Each perspective starts with a definition of ODSS, derives a statement of requirements for ODSS, and then describes some technologies and research opportunities to satisfy these needs. Taking the union of these ideas and perspectives gives us a good idea of an emerging field of research that places IT in the context of organizational design.

Before summarizing the main themes of this chapter, we will discuss the question of the definition of ODSS since this to some extent colors our interpretation of the various contributions. There seem to be two conflicting views:

- an ODSS is a system designed to support organization-wide decisions, decisions involving many people, and decisions that are of great importance to the organization; or
- an ODSS is a system designed to support organizational (as opposed to individual or single-group) decision processes.

Given the emphasis in this book, it should come as no surprise that we embrace the latter view. We believe that this implies first the development of a sociotechnical architecture within the organization to support ongoing decision making, and second the idea that decisions evolve over time from a process involving cultural and political factors, as well as economic or rational factors.

Are there examples of ODSS in organizations? In our mind, the answer is yes—in a trivial sense every organization is an ODSS. A better question seems to be, "Are there examples of consciously designed ODSS in real organizations?" Again, we believe the answer is yes. Command and control systems in the armed services and in NASA are highly developed examples of ODSS for rigid, hierarchical organizations. In industry, the Frito-Lay executive support system [*New York Times*, 1990] is a much-published example of an ODSS that coordinates many members of the organization around a class of decisions focused on market feedback and response. Incidentally, these two examples reveal two dimensions that must be considered in discussions of ODSS—that organizational environment, purpose, and culture impact the kind of ODSS that is needed, and that there are different classes of decision processes in organizations that might be served by an ODSS. Both of these themes are evident in the contributions in Chapter 5.

Chapter 5 begins from a historical perspective. The area of ODSS is emerging at the present time both because the enabling technology, particularly in the communications area, is now available, and because of organizational needs in the face of a rapidly changing and turbulent environment. Organizations are becoming leaner, have fewer management levels, are relying less on rigid hierarchical structures and more on semiautonomous teams, and are extending their scope to include international operations. All of these developments give rise to increasing demands for information to help organizations react in a timely and coordinated fashion to rapid changes in their external environment.

In their section in Chapter 5, Swanson and Zmud discuss the role of ODSS in supporting distributed decision making. Traditionally, decision-making responsibility has been distributed hierarchically. Nowadays, however, to handle decision processes that cross organizational boundaries, "virtual positions" that may not exist formally on organization charts and may have only an ephemeral existence are being created. Examples are task forces, standing committees, and groups that engage in conferencing activities. The authors describe some strategies that may be useful in supporting distributed decision making performed by such teams, suggest that an ODSS should support the development of shared agendas and social networks, and propose a possible ODSS architecture.

In their section, Culnan and Gutek discuss four basic motivations that lead organizations to collect and store information. These are for use in specific problem-solving tasks, to create a "store" of information for anticipated or unanticipated use later on, to communicate across organizational subunits for the purpose of coordination and decision implementation, and to further political aims. These requirements give rise to a need for the ODSS to comprise a multiplicity of different kinds of information collection and dissemination entities including traditional DSS objects such as databases, models, and executive support systems, but also including environmental scanning units, libraries, public affairs departments, common access databases, bulletin boards, and so on.

In another section, Fedorowicz and Konsynski describe four basic types of system that comprise an ODSS architecture emphasizing the impact that each of these types has on organizational structure: (1) traditional information systems (structure enforcing), (2) "organization-wide systems" such as executive support systems (structure preserving), (3) "spanning systems" such as electronic mail systems that cross organizational boundaries (structure independent), and (4) systems that support "new organizational structures" such as teleconferencing systems that permit teams to be formed independent of geographic or traditional hierarchical relationships (structure transforming). For each class of system, they state some research questions and priorities.

Nunamaker, George, and Valacich, in their section, discuss the role of IT in supporting changes in the structure of organizations. In particular, they see three current trends that impact organization structure: (1) downsizing or reducing both the total number of people in the organization and the number of hierarchical layers, (2) the development of the teamwork concept, and (3) outsourcing or farming out functions that were formerly handled by the organization itself. They note that downsizing implies a need for intraorganizational communication, information filtering, and operational monitoring that are facilitated by current developments in communications systems, and software to support group work (groupware). The teamwork concept requires an emphasis on technologies to support intragroup communication, coordination, and decision making. The outsourcing trend requires an emphasis on interorganizational communication and coordination technologies. The matrix in Figure 2 of Chapter 5 relates various ODSS technologies to these requirements.

In their section, King and Star discuss the need to support decision processes at an organizational level which may differ qualitatively from those at the group and individual levels. In particular, organizational decision processes employ boundary objects and mechanisms for due process and articulation. Boundary objects are mutually recognized by different social worlds and permit communication between those two worlds. By due process is meant decision-making protocols (such as Robert's Rules of Order in group meetings) that make adequate provision for recognizing, gathering, and weighing evidence from conflicting sources and constituencies. Articulation is the process of facilitating, scheduling, and coordinating such decision processes. King and Star conclude by stating some requirements for ODSS to support organization-wide decision processes of this kind. They suggest, for example, that ODSS should preserve social context (in contrast to GDSS and e-mail systems, which tend to eliminate it) and that ODSS systems should employ boundary objects that help span different social worlds.

Applegate and Henderson introduce their section by listing a number of recent organization design proposals, all of which place an increased emphasis on teams and depend critically on information technology for their success. They propose a framework for ODSS that builds on previous DSS and GDSS research (see Figure 3 in Chapter 5). The model describes DSS along two dimensions, a technology hierarchy dimension, consisting of communications, data management, and process layers, and a functional dimension described in terms of three categories of functionality that are to be provided—production, coordination, and policy. To support multiple interacting teams, they emphasize the importance of the policy function "the procedures, standards, and guidelines that enable a firm to achieve portability of processes, data, and communications across organizational boundaries."

To summarize these contributions, an ODSS is seen as a purposeful, designed network of heterogeneous processing and communication units that support the organization's needs for coordination and decision making. In a sense, to design the ODSS is to design the nervous system for the organization. The policies and standards enable communication between subunits and direct the forms of processing and communication protocols that enable communication and decision making. Many kinds of information and many reasons for maintaining that information may be important. All classes of information technology can play a role—from traditional information systems through model management systems to organizational units that handle soft information. An ODSS enables organization structure to be realized and is particularly relevant for modern organization structures that involve distributed decision processes, virtual positions, and interacting teams. Some basic research questions are, What are the evolving organizational structures? How can information technology facilitate the development, operation, and coordination of these organizational structures?

Technology environments to support decision processes. In Chapter 6, the members of the information technology support environment team characterize the technology support environment as "the set of technology capabilities and the manner in which they are used by people in performing these tasks." Their concept of technology environment includes the interface and interaction between the users and the system, and their use of the word environment emphasizes the blending or merging of mental and computer-based processes rather than their differentiation.

In his section, King discusses technology in terms of the functionality provided and the philosophical vision underlying the approach to providing that functionality. He first proposes that degree of control is an important issue in distinguishing system approaches. DSS provide assistance to users in decision tasks, leaving users with a substantial degree of control over what to look at, how to look at it, and how to interpret it. Expert systems, on the other hand, attempt to automate these decision-making processes, leaving little control in the hands of the users. The concept of "augmented systems" [Engelbart, 1988] lies in between these two extremes in terms of control. Here, the essential idea is that tool systems should be designed to extend human capabilities in intended and unintended ways, to change the basic character of communities, and to make humans and communities more effective. King then describes the "desktop metaphor" as the dominant design paradigm underlying current tools. This has been successful in the world of the office, but is restricting for decision processes because (1) it does not deal with the objects of such a world, which include goals, plans, opportunities, and so on; (2) its input-output capabilities are inadequate; and (3) its limited intelligence and processing abilities provide a poor match for those of humans. King describes some examples of AI research aimed at alleviating these problems. Finally, he describes an entirely different philosophical stance to the use of technology to support decision processes in which computers are not used to augment human rationality but rather to enrich communications between humans.

In their section, Benbasat and Todd describe alternative theories of the individual human decision-maker component of the information technology environment, developing a "technology-independent perspective to understanding the use and effects of DSS." The influence of technology is through its effects on decision-makers' perceptions and abilities; conversely, the motivations, goals, and abilities of decision-makers determine the way they use technology. Bottom-up theories are reductionist in nature, focusing on elementary cognitive processes with a view to designing more effective decision aids. Middle-out theories address issues (such as the degree of consciousness and control users have over their cognitive processes, their motivation, and their perception of decision making) that influence the way in which a DSS might be utilized. Top-down theories view the user as acting within and being influenced by their organizational and social context. Benbasat and Todd describe several theories in each of these categories and conclude by stating that such theories provide a stable, technology-invariant base for understanding DSS use and influence, and represent a fertile area for research.

In their section, Sprague and Hill discuss the task component of the technology environment. They classify work into two main categories. Procedure-driven (Type I) work is transaction-oriented work that can be performed by known procedures. Problem-driven (Type II) work consists of problem-solving and goal attainment activities for which no single procedure is known a priori; it can only be specified by stating the desired outcomes. This dichotomy differs from the "clerical" versus "professional-managerial" classification of tasks since clerical work often contains Type II components and professional-managerial work contains Type I components. DSS are directed mainly toward problem-driven work. Two important issues are how best to represent such work and how to align the technology to support people in its performance. Sprague and Hill suggest four dimensions that are key to an adequate representation of problem-driven work: (1) decomposability of abstract tasks into less abstract subtasks, (2) gradual accomplishment of subtasks and thresholds (or degrees) of subtask achievement, (3) the interaction between subtasks, and (4) simultaneity or concurrent accomplishment of several subtasks. They suggest that neural networks exhibit these properties and might give clues to a suitable representation scheme.

Sol, in his section, discusses the need to use multiple perspectives in the design of systems to support decision processes. The first perspective is the need for design techniques that address issues at three different levels: (1) the micro level, which focuses on task improvement of knowledge workers; (2) the meso level, which is concerned with the coordination of workplaces in their natural setting; and (3) the macro level, which focuses on information infrastructures between and above several organizations. The second perspective concerns the pattern of problem solving to be used and the need to provide degrees of freedom for the user with regard to metatheoretical and conceptual issues, and modeling and solution-finding activities. The final perspective concerns the methods and tools that are needed to design and implement information systems that support decision processes. These methods and tools must support our way of thinking about the design process, modeling the real-world objects, and implementing and controlling systems building efforts.

In his section, Omar El Sawy suggests an "ISDP research generator" that comprises four dimensions for characterizing research: the causal theory to be used, perceptions of the role of decision support, the model of work activity to be adopted, and conceptions of the technology environment. The last three dimensions are directly related to the discussions in the prior sections and allow them to be placed in the perspective of a larger program of research in ISDP.

To summarize, a major thrust of Chapter 6 is that the technology environment should be considered as the product of both objective technical factors and subjective mental factors. This echoes a recurrent theme in the ISDP workshop and is a major challenge for research aimed at developing theories of technology environments and their impact on organizational efficiency and effectiveness.

Model management systems. Chapter 7 introduces the concept of model management systems (MMS) by briefly tracing its origins. The field of MMS grew from the idea that there should be software that insulates users from the details of managing and running models, just as database management systems serve to insulate users from the details of managing and processing stored data. Some progress has been made in formalizing this concept. Blanning developed a "relational theory" of model management that extends relational database theory to provide a rigorous framework for organizing model bases and combining models [Blanning, 1984, 1987a]. The early work in MMS drew mostly on the background disciplines of computer science and management science. Current efforts in the field draw on developments in artificial intelligence and cognitive science to extend the concept of model management on three dimensions:

1. Functional dimension: To support a broader range of cognitive functions and all phases of the life cycle of a model—model selection, formulation, construction, use, interpretation, and maintenance.

2. Informational dimension: To include different forms of information as well as models as the objects to be managed—data, models, knowledge, documents, messages, multimedia, and so on.

3. Symbiotic dimension. To build a more intimate relationship with the user, moving beyond merely providing a user-friendly interface toward a vision in which the DSS becomes an extension of the human mind.

The hyperknowledge environment perspective developed by Whinston and Holsapple in their section provides a formal statement of one way of moving on all three dimensions of function, information, and symbiosis—with most emphasis on the latter two dimensions. The hyperknowledge metaphor extends the idea of hypertext (forming networks of associations in which the nodes contain textual information) to networks of "concepts," which are nuggets of descriptive, linguistic, algorithmic, and rule-based knowledge. The idea is to develop a system that allows users to access the knowledge in the DSS either directly or associatively in a manner that is a seamless extension of our own cognitive processes. The formal framework provides an architecture for such a system and imposes some requirements on that architecture. To provide interface independence and to handle the various knowledge types in a uniform way, the architecture separates "surface" input and output elements that are understood by users from "deep" concepts that are understood and manipulated by the system.

In their section "Conceptual Modeling and Change Propagation," Dhar and Jarke focus on the design and maintenance phases of the modeling cycle (the functional dimension above). The goal is to enhance the utility of models by providing the MMS with sufficient knowledge about the processes used by model developers so that models can be richer statements of meaning and also be more flexible and adaptive in the face of change. If an underlying design assumption can no longer be held, the system should be able either to mend itself or to provide sufficient information about the underlying model (the *why* as well as the *what*) so that redesign can be facilitated. The MMS design described in this section has been implemented as a prototype. To capture the (design) process knowledge, it contains a model of the collaborative activity used by people when they impose structure on unstructured problems (i.e., goals, issues, and arguments supporting the positions are explicitly modeled). Expert-system-like representations and mechanisms are used to represent design and model knowledge and to react to changes.

In his section "Modeling Model Management," Kimbrough provides another philosophical framework for the design of model management systems. This is based on a different cognitive model, "the language of thought" hypothesis (LoT), which asserts that "thought consists of the manipulation of sentences in the language of thought." Kimbrough then discusses how mathematical models, the basic components of MMS to date, can be represented linguistically as an "embedded" language (or multiple alternative embedded languages) that are then manipulated by a higher level (meta) "embedding" language. The embedded languages approach formalizes the idea that users conceive and mentally manipulate models (through the various stages of the modeling life cycle) in a language that is quite different from the formal languages used to define those models in the management science tradition.

In the final contribution in this chapter, "Designing DSS Interfaces," Lerch and Prietula focus on the high-level exchange of conceptual information between a DSS and its users as the basis for MMS design. The human processor is considered as part of the problem-solving architecture, and the approach concentrates on the design of the machine component so that it is cognitively compatible with the human processor. The interaction between the machine and human processors must be designed so that mutual understanding can be attained and learning facilitated. A cognitive metaphor, based on a long tradition of work in AI [Newell and Simon, 1975], is used as the basis for the MMS design. Under this model, users have tasks that they want to accomplish and the solution process involves representing the problem in a problem space and using search control procedures and operators to iteratively transform the problem into a solution. DSS interaction is then cast as a problem-solving process involving communication of goals, results, and knowledge between the human and machine processors. Problem solving is a distributed process in which the machine's capabilities for rapid computation, large working memory, and so on complement abilities for pattern recognition and judgment. Design and research problems involve the development of the machine processor and the learning mechanism, and how the coordination between the two processors should be conceived and managed.

What can we learn from these four models of future MMS? In each model, a cognitive metaphor is used as the foundation for the MMS design to provide (1) a robust approach valid across multiple task-specific situations, and (2) a more natural, helpful, and intelligent interface. These cognitive metaphors are implemented in an electronic form that obviously differs from the biological mechanisms used by humans. The idea, however, is that there should be enough conceptual veracity to make the systems easy to use by a broad range of people in a wide variety of task situations and throughout all the stages of the life cycle. In addition, of course, the cognitive metaphors provide design guidelines that help maintain conceptual integrity in the development of the MMS architecture.

Returning to the three thrusts of model management listed above, all four approaches provide a framework for MMS in which greater functionality can be achieved. The Dhar and Jarke (design and maintenance) and Lerch and Prietula (use and learning) approaches are more specific in this area. With regard to informational aspects, the Holsapple and Whinston hyperknowledge model addresses the idea of a progression from model to knowledge management more directly than the other three. At a high level—of generality, at least—the kind of information that is maintained by the MMS is more a technical than a conceptual issue. If the functionality to manage one kind of knowledge is mastered, the same design metaphor and principles might be used with other media. In the area of symbiosis, all four approaches have underlying cognitive metaphors that presumably will help higher level (more conceptual) uses of the system. The Holsapple and Whinston and Kimbrough contributions recognize the need to store internal knowledge about the intent of users, while Lerch and Prietula attempt an explicit recognition of the human-machine coordination process.

What are the implications of pursuing a research program based on the shared vision that seems to underlie these contributions? First, the functionality that is being proposed will also be useful for other kinds of knowledge beyond models per se. It seems useful therefore to replace model management systems (MMS) as a major research thrust by the more general concept of knowledge management systems (KMS), as suggested by Holsapple and Whinston. Second, given sufficient progress on the above dimensions (functional, informational, and symbiotic), we can envision a general layer of software (the KMS) in which much but not all computer systems activity would take place. We say not all because what is lacking in the four models is a multiperson dimension. For this, we need explicit models of multiperson and group interaction processes embedded in a network-based system that supports management communication and coordination activities (a communication/coordination management system or CMS). Extending this train of thought, a future management support system might consist of a CMS layer of software on top of a KMS on top of the basic computer operating and communication systems. The KMS would subsume functions now performed by the DBMS, MMS, and user-interface components. The CMS would subsume the functions now performed by electronic mail and other network-based systems; it would be the primary interface for the users.

Such a pie-in-the-sky vision has no theoretical foundation—there may be better ways of achieving the ultimate in management support systems (or perhaps we will never achieve such a vision). But perhaps this overly simple model can serve as a vision around which a very long-term program of research could be built. The four sections in Chapter 7 make a tentative start on the KMS portion, leaving a myriad of questions concerning such things as the best cognitive model yet to be decided. Current work in the computer-supported collaborative work (CSCW) [Olson, 1989] area (electronic mail systems, computer and video conferencing, etc.) and the ODSS chapter in this book make a tentative start on the CMS portion of the vision.

ISDP research framework

In this section, we sketch a simple framework from which to view ISDP research. We call this an entity-relationship-property (ERP) framework because we use the entity relationship technique from database theory [Chen, 1976] to model the objects (entities and relationships) that are of interest in research on information systems. We focus first on *what* is studied—on entity classes and relationships in real-world systems. We next make some assertions about properties of these entity classes and relationships, and use this as a second level of the classification scheme. Any finer nuances or properties of the entities and relationships are omitted, as is any attempt to define independent and dependent research variables. Other frameworks that provide finer detail in some topic areas together with definitions of research variables can be used to augment our framework [Mason and Mitroff, 1973; Ives et al., 1980; Ariav and Ginzberg, 1985 (see Chap. 1); Pinsonneault and Kraemer, 1989 (see Chap. 5); Culnan and Swanson, 1986; Culnan, 1987]. Barki and Rivard provide a comprehensive classification scheme of IS research topics with roughly 600 detailed classifications, many of which are relevant to ISDP research [Barki and Rivard, 1988].

The objective of the framework is to allow us to identify and discuss *classes* of research topics that we believe have relevance to ISDP research and also to show how the work of the ISDP teams fits in this framework. In accordance with these limited objectives, we will not attempt an exhaustive enumeration of all the various types of entity and relationship. Rather, we provide broad categories together with some indication of the more detailed substructure we have in mind.

We now expand the research framework outlined in Chapter 2 in several directions. First, we introduce a group level of analysis into the modified Leavitt model (Figure 1, Chapter 2) and describe the entities and relationships in that model in more detail (see Figure 1). We consider an information system to be composed of a set of information technologies (IT) supporting one or more individuals (I) and one or more groups (G), in the context of an organization (O). Each of these entities communicates with, affects, and is affected by the other entities including its portion of the environment (denoted by E_t, E_i, E_g, and E_o, respectively). The overall environment (E) is the union of these separate environments.

Second, we develop the dynamic aspects (depicted in Figure 2, Chapter 2), by formalizing the concept of decision processes. The IT and human elements in the system jointly perform *tasks* using *information* as input to *decision processes* that determine actions and result in *outcomes*. Third, recognizing that any system consists of an arrangement of components, we introduce system architecture as a separate area of study that can only be approached in a holistic fashion. Systems development and implementation issues constitute the fourth component in our framework. Finally, we recognize the role of the researcher (R) who observes the different components and the total system for the purposes of understanding existing systems and designing new ones. The elements in our ISDP research framework are depicted in Figure 1 in outline form.

In the remainder of the chapter we discuss the structural, dynamic, and architectural elements of the framework. We omit systems design and development issues, not because they are unimportant, but because our focus is more on direction finding with regard to the emerging concept of decision processes and not on how systems to support decision processes can or should be developed. The problems of the researcher will be discussed in the next chapter.

Structural aspects of research framework. The nodes in the diagram represent entity classes and the arcs represent many-to-many relationships in the usual sense of the entity relationship model [Chen, 1976]. By IT we mean the hardware, software, and communications systems components of the MIS, DSS, GDSS, ODSS or other *type of system* of interest to the researcher. There are various *functional components* of the IT such as the dialogue, data, and model management components of an MMS. Each IT system has a number of *functional capabilities*. IT systems have a *support role* in decision processes, for example, to automate, inform, coordinate, formalize, or facilitate.

By I we designate an individual user or class of individual users of the IT. (We use "individual" rather than "decision-maker" to emphasize that people have many roles and activities besides decision making or choice.) Each I has a number of *personal characteristics* (knowledge, attitudes, abilities, and motives), an *organizational role* (title, authority, status, and functional responsibilities), and a *group role* (leader, adviser, member) in every group in which he or she participates. Each I participates in one or more decision processes and has *decisional responsibilities* vis-à-vis one or more phases of that decision process (intelligence, design, choice, implementation). Example decisional responsibilities are to direct, approve, coordinate, advise, execute, or observe and report. Thus, an I who executes the choice phase of a decision process makes a decision choice (is a decision-maker for that decision process) in the normal sense. Different individuals may have the responsibility to approve that choice, or provide advice on the choice, and so on.

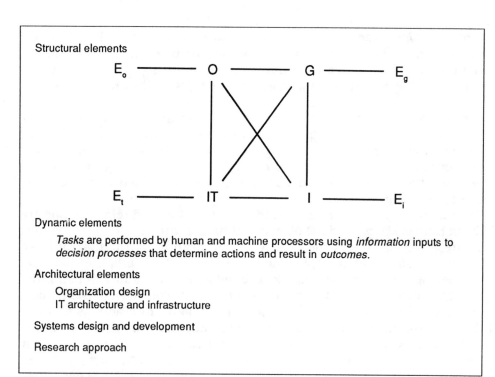

Figure 1. ISDP research framework.

By G we mean one or more groups of various *types* (such as work cells, departments, informal work groups, committees, ad hoc and permanent teams, members of a meeting, etc.) that interact with the IT. *Group characteristics* include size, structure, status relationships, power relationships, group norms, cohesiveness, and goal congruity of members. Groups have *organizational roles, group roles* (as subgroups of larger groups), and *decisional responsibilities* that mirror those of individuals. In addition, groups have *conflict resolution roles* that involve bargaining, negotiation, and conciliation.

By O we mean an organization of a given type, consisting of one or more groups of individuals. *Organizational characteristics* include size, resources, geographic location, industry, formal structure (hierarchy and teams), corporate strategy and objectives, policies, standards, culture, and interorganizational relationships.

By E we mean all aspects of the environment that might be relevant to a given study. What is considered to be environment and what is part of the system varies with the level and scope of the research study. *Environmental characteristics* include economic, legal, political, and social factors, the technological environment of the particular IT being studied (both inside and outside the firm), and the organizational environment consisting of the organizational characteristics listed above. Unlike some other frameworks, we do not include tasks as part of the environment but prefer to think of them as being generated by the man-machine system itself in reaction to events in the environment.

Influence patterns and research subjects. We interpret the arcs (relationships) in Figure 1 as "patterns of influence" rather than just information flows. We are interested in interactions that change the objects in the system. Furthermore, we distinguish three forms of interaction between the components in our framework and three corresponding modes of research.

In the first research mode, the individual entities and relationships are the objects of study, and the objective of the research is either descriptive or prescriptive. This is the most obvious meaning of the diagram. We study IT using, for example, the methods of MIS, computer science, management science, and artificial intelligence. We study G using the reference disciplines of behavioral science, decision theory, economics, and so on. The relationships represent the dynamic interactions between the different classes of object; these interactions involve both semantic and syntactic information exchanges and the protocols that exist for those exchanges. We will denote research on the interfaces between entities by two-way arrows: IT $\leftrightarrow$ I, O $\leftrightarrow$ G, and so on. More generally, we interpret IT $\leftrightarrow$ I, IT $\leftrightarrow$ G, and IT $\leftrightarrow$ O as representing the use of IT to support individuals, groups, and organizations, respectively. Thus, we might use theories from MIS, human factors, decision theory, cognitive science, or semiotics to study the interface between a specific type of IT (say a DSS model) and a single class of users I.

In the second research mode, the *impacts* of one class of entity on another are studied, and the relationship arcs represent impact. We will denote this kind of relationship by A $-*$ B, meaning that objects in the realm of class A impact the state and behavior of objects in the realm of class B (the asterisk is meant to convey the idea of collision). This mode of research usually has a descriptive flavor but is also prescriptive in the longer run sense that if we discover dysfunctional impacts we can suggest changes to the system. We will expand on the two-way impacts between IT and the human components of the system because this is of central importance to the decision process view of IT in organizations.

The organizational structure and culture as well as group and individual abilities, norms, customs, and beliefs impact IT by (1) determining the value and nature of the IT investments that are made and (2) governing how the IT is perceived and used. The latter point is worth emphasizing. Different individuals and groups have different perceptions of the functionality of IT and different beliefs as to its proper role and appropriate uses. While these perceptions are subjective, they give rise to a structure of roles, uses, formal rules, and policies with regard to IT that may be studied and that is, in this sense, objective. Thus, the human components of the system, which we will designate collectively as H, influence the shape and performance of the technological components. We designate this impact influence pattern by the notation H −∗ IT. (i.e., humans shape their tools). Conversely, human activities and relationships are shaped by the nature of the tools they use. Tools alter work patterns, endow us with new capabilities, and can change power relationships between individuals and groups. We designate this impact influence pattern by IT −∗ H (i.e., humans are the products of the tools they use). The two-way interaction between IT and H (between objective and subjective factors) jointly determines the structure of IT use in the support of organizational activities. This concept is discussed in more detail elsewhere [Markus and Robey, 1988; Orlikowski and Robey, 1991].

The idea for the third mode of research comes from Elam, Jarvenpaa, and Schkade in Chapter 3 of this volume. They introduce an important concept regarding both what should be studied in ISDP research and how to go about that study. The underlying motive for this research approach is prescriptive. First, they suggest that we should study the human components and their interrelationships in order to devise better IT tools. An example might be to measure eye-hand reaction times in the course of an ergonomic study aimed at developing a better keyboard. Following their notation, we designate this pattern of research by the notation H → IT. (i.e., study the human component to learn what the IT component should be). Here, the arrow has an implication or inference connotation. Conversely, they also suggest that we can use the fact that humans are impacted by the tools they use to learn more about the human components of the system. Again following Elam, Jarvenpaa, and Schkade, we designate this pattern of research by IT → H (i.e., study the impact of IT interventions—IT −∗ H—in order to formulate more general rules about human behavior).

In essence, we endorse their suggestion that a promising set of topics for a multidisciplinary program of research can be derived by considering the implications of alternating IT → H and H → IT forms of study in specific contexts. Thus, we might have CAD (computer-aided design) as the information technology and an engineering design team as the type of H. We could determine functional requirements for CAD by studying verbal protocols of engineers as they make design decisions (H → IT) and follow this by an IT → H study using a prototype CAD system to confirm our initial theories about the support needs of engineers or to build entirely new theories about their cognitive processes in design activities.

Illustration of structural part of framework. The above research framework allows us to partially identify the (real-world) subject or "level of analysis" of a research study. All components of the model depicted in

Figure 1 need research. Table 1 lists some of the nodes and arcs in Figure 1 together with one or two examples of the almost limitless number of possible research studies in each category. Note that different research modalities are indicated in the table. Research might also focus on more than one structural component. For example, we might study both IT → H and H → IT in order to understand ideas of structuration [Giddens, 1984; Orlikowski and Robey, 1991].

At this highly aggregate level, the framework can serve to classify research in only a very gross fashion. To convert the framework into a comprehensive classification scheme, we would need to list the various types of IT, I, G, O, E, relationships, tasks, processes, and so on that are possible. The number of combinations of possible research topics would then be enormous. (Consider every class of IT, individual, group, organization, task, information, and process; every relationship in Figure 1; and every reference discipline that might be applicable!). While developing these lists may not be particularly difficult, it is only necessary here to speak in generic terms. For example, we can already point to areas where past research emphasis has been light—for example, research that infers desired properties of IT from the known (or discovered) properties of groups and organizations (G → IT and O → IT).

At a different level of abstraction, one might ask if the framework says anything about the concerns of MIS as a field of study. In our opinion, the answer is yes. From this viewpoint, MIS is the primary academic discipline concerned with issues surrounding *information*, IT, and its (two-way) connections of influence patterns with the I, G, and O components in Figure 1. Its interest in the *task*, *information*, and *process* components is shared with a number of other disciplines including computer science, operations management, artificial intelligence, and organizational theory.

Dynamic aspects of research framework. *Decision processes* result in actions that define the behavior of the organization. Actions are needed to perform tasks. Thinking of the organization as a man-machine system, tasks are formulated and performed by groups, individuals, or machines acting either jointly or alone. Tasks are generated as a result of a perceived need to maintain or alter the state of the organization or a group, individual, or machine within the organization. Tasks are triggered by the passage of time, the completion of other tasks, or the receipt of information from the environment or from within the organization. The nature of the task that is initiated depends both on the trigger and the internal state of the initiating organization, group, individual, or machine. Tasks can be decomposed (1) over time into subtasks corresponding to each phase of decision making (intelligence, design, choice, implementation) and also (2) into subtasks that depend on the innate

Table 1. Topics related to microstructure.

Component	Sample Research Studies
IT	Novel systems, algorithms, technologies, networks
IT $\leftrightarrow$ I	Human factors study of interface design
IT $-*$ I	Stress from CRT use, task efficiency
IT $-*$ G	Impact of GDSS on group performance
G $\rightarrow$ IT	Study group processes and apply findings to IT design
IT $-*$ O	How IT impacts organizational structure
O $-*$ IT	Organizational determinants of network topography
IT $-*$ E_t	Competitive or social impacts of technology
E_t $\leftrightarrow$ IT	Electronic data interchange
I	Study human cognitive processes
I $-*$ G	How asymmetrical information affects power relationships
G $-*$ I	How individuals are affected by group norms
I $-*$ O	Role of individual innovators in technology adoption
O $-*$ I	Influence of organizational norms on IT use
E_i $-*$ I	Cultural factors as a determinant of IT use
G	Small-group research
G $\leftrightarrow$ O	Role of team in organization
O $-*$ G	How organization structure affects group behavior
E_g $-*$ G	Political/social impacts on group behavior
O	Organizational design, organizational strategy
E_o $-*$ O	How electronic markets impact organization structure
O $-*$ E_o	How organizational strategy impacts competitors
E	Technology scanning, survey of attitudes toward IT

structure of the task as in the division of labor in clerical work, PERT networks, manufacturing jobs, and so on.

We believe it makes sense to think of each task and subtask as being executed by a single decision process. The decision process determines the actions needed to perform the task. Each chosen action represents a task for which another decision process is required, and so on. If the original task is complex it will be decomposed into subtasks. As tasks are decomposed recursively, there is a matching decomposition of the higher level decision processes into lower level decision processes. Machines, individuals, and groups have different decisional responsibilities (e.g., to approve, advise, execute, etc.) with regard to the performance of each task/decision process at each level in this decomposition. Each task/decision process also has a time frame in which it is executed. Decision processes are not independent of each other in the sense that there may be mutual interference, and many decision processes trigger

Table 2. Sample research topics related to dynamic aspects.

Task: Understanding task structure, task decomposition, strategies for distribution of work, methods for job design, how to determine goals and critical success factors

Information: Classification of information types, development of performance measures, new problem representation schemes, information filters

Process: Individual processing strategies, group processes, organizational processes, political processes, IS processing requirements, management science techniques, expert systems, simulations

Outcomes: Organizational, group, and individual effectiveness measures; productivity issues; process cycle times; quality measures

---

or terminate other decision processes. The organizational structure and culture as well as group and individual abilities, norms, customs, and beliefs influence the nature of the tasks that are performed (or, equivalently, the decision processes that are executed).

The study of decision processes involves, first, the holistic study of tasks and of all of the determinants of each action choice. For each task, this involves analyzing the task to be performed, the *information* needed to perform the *task*, and the *process* to be performed. Note that in the man-machine system some processes are performed by machine and others by the human actors. The actions that are taken result in *outcomes* that may be favorable or unfavorable to the organization, group, or individual concerned. Some examples of research topics at this level of analysis are shown in Table 2.

Usually, all of these elements have to be jointly studied in the context of one or more of the above structural elements. For example, a research study in GDSS might investigate the relationships between a particular kind of GDSS software system (e.g., electronic brainstorming), group task, group processes in performing the task, and the type of information used by the group.

System architecture and infrastructure. While research on the microstructure in Table 1 is important, we also need more global research directed to overall information systems architecture at an organizational level or to developing infrastructure technologies that support those architectures. Table 3 lists some research topics in this area.

Research on these topics is essential if progress is to be made in the ISDP area. In fact, one plausible strategy proposed in the discussion of the ODSS chapter is to concentrate research efforts on infrastructure

Table 3. Architecture/infrastructure topics.

IT architecture for an organization
Organization design and IT
Communication system infrastructure (LANs, WANs)
Network-based systems (e-mail, GDSS, etc.)
Distributed processing systems
Database management systems
Model management systems
Knowledge base management

development in order to provide an environment in which users can experiment and evolve their own specialized forms of support.

Properties of system elements. The above research topic framework is quite coarse-grained. To refine the scheme, we state some basic assertions about properties of the system (IT, I, G, O, etc.) and the researcher, R, that are always or almost always true and that have varying degrees of significance in different situations. To simplify matters, we will use the generic term DSS to represent any MIS, DSS, GDSS, or ODSS, and H to designate any one or more of the human elements in the framework (I, G, or O). Finer distinctions are possible, but the following will be a sufficient set of properties for the present discussion.

Nature of the System

1. Goal: The DSS is designed to support H in the execution of one or more tasks.
2. Man-machine system: The DSS consists of the two processors, IT and H, and the dynamic interaction that takes place between them.

Properties 3 through 19 below represent deviations away from a perfectly "rational model" of the world [Kling, 1980, and Chapter 9]. In some sense they represent "vulnerabilities" or points where the rationalist research/design paradigm might come unstuck.

User-IT Roles

3. Problem setting: H sets the goals and the tasks for the DSS.
4. Locus of control: H is the ultimate decision-maker.
5. Voluntary use: H can choose not to use the DSS but rather to use the information from the environment (E_d, E_g, and E_o) and its own processing abilities and judgment to perform its tasks.

Properties of System Elements

6. Idiosyncrasy: Individual I's, G's, and O's differ from each other.
7. Cognitive processes: H has limited cognitive abilities and exhibits biases in processing information; different H's may have different cognitive styles; H learns from experience.
8. Affective processes: The decisions H makes are affected by non-cognitive factors such as motivation, social pressures, cultural norms, and emotions.
9. Group processes: Group processes and dynamics are uncertain; leadership, politics, and social and legal conventions may play a large role.
10. Interface: The communication between IT and H is noisy and of low bandwidth.
11. IT imperfection: IT may be imperfectly designed or unreliable, or it may even give wrong answers.

Dynamics of Change

12. Environmental impacts: Both the IT and H processors are affected by uncertain information received from the environment:
    - Changes in E_t may invalidate the design assumptions of IT.
    - Environments E_d, E_g, and E_o affect the behavior of H through the impact of cultural norms, economic factors, bureaucratic pressures, and so on.

13. Social impacts: Communications within the organization (between IT and H and between different I's and G's, etc.) change motivations and values, and thereby the behavior patterns of H.
14. Nonneutrality: H is affected (changed) by its interaction with IT.

Uncertain Knowledge

15. User uncertainty: The IT designer cannot understand H:
    - Motivations and goals of H are unknown or uncertain.
    - Cognitive style, biases, and limitations of H are unknown or uncertain.

16. Task uncertainty: Neither R nor H has a good understanding of the tasks (and goals) for the DSS.
17. Model uncertainty: H does not understand DSS models nor the results of those models.

Researcher

18. Imperfect observations: R has an imperfect view of the world.

19. Training: Each R has a unique background and training and a predisposition to use certain research methods.
20. Viewpoint: Different R's may consciously or unconsciously exhibit different views of the world (e.g., that the scientific method is directly applicable in social science research or vice versa).

Note that each of these properties can be broken down into more detailed classifications. For example, the "stylized facts" in Table 2 of Chapter 3 represent a breakdown of what we know about item 7, cognitive processes. Table 4 gives some examples of research streams that have been oriented around these properties (again, research methods are treated in the next chapter).

Research topic classification scheme. Combining the structural model of Figure 1 with the system properties just described, we obtain a method for describing research topics at a more detailed (but still quite high) level of aggregation. Namely, we suggest that research topics can usefully be described by the notation:

Objects studied/properties investigated.

Table 5 describes each of the individual contributions to the ISDP research project using this notation. The next chapter (on research approaches) suggests a third "research paradigm" dimension for the classification scheme that (together with the research topic scheme in this section) will further help to classify research studies.

Implications of the research framework. We now use the above framework to discuss some broad issues arising from the work of the teams, the discussion at the workshop, and subsequent thinking about ISDP.

What is reality? Properties 4, 12, 13, and 14 (locus of control, environmental impacts, social impacts, and nonneutrality) together make for indeterminacy and problems in deciding what is "real." Humans are affected by their interaction with the environment, with each other, and with the system in ways that are poorly understood. Yet if H is the ultimate decision-maker, then this is the only "reality" that matters. This leads some researchers to propose that DSS designers are really involved in "image management." Users have dynamically changing images of the problem that may differ from the image engineered into the IT and that may be affected by things that are going on outside the IT in the environment of the user. To be effective according to this argument, the IT needs knowledge of H—to understand goals, cognitive processes, and so on, and to help develop useful mental images or representations of the problem.

Table 4. Examples of research related to system properties.

Property	Research Stream Examples
User-IT Roles	
3. Problem setting	Multicriteria research (goals), prototyping design approach (goals/tasks)
4. Locus of control	Basis for DSS (supporting rather than automating decisions), sensitivity techniques
5. Voluntary use	IT adoption research, DSS satisfaction measure
Properties of System Elements	
6. Idiosyncrasy	User-modifiable systems
7. Cognitive processes	Behavioral decision making, cognitive styles research, problem representation research, learning research
8. Affective processes	Motivation studies, expectancy theory (see Chapters 5 and 6)
9. Group processes	Small-group research, leadership studies, GDSS
10. Interface	Human factors, interface design

Are rational design approaches viable? Not only do we have to deal with images, according to property 7 (cognitive processes); we also manipulate information in ways contrary to "rational" predictions based on theories such as Bayesian decision making. Worse still, according to property 8 (affective processes), decisions may be affected by all sorts of emotional and political forces that lie completely outside normal rational models.

Table 4. Examples of research (continued).

Property	Research Stream Examples
11. IT imperfection	Requirements analysis, systems reliability, error reporting and recovery
Dynamics of Change	
12. Environmental impacts:	
• On IT:	Design process capture [Dhar and Jarke, Chap. 7]
• On H:	Cultural, political factors as determinants of system outcomes
13. Social impacts	Sociotechnical systems design, human communications research
14. Nonneutrality	User satisfaction research, IT impact research
Uncertain Knowledge	
15. User uncertainty	"Symbiotic systems" [Manheim, 1989], evolutionary/participatory design
16. Task uncertainty	Evolutionary/participatory design, job design, task analysis (see Chapter 6), utility theory
17. Model uncertainty	Model representation research, help and documentation features, "hyperknowledge," and other approaches in Chapter 7.

What is important? A moment's consideration of the framework reveals the complexity of the research problem. There are many kinds of systems and many interesting interrelationships. Moreover, new technology and our own inventiveness are continually creating more topics to research. Choosing a design topic that will be significant from either a theoretical or practical point of view may be like finding a needle in a haystack.

While the above discussion highlights some important concerns, it is, of course, overly pessimistic. It seems to indicate either that there is very little we can do, or that we have to radically change our theories to take into account behavioral complexities that are not well understood. As our objective in this chapter is to highlight important design issues, we briefly revisit the question of finding an important research topic by suggesting that we need to be aware of "first-order" and "second-order" effects. As a simple example, consider property 6 (idiosyncrasy) and its impact on the popularity and usefulness of spreadsheets. While we know that people are different, this was a second-order (or maybe a tenth-order!) effect, simply because the idea behind the spreadsheet was so powerful that it had universal appeal. On the other hand, the designer of a GDSS to support conflict negotiation should be aware that a system based on mathematical game theory (rational) approaches may have a second-order effect in the face of emotional and cultural factors (property 8) and group dynamics (property 9).

This leads us to an obvious and important research topic. What can we learn from history, prior research, and our own intuition about factors that really make a difference in the success of technology? It seems, from the spreadsheet example, that problem representation (or user interface, or a mixture of both) can be important. What are the other important factors?

How does the adoption of a decision process view influence the choice of research topic? Following the conceptual discussion of decision processes given above, we believe that it is important that decision processes arise out of the tasks that have to be performed. In other words, the driving force in research topic selection is task-oriented rather than decision-oriented. In a decision-making view one searches for key decisions to be supported and tends to focus on complex decision models and/or strategic issues to the exclusion of many other activities that are vital to organizations. Using tasks as the driving force immediately changes the emphasis to a broader array of topics and to a more holistic view of the processes that need to be supported. The task to be researched can be of the problem-oriented variety (see Chapter 5), in which case the resulting research may include models and have traditional DSS topics as a major but not exclusive interest. Alternatively, the chosen task may be process-oriented, in which case the research focus may be more on issues of coordination and communication of work, as in CSCW research. In either case, organization members engage in decision processes.

Research directions in ISDP

Scope and organization of discussion. In the last section we used a general research framework to propose some broad challenges and approaches arising from a consideration of the ISDP papers and work-

---

Table 5. Classification of ISDP research contributions.

Chapter: Title / Objects / Properties

Chapter 3: Behavioral Decision Theory and DSS
    I, IT → DM, DM → IT / property 7: cognitive processes

Chapter 4: Group Decision Support Systems
    G, IT ↔ G / property 9: group processes

Chapter 5: Organizational Decision Support Systems
    ODSS Concepts and Architecture
        Org. design, IT ↔ G /
    Why Organizations Collect and Store Information
        Information /
    ODSS Technology and Decision Processes
        IT architecture
    Information Technology and ODSS
        IT architecture
    Organizational Decision Process as an Open System Problem
        G, *process* / property 9: group processes
    Organizational Decision Support: An Interacting Team Perspective
        Org. design, IT ↔ G / property 9: group processes

Chapter 6: Technology Environments to Support Decisions
    Evolving Functionality for the Technology Environment
        IT, H ↔ IT / property 4: locus of control; property 7: cognitive
        processes; property 13: human communications
    Theories of DSS Use By Individual Decision-Makers
        I / property 8: affective processes
    The Nature of the Work
        Task
    Design Perspectives for Systems to Support Decision Processes
        System design
    ISDP Research Generator
        Research

Chapter 7: Model Management Systems
    The Hyperknowledge Environment of Model Management Systems
        MMS / property 7: cognitive processes; property 17: model
        uncertainty
    Conceptual Modeling and Change Propagation
        MMS / property 12, first item: environmental change
    Modeling Model Management
        MMS / property 7: cognitive processes; property 17: model
        uncertainty
    Designing DSS Interfaces
        MMS ↔ I / property 7: cognitive processes

Note: MMS stands for model management systems, a type of IT.

---

shop discussion. We now suggest some research challenges that are more directly related to the focus of the workshop on information systems and decision processes. These research suggestions will again be general in nature and more in the form of research areas than specific research topics. Each of these research areas will probably require a research program involving a number of different researchers from different research disciplines over a number of years. Such a research program might involve a combination of research approaches starting with exploratory field and case studies, proceeding with mathematical model building and/or laboratory and field experiments, and concluding with studies to test the results and revise the theory against the realities of actual organizations.

Making predictions about what will be fruitful areas of research is at best a risky business. We give our cut at this here and invite others both to criticize our approach and to use the material accumulated in this book to reach other conclusions, draw alternative research frameworks, and call for entirely new approaches and directions for research.

Before proceeding, we give some alternative sources of suggestions for research in DSS-related areas that have been useful to us in writing these conclusions. An excellent discussion of relevant research opportunities is contained in a report on a workshop that sought to identify research funding opportunities for the National Science Foundation's Decision and Management Sciences Program [Little, 1988]. (The ISDP project was funded in part by the DMS program within NSF.) The paper by Elam et al. that seeks a new "vision for DSS" was influential in generating the idea for the ISDP workshop [Elam et al., 1984]. Finally, a report by the Committee on the Next Decade in Operations Research [CONDOR, 1988] contains a number of relevant research suggestions in the areas of modeling, AI, and DSS.

One way to describe a multidisciplinary program for ISDP research is to proceed discipline by discipline, suggesting relevant research questions and showing how they relate to the central mission of ISDP. This was our approach in the last section, when we suggested that research related to each H $\rightarrow$ IT component was needed and that the list of propositions in the previous section, suitably expanded, provided a good source of research ideas. Rather than continuing in that mode, to provide more focus and a greater sense of purpose, we organize the discussion in this section around our concept of decision processes in organizations (see Chapter 2) and let the resulting organizational and information systems design issues drive the research questions.

The choice of a design-oriented organization for the discussion does not mean that we advocate only a prescriptive approach to research. The same research questions can also be approached from a "pure research" standpoint. That is, one can pursue research to gain understanding of real-world phenomena or to explore theoretical relationships without any thought of immediate applications. Alternatively, we could direct efforts toward providing a suitable communications and software infrastructure and then adopt a descriptive approach to study the thousands of natural experiments that arise from the inventiveness of hardware and software vendors and the innovations introduced by users.

Enhanced hardware and communications capabilities are a sine qua non of any idealized vision of IT in organizations. As these are outside of the DSS research domain, we will simply assume that organizations in the relatively near future will have untold computing power, be totally networked, and have access to vast internal and external data sources. In other words, we will not concern ourselves with questions of hardware and software infrastructure. However, improving our ability to rapidly design, develop, and deliver high-quality software capabilities (applications) in the decision support area is within the scope of our discussion, as is research aimed at determining what those software applications should be and how they can be related to organizational objectives.

Major research questions

What would signify the success of a research program to support decision processes in organizations? Would we recognize success if we saw it?

The most ambitious view of what constitutes success would be the broad adoption of a decision process framework for organizational design. Given the organizational mission and tasks to be performed, organizational design would be seen as a matter of designing the organizational structure, building a technical infrastructure, and designing policies and operating standards that would foster efficient formal and informal decision processes. The formal decision processes would be designed just as we currently design the organization's production processes. The overall design would ensure mechanisms for continuous improvement in the performance of the decision processes through organizational learning. Furthermore, the decision processes would continuously adapt their form and output to the changing needs of the organization. To cope with the need to execute informal and ad hoc decision processes, organization members would be educated in decision processes and know what decision technology is designed to be used in a given situation—or if the situation is novel, what decision process is most likely to be successful.

Without any pretense that this dream is in imminent danger of being realized, let us pursue its consequences as a means of generating some interesting research possibilities. (Daft and Lewin present some sobering reflections on the impacts of organizational design theory on practice [Daft and Lewin, 1990].)

Assume for the moment that we know what it means to design a decision process. The above vision requires the development of a theory relating organizational strategies, organizational structure, and decision processes. Possible foundations for such a theory have been around for a long time. Organizations were seen as problem solving and decision-making systems by Simon, March, Huber, and McDaniel [Simon, 1957; March and Simon, 1958; Huber and McDaniel, 1986]. Galbraith proposed an information processing approach to organization design [Galbraith 1973, 1974]. The economics-of-information approach [Marshak and Radnor, 1972] appears to embrace both decision-making and information processing views. What is the difference between our conception of decision processes and previous approaches? Mainly, a matter of degree and emphasis. Compared with most previous decision-making approaches, we want to recognize the whole time line of a decision process (from intelligence through execution and feedback) and a broader array of political, psychological, and social processes as determinants of the actions taken by organizations. Compared with the information design approaches mentioned above, we would emphasize recent advances in organization theory, insights gained from the fields of DSS and AI, and the capabilities of new communication technologies.

One possible line of ISDP research then is to revisit previous decision-based and information-based theories (as well as competing organization design theories) in the light of present organizational needs, the capabilities of modern technology, and what has so far been learned in the area of organization theory. Perhaps a better theory can emerge as a synthesis of existing theories (or out of an understanding of their weaknesses).

What kind of theory would enable an organizational design of the type we have in mind?

First, we need to know how to match the organizational tasks set by strategic analysis to the organizational structures, decision processing capabilities, and execution processes that are needed to perform those tasks. In the decision process view, organizational/information systems design must have a very broad conception of organizational architecture, managerial processes, and their information inputs, and the determinants of success and failure. Information—hard and soft, factual and emotive, computerized and noncomputerized—is one common thread linking all of this. Furthermore, every form of information processing technology—including informal face-to-face meetings, formal meetings using due process protocols, and the whole panoply of computer- and communications-based processing systems from traditional MIS through e-mail, DSS, GDSS, mathematical models, computer conferencing, and so on—would be available to process information, and help make decisions and execute actions. One important facet of the organization/information systems design problem is to decide how much should be invested in each of these technologies. Some technologies require up-front dollar investments in computer and communications systems that can be measured relatively easily. However, one might also set organizational policies that implicitly or explicitly cause the organization to invest heavily in management time spent in conversation as the major information processing technology (in an organization whose tasks are mainly political, this might make a lot of sense).

The implications of this line of thought are far reaching. Perhaps it is time to drop "computer-based" as the implicit qualifier for the information systems field. In any case, thinking broadly in this fashion, we need to understand how to invest in a portfolio of organizational structure, human competence, computer and communications infrastructure, and directive policies that would allow an efficient and dynamically changing mix of all of the above technologies to be used in the execution of organizational tasks.

To design a decision process in this context is a complex task, but it is one that is done every day in organizations in either an explicit or implicit fashion. It might be thought of as organizational design or project planning, depending on the permanence of the resulting organizational substructure. First, it requires the design of a new organizational substructure or the assignment of roles and responsibilities to humans and machine components within an existing organizational structure. These roles include the execution of subtasks involving information collection and processing, communicating, coordinating, deciding, executing, and evaluating. Second, it requires the assignment or design and development of the appropriate information processing technology to support each role. Third, it requires the development of a set of policies or metarules on how these roles are to be sequenced and carried out. Finally, in all of the above, it requires explicit consideration of the properties of the human elements in the system—taking into account the social, political, behavioral, and cognitive determinants of human behavior.

We want to emphasize that there is nothing really new in any of this. However, we believe that it represents a major change in the worldview of DSS to one that is more closely oriented toward organizational design and performance and is more holistic in nature.

We now follow the framework of the previous section to consider research questions around each of the components of the framework. We concentrate on the dynamic aspects of the framework since this is more relevant to a decision process view. The structural components (the nodes IT, I, G, and O in Figure 1) are subjects for research by various reference disciplines. From the design point of view, task and environment are considered to be independent variables driving the design of the organization structure, information, and process variables.

Tasks

What do individuals and groups do? What should they do? What could they do?

Studies aimed at understanding the activities of groups, with and without the use of IT, are needed to identify opportunities for support. According to Mintzberg, managers spend the majority of their time in communication activities and meetings rather than in decision-making or analytic activities per se [Mintzberg 1971]. Perhaps we should invest more in systems to support these kinds of activities? Determining what groups do in and out of meetings was one of the main research questions for the GDSS (Chapter 4) and ODSS (Chapter 5) teams, and the reader is referred to these chapters for many specific research suggestions. The literature on CSCW also contains many suggestions [Olson, 1989].

What is an appropriate categorization of tasks for design purposes?

To use the tasks that an organization must execute to guide the design of decision processing systems, we need to understand those tasks better. Simon's classification of structured versus unstructured tasks and the phases of decision making has provided a useful scheme for many purposes. The distinction between goal-oriented and process-oriented tasks in Chapter 5 certainly tells us something about the kinds of decision processes that might be used (in one we need to provide deeper levels of cognitive support than in the other, for example). A one-dimensional categorization of tasks based on their uncertainty (defined as the difference between the amount of information required for their successful execution and the amount of information at hand in the organization) was sufficient to drive Galbraith's theory of organizational design. The categorizations of tasks used in team theory, game theory, bargaining theory, and negotiation theory may also be useful.

For more detailed design issues we probably need finer distinctions. The Ariav and Ginzberg list of task characteristics given in Chapter 1 provides a start; it includes the Simon dimensions and adds dimensions for organizational level and functional area. What other dimensions or classification schemes might be useful? How about classical management theory's classification of managerial tasks into five types: motivating, planning, organizing, coordinating, and controlling? Individual versus group versus organizational tasks is another useful distinction pertinent to much of the ISDP discussion. At the organizational design level, we might assume that the organizational processing system is also designed to execute metatasks (e.g., discover new tasks to be performed, prioritize known tasks, schedule tasks) and structure-transforming tasks (e.g., add a new overseas division, form new teams around an unanticipated task). Finally, the importance and urgency of the task need to be taken into account.

The research problem here is to identify the important task categories and to understand the general principles that apply to the design of decision processes in each category. For instance, decision processes for crisis management (e.g., studying systems for the control of nuclear power plants) seems to be a well-focused and important area for research.

Thinking more proactively, we have the following design issues.

How can tasks be represented?

Representing tasks is of first importance if the system is to support task decomposition, assignment of subtasks, and coordination of these tasks. The Sprague and Hill discussion in Chapter 6 contains some interesting observations concerning hierarchical decomposition, the interaction of subtasks, the gradual attainment of goals, and thresholds of achievement. More work needs to be done in this area and actual systems developed and tested. Any form of collaborative activity requires a language for sharing goals, tasks, and progress on tasks. The PERT graphical representation of project activities is an important tool; how could it be improved using modern technology such as multimedia and hypertext?

As suggested in Chapter 7, an entirely different and equally important reason for improving our ability to represent tasks is to enable the system to perform analogical or case-based reasoning—to recognize similar situations and to explain what actions were taken or to suggest new actions based on past experience. Automatic generation of rule-based expert systems for highly structured situations is already possible [Messier and Hansen, 1988]. Recognizing patterns in less-structured domains is an even more important research challenge.

How should tasks be allocated to human and machine processors? How can task execution be coordinated?

Systems to help allocate tasks have been in use for years in the area of production management and especially job scheduling [Baker, 1974]. Can similar, more human-oriented systems be used in other domains, for example, to manage work flows in an office? Do techniques from manufacturing such as just-in-time management apply in the service sector? Should such systems be organized hierarchically or should alternative organizing principles be employed? For example, we can envision a market-oriented organization in which distributed machine and human experts submit "bids" to perform knowledge work tasks.

How does technology impact the tasks performed?

In the previous paragraphs, we have looked at organizational tasks as a way of organizing our thoughts about how decision processes can be designed to support the performance of those tasks (i.e., task → IT research). But because IT is a powerful intervention that changes the way that humans perform current tasks and creates potential for entirely new kinds of tasks, we need to investigate the implications of IT on the tasks that are executed (i.e., IT → task research). For each form of IT in which we are interested, we need to investigate at least the following questions: How are changes in work manifested? How do people and groups rearrange their time? How are time savings achieved? What is the effect on satisfaction? on performance? on quality of work? What old tasks are eliminated? What new tasks are performed? How are internal patterns of communications affected? What are the beneficial effects? What are the undesirable side effects? What tasks that were hitherto impossible are now enabled by advances in technology? What tasks that are now being performed can be eliminated?

Environment

How does one describe the environment?

From a research point of view, it is important to be able to compare results across different situations. In practice, a support system that could recognize similarities and differences in past and present market situations would be invaluable. Can we develop a common language to help us describe social forces? Legal forces? Information technology futures? Production technology features and futures? The competitive situation? All of these factors influence strategy choice and impact the organization and its employees in an ongoing fashion.

How does environment impact the choice of decision processes?

Internationalization, major political events, intensified competition, rapid changes in technology, and the uncertain economic climate are all impacting organizational structure and processes at a rapid rate. There are opportunities to observe many natural experiments as firms respond to the turbulent environment in different ways. It is important to understand the conditions under which different responses such as outsourcing and team-based organizations are viable. On the prescriptive side, the ODSS chapter sketched some ways in which information technology might be helpful in restructuring organizations. Empirical evidence that these forms of support are in fact useful, their refinement in the light of experience, and the discovery of new forms of support are interesting research possibilities. The need to design organizational systems that respond to the increasing frequency and criticality of the decision-making process is also emphasized by a number of other researchers. Huber and McDaniel describe an organizational design approach based on the decision-making paradigm that includes 10 explicit guidelines, each of which poses a research challenge in itself [Huber and McDaniel, 1986]. Finally, the whole area of interorganizational systems challenges existing notions of organizational boundaries and information processing and needs further research.

Organization structure. In Chapter 5 on organizational decision support systems (ODSS), the need to restructure organizations was seen as a driving force for many interesting research possibilities (see also the discussion section at the end of the chapter).

What is the relationship between decision processes and organizational structures?

Marshak and Radnor investigate issues of centralization and decentralization under varying assumptions with regard to information uncertainty and collection and communication costs [Marshak and Radnor, 1972]. Galbraith discusses organization structure and the need to create hierarchical information systems and lateral (across organizational boundaries) information flows as a means of coping with task uncertainty [Galbraith, 1974]. More work is needed to understand the information and decision processing capacity of modern organizational structures that involve fewer organizational layers, interacting teams, and interorganizational systems.

How can support be provided for interacting teams?

Research is urgently needed on networked-based systems that help achieve coordination of remotely located teams working on common tasks in a distributed processing mode. Both coordination and joint problem-solving tasks need to be supported. The first requirement is to achieve a shared vision of the task and mutually understood mechanisms for communicating work progress and problems. A second requirement is the need to reduce complexity and make the division of labor as modular as possible so that information transfer and coordination requirements are reduced. Swanson and Zmud in Chapter 5 suggest some strategies (blackboards using cognitive maps for shared vision and decision ordering, information sharing, and negotiated choice for coordination), while Applegate and Henderson suggest a need for shared standards and policies. Collaborative support might be provided synchronously using telephones, video conferencing, or shared computer screens on a LAN, for example, or asynchronously using voice messaging, electronic mail, computer conferencing, and so on. Mixtures of these technologies might also be employed to increase communication bandwidth. While technology can help, we believe that success in this area requires (1) field and laboratory research leading to a basic understanding of the habits, needs, and activities of interacting work groups, and (2) the design of work representation schemes and protocols for coordinating computer-mediated work.

How should internal support for teams be provided?

This is a primary focus of the emerging area of collaborative work [Olson, 1989]. In the same reference, Johansen suggests 17 different forms of computer support for teams, most of which have received only meager attention from researchers [Johansen, 1989]. Chapter 4 in this volume provides an extensive discussion of support for group meetings [see also Stefic and Seely Brown, 1989].

Process. In accord with the concept of organizations as man-machine systems, we use the term "process" very broadly to include organizational, group, and individual decision processes, as well as processes that are executed within computers. This emphasizes a distributed processing view of organizations.

What classes of decision processes can be identified in real organizations?

There is a need for more information on the alternative decision processing strategies that are—or might be—employed in organizations. For example, there are formal decision processes associated with routine data processing tasks, such as budgeting and capital acquisition activities, and more or less formal decision processes for problem-solving tasks, such as the introduction of new products. In addition, there are bureaucratic decision processes involving due process for resolving certain classes of decisions, as pointed out by King and Star in Chapter 5. Finally, there are many informal decision processes designed on the spot, for such things as getting out a report by next week's deadline or arranging a promotional event. What other classes of decision process are there?

Given that it makes sense to identify different classes of decision processes, what are their properties? What are their advantages and disadvantages?

How can one choose among a myriad of possible decision process designs and technologies that are available (or could be designed) for the execution of each task? These decision processes are to some extent substitutes for each other—one could substitute individual for group decision making, for example—but we can also be sure that the effectiveness of each decision process choice will depend heavily on situational factors. Note that one way to approach this question is to discover the trade-offs between specific decision process technologies for different phases of the decision process and different subtasks of the overall task. There is already a lot of work at this more specific level. For example, we are beginning to explore the advantages and disadvantages of computer conferencing versus face-to-face meetings, and GDSS meeting rooms versus traditional forums. Accumulating this knowledge could help in the design of decision processes that employ multiple technologies both in parallel and over time. However, the appropriate choice of decision process type also depends on

- environmental factors such as legal requirements, competitive pressures, and so on;
- the available internal resources, including the installed IT systems and the nature and quality of the human resources;
- the time frame of the decision process (urgent, nonurgent, intermittent, regular);
- the magnitude of the decision;
- the kind of problem solving involved;
- the political nature of the groups performing the decision process; and
- cultural norms.

How can we support the transition between choice and implementation?

Almost all discussions of decision making end with the choice phase. Problems of implementation and feedback of information concerning success or failure have been a concern of DSS research, but it is almost as if there are two separate problems involved, separated by the magical moment of truth when the decision is made. Some other areas of management have suffered from the same schizophrenic behavior. For example, product design has often been separated from manufacturing process design with attendant problems in increased time to market and increased production costs. Other areas have been more careful. For example, CASE tools with application generators are creating a seamless integration of the system design and implementation phases. These lessons have value in all areas of management.

Dhar and Jarke make a valuable contribution in Chapter 7 of this volume when they describe how knowledge of a design or planning process can be captured and used to modify the design or plan when design assumptions are no longer valid. Extending this concept slightly, we believe that decision processing systems should not only make choices but also design and even implement the control systems useful for implementation. For some simple but very common situations, this may not be as hard as it sounds. For example, the task of producing a report might be decomposed into several subtasks that are assigned to different people. If this plan were known to an automated planning assistant, the employees' work schedules could be updated, required materials automatically ordered, and reminders sent to the employees when work on their subtask was required. While the example is simple, we believe that the general principle involved—of integrating the intelligence, design, choice, and implementation phases of decision processes—has large potential payoffs.

What are the real determinants of decision outcomes and what is an appropriate viewpoint for analysis of decision process needs?

In his book on the Cuban missile crisis, Allison points out that the decisions made by the two parties (Kennedy and Khrushchev) can be justified and explained from three points of view—rational, organizational process, and political [Allison, 1971]. Each of these viewpoints has different implications with regard to cause and effect mechanisms and different implications therefore for the kinds of support that should be provided. Research on this question would require intensive case studies and difficult analyses. If successful, it might be possible to identify those processes for which current rational approaches to decision support seem adequate as a first approximation and those for which other approaches are needed.

How does one support decision processes for which the main determinants of outcomes are political or social and cultural?

We should point out that there is already a very rich literature on game theory, bargaining theory, and so on and that there is a promising body of work on extending GDSS to provide support in overt conflict and negotiation situations [Shakun, 1985]. But there are probably many decision situations where political influences are important but hidden. Whether the politics are overt or not, this research question leads to other interesting research issues. How does one determine the objectives of such support? Should the system somehow remain neutral and unbiased? Or should the system predispose the outcome toward some rational (e.g., profit-maximizing or satisficing) objective? Are there classes of decision that we should not try to support at all?

What are the most important classes of decision process from the point of view of research and development payoff?

The traditional focus of DSS research has been on decision processes involving modeling and more recently on GDSS to support face-to-face meetings. A promising new area of research is developing in the area of computer-supported collaborative work (CSCW). How can the outputs of DSS research (for example, model management ideas and artificial intelligence techniques) be integrated into the CSCW work? What are the hidden or neglected decision processes where support can have big payoffs?

Are there generic aids that can be applicable across a broad variety of decision domains and classes of decision process?

The concept of providing general, non-domain-specific support was introduced in Chapter 1 in the discussion of cognitive aids for individual users. Examples are systems that provide support for multicriteria decision making and that attempt to enhance individual creativity. What general classes of cognitive aid can be useful in the support of group or organizational decision processes? Some obvious examples are systems to assist in scheduling meetings or to help in coordinating activities. Johansen provides 17 different examples [Johansen, 1989]. Other examples of group cognitive aids will be discussed at various points below. Research is needed to understand the potential and requirements for such tools and to identify the most promising opportunities for new tools.

How can we improve human information processing capabilities?

In a sense, the whole DSS movement addresses this problem. More specifically, we are concerned here with the cognitive processes used by humans while participating in decision processing tasks. Empirical studies have shown that human decision making differs from the predictions of rational models, casting doubt on the applicability of traditional approaches such as decision theory and expected utility theory. One theoretical approach is to recast normative decision-making theory to make it correspond more closely with reality. An alternative is to try to understand human information processing biases and to compensate for them in the interface to the DSS. Chapter 3 in this volume addresses these issues and suggests a comprehensive program of research involving the two disciplines of behavioral decision making and DSS. Similar programs of study in other areas of psychology are possible and desirable. Other related areas are marketing (the study of consumer choice behavior) and management science (determination of utilities and decision making in the face of multiple conflicting criteria).

Information

Why do organizations collect information?

This was the question posed by Culnan and Gutek in Chapter 5. Their answer indicated several reasons for gathering and using information that have not hitherto been seriously considered in DSS and MIS research. Continuing this line of inquiry, how can we assign economic values to these different classes of information? How can we develop systems to support its collection, processing, and dissemination?

How can we simplify information?

Information is becoming a cheap good. On-line databases that provide instant access to detailed marketing and financial information are commonplace. Executive information systems are feeding the outputs of traditional MIS systems to executive desks. We are deluged with information beyond anyone's capability to comprehend it. Research on techniques to detect, display, and explain underlying patterns in voluminous data is urgently needed. Such research will probably require the combination of statistics and AI techniques. Problem representation is another important area—in many modeling situations, there is a huge payoff to be obtained from the invention of more effective ways of displaying multiple relationships in complex spaces. Methods of representing information in multiple dimensions or using different types of media simultaneously (e.g., voice and graphics) are available and need research. New forms of hypertext systems that dynamically form associations between data in different formats on different media show promise [Conklin, 1987], as does visual interactive modeling [Turban and Carlson, 1988].

How can we filter information?

In addition to aggregating and analyzing information as discussed in the last paragraph, we can seek ways to avoid junk data and selectively collect data of interest. The "information lens" system which uses rule-based reasoning to filter each user's incoming electronic mail is a well-known example [Malone et al., 1987]. Systems that can understand and interpret text are currently under development. In the meantime, there are many other opportunities in document-based imaging and networked-based systems that must be waiting for discovery and exploitation.

How can we structure information?

Our experience during the ISDP workshop confirms the claim that GDSS systems are efficient generators of information. Techniques to summarize, rearrange, and understand text of this type or to structure the conversation and ideas of a group are sorely needed. Dynamic hypertext or even relatively simple interactive graphical representations could be useful in this regard. The Cognoter software tool at Xerox PARC that helps organize ideas from brainstorming sessions in a graphical format may be a precursor of future collaborative support tools [Stefic and Seely Brown, 1989]. Other applications for systems that can structure information in ways that assist human beings abound—for example, on-line graphical display of opposing arguments in a debate is one possibility.

How can we represent and store knowledge?

Going beyond information representation, there is a need for improved techniques for knowledge representation—that is, the representation of information plus the rules or meta-information necessary to use that information in an intelligent manner. This is the basis for systems that might be able to learn and to supply more intelligent forms of expert support. The reference discipline of AI is concerned with this question, and we will not explore it in any more detail here except to state its importance to the future of DSS (see also Chapter 7 in this volume).

Outcomes. Approximately 50 percent of all new investment in corporations today is being spent in information technology. Measuring the effectiveness of information technology use is therefore of the utmost importance but has so far proved to be extremely difficult. This difficulty arises not only from the problems of empirical measurement, but also because there are usually multiple system goals and the measures of effectiveness are often not independent of the observer. Obtaining feedback on outcomes in decision processes is a key to their control and adaptive improvement and presents a number of important research challenges.

How can one measure the effectiveness of decision processes?

At the organizational level, Quinn and Rohrbaugh describe a "spatial model" showing competing means-ends dimensions for four different management emphases: human resources, adaptive system, integrative system, and goal attainment [Quinn and Rohrbaugh, 1983]. Lewin and Minton [Lewin and Minton, 1986] discuss this and other organizational effectiveness measures and propose a method of measuring organizational effectiveness that involves tracing efficient production frontiers [Charnes et al., 1978]. These general ideas seem applicable at the level of organizational processes. For production processes, any or all of the following effectiveness criteria may be important: cost or profit, quality of output, productivity of work force, user satisfaction, process cycle time, responsiveness, reliability, and flexibility. Note that the recent emphasis on "total quality" is making this kind of process measurement much more common. These same criteria apply to knowledge work in general and to our conception of decision processes. However, if we consider decisions as the major output of a decision process, we face the same difficulties that have plagued empirical research in DSS (see Chapter 1). It may be possible to measure cost, user satisfaction, process cycle time, and responsiveness in some cases, but the measurement of decision quality, reliability, and flexibility presents severe challenges.

How does information technology impact users?

The presumption of most DSS research is that DSS can be designed to support cognitive processes and improve decision making. However, this implies that users will adopt the technology and use it in the way intended by the designers. The reader is referred to Benbasat and Todd's discussion of theories of DSS use in Chapter 6 for an overview of theory and suggestions for research in this area.

How can we ensure desirable outcomes?

If we are to design decision processes, then we should also try to establish an environment that is conducive to their successful employment. There are a number of important research questions. First, how can we motivate desirable uses of the system? As suggested by Huber and McDaniel, a reward system for good decision making is probably desirable [Huber and McDaniel, 1986]. What are the attributes of good decision making that should be rewarded and how should they be measured? How can we prevent possible undesirable side effects of the reward system (such as gaming)? A second direction for research in this area is to discover how decision processes can be designed to support notions of equity and fairness (see the discussion on due process by King and Star in Chapter 5). Finally, decision process systems are multiperson man-machine systems that require good "human engineering," probably even more than do individual software programs. The policies, organizational framework, and human task assignments must all be designed to be user friendly and supportive. We have only just begun to learn what "user friendly" means in a group context (see Chapter 4). In this area, we need a better understanding of how information technology can be used to make jobs more interesting, to reinforce group and organizational cohesiveness, and to promote a sense of mission and purpose.

Final thoughts and a "blue rose"

Our interpretation of the major changes in research directions suggested by the ISDP research program was listed at the beginning of this chapter. In our opinion, the changes do indeed constitute a paradigm shift of major proportions. In the remainder of the chapter we developed a research framework to organize our discussion and suggest interesting research questions at a more detailed level. This book has provided many specific suggestions for research topics, and in the final chapter we will have more to say on research methods that may help us understand these topics and accumulate knowledge in the information systems and decision processes area. In this section, we give some final thoughts on the subject of research directions and propose a vehicle for a joint program of research that could serve to stimulate and focus research efforts.

In the words of baseball philosopher Yogi Berra, "You can observe a lot just by watching." The first of our two final recommendations for ISDP research is that Berra's advice should be taken very seriously. Information systems are man-made artifacts that exist in a social world, and they cannot be studied in isolation from that world. Useful theory must be grounded in observation and must, at least in the not too distant future, have significant practical implications. Apart from anything else, there is just too much of interest to waste time adding footnotes to previous research where the payoff is known to be insignificant. Following this recommendation means that more researchers should work closely with practitioners as both observers and as active partners in real decision making.

Our second recommendation is to concentrate on unstructured rather than structured problems—as DSS researchers, we should swallow our own medicine! Real progress can be made by bringing structure to hitherto fuzzy and uncertain areas. One unstructured area with huge potential payoffs in terms of better systems and increased acceptance of systems involves gaining a better understanding of the human component of the information system, and especially the interaction between technology and the mental, social, and political worlds in which human actions take place. A second unstructured area involves problems that should be at the root of the information systems field. We should take the stuff of information systems—information—more seriously. Understanding how to add value to data and to refine it for decision-making purposes should be major preoccupations of the field. To guide this work, we need a deeper understanding of (1) the structure of tasks and how they can be represented, decomposed, and processed; (2) human problem-solving processes; and (3) techniques for problem representation. A third unstructured area lies in our understanding of knowledge itself. Our field has progressed from a preoccupation with data in the early days of data processing to an interest in information during the MIS era and in decision making in the DSS era. More recently, in the last decade, we have become interested in knowledge-based systems. But, at best, our understanding of the structure of knowledge is a poor imitation of reality. The meaning and structure of knowledge have been preoccupations of philosophy throughout history, and they are central concerns of many other fields including education, psychology, psychiatry, and artificial intelligence. While information systems researchers may not take the lead in this area, we should be very aware of progress in other fields because, in some real sense, knowledge, its discovery, accumulation, and communication are at the heart of the information systems idea.

To focus our research ideas, we need a "blue rose." In the field of bioengineering, a challenge was let out that competency in this area might be demonstrated by accomplishing a task that could not be accomplished in the absence of new skills. The challenge was to "engineer" a blue rose. Blue roses have not existed in nature, and the ability to develop such a specimen would clearly demonstrate the attainment of new competencies in the field. Thus, bioengineers established a classic problem that offered a common direction and vocabulary, agreed-upon measures, and an event that would clearly signal that a significant advance in knowledge had been achieved.

Another example of such a challenge is the famous Turing test [Turing, 1950] to recognize examples of artificial intelligence. In this test, the "system" responds to questions, as does a human "foiler." If the testing agent is unable to identify which responding entity is the human imposter within five minutes (i.e., if the system can fool the questioner for five minutes), then the system may be said to be intelligent. Other fields have made frequent use of such challenges—the four-color theorem in mathematics, the traveling salesman problem in operations research, building strong structures out of x ounces of balsa wood in engineering. So too in the information systems field, we need to establish research challenges, the achievement of which will stimulate the attainment of new skills and the accomplishment of milestones in knowledge attainment.

We now offer some ideas for significant research projects that will provide a challenge and focus for dialogues on the future role and practice for a decision process view of the firm. It is up to the research community as a whole either to accept these challenges or to find better ones:

- Demonstration that a novice with a decision support tool can perform as well as an expert decision-maker in some domain.
- The complete relocation of judgment and decisions from historically human decision-makers to systems for a narrow function, say, underwriting (loans or insurance policies).
- The development of a commercially viable model management system.
- The development of an interactive system to support the worldwide community of information systems researchers. The system would maintain bibliographic information, facilitate the review and publication of research papers, and provide extensive computer conferencing opportunities for researchers.
- Representation of the knowledge that should be gained in a subject area within the information systems curriculum (or any other knowl-

edge domain) in a manner that would be concrete, readily understand-able, and verifiable in the light of the best research to date in the field. Such a representation might utilize ideas on knowledge representa-tion from the fields of semantic databases and artificial intelligence. It might employ hypertext and multimedia techniques to assist the exploration of ideas and to make the interface and learning experience more enjoyable. Success at one level would be achieved if the system proved useful as a medium of communication both within the field and outside it. Even greater success would be indicated if the knowl-edge representation system proved to be a significantly better learning device than a textbook.

We make progress by answering questions or solving problems that are important or interesting, or both. It is incumbent upon the community of researchers in the ISDP arena to identify the meaningful challenges that will provide the needed communication of ideas and results that will advance the level of discussion and the knowledge of the discipline.

Chapter 9

Research Approaches in ISDP

Benn R. Konsynski and Edward A. Stohr

Up to this point, this book has been primarily concerned with developing ideas for research directions in some of the subareas of the emerging field of research that deals with decision processes in organizations. In other words, we have been dealing with "the what" of a possible research program. In this final section of the book, we present some ideas on how IS researchers can use traditional and newly emerging research methodologies to advance knowledge. This leads to some specific recommendations for the ISDP subfield.

This chapter is not a tutorial on research methods. Rather, it is an overview of research options that are frequently exercised in the conduct of research on information systems and organizations. It is our intent to encourage consideration of a broad range of research approaches and to suggest multimethod research programs targeted at the issues raised in Chapter 8 and elsewhere in this book. Research methods are not ends in themselves nor guarantors of truth in any sense; they merely help establish a degree of confidence in the information gained from our investigations. ISDP research is concerned with the intersection of technical and social systems and involves a broad range of physical, systemic, social, cognitive, philosophical, and even aesthetic and moral issues. Each of these dimensions offers challenges in terms of research method selection that we leave up to the skill and taste of the researcher.

The chapter is organized as follows. We start with a simple model of how different categories of research can be thought of as combining to generate knowledge. We follow this by a brief discussion of the implications of this model and a call for a better understanding of the process of knowledge generation in the IS field. In the next subsection, we provide a more in-depth discussion of the various techniques, followed by a discussion of research methodology paradigms. A final subsection draws some conclusions relevant to the research program that is needed in the ISDP area.

A knowledge acquisition model for IS research

There are a bewildering number of research methods available to IS researchers. Table 1 contains a brief summary of the major types. We distinguish between empirical research methods and analytic research methods. In empirical research, the researcher uses data and observations from the laboratory and/or the real world to develop knowledge using a mixture of inductive and deductive reasoning. The knowledge generated by empirical research usually consists of statements about the behavior of the phenomenon given certain contingent conditions. In analytic research one develops assumptions and axioms about the phenomenon of interest and deductively develops propositions about its behavior. The knowledge produced by analytic research is usually encapsulated in models that can be used to explain and predict real-world phenomena. It is not our intention to provide a detailed overview of research methodology; however, some discussion of specific research methods will be provided in later sections together with relevant sources of reference material.

We now describe a simple, idealized view of IS research as a knowledge generator. The overview assigns different roles to various research methodologies and emphasizes their interaction in advancing knowledge (see Figure 1). In practice, of course, there is no such "grand design"; researchers choose research methods based on the research question they want to answer and are influenced in this choice by their own backgrounds and the prevailing research paradigms of the field.

Table 1. Summary of research methods.

Empirical Research Methods

Sample surveys:	Analysis of questionnaire and interview data
Experimental:	Laboratory experiments
	Field experiments
Nonexperimental:	Field and case studies
	Interpretive methods
Econometric:	Regression analysis/other
AI techniques:	Protocol analysis
	Knowledge acquisition techniques

Analytic Research Methods

Computer simulation
Mathematical modeling: Economic models
Optimization models

Computer science models
Logical systems modeling

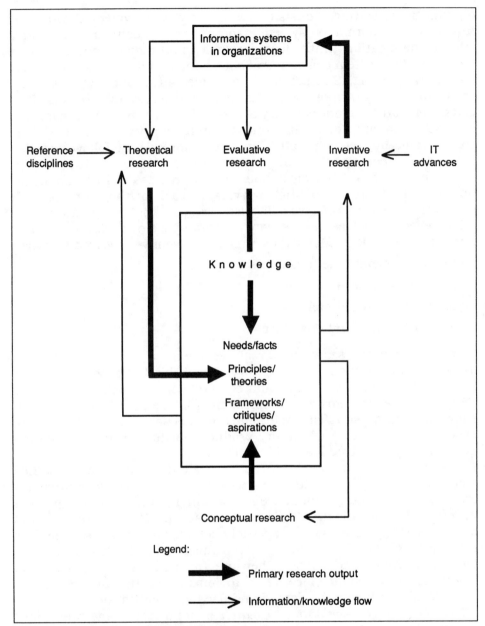

Figure 1. IS research as a knowledge generator.

We adopt Keen's view that the goal of IS research is to improve the design, delivery, and use of computer systems and information technology in organizations [Keen, 1980]. The box at the top of Figure 1 represents the primary research objects (information systems) in their organizational setting. Consistent with the view prevalent throughout this book, an information system is more than just software, hardware, and communications links; it is a complex and dynamically changing sociotechnical system consisting of both human and machine elements.

Broadly speaking, IS research can be divided into four categories based on the underlying purpose of the research. Single research projects often consist of more than one category of research, and most MIS researchers conduct research in more than one research category. Because of their considerable impact in practice, in the examples that follow, we also consider the contributions of practitioners, software developers, and researchers from related disciplines to the progress of IS in organizations. We first provide a brief overview of each of the four research categories; following this, we will briefly examine their interaction.

The objective of *inventive research* is to propose or design innovative uses of IT technology. Major topic areas for inventive research include

- new development methodologies,
- technology innovations,
- innovative applications, and
- innovative organizational forms.

The dynamics of research in IS requires invention and implementation as well as understanding and theory. Which kind of research should precede the other is a chicken and egg problem that defies resolution. Thus, database systems were implemented in the field before research efforts produced a satisfying relational theory of data. On the other hand, expert systems were a laboratory product that took years of gestation before they were introduced into the field.

Researchers working in the inventive mode draw on theory, codified design principles, the results of evaluative testing of specific approaches and systems, personal experience and intuition, and new developments in information technology. They conceive and design new solutions to organizational problems using a variety of tools and methods, including mathematical modeling, organizational theory, the findings of human factors research, and so on. They are the applied researchers and engineers whose main objective is to impact practice by having the outputs of their research adapted and used in organizations.

The objective of *evaluative research* is to perform an intelligence function by testing and probing both the environment of organizations and the performance of specific information systems or approaches to developing and managing information systems. Typical research topics in this category are the following:

- Spotting macro and micro trends that may impact IS—technology innovations, demographic and job market trends, skills shortages, future educational requirements, and so on.

- Gathering information on current problems and opportunities for IS research and development through opinion surveys and other means.

- Discovering what works and what doesn't work—methodology testing, software testing, and so on.

- Evaluating the impacts of IT and determining the value of IT investment.

The primary research methods employed in evaluative research include sample surveys, field and laboratory experiments, field studies, case studies, and mathematical modeling (usually followed by empirical testing of the model). As is evident from the above, there are really two subcategories of evaluative research. Some research in this category involves environmental scanning—seeking to alert IS researchers and practitioners to the real state of the world. This subcategory of research is often labeled "descriptive" because there is little opportunity for theoretical grounding or interpretation of the phenomena of interest. The second subcategory of evaluative research is more product-oriented—aiming at incremental improvements in products, procedures, and management methods. Thus, the followers of the evaluative research tradition are both sleuths who discover directions and trends, and critics who provide feedback to other researchers and developers.

The objectives of *theoretical research* are to discover and test lasting principles and causal theories of IS design, implementation, and practice. There are a number of aspects of information systems on which theoretical research can be focused [Ginzberg and Zmud, 1988]:

- individual, work group, or organizational levels of aggregation;

- technological, operational, managerial, or institutional concerns;

- transaction, communication, or decision targets; and

- work life, quality of work life, motivational, and political impacts.

We also should add the dichotomy, mentioned a number of times in this book, between research that focuses on understanding the processes used by individuals and groups when they interact with information technology, and research that focuses on the outcomes of that interaction. Research topics can also differ according to the "reference disciplines" adopted by the researcher. These include organization theory, behavioral theory, communications theory, economics, management science, and computer science. One of the major themes of this book has been the necessity for IS researchers to build upon the work of such reference disciplines.

All of the methods mentioned in Table 1 are of possible use in theory building and testing. In general, some subcategories such as qualitative and analytic research methods are more concerned with the discovery of theory and relationships, while others, such as experimental and survey research, are more concerned with theory testing.

Whatever topic is addressed, reference discipline followed, or research methodology adopted, researchers in the theory building mode, of necessity, take a longer range view of their research. Their objective is to produce knowledge and understanding about the way information technology impacts work, communication, and decision-making activities at both the individual and group levels. Only after this knowledge is accumulated can it be used to guide the development and implementation of applications.

The objectives of *conceptual research* are to generate research frameworks, to provide critiques, and to set aspirations for the overall research field. Meaningful research frameworks are not obvious or easy to develop in any scientific field. This is particularly so for IS because of its relative youth, because so many reference disciplines have important contributions to make, and because of the rapid changes in technologies that continually shift the target of research. (Are there any of us still interested in the efficiency of batch processing or in strategies for time-sharing?)

In an important sense, the inventive role of IS research continually changes the rules of the game, making it harder to develop theory and principles that have long-term efficacy. Frameworks can be useful in drawing together a field of knowledge, in identifying gaps in current knowledge, and in pointing to meaningful directions of research. Good frameworks can also be very persuasive; an example immediately relevant to this book is the Gorry and Scott Morton framework for IS that is perhaps the starting point for the DSS field [Gorry and Scott Morton, 1971]. (We distinguish between frameworks and models in that the latter specify relationships between concepts, whereas frameworks do not.) There have been many critiques of the IS field and of DSS in particular. Some are concerned with research quality and relevance [e.g., Keen, 1991]. Others contend that there is a need for a shift in paradigm regarding the field's basic concepts and objectives [Hirschheim and Klein, 1989] or how research should be conducted [Orlikowski and Baroudi, 1990, 1991].

We include setting aspirations as a useful function of conceptual research because it is easy to think short term and to languish in yesterday's problems as a result. The realization in practice of many ideas from science fiction demonstrates the importance of considering the limits of what is possible in using IT. Johansen provides a good example of conceptual research that sets aspirations in the area of collaborative technologies [Johansen, 1989].

Conceptual research is difficult because there is no standard by which its scientific quality can be judged a priori. Quality can often be judged only ex post facto if the proposed frameworks and ideas are accepted and assert an influence on the field. Those who engage in conceptual research use their own intuition and scholarship and their knowledge of the philosophy of science and other reference disciplines. These are the armchair philosophers of the field. (It is often argued that there are far too many of them!)

In summary, evaluative research provides a scanning and testing function, inventive research produces new information products and new implementation and management techniques, theory building research develops long-term principles and theory to improve IS practice and to guide inventive research, and finally, conceptual research provides over-all guidance on research directions and paradigms. We have separate categories for evaluative and theory building research largely because we see the need for a quicker feedback to practice than seems possible from theory building and testing research in its current state of development. This is not to say that evaluative research should not be theory driven— only that the development of generalizable, certifiable, and useful knowledge seems to require a qualitatively different frame of reference and level of effort. The boundary between theoretical and concept research may also be blurred at times. Still we think that it is useful to distinguish between contributions that are direction setting and those that are concerned more directly with the production of knowledge. In practice, many, if not most, research projects involve more than one of the four categories of research. Methodology development and product development research are usually accompanied by evaluative research on the methodology or product produced. Thus, inventive and evaluative research together advance IT knowledge and practice in an evolutionary "generate and test" manner. The contributions on model management in Chapter 7 combine conceptual, analytic theory building, and inventive research elements. Research programs on GDSS at Arizona, Minnesota, Claremont, and other sites combine inventive, evaluative, and theory building research tasks (see Chapter 5).

Implications of the knowledge generation model

In theory, the above picture of the various research methods combining to form a dynamic knowledge acquisition system has some appeal. At least, it points out the need for multiple research approaches and the need for tolerance among researchers who may favor one category of research over another. It also might explain to some extent why the overall IS research field appears chaotic to many observers.

The framework in Figure 1 immediately gives rise to a number of interesting questions. First, what should be the objective of the IS research field? Should we concentrate our efforts on increasing the total store of IS knowledge or should our primary objective be to assist IS practice? The choice of topics and therefore the choice of research methodology will change quite markedly if we make one choice or the other. In essence, this is the old debate concerning "pure" and "applied" research. Given the difficulties that have been experienced in adding to the store of IS knowledge in the form of firm principles and causal theories (and the cost of any program of theoretical research), it is obvious that the topics for such research programs should be chosen with care. In our opinion, this means that topics should be chosen not only for their contribution to knowledge, but also to maximize potential benefits in practice. If the connection between a given piece of theoretical research and its eventual (perhaps long-term) effect on practice is not clear and significant, then it should not be pursued. Just as truth is often stranger than fiction, so too are real problems often more interesting, deeper, and more satisfying than contrived problems that fill in small and inconsequential gaps in knowledge.

It is perhaps interesting to speculate on the ideal mix of research methods if, for a given set of research questions, it were possible to design the knowledge acquisition process in Figure 1 according to some criterion of optimality. To begin by looking at current practice, surveys of IS research [Orlikowski and Baroudi, 1991; Culnan, 1987; Culnan and Swanson, 1986; Weill and Olson, 1989; Zmud et al., 1989; Vogel and Wetherbe, 1984] show that a little more than 50 percent of all IS research is empirical, with the remainder consisting of conceptual and model building research. According to Orlikowski and Baroudi, empirical research consists mainly of surveys (49 percent), laboratory experiments (27 percent), case studies (13 percent), and field experiments (3 percent) [Orlikowski and Baroudi, 1991]. Unfortunately, these figures do not map neatly on to the four categories of research in Figure 1. In any case, the above question is obviously unanswerable in any absolute sense. While this may be true, many researchers do have strong feelings about the relative mix of research methodologies that should be used to advance the field. A number of authors have criticized the relatively high proportion of conceptual and descriptive surveys in IS research [Dickson, 1989]. Within the behavioral research area, there have also been calls for more laboratory studies [Dickson, 1989], field experiments [Zmud et al., 1989], and interpretive studies [Orlikowski and Baroudi, 1990].

Another criticism of IS research that is sometimes heard is that it is "technology driven." Presumably, this equates to a call for less inventive research and more theoretical research. But if the objects studied in IS research are sociotechnical systems, it seems equally important (and much easier) to improve the technology component as it does to develop theories about individual and group behavior or about the interaction of the human and technology components. Who can doubt the tremendous impact of inventions such as the mouse or windows? And once an IT invention is in the field, it is incumbent on IS researchers to investigate its uses and impacts.

It must be emphasized that the appropriate choice of a research methodology depends on the phenomena of interest and the research task at hand [Benbasat, 1985]. Given the broad range of research tasks in the IS field and the complexity of social research in general, this leads to the conclusion that IS researchers should broaden the array of research methods that they use. For example, given the above data, this would mean a move in the behavioral research area toward more studies that have greater realism (field experiments, case studies, and interpretive techniques). In the next section, we will attempt to give this prescription more weight.

To conclude, we believe it important to consider the questions raised in this section. For individual research centers engaged in long-term programs of research involving numbers of researchers, proper directions for research and selection of the appropriate mix of research approaches can, to some extent, be planned and managed. For the IS field as a whole, more knowledge of the choices and better education as to the role of the various research methods in furthering knowledge would be beneficial. In this regard, it might be useful to perform a careful analysis of selected research methods aimed at determining the tasks for which they are most suited and to gain some appreciation for their productivity in terms of "knowledge yield" per unit of effort.

Discussion of research methods and paradigms

In this section, we provide a brief overview of the various research methods listed in Table 1 with examples and reference sources. Our purpose is not to provide a comprehensive survey but rather to illustrate a number of very different research methods. This leads to a discussion of some research methodology paradigms that are present in IS research and some suggestions for approaches that might be suitable in the ISDP area.

Empirical research methods. Two classic texts on empirical research methods are Campbell and Stanley [Campbell and Stanley, 1966] and Kerlinger [Kerlinger, 1986]. Stone provides an excellent overview of empirical research methods [Stone, 1978]. Overviews of empirical research methods in IS are contained in Weick [Weick, 1985] and Mumford et al. [Mumford et al., 1985]. In-depth discussions of the experimental, qualitative, and survey approaches to IS research are contained in Benbasat [Benbasat, 1989], Cash and Lawrence [Cash and Lawrence, 1989], and Kraemer [Kraemer, 1991], respectively.

Experimental methods were first developed in the physical sciences and have been a mainstay of scientific research. In a typical behavioral experiment, a small number of dependent and independent variables that are thought to be associated with the phenomenon to be investigated are isolated (independent variables cause changes in the values of dependent variables). Causal behavior is posited in advance on the basis of prior experimental results, received theory, or deductive reasoning. This causal behavior is usually stated in the form of hypotheses that are then tested in the experiment by manipulating the independent variables and measuring the effects on the dependent variables. Control is asserted by the random assignment of subjects to treatment and control groups and by eliminating or controlling for nuisance or intervening variables. Inference is possible (high "internal validity" is attained) to the extent that statistically significant changes in a dependent variable are found when an independent variable is changed, and the control is good enough to eliminate all other possible explanations of the observed changes. The "external validity" of an experiment is the degree to which the causal relationships observed in the experimental setting can be generalized to other populations and situations of interest. A number of variants on experimental designs such as quasi-experimental designs are possible [Cook and Campbell, 1979].

In a *laboratory experiment*, the researcher establishes an artificial environment and develops artificial experimental tasks to be performed by subjects (who for economic and other reasons are usually students). The advantage of laboratory experimentation is the high degree of internal validity that can be attained; on the other hand, the generalizability (external validity) of the results may be low. For this reason, a number of researchers [e.g., Zmud et al., 1989] have advocated greater use of *field experiments*, in which experiments are performed in a natural setting (e.g., the site of the experiment is an actual company, the subjects are managers, and the experimental tasks are real problems faced by the managers). Unfortunately, field experiments are difficult and expensive to set up, and it may be difficult to assert as high a degree of control as is possible in the laboratory. Thus, external validity may be gained only at the expense of internal validity. (This trade-off between control and generalizability is common to all empirical methods [Mason, 1989].)

Nonexperimental research studies are characterized by the fact that the experimenter cannot control the independent variables of the study but rather must infer them (for example, from self-reports of the subjects). This makes inference of causality between the independent and dependent variables difficult [Stone, 1978]. *Field studies* are carried out in natural settings, the dependent and independent variables are measured in a nonobtrusive manner, and the focus of the work may be descriptive, exploratory, or hypothesis testing. A *case study* involves the extensive study of a specific group or organizational unit, generally over a long period of time. Data can be collected by multiple means such as interviews, document search, or questionnaires. The objective of the case study is usually exploratory—to generate hypotheses or discover relationships that might not be found by other research methods—and the output is often qualitative rather than quantitative in form. However, it is sometimes possible to perform inference in case study research. Since data can be gathered on many different dependent variables, alternative theories that purport to explain those phenomena can be systematically tested [Campbell, 1975].

According to the data presented in the previous section, *sample surveys* (collection and analysis of questionnaire or interview data) constitute the most popular research method for IS researchers. The objectives of sample survey research include description (e.g., determining the opinions, attitudes, and demographic characteristics of a target population of individuals), prediction, and hypothesis testing. Questionnaires can be administered personally or mailed to respondents, and are a relatively simple and cheap method of objectively gathering data. Standardized questionnaires have been developed to measure variables such as job stress, user satisfaction, and cognitive style, thereby encouraging the use of common measurement systems by different researchers. Disadvantages of survey techniques as a means of gathering data include (1) problems of low return rates for mailed questionnaires giving rise to low external validity and (2) their inflexibility compared with subjective means of gathering data such as interviews and observer-participant methods. Only the predetermined questions can be answered so that important information may be overlooked by the researcher.

Orlikowski and Baroudi categorize empirical research studies into three epistemological approaches: descriptive, logical positivist, and interpretive [Orlikowski and Baroudi, 1990]. Descriptive studies are aimed at gathering facts, have little theoretical grounding, and provide little opportunity for theory building or theory testing. Empirical researchers interested in theory may work deductively, moving from a foundation of established knowledge and theory to carefully reasoned hypotheses of what should occur in their experiments. Or alternatively, they may take an inductive, exploratory approach to their research, "letting the data tell the story." The former *logical positivist* approach is the basis of the experimental methods discussed above. It has a strong appeal for those who see a need to work methodically to tease reliable threads of knowledge from the complex fabric of reality. The latter *interpretive* approach is the major motivation for some (not all) case studies and for some other qualitative research methods that will be outlined below.

The objective of *interpretive methods* is to obtain a "deep" understanding of the phenomena being investigated. As mentioned above, no prior assumptions are made so that the investigator can be free of any preconceptions. It is important to note also that interpretivism often ascribes a different meaning to reality. While logical positive approaches require independent variables that can be manipulated or at least observed, interpretivists assert that there are internal mental, conscious or unconscious determinants of human actions that cannot be so manipulated or (easily) observed. They also question logical positivist notions of one-way causality in social dynamics. (Is job performance a result of job satisfaction, job satisfaction a result of job performance, or are both statements simultaneously true?) Finally, in contrast to logical positivism, which requires few explanatory variables, interpretivists can develop "high-variety" languages that have sufficient richness to explain complex social phenomena [Daft and Wigington, 1979]. Interpretive methods come in several flavors [Orlikowski and Baroudi, 1990]: *phenomenology* is concerned with systematically studying consciousness; *ethnomethodology* is concerned with the study of the processes and conventions that people use to negotiate and reach consensus; *symbolic interactionism* examines the process by which individuals interpret the situation they are in through the exchange of shared interpretations and the development of social roles; *contextualism* takes a historical approach to the study of change; *ethnographics* is an anthropological method for studying the determinants of behavior which involves the researcher actually living in the organization for an extended period of time. An example of interpretivist research in IS is given by Boland and Day, who studied a year in the life of a systems designer unearthing issues regarding motivations and performance enhancers and inhibitors that may not have been discovered by other research approaches [Boland and Day, 1982].

Interpretive approaches address more complex situations than the other research methods and can enrich understanding of important issues. However, while interpretive methods are high in realism, it may be hard to generalize their results to other populations and situations. It is relatively easy for other researchers to understand and test the causal results of positive methods of generating knowledge. The rich results of interpretive research methods may make the accumulation of transferable knowledge through these methods more difficult.

Econometric techniques are familiar from economics and will not be discussed in great detail here. Regression analysis is useful for developing and testing mathematical models of phenomena involving variables for which either time series or cross-sectional data can be collected.

The field of *artificial intelligence* is directly concerned with understanding and emulating or simulating human intelligence. Protocol analysis involves the detailed collection and subsequent analysis of verbal explanations from subjects who are engaged in problem-solving activities. These techniques have been highly developed to the point where there is a standard methodology [Erickson and Simon, 1982]. Knowledge acquisition techniques that have been developed in the expert systems area include the automatic recognition of patterns and concomitant production of the rules used by expert decision-makers [Quinlan, 1979].

Analytic research methods

In analytic research one develops a model of a real-world phenomenon by representing it in terms of variables and making assumptions about the relationships between these variables using a largely deductive process. The model can then be used

- to test the assumptions of the model in order to confirm our understanding of the real world,

- to generate prescriptions in the form of optimal (or near optimal) decisions that should be made, or

- to make predictions about the future course of events (as in forecasting).

CONDOR provides a good overview of analytic research methods that contains many prescriptions for research and also discusses the relationship between DSS and operations research [CONDOR, 1988].

Empirical research has been the subject of many tomes, and there exist explicit methods of doing research that are recognized by all researchers. In contrast, relatively little has been written about the process of conducting analytic research. Many methods (algorithms and so on) are available, but the literature is strangely silent on the human process of modeling. (Polya is a notable exception [Polya, 1957].) Perhaps the paucity of epistemological investigations in the analytic research area reflects the largely introspective and often individualistic nature of work in this field.

The objective of much analytic research is to provide methods of solving classes of problems (such as job scheduling in computer systems, the development of optimal topographies in communication networks, or methods for representing knowledge in expert systems). Each problem technique contributes to the certified store of IS knowledge, just as do the propositions of behavioral theory. Concepts of internal and external validity apply to analytic models just as they do to empirical models. For some classes of analytic models, internal validity can be unambiguously established in the form of a mathematical proof. In many operations research applications (such as refinery scheduling and portfolio analyses), external validity is also relatively easy to establish. It is of course a different matter when analytic modeling techniques are applied in a social context—in general, both internal and external validity will be in question.

Computer simulations model assumed relationships in a real-world system, the properties of which can then be explored by manipulating independent variables in a manner similar to laboratory experiments. The problem with simulation models is that, until recently, the models were expensive to develop and difficult to validate. Cohen and Cyert discuss possible applications to organizational design [Cohen and Cyert, 1965], but there have been relatively few applications of simulations in either the social sciences or IS. New graphics-oriented simulation systems are now available that make certain classes of simulation model easy to develop and test. Eventually, it can be expected that the information systems development process will routinely involve the development and testing of simulation models of alternative systems before they are implemented in organizations. Including human behaviors in such models will, however, remain a problem in the foreseeable future.

Some examples of *optimization models* have already been mentioned. *Economic models* also have relevance for IS. Information economics is thought by some to provide a theoretical underpinning for IS. (See Chapter 2 for an application of this model to building a framework for IS research and Marshak and Radnor [Marshak and Radnor, 1972] for an exposition of team theory.) The models based on agency theory [Jensen and Meckling, 1973] that are beginning to be used in IS research have their roots in the information economics stream of research.

Computer science and its subfield of artificial intelligence provide many successful examples of models that are useful in IS research. These include models of computer networks, database modeling, models of how knowledge can be represented, models of human and machine learning, and so on.

By *logical systems modeling* we mean an analytic approach to the development of models of organizations and complex man-machine systems. Influential examples of logical systems models are contained in the books by March and Simon [March and Simon, 1958] and Cyert and March [Cyert and March, 1963]. More current examples are contained in Huber's theory relating IT to organizational design, intelligence, and decision making [Huber, 1990] and Holsapple and Whinston's hyperknowledge-based system model in Chapter 7 of this text. Good models of this type build on received theory and the lessons of history. They require scholarship together with imagination to see things as a united whole. The propositions that they contain provide guidelines for research and practice challenging empirical verification or providing architectures for advanced systems implementation.

Research methodology paradigms

In the previous section we discussed a number of empirical and analytic research methods. Both good empirical research and good analytic research are required if we are to improve the performance of IS as an academic field. We regard both classes of research as being equally important. Both contribute to theory, both require scholarship, and both exhibit a similar trade-off—between realism and control in empirical research and between realism and tractability in analytic research.

In practice, the conduct of IS research seems to be improving in quality [Benbasat 1989]. The young researchers entering the field are better educated in research methods, and expectations of what constitutes acceptable research methodology have risen. However, empirical research in MIS appears to have had little impact on practice [Dickson, 1989]. Theory building research relevant to IS seems to have been performed more successfully outside the IS field than within it. (After all, we do have a theory of databases, information economics does provide some legitimacy for our field, and cognitive science and behavioral decision theory have developed some lasting principles that are useful for IS researchers.) Obviously, theory building is an important objective of IS research, and it seems reasonable that such research should be applicable in practice. Dickson and others believe that the complexity of research problems in the IT field, as in the other social sciences, is such that only concentrated *programs* of research involving a number of experiments on the same phenomenon by a number of researchers over an extended period of time can advance the state of knowledge.

While we have singled out experimental research above, we believe that analytic research in our field has also contributed less than it might. Such research is often short-term in nature and directed at problems that are not of great moment in practice. Moreover, as in empirical research, there is a need for both scholarship and hard work; advances in knowledge are, for the most part, cumulative and incremental, and produced by a number of researchers working on a common problem and developing a shared language of communication.

Research in IS is a difficult enterprise requiring better direction, more skill, more resources, and more time than we have hitherto thought necessary. But it is also possible that we need to think in terms of a paradigmatic shift in the manner in which research is conducted (just as in the last chapter, we advocated a need to change our paradigm concerning the substantive issues to be researched by DSS researchers).

In their study of IS behavioral research, Orlikowski and Baroudi found that the overwhelming majority (72.9 percent) were in the positivist tradition, followed by descriptive studies (23.9 percent) and interpretive studies at only 3.2 percent [Orlikowski and Baroudi, 1991]. Furthermore, an investigation of the time period of the studies revealed that the overwhelming majority (90.3 percent) were cross-sectional single-snapshot studies; longitudinal studies constituted 4.5 percent of the sample; cross-sectional multiple-time-period studies, 3.9 percent; and protocol analyses, 1.3 percent. Thus, most behavioral research is positivist in its approach and largely ignores the time dimension.

Given the wide range of research questions in IS, there is a need for a broader use of the available research methodologies. No one methodology appears a priori to be superior to another—each has a different worldview and can yield different kinds of knowledge when used to investigate the same real-world phenomenon. The research method should match the research question under study. What we are advocating is a greater awareness of and education in the broad array of research methodologies that are available. In the behavioral research area, this means a shift from a state of affairs in which there is a dominating positivist paradigm to a state in which at least two paradigms (positivist and interpretive) coexist. Note that the two approaches can be used jointly to add both richness and certifiability to research results. (Interpretive methods might be used to generate theories that are later tested experimentally, or experimental results might be elaborated and confirmed by interpretive studies.) Nevertheless, the logical positivist and interpretive epistemologies involve fundamentally different assumptions about how knowledge can best be accumulated in the social sciences.

In both the empirical and analytic research areas, there is a great need to understand the research paradigms used by the reference disciplines that are important to the field. Without this understanding, IS researchers are in constant danger of misinterpreting the research of other disciplines. One interesting strategy for carrying out interdisciplinary research was discussed by Elam et al. in Chapter 3 of this volume. They suggested a research program involving two teams of cooperating groups of researchers. The first team, from the DSS area, would study the impact of a specific form of IT on decision-makers in order to test existing theories and develop new theories about human behavior. The second, from the behavioral decision-making discipline, would study the human decision-maker directly, to develop theory and suggest forms of IT based on that theory. The same approach can be applied in other areas and with other reference disciplines. While the difficulty and expense of conducting an interdisciplinary research program should not be underestimated, we believe that an orchestrated approach like this could yield important insights.

We also need to understand the role that different research methods can have in breaking the "normal straight jacket of science" [Daft and Lewin, 1990]. In their introduction to the inaugural issue of *Organization Science*, Daft and Lewin address the need for new paradigms in organization theory. Among other approaches, they advocate "heretical research methods" that attempt to find surprising results by examining outliers rather than central tendencies, by prescriptive research that includes implementation in a real organization, and by longitudinal case studies across several organizations.

Another general strategy for acquiring understanding is to attempt explanations of the same phenomenon from entirely different viewpoints—either with respect to the model of the phenomenon itself or with respect to the epistemology that is applied to pursue knowledge about that phenomenon. There are several different models of group decision processes. In earlier chapters, we mentioned Allison's study of the Cuban missile crisis in which he explained the decision processes of the Kennedy administration using three different models—the rational actor model, the political model, and the bureaucratic model [Allison, 1971]. We also mentioned an alternative model in which decision processes are viewed from four different perspectives: the rational, the consensual, the political, and the empirical [Rohrbaugh, 1985].

There are also several frameworks for describing different research paradigms. Churchman proposes four basic mechanisms for acquiring knowledge which he labeled Leibnizian (formal-deductive), Kantian (synthetic-representational), Hegelian (dialectical-conflictual), and Lockean (empirical-inductive) [Churchman, 1971]. Burrell and Morgan state that sociological research can be viewed along two dimensions [Burrell and Morgan, 1979]. In the first, the epistemological dimension, the researcher adopts either an objective view of the world in which the methods of the physical sciences are applicable, or a subjective view in which understanding can only be obtained by examining subjective experience. In the second, the ontological dimension, the researcher can view the world either as ordered and stable or as conflicting and coercive. These two dimensions then yield four different research points of view: objective-ordered, objective-conflicting, subjective-ordered, and subjective-conflicting. Hirschheim and Klein applied this model to discuss four different paradigms for systems development [Hirschheim and Klein, 1989].

There are other possible perspectives concerning decision processes and other ways of viewing research paradigms. We simply suggest here that research programs adopting multiple-perspective approaches can provide insights that are not possible from a single perspective and that such approaches should be seriously considered in the ISDP area.

Finally, almost all research to date in the social sciences assumes that small pieces of knowledge can be accumulated to form a complete contingency theory that will explain the phenomena of interest. Recent discoveries in physics (chaos theory) bring this fundamental assumption into question. Many natural phenomena can only be studied holistically [Gleick, 1987]. If this were also true of social systems, completely new research approaches would be needed.

Implications for the ISDP research program

In Chapter 2, we described the concept of decision processes as complex social interactions existing through time and being performed by multiple individuals and groups interacting with a broad array of technologies. Some research questions related to decision processes were discussed in the last chapter.

Returning to the concept of the research process embodied in Figure 1, we believe that the products of the five research teams will prove to be good examples of *conceptual research* that will help set directions for their particular research areas. While we have tried to summarize these contributions in the previous chapter, more work needs to be done to integrate the ideas of the research teams. Obviously, we need better frameworks to guide research, we need to continually raise our aspirations, and we need to develop new substantive and methodological research paradigms.

With regard to *theoretical research*, we advocate the use of a broader range of empirical and analytic research tools. Within the behavioral research area, the previous section makes the case for a switch from a single positivist paradigm to one in which both logical positive and interpretive paradigms coexist. More specifically:

- Traditional, logical positivist research involving laboratory and field experiments and field studies is being successfully applied now in many ISDP areas (e.g., GDSS) and should be continued.

- Many of the technologies for meeting support, for collaborative work, and for distributed decision making are recent innovations that are not well understood. This implies a need for exploratory studies employing qualitative techniques aimed at theory formation.

- Since decision processes occur through time, longitudinal case studies should be helpful in unearthing dynamic effects.

- The use of high-variety research methodologies that help reveal underlying behavioral and cognitive issues is particularly necessary if we are to make progress with our concept of decision processes.

- Studies involving multiple perspectives on decision processes and/or employing multiple research paradigms are needed.

- It is incumbent on ISDP researchers to learn more about the research paradigms of other fields. Interdisciplinary research studies are needed to understand IT in an organizational context.

- The development of long-range research programs (such as we are beginning to see in the GDSS area) should be encouraged.

- Given the state of advancement of ISDP research, it is necessary to develop close relationships with practice. Field and case studies that promote communication between managers and researchers are vital.

- We need pioneering research aimed at developing "logical systems models" that provide a comprehensive model of each of the thematic areas in ISDP.

The last recommendation concerning the need for logical systems models needs elaboration. First, such models must be based on a comprehensive study of the results to date in both IS and related disciplines (and should be attempted only by the brightest scholars in the field). Second, while they must provide bold statements and assertions about reality, the propositions they contain must be grounded in research and make sense within some logical framework. Since the reality with which we deal involves the interpersonal communications and psychological and cognitive processes that lead to decisions, the models must take account of these factors. Such models are examples of what Daft and Lewin call "symbol creating" research, which develops new concepts and vocabularies, as opposed to "symbol communicating research," in which the meaning of the research is widely agreed on [Daft and Lewin, 1990]. It must be recognized at the outset that these models will be largely incorrect. They are nevertheless necessary to the advancement of knowledge in our area because of the effect that they will have in promoting communication between researchers and guiding research efforts. In other words, successful symbol creation research will lead to symbol communication research.

The ISDP concept is exciting because, as we have seen in the previous chapter, there are so many possibilities for invention. With regard to the methodology of *inventive research* in ISDP, we must be concerned with questions of both relevance and certifiability:

- *Relevance* stems from the probability of commercial adaptation of the software product, expert system, or methodology *prototype* produced by the researcher. To ensure this, we should encourage close collaboration and support for research efforts from software and hardware vendors, consulting houses, and organizations that are likely to implement the products of our research.

- *Certifiability* depends on the actual development of a prototype and its testing in the laboratory or field. With regard to attempts to design interesting software or expert systems, running models are required. Papers describing "vaporware" should not be accepted as valid research products.

It should be noted that inventive research does *not* involve the development of complete methodologies or commercial-quality software. Such products require order of magnitude increases in effort and are a waste of time from an applied research point of view. Rather, the researcher should develop and test a "skeleton" that is sufficient to demonstrate feasibility and usefulness of the idea. The field of artificial intelligence has handled the certifiability problem by refusing to accept research papers that do not describe a running prototype. This concept of "program as proof" is a useful form of quality control that should be emulated by ISDP researchers.

The role of *evaluative research* in ISDP is no different from that in other areas of IS research. We need a stream of research that will provide reliable feedback to practitioners and other researchers on environmental factors, and reports on products and methodologies that are flops as well as successes. An idea that might be useful is to encourage competitions that test rival approaches and software. An example is provided by the area of integer programming, where an informal international challenge is taking place involving the best way to solve the traveling salesman problem.

More globally, we have argued for

- the selection of research topics based on their potential for contributing to practice,
- the selection of research methodologies that fit the problem to be researched and are likely to bring surprising results, and
- the use of multiple research methods and paradigms on the same research project.

Conclusions

This chapter has described a number of research methodologies and has made some specific recommendations for a program of research in ISDP. Probably the most important theme has been that multiple research methods are needed for further progress. This will necessitate education in multiple research paradigms, including those of other disciplines relevant to IS. It also requires a different approach to the assessment of what constitutes a useful contribution to knowledge. While we obviously need to pay attention to questions of quality in the conduct of research, we must also be careful not to confuse method with substance. In the final analysis, it is contributions to knowledge that count; orthodoxy in research themes or research methods can be a deadly palliative.

Names and Affiliations
of Contributors

Chapter 1: Review and Critique of DSS

Benn R. Konsynski, *Harvard University/Emory University*
Edward A. Stohr, *New York University*
James V. McGee, *Ernst & Young*

Chapter 2: Decison Processes: An Organizational View

Benn R. Konsynski, *Harvard University/Emory University*
Edward A. Stohr, *New York University*

Chapter 3: Behavioral Decision Theory and DSS:
New Opportunities for Collaborative Research

Joyce J. Elam, *Florida International University*
Sirkka L. Jarvenpaa, *University of Texas at Austin*
David A. Schkade, *University of Texas at Austin*

Chapter 4: Group Decision Support Systems

Paul Gray, *Claremont Graduate School*
Steven Alter, *University of San Francisco*
Gerardine DeSanctis, *University of Minnesota*
Gary W. Dickson, *University of Minnesota*
Robert Johansen, *Institute for the Future*
Kenneth L. Kraemer, *University of California, Irvine*
Lorne Olfman, *Claremont Graduate School*
Douglas R. Vogel, *University of Arizona*

Chapter 5: Organizational Decision Support Systems

Jay F. Nunamaker, *University of Arizona, Tucson*
Lynda M. Applegate, *Harvard University*
Mary J. Culnan, *Georgetown University*
Jane Fedorowicz, *Boston University*
Joey F. George, *University of Arizona, Tucson*
Barbara Gutek, *University of Arizona, Tucson*

John C. Henderson, *MIT Sloan School of Management*
John L. King, *University of California, Irvine*
Benn R. Konsynski, *Harvard University/Emory University*
Susan L. Star, *University of Arizona, Tucson*
E. Burton Swanson, *University of California*
Joseph S. Valacich, *Indiana University*
Robert W. Zmud, *Florida State University, Tallahassee*

Chapter 6: Technology Environments to Support Decision Processes

Ralph H. Sprague, Jr., *University of Hawaii*
Izak Benbasat, *University of British Columbia*
Omar A. El Sawy, *University of Southern California*
David King, *Comshare Inc.*
Timothy R. Hill, *University of Hawaii*
Henk G. Sol, Delft University of Technology
Peter A. Todd, *Queens University*

Chapter 7: Model Management Systems

Robert W. Blanning, *Vanderbilt University*
Andrew B. Whinston, *University of Texas at Austin*
Ai-Mei Chang, *University of Arizona, Tucson*
Vasant Dhar, *New York University*
Clyde W. Holsapple, *University of Kentucky*
Matthias Jarke, *University of Passau*
Steven O. Kimbrough, *University of Pennsylvania*
Javier Lerch, *Carnegie Mellon University*
Michael J. Prietula, *Carnegie Mellon Institute*

Chapter 8: Research Challenges

Benn R. Konsynski, *Harvard University/Emory University*
Edward A. Stohr, *New York University*

Chapter 9: Research Approaches in ISDP

Benn R. Konsynski, *Harvard University/Emory University*
Edward A. Stohr, *New York University*

Discussants

Gadi Ariav, *Tel Aviv University*
Frederick J. Duhl, *Boston Family Institute*
Douglas C. Engelbart, *Stanford University (Keynote speaker)*
Michael J. Ginzberg, *Case Western Reserve University*
Rudolph A. Hirschheim, *University of Houston*
Blake Ives, *Southern Methodist University*
William R. King, *University of Pittsburgh*
Arie Y. Lewin, *Duke University*
Marvin L. Manheim, *Northwestern University*
Richard O. Mason, *Southern Methodist University*
Daniel Robey, *Florida International University, Miami*
Andrew P. Sage, *George Mason University*
Lee S. Sproull, *Boston University*
Charles B. Stabell, *Norwegian School of Management*
Jon A. Turner, *New York University*
Nicholas P. Vitalari, *University of California, Irvine*
Hugh J. Watson, *University of Georgia*

References

Abelson, H., et al., "Intelligence in Scientific Computing,"*Comm. of the ACM*, Vol. 32, May 1989, pp. 546-562.

Abelson, R.P., "Psychological Status of the Script Concept," *American Psychologist*, Vol. 36, 1981, pp. 715-729.

Aldag, R.J. and D.J.Power, "An Empirical Assessment of Computer-Assisted Decision Analysis," *Decision Sciences*, Vol. 17, No. 4, 1986, pp. 572-588.

Allison, G.T., *Essence of Decision: Explaining the Cuban Missile Crisis*, Little, Brown and Co., Boston, Mass., 1971.

Alter, S., "A Taxonomy of Decision Support Systems," *Sloan Management Rev.*, Vol. 19, 1977, pp. 39-56.

Alter, S., *Decision Support Systems: Current Practice and Continuing Challenges*, Addison-Wesley, Reading, Mass., 1980.

Anderson, J.R., "A Theory on the Origins of Human Knowledge," *Artificial Intelligence*, Vol. 40, Sept. 1989, pp. 313-352.

Anderson, J.R., *The Architecture of Cognition*, Harvard Univ. Press, Cambridge, Mass., 1983.

Anderson, J.R., *Cognitive Psychology and Its Implications*, 2nd ed., W.H. Freeman and Company., New York, N.Y., 1985.

Anthony, R.N., *Planning and Control Systems: A Framework for Analysis*, Division of Research, Harvard Business School, Boston, Mass., 1965.

Applegate, L.M., J.I. Cash, Jr., and D.Q. Mills, "Information Technology and Tomorrow's Manager," *Harvard Business Rev.*, Nov.-Dec., 1988, pp. 128-136.

Argyris, C. and D.A. Schon, *Organizational Learning: A Theory of Action Perspective*, Addison-Wesley, Reading Mass., 1978.

Ariav, G. and M.J. Ginzberg, "DSS Design: A Systematic View of Decision Support," *Comm. of the ACM*, Vol. 28, No. 10, Oct. 1985, pp. 1045-1052.

Aronson, J.E., J.S. Aronofsky, and P. Gray, "An Exploratory Experiment in Group Decision Support Systems Using the SMU Decision Room," *Proc. Decision Sciences Institute*, Boston, Mass., November 1987.

Athey, S., "A Consultant to Assist Students in Solving Statistics Problems," *Proc. 22nd Ann. Hawaii Int'l Conf. System Sciences*, IEEE CS Press, Los Alamitos, Calif., 1989, pp. 439-448.

Baddeley, A.D., "The Concept of Working Memory: A View of its Current State and Probable Future Development," *Cognition*, Vol. 10, 1981, pp. 17-23.

Baecker, R. M. and W.A.S. Buxton, *Readings in Human-Computer Interaction: A Multidisciplinary Approach*, Morgan Kaufmann, Los Altos, Calif., 1987.

Baker, K.R., *Introduction to Sequencing and Scheduling*, John Wiley & Sons, New York, N.Y., 1974.

Balakrishnan, A. and A.B. Whinston, "Information Issues in Model Specification," *Information Systems Research*, Vol. 2, No. 4, December 1992, pp. 263-286.

Barnard, C.I., *The Functions of the Executive*, Harvard Univ. Press, Cambridge, Mass., 1938.

Beauclair, R., "An Experimental Study of the Effects of Group Decision Support System Process Support Applications on Small Group Decision Making," Unpublished Doctoral Dissertation, Indiana Univ., 1987.

Beer, S., *Platform for Change*, John Wiley & Sons, New York, N.Y., 1983.

Benbasat, I. and R. Schroeder, "An Experimental Investigation of Some MIS Design Variables," *MIS Quarterly*, 1977, pp 37-50.

Benbasat, I. and B.R. Nault, "An Evaluation of Empirical Research in Managerial Support Studies: Decision Support Systems, Group Decision Support Systems and Expert Systems," Working Paper, Faculty of Commerce and Business Administration, Univ. of British Columbia, B.C., Canada, 1990.

Benbasat, I. and R.N. Taylor, "The Impact of Cognitive Styles on Information Systems Design," *MIS Quarterly*, Vol. 2, No. 2, 1978, pp. 43-54.

Benbasat, I., ed., "Laboratory Experiments in Information Systems Studies with a Focus on Individuals: A Critical Appraisal," in *The Information Systems Research Challenge: Experimental Research Methods*, Harvard Business School Press, Boston, Mass., 1989, pp. 33-52.

Benbasat, I., "An Analysis of Research Methodologies," in *The Information Systems Research Challenge*, F. Warren McFarlan, ed., Harvard Business School Press, Boston, Mass., 1985, pp. 47-85.

Benbasat, I. and A.S. Dexter, "An Experimental Evaluation of Graphical and Color-Enhanced Information Presentation," *Management Science*, Vol. 31, Nov. 1985, pp. 1349-1364.

Benbasat, I. and A.S. Dexter, "Individual Differences in the Use of Decision Support Aids," *J. of Accounting Research*, Vol. 20, 1982, pp. 1-11.

Benbasat, I. and B.R. Nault, "An Evaluation of Empirical Research in Managerial Support Technologies," *Decision Support Systems*, Vol. 6, No. 3, 1990, pp. 24-46.

Bennett, J.L., ed., *Building Decision Support Systems*, Addison-Wesley, Reading, Mass., 1983.

Bennett, J., "User-Oriented Graphics, Systems for Decision Support in Unstructured Tasks," in *User-Oriented Design of Interactive Graphics Systems*, Treu, ed., Assoc. for Computing Machinery, New York, N.Y., 1977.

Bettman, J.R., *An Information Processing Theory of Consumer Choice*, 1979.

Bhargava, H.K., M.P. Bieber, and S.O. Kimbrough, "Oona, Max, and the WYWWYWI Principle: Generalized Hypertext and Model Management in a Symbolic Programming Environment," *Proc. Ninth Int'l Conf. Information Systems*, 1988, pp. 179-191.

Bhargava, H.K., S.O. Kimbrough, and R. Krishnan, "Unique Names Violations: A Problem for Model Integration or You Say Tomato, I Say Tomahto," *ORSA J. on Computing*, Vol. 3, No. 2, Spring 1991, pp. 107-120.

Bhargava, H.K. and S.O. Kimbrough, "On Embedded Languages for Model Management," *Proc. 23rd Ann. Hawaii Int'l Conf. System Sciences*, IEEE CS Press, Los Alamitos, Calif., 1990, pp. 443-452.

Bieber, M.P. and S.O. Kimbrough, "On Generalizing the Concept of Hypertext," *Management Information Systems Quarterly*, Vol. 16, No. 1, Mar. 1992, pp. 77-93.

Bieber, M.P. and S.O. Kimbrough, "Towards a Logic Model for Generalized Hypertext," *Proc. 23rd Ann. Hawaii Int'l Conf. System Sciences*, IEEE CS Press, Los Alamitos, Calif., 1990, pp. 506-515.

Binbasioglu, M. and M. Jarke, "Domain-Specific DSS Tools for Knowledge-Based Model Building," *Decision Support Systems*, Vol. 2, No. 3, 1986, pp. 213-223.

Bisschop, J. and A. Meeraus, "On the Development of a General Algebraic Modeling System in a Strategic Planning Environment," *Mathematical Programming Study*, Vol. 20, 1982.

Blanning, R.W., "The Functions of a Decision Support System," *Information and Management*, Vol. 2, 1979, pp. 87-93.

Blanning, R.W., "Issues in the Design of Relational Model Base Systems," *Proc. Nat'l Computer Conf.*, 1983, pp. 395-407.

Blanning, R.W., "A Relational Framework for Model Bank Organization," *Proc. IEEE Workshop Languages for Automation*, IEEE CS Press, Los Alamitos, Calif., 1984, pp. 141-146.

Blanning, R.W., "A Relational Theory of Model Management," in *Decision Support Systems: Theory and Application*, C.W. Holsapple and A.B. Whinston, Eds., Springer-Verlag, Berlin, 1987a, pp. 19-53.

Blanning, R.W., "A Framework for Expert Modelbase Systems," *Proc. Nat'l Computer Conference*, June 1987b, pp. 13-17.

Blanning, R.W., "A Relational Theory of Model Management," in *Decision Support Systems: Theory and Applications*, C.W. Holsapple and A.B. Whinston, eds., Springer-Verlag, Berlin, 1987c, pp. 19-53.

Blanning, R.W., "Model Management Systems," Working Paper, Vanderbilt Univ., 1988.

Blanning, R.W., "Model Management Systems," Working Paper No. 89-23, Owen Graduate School of Management, Vanderbilt Univ., Nashville, Tenn., 1989; also to appear in *Decision Support Systems: Putting Theory into Practice*, 2nd ed., R.H. Sprague, Jr. and H.J. Watson, eds., Prentice-Hall, Englewood Cliffs, N.J., 1990.

Boehm, B.W., "A Spiral Model of Software Development and Enhancement," *Software Engineering Notes*, Vol. 11, No. 4, 1986, pp. 22-42.

Boland, R.J. and W. Day, "The Phenomenology of Systems Design," *Proc. Third Int'l Conf. Information Systems*, 1982.

Bonczek, R.H., C.W. Holsapple, A.B. Whinston, "Future Directions for Developing Decision Support Systems," *Decision Sciences*, October 1980.

Bonczek, R.H., C.W. Holsapple, and A.B. Watson, *Foundations of Decision Support Systems*, Academic Press, New York, N.Y., 1981.

Bots, P.W.G., F.D.J. van Schaik, and H.G. Sol, "A Gaming Environment for Testing," *Decision Support Systems*, Edinburgh, UK, 1989.

Bots, P.W.G., "An Environment to Support Problem Solving," PhD Thesis, Delft Univ. of Technology, Delft, The Netherlands, 1989.

Bots, P.W.G. and H.G. Sol, "Shaping Organizational Information Systems through Coordination Support," *Proc. IFIP WG 8.3 Working Conference on Organizational Decision Support Systems*, North-Holland, Amsterdam, The Netherlands, 1988.

Bower, J.L. and T.M. Hout, "Fast-Cycle Capability for Competitive Power," *Harvard Business Rev.*, Vol. 66, No. 6, 1988, pp. 110-118.

Brachman, R.J. and J.G. Schmolze, "An Overview of the KL-ONE Knowledge Representation System," *Cognitive Science*, Vol. 9, No. 2, 1985.

Bradley, G.H. and R.D. Clemence, Jr., "Model Integration with a Typed Executable Modeling Language," *Proc. 21st Ann. Hawaii Int'l Conf. System Sciences*, Vol. II, IEEE CS Press, Los Alamitos, Calif., 1988, pp. 403-410.

Bradley, G., "Mathematical Programming Modeling Project," *Proc. Conf. on the Impact of Recent Computer Advances on Operations Research*, Jan., 1989.

Buehner, R. and P. Kleinschmidt, "Reflections on the Architecture of a Decision Support System for Personnel Assignment Scheduling in a Production Cell Technology," *Decision Support Systems*, Vol. 4, No. 4, 1988, pp. 473-480.

Bui, T.X. *Co-op*, Springer-Verlag, Berlin, 1987.

Business Week, "The Payoff from Teamwork," July 10, 1989, pp. 56-62.

Campbell, D.T. and J.C. Stanley, *Experimental and Quasi-Experimental Designs for Research*, Rand McNally, Chicago, Ill., 1966.

Campbell, D.T., "'Degrees of Freedom' and the Case Study," *Comparative Political Studies*, Vol. 8, 1975, pp. 178-193.

Carlson, E.D., B. Grace, and J. Sutton, "Case Studies of End User Requirements for Interactive Problem-Solving Systems," *MIS Quarterly*, 1977, pp. 51-63.

Carlson, E.D., "An Approach for Designing Decision Support Systems," *Data Base*, Vol. 10, No. 3, Winter 1979, pp. 3-15.

Carroll, P.B. and J.R. Wilke, "Computer Firms Find Service is What Sells, Not Fancier Hardware," *The Wall Street Journal*, Aug. 15, 1989, pp. A1 and A9.

Cartwright, D. and A. Zander, *Group Dynamics: Research and Theory*, 3rd ed., Harper & Row, New York, N.Y., 1968.

Cash, J.I. Jr. and P.R. Lawrence, eds., *The Information Systems Research Challenge: Qualitative Research Methods*, Harvard Business School Press, Boston, Mass., 1989.

Cats-Baril, W.L. and G.P. Huber, "Decision Support Systems for Ill-Structured Problems: An Empirical Study," *Decision Sciences*, Vol. 18, No. 3, 1987, pp. 350-372.

Chang, A., C.W. Holsapple, and A.B. Whinston, "A Decision Support System Theory," *Kentucky Institute for Knowledge Management*, Paper No. 5, 1988.

Charnes, A., W.W. Cooper, and E. Rhodes, "Evaluating Program and Managerial Efficiency: An Application of Data Envelope Analysis," *Management Science*, Vol. 27, No. 6, 1981, pp. 668-697.

Chen, P.P., "The Entity Relationship Model: Toward a Unified View of Data," *ACM Trans. Database Systems*, Vol. 1, No. 1, 1976. pp. 9-36.

Chinneck, J.W., "Formulating Processing Network Models: Viability Theory," forthcoming in *Naval Research Logistics*.

Chinneck, J.W. and E.W. Dravnieks, "Locating Minimal Infeasible Constraint Sets in Linear Programs," Carleton Univ., Ottawa, Canada, Dept. of Systems & Computer Engineering, working paper, Nov. 1989.

Chinneck, J.W., "Viability Analysis: A Formulation Aid for All Classes of Network Models," Carleton Univ., Ottawa, Canada, Dept. of Systems & Computer Engineering, working paper, Aug. 1989.

Churchman, C.W., *The Design of Inquiring Systems*, Basic Books, New York, N.Y., 1971.

Clippinger, J.H. and B.R. Konsynski, "Information Refineries: Electronically Distilling Business' Raw Material to Make it More Usable," *Computerworld*, Aug. 28, 1989, pp. 73-77.

Cohen, M., et al., "Research Needs and Phenomena of Decision Making and Operations," *IEEE Trans. Systems, Man, and Cybernetics*, Vol. 15, No. 6, 1983, pp. 764-775.

Cohen, K.J. and R.M. Cyert, "Simulation of Organizational Behavior," in *Handbook of Organizations*, J.G. March, ed., Rand McNally, Chicago, Ill., 1965, pp. 305-334.

Cohen, M.A. H. and H.G. Sol, "A Simulation Environment for the Development of Information Systems," *Simulation Environments and Symbol and Number Processing on Multi Array Processors, Proc. European Simulation Multiconference*, 1988, pp. 204-210.

CONDOR: Committee on the Next Decade in Operations Research, "Operations Research: The Next Decade,"*Operations Research*, Vol. 36, No. 4, July-Aug. 1988, pp. 619-637.

Conklin, J., "Hypertext: An Introduction and Survey," *Computer*, Vol. 20, No. 9, 1987, pp. 17-42.

Conklin, J., and M.L. Begeman, "gIBIS: A Hypertext Tool for Expiratory Policy Discussion," *ACM Trans. Office Information Systems*, Vol. 6, No. 4, 1988, pp. 303-331.

Connolly, T., L. Jessup, and J. Valacich, "Idea Generation in a GDSS: Effects of Anonymity and Evaluative Tone," working paper, Univ. of Arizona, 1989.

Cook, T.D., and D.T. Campbell, *Quasi-Experimentation*, Houghton Mifflin, Boston, Mass., 1979.

CSCW '86, Proc. Conf. on Computer Supported Work, MCC Software Technology Program, Austin, TX, 1986.

CSCW '88, Proc. Conf. on Computer Supported Work, Assoc. for Computing Machinery, New York, N.Y., 1988.

Culnan, M.J., "Mapping the Intellectual Structure of MIS, 1980-1985: A Co-Citation Analysis," *MIS Quarterly*, Sept. 1987, pp. 341-353.

Culnan, M.J. and E.B. Swanson, "Research in Management Systems, 1980-1984: Points of Work and Reference," *MIS Quarterly*, Sept. 1986, pp. 289-302.

Cyert, R. and J.G. March, *The Behavioral Theory of the Firm*, Prentice-Hall, Englewood Cliffs, N.J., 1963.

Daft, R.L. and K.E. Weick, "Toward a Model of Organizations as Interpretive Systems," *Academy of Management Rev.*, Vol. 9, No. 2, 1984, pp. 284-295.

Daft, R.L. and A.Y. Lewin, "Can Organization Studies Begin to Break Out of the Normal Science Straightjacket? An Editorial Essay," *Organization Science*, Vol. 1, No. 1, 1990, pp. 1-9.

Daft, R.L. and J.C. Wigington, "Language and Organization," *Academy of Management Rev.*, Vol. 4, No. 2, 1979, pp. 179-191.

Dalkey, N. and O. Helmer, "An Experimental Application of the Delphi Method to the Use of Experts," *Management Science*, Vol. 9, No. 3, Apr. 1963, pp. 458-467.

Davenport, T.H. and J.E. Short, "The New Industrial Engineering: Information Technology and Business Process Redesign," *Sloan Management Rev.*, Summer 1990, pp. 11-27.

Dawes, R. and A. Corrigan, "Linear Models in Decision Making," *Psychological Bulletin*, Vol. 81, 1974, pp. 95-106.

deKleer, J., "An Assumption-Based TMS," *Artificial Intelligence*, Vol. 28, No. 2, 1986.

Delbecq, A.L., A.H. Van de Ven, and D.H. Gustafson, *Group Techniques for Program Planning*, Scott Foresman and Company, Glenview, Ill., 1975.

DeSanctis, G., "Expectancy Theory as an Explanation of Voluntary Use of a Decision Support System," *Psychological Reports*, Vol. 52, 1983, pp. 247-260.

DeSanctis, G., "Computer Graphics as Decision Aids: Directions for Research," *Decision Science*, Vol. 15, No. 4, 1984, pp. 463-487.

DeSanctis, G. and R.B. Gallupe, "A Foundation for the Study of Decision Support Systems," *Management Science*, Vol. 33, No. 5, 1987, pp. 589-609.

DeSanctis, G. and R.B. Gallupe, "Group Decision Support Systems: A New Frontier," *Data Base*, Winter 1985.

Dhar, V. and N. Ranganathan, "Experiments with an Integer Programming Formulation of an Expert System," *Comm. of the ACM*, 1989.

Dhar, V., "A Truth Maintenance System for Supporting Constraint-based Reasoning," *Decision Support Systems*, Vol. 5, No. 3, 1989.

Dhar, V., "PLANET: An Intelligent Decision Support System for the Formulation and Investigation of Formal Planning Models," PhD Thesis, Graduate School of Business, Univ. of Pittsburgh, Pittsburgh, Penn., 1984.

Dhar, V. and H.E. Pople, "Rule-Based Versus Structure-Based Models for Generating and Explaining Expert Behavior," *Comm. of the ACM*, Vol. 30, No. 6, 1987, pp. 542-555.

Dhar, V. and M. Jarke, "Dependency-Directed Reasoning and Learning in System Maintenance Support," *IEEE Trans. Software Eng.*, Vol. 14, No. 2, 1988, pp. 211-227.

Dickson, G.W., "A Programmatic Appeal to Information Systems Research: An Experimentalist's View," in *The Information Systems Research Challenge: Experimental Research Methods*, I. Benbasat, ed., Harvard Business School Press, Boston, Mass., 1989, pp. 147-172.

Dickson, G.W., G. DeSanctis, and D.J. McBride, "Understanding the Effectiveness of Computer Graphics for Decision Support: A Cumulative Experimental Approach," *Comm. of the ACM*, Vol. 29, 1986, pp. 40-47.

Dolk, D.R. and B.R. Konsynski, "Knowledge Representation for Model Management Systems," *IEEE Trans. Software Eng.*, SE-10, 1984, pp. 619-628.

Dos Santos, B.L. and M.L. Bariff, "A Study of User Interface Aids for Decision Support Systems," *Management Science*, 1988.

Dos Santos, B.L. and C.W. Holsapple, "A Framework for Designing Adaptive DSS Interfaces," *Decision Support Systems*, Vol. 5, No. 1, 1989.

Doyle, J., "A Truth Maintenance System," *Artificial Intelligence*, Vol. 12, No. 3, 1979.

Dreyfuss, J., "Catching the Computer Wave," *Fortune*, Sept. 26, 1988, pp. 78-79, 82.

Drucker, P.F., "How to Measure White Collar Productivity," *The Wall Street Journal*, Nov. 26, 1985, p. 30.

Drucker, P.F., "The Coming of the New Organization," *Harvard Business Rev.*, Jan.-Feb., 1988, pp. 45-53.

Drucker, P.F., *The New Realities*, Harper & Row, New York, N.Y., 1989.

DSS'86, "Special Issue on Model Management," *Decision Support Systems*, Vol. 2, No. 1, 1986.

Dur, R.C.J. and H.G. Sol, "Dynamic Modelling in Office Systems Analysis," *Proc. First Dutch Conf. on Information Systems*, 1989.

Dur, R.C.J. and J.M. Versendaal, "Specifying Highly Interactive Systems Using an Object Oriented Approach," *Proc. Conf. Technology of Object-Oriented Languages and Systems Tools*, 1989.

Dur, R.C.J. and H.G. Sol, "Supporting the Office System Design Process," *Proc. IFIP 8.3 Working Conf.*, 1990.

Dutton, W. and K.L. Kraemer, *Modeling as Negotiating: The Political Dynamics of Computer Models in the Policy Process*, Ablex, Norwood, N.J., 1985.

Easton, A., "An Experimental Investigation of Automated versus Manual Support for Stakeholder Identification and Assumption Surfacing in Small Groups," Unpublished Doctoral Dissertation, Univ. of Arizona, 1988.

Easton, G., "Group Decision Support System versus Face-to-Face Communication for Collaborative Group Work: An Experimental Investigation," Unpublished Doctoral Dissertation, Univ. of Arizona, 1988.

Eccles, R. and D. Crane. "Managing through Networks," *California Management Rev.*, Vol. 30, No. 1, 1987, pp. 176-195.

Edelman, F., "Managers, Computer Systems, and Productivity," *MIS Quarterly*, Vol. 5, No. 3, 1981, pp. 1-19.

Edwards, W. "The Theory of Decision Making," *Psychological Bulletin*, Vol. 51, 1954, pp. 380-417.

Edwards, W. "Behavioral Decision Theory," *Ann. Rev. of Psychology*, Vol. 12, 1961, pp. 473-498.

El Sherif, H. and O. El Sawy, "Issue-Based Decision Support Systems for the Egyptian Cabinet," *MIS Quarterly*, Vol. 12, No. 4, Dec. 1988, pp. 551-569.

Elam, J.J. and M. Mead, "Can Software Influence Creativity," *Information Systems Research*, Vol. 1, No. 1, 1990. pp 1-22.

Elam, J.J. and B.R. Konsynski, "Using Artificial Intelligence Techniques to Enhance the Capabilities of Model Management Systems," *Decision Sciences*, Vol. 18, No. 3, Summer 1987, pp. 487-502.

Elam, J.J., G.P. Huber, and M.E. Hurt, "An Examination of the DSS Literature (1975-1985)," in *Decision Support Systems: A Decade in Perspective*, E.R. McLean and H.G. Sol, eds., Elsevier Science Publishers, New York, N.Y., 1987, pp. 1-17.

Elam, J.J., et al., "A Vision for DSS," 1984. (private communication)

Elofson, G.S. and B.R. Konsynski, "Organizational Learning in the Extended Enterprise," *Proc. Second Ann. Conf. Economics and Artificial Intelligence*, 1990, pp. 193-199.

Engelbart, D., "The Augmentation System Framework," in *Interactive Multimedia*, S. Ambron and K. Hooper, eds. Microsoft Press, Redmond, Wash., 1988.

Eom, H.B. and S.M. Lee, "A Survey of Decision Support System Applications," *Interfaces*, Vol. 20, No. 3, May-June, 1990.

Ericsson, K.A. and H.A. Simon, *Verbal Protocols as Data*, MIT Press, Cambridge, Mass., 1984.

Ericsson, K.A., and H.A. Simon, "Verbal Reports as Data," *Psychological Rev.*, Vol. 84, 1982, pp. 215-251.

Feigenbaum, E. and D. Lenat, "On the Thresholds of Knowledge," in *Applications of Expert Systems: Vol. 2*, J. Quinlan, ed., Addison-Wesley, New York, N.Y., 1989.

Fellers, J.W., R.P. Bostrom, and B.E. Wynne, "An Exploratory Investigation of Critical Success Factors for Knowledge Acquisition in Expert Systems Development," IRMIS Working Paper 813, Graduate School of Business, Bloomington, IN, Univ. of Indiana, Oct. 1988.

Feurzeig, W., "Algebra Slaves and Agents in Logo-Based Mathematics Curriculum," in *Artificial Intelligence and Education*, Vol. 1, R. Lawler and M. Yazdani, eds., Ablex Publishers, Norwood, N.J., 1987.

Fischer, G. and T. Mastaglio, "Computer-Based Critics: Decision Support and Knowledge Based Systems," *Proc. 22nd Ann. Hawaii Int'l Conf. System Sciences*, Vol. III, IEEE CS Press, Los Alamitos, California, 1989, pp. 427-436.

Fischer, G., "Human-Computer Interaction Software: Lessons Learned, Challenges Ahead," *IEEE Software*, Jan. 1989, pp. 44-52.

Fishbein, M. and I. Ajzen, *Belief, Attitude, Intention and Behavior: An Introduction to Theory and Research*, Addison Wesley, Reading, Mass., 1975.

Fodor, J.A., *Psychosemantics*, The MIT Press, Cambridge, Mass., 1987.

Foley, J.D. and A. Van Dam, *Fundamentals of Interactive Computer Graphics*, Addison-Wesley, Reading, Mass, 1982.

Foley, J.D., "Interfaces for Advanced Computing," *Scientific American: Trends in Computing*, Vol. 1, 1988.

Fourer, R., "Modeling Languages versus Matrix Generators for Linear Programming," *ACM Trans. Mathematical Software*, Vol. 9, No. 2, 1983.

Fourer, R., D. Gay, and B.W. Kernighan, "AMPL: A Mathematical Programming Language," *Managment Science*, Vol. 36, No. 5, 1990, pp. 519-534.

Fukushima, K., "A Neural Network for Visual Pattern Recognition," *Computer*, Vol. 21, No. 3, 1988, pp. 65-75.

Galbraith, J.R., "Organizational Design: An Information Processing View," *Interfaces*, Vol. 4, 1974. pp. 28-36.

Galbraith, J.R., *Designing Complex Organizations*, Addison-Wesley, Reading, Mass., 1973.

Gale, W. "REX Review" in *Artificial Intelligence and Statistics*, W. Gale, ed., Addison-Wesley, Reading, Mass., 1986.

Gallupe, R.B., "The Impact of Task Difficulty on the Use of a Group Decision Support System," Unpublished Doctoral Dissertation, Univ. of Minnesota, 1985.

Gallupe, R.B., "Suppressing the Contributions of the Groups: Is GDSS Best Member Use Appropriate for All Tasks?" *Proc. 23rd Ann. Hawaii Int'l Conf. System Sciences*, IEEE CS Press, Los Alamitos, Calif., 1990, pp. 13-22.

Gardner, M.M. and B. Christie, *Applying Cognitive Psychology to User-Interface Design*, John Wiley & Sons, New York, N.Y., 1987.

Geoffrion, A., "An Introduction to Structured Modeling." *Management Science*, Vol. 33, No. 5, 1987, pp. 547-585.

Geoffrion, A.M., "SML: A Model Definition Language for Structured Modeling," Working Paper No. 360, Western Management Science Institute, UCLA, 1988.

George, J.F. and J.F. Nunamaker, "Group Decision Support Systems in Pacific Rim Nations," in *Group Decision Support Systems in Pacific Rim Nations*, J.F. George and J.F. Nunamaker, eds., Honolulu: Pacific Research Institute for Information Systems and Management (PRIISM), 1988, pp. 3-17.

Gerrity, T.P., "Design of Man-Machine Decision Systems: An Application to Portfolio Management," *Sloan Management Rev.*, Vol. 12, No. 2, 1971, pp. 59-75.

Giddens, A., *The Constitution of Society: Outline of the Theory of Structure*, Univ. of Calif. Press, Berkeley, CA, 1984.

Ginzberg, M.J. and E.A. Stohr, "Decision Support Systems: Issues and Perspectives," in *Decision Support Systems*, M.J. Ginzberg, W. Reitman, and E.A. Stohr, eds., North-Holland, Amsterdam, The Netherlands, 1981, pp. 9-32.

Ginzberg, M.J., "DSS Success: Measurement and Facilitation," in *Database Management: Theory and Applications*, C.W. Holsapple and A.B. Whinston, eds., Reidel, Hingham, Mass., 1983, pp. 367-387.

Ginzberg, M.J. and R.W. Zmud, "Evolving Criteria for Information Systems Assessment," in *Informations Systems Assessment: Issues and Challenges*, N. Bjorn-Andersen and G.B. Davis, eds., North-Holland, Amsterdam, The Netherlands, 1988.

Gleick, J., *Chaos: Making a New Science*, Penguin Books, New York, N.Y., 1987.

Glenn, J., *Future Mind*, Acropolis Books, Washington, D.C., 1989.

Goldstein, W.M. and H.J. Einhorn, "Expression Theory and the Preference Reversal Phenomena," *Psychological Rev.*, Vol. 94, 1987, pp. 236-254.

Gorry, G.A. and M.S. Scott Morton, "A Framework for Management Information Systems," *Sloan Management Rev.*, Vol. 13, No. 1, 1971, pp. 55-71.

Goslar, M.D., G.I. Green, and T.H. Hughes, "Decision Support Systems: An Empirical Assessment for Decision Making," *Decision Sciences*, Vol. 17, 1986, pp. 16-32.

Gray P., et al. "The SMU Decision Room Project," in *DSS-81 Trans.*, D. Young and P.G.W. Keen, eds., The Institute of Management Sciences, Providence, R.I., 1981, pp. 122-129.

Gray, P., D. Vogel, and R. Beauclair, "Assessing GDSS Empirical Research," *European J. Operations Research*, Vol. 45, 1990.

Gray, P. and L. Olfman, "The User Interface in Group Decision Support," *Decision Support Systems*, Vol. 5, No. 2, 1989, pp. 119-138.

Gray, P. and J.F. Nunamaker, "Group Decision Support Systems," in *Decision Support Systems*, 2nd ed., R.H. Sprague and H.J. Watson, eds., Prentice Hall, Englewood Cliffs, N.J., 1989.

Gray, P., L. Olfman, and H. Park, "The Interface Problem in International Group DSS," in *Group Decision Support Systems in Pacific Rim Nations*, J.F. George and J.F. Nunamaker, eds., Honolulu: Pacific Research Institute for Information Systems and Management (PRIISM), 1988, pp. 61-89.

Greenberg, H.J., "A Natural Language Discourse Model to Explain Linear Programming Models and Solutions," *Decision Support Systems*, Vol. 3, 1987, pp. 333-342.

Greenberg, H.J. and F.H. Murphy, "Mathematizing Infeasibility: Criteria for Diagnosis," Univ. of Colorado at Denver, Mathematics Dept., working paper, Sept. 1989.

Greenberg, H.J., "A Functional Description of ANALYZE: A Computer Assisted Analysis System for Linear Programming Models," *ACM Trans. Mathematical Software*, Vol. 9, No. 1, Mar. 1983.

Greif, I., ed., *Computer-Supported Cooperative Work: A Book of Readings*, Morgan Kaufmann, San Mateo, Calif., 1988.

Gurbaxani, V. and S. Whang, "The Impact of Information Systems on Organizations and Markets," *Comm. of the ACM*, Vol. 34, No. 1, 1991, pp. 59-64.

Hackman, J.R. and G.R. Oldham. "Motivation through the Design of Work: Test of a Theory," *Organizational Behavior and Human Performance*, Vol. 16, 1976, pp. 250-279.

Hammer, M., "Reengineering Work: Don't Automate, Obliterate," *Harvard Business Rev.*, July-Aug. 1990, pp. 104-112.

Hammond, K., *Case-Based Planning: Viewing Planning as a Memory Task*, John Wiley & Sons, New York, N.Y., 1989.

Hansen, J.V., L.J. McKell, and L.E. Heitger, "ISMS: Computer- Aided Analysis for Design of Decision-Support Systems," *Management Science*, Vol. 25, No. 11, 1979, pp. 1069-1081.

Hartson, H.R. and D. Hix, *Advances in Human-Computer Interaction*, Vol. 2, Ablex Publishing, Norwood, N.J., 1988.

Hartson, H.R., *Advances in Human-Computer Interaction*, Vol. 1, Ablex Publishing, Norwood, N.J., 1985.

Hastie, R., S. Penrod, and N. Pennington, *Inside the Jury*, Harvard Univ. Press, Cambridge, Mass., 1983.

Hayes-Roth, F., D.A. Waterman, and D.B. Lenat, eds, *Building Expert Systems*, Addison-Wesley, Reading, Mass., 1983.

Helander, M., *Handbook of Human-Computer Interaction*, North-Holland, New York, N.Y., 1988.

Heminger, A., "Group Decision Support System Assessment in a Field Setting," Unpublished Doctoral Dissertation, Univ. of Arizona, 1988.

Henderson, J.C., "Finding Synergy Between Decision Support Systems and Expert Systems Research," *Decision Sciences*, Vol. 18, No. 3, 1987, pp. 333-349.

Henderson, J.C. and J.G. Cooprider, "Dimensions of IS Planning and Design Technology," *Information Systems Research*, 1990.

Hiltz, S.R., M. Turoff, and K. Johnson, "Experiments in Group Decision Making, 3: Disinhibition, Deindividualization, and Group Process in Pen Name and Real Name Computer Conferences," *Decision Support Systems*, Vol. 5, No. 2, 1989, pp. 217-232.

Hirschheim, R. and H.K. Klein, "Four Paradigms of Information Systems Development," *Comm. of the ACM*, Vol. 32, No. 10, 1989, pp. 199-1218.

Hogarth, R., Personal Interview, 1989.

Hogue, J.T. and H.J. Watson, "An Examination of Decision Makers' Utilization of Decision Support Systems," *Information and Management*, Vol. 8, No. 4, 1985, pp. 205-212.

Holsapple, C.W., "Adapting Demons to Knowledge Management Environments," *Decision Support Systems*, Vol. 3, No. 4, 1987.

Holsapple, C.W., "Decision Support in Multiparticipant Decision Makers," Kentucky Initiative for Knowledge Management, Paper No. 12, Univ. of Kentucky, Lexington, Kentucky, 1989.

Holsapple, C.W. and A.B. Whinston, "Knowledge Representation and Processing in Economics and Management," *Proc. Conf. Integrated Modeling Systems*, 1986.

Holsapple, C.W. and A.B. Whinston, "Toward an Environment Theory of Decision Support," *Proc. Conf. Integrated Modeling Systems*, 1987a.

Holsapple, C.W. and A.B. Whinston, *Business Expert Systems*, Irwin, Homewood, Ill., 1987b.

Holsapple, C.W. and A.B. Whinston, *The Information Jungle*, Dow Jones-Irwin, Homewood, Ill., 1988a.

Holsapple, C.W. and A.B. Whinston, "Model Management Issues and Directions," Kentucky Initiative for Knowledge Management, Paper No. 7, Univ. of Kentucky, Lexington, Ky., 1988b.

Holsapple, C.W., S. Park, and A.B. Whinston, "Developing User Interfaces for Decision Support Systems," *Proc. First Asian Federation of Operations Research Society Conf.*, 1988.

Holyoak, K.J. and P. Thagard, "Analogical Mapping by Constraint Satisfaction," *Cognitive Science*, Vol. 13, 1989, pp. 295-355.

Homans, G., *The Human Group*, Harcourt, Brace, Jovanovich, New York, N.Y., 1950.

Huber, G.P., "Cognitive Style in Information Systems Research: Much Ado About Nothing?," *Management Science*, Vol. 29, 1983, pp. 567-579.

Huber, G.P., "The Nature and Design of Post-Industrial Organizations," *Management Science*, Vol. 30, No. 8, 1984a, pp. 928-951.

Huber, G.P., "Issues in the Design of Group Decision Support Systems," *MIS Quarterly*, Vol. 8, No. 3, Sept. 1984b, pp. 195-204.

Huber, G.P., "A Theory of the Effects of Advanced Information Technologies on Organizational Design, Intelligence and Decision Making," *The Academy of Management Rev.*, Vol. 15, No. 1, Jan. 1990, pp. 47-71.

Huber, G.P. and R.R. McDaniel, "The Decision-Making Paradigm of Organizational Design," *Management Science*, Vol. 32, No. 5, 1986, pp. 572-589.

Ives, B., S. Hamilton, and G.B. Davis, "A Framework for Research in Computer-Based Management Information Systems," *Management Science*, Vol. 26, No. 9, 1980, pp. 910-934.

Ives, B., "Graphical User Interfaces for Business Information Systems," *MIS Quarterly*, Special Issue, 1982, pp. 15-47.

Jacoby, J. and W. Hoyer, "Rev. of Consumer Behavior Literature," *Handbook of Industrial and Organizational Psychology*, 1989.

Jarke, M. and DAIDA Team, "The DAIDA Demonstrator: Development Aids for Database-intensive Information Systems," *Proc. ESPRIT Conference Week '89*, 1989.

Jarke, M., "Coupling Conceptual and Numerical Models in Decision Support," *Proc. CompEuro '88*, IEEE CS Press, Los Alamitos, Calif., 1988, pp. 175-182.

Jarke, M., M. Jeusfeld, and T. Rose, "A Software Process Data Model for Knowledge Engineering in Information Systems," *Information Systems*, Vol. 14, No. 3, 1989.

Jarvenpaa, S.L., G. Dickson, and G. DeSanctis, "Methodological Issues in Experimental IS Research: Experiences and Recommendations," *MIS Quarterly*, Vol. 9, 1985, pp. 141-156.

Jarvenpaa, S.L., "The Effect of Task Demands and Graphical Format on Information Processing Strategies," *Management Science*, Vol. 35, No. 3, 1989.

Jenkins, A.M., *MIS Design Variables and Decision Making Performance*, UMI Research Press, Ann Arbor, Mich., 1983.

Jensen, M.C. and W.H. Meckling, "Theory of the Firm: Managerial Behavior, Agency Costs, and Ownership Structure," *J. Financial Economics*, Vol. 3, Oct. 1973, pp. 305-360.

Jessup, L.M., D. Tansik, and T.D. Laase, "Group Problem Solving in an Automated Environment: The Effects of Anonymity and Proximity on Group Process and Outcome with a Group Decision Support System," *Proc. Academy of Management*, 1988.

Johansen, R., "Groupware and Collaborative Systems: A Big Picture View," Inst. for the Future Paper, P-163, Aug. 1989.

Johansen, R., "User Approaches to Computer Supported Teams," in *Technological Support for Work Group Collaboration*, M.H. Olson, ed., Lawrence Erlbaum Associates, Hillsdale, N.J., 1989, pp. 1-32.

Johansen, R., *Groupware*, Free Press, New York, N.Y., 1988.

Johnson, E.J. and J.W. Payne, "Effort and Accuracy in Choice," *Management Science*, Vol. 31, No. 4, 1985, pp. 395-414.

Johnson-Laird, P.N., *Mental Models*, Harvard Univ. Press, Cambridge, Mass., 1983.

Johnson-Laird, P.N., *The Computer and the Mind: An Introduction to Cognitive Science*, Harvard Univ. Press, Cambridge, Mass., 1988.

Kahneman, D. and A. Tversky, "Prospect Theory: An Analysis of Decision Under Risk," *Econometrica*, Vol. 47, 1979, pp. 263-291.

Kahneman, D., P. Slovic, and A. Tversky, *Judgment Under Uncertainty: Heuristics and Biases*, Cambridge Univ. Press, 1982.

Kanter, R.M. "When a Thousand Flowers Bloom: Structural, Collective and Social Conditions for Innovation in Organizations," *Research in Organizational Behavior*, Vol. 10, 1988, pp. 169-211.

Kay, A. "Computer Software," *Scientific American*, Vol. 251, 1984, pp. 52-59.

Keen, P.G.W. and M.S. Morton, *Decision Support Systems: An Organizational Perspective,* Addison Wesley, Reading, Mass., 1978.

Keen, P.G.W., "Decision Support Systems: Translating Useful Models into Usable Technologies," *Sloan Management Rev.,* Vol. 21, No. 3, Spring 1980, pp 33-44.

Keen, P.G.W., "Value Analysis: Justifying Decision Support Systems," *MIS Quarterly,* Vol. 5, No. 1, 1981, pp. 1-15.

Keen, P.G.W., "MIS Research: Reference Disciplines and a Cumulative Tradition," *Proc. First Int'l Conf. Information Systems,* 1982.

Keen, P.G.W., "Decision Support Systems: A Research Perspective," in *Decision Supports Systems: Issues and Challenges,* G. Fick and R.H. Sprague, Jr., eds., Pergamon Press, London, U.K.

Keeney, R.L. and H. Raiffa, *Decisions with Multiple Objectives: Decisions and Tradeoffs,* John Wiley and Sons, New York, N.Y., 1976.

Kelly, H.H. and J. Thibaut, "Group Problem Solving," in *The Handbook of Social Psychology,* 2nd ed., G. Lindsey and E. Aronson, eds., Addison-Wesley, Reading, Mass., 1969.

Kerlinger, N.D., *Foundations of Behavioral Research,* 3rd ed., Holt Rinehart and Winston, New York, N.Y., 1986.

Kieras, D.E. and P.G. Polson, "An Approach to the Formal Analysis of User Complexity," *Int'l J. of Man-Machine Studies,* Vol. 22, 1985, pp. 365-394.

Kiesler, S., J. Siegel, and T. McGuire, "Social Psychological Aspects of Computer-mediated Communication," *American Psychologist,* Vol. 39, 1984, pp. 1123-34.

Kimbrough, S.O., "On Model Management and the Language of Thought Hypothesis," working paper, Univ. of Pennsylvania, The Wharton School, Dept. of Decision Sciences, 1990.

King, D., "Intelligent Decision Support: Strategies for Integrating Decision Support, Database Management and Expert Systems Technologies," *Expert Systems with Applications: An International Journal,* Vol. 1, May 1990.

King, D., "Evolving Functionality for the Technology Environment," ISDP Working Group paper, 1990.

Klein, H. and R. Hirschheim, "Fundamental Issues of Decision Support Systems: A Consequentialist Perspective," *Decision Support Systems,* Vol. 1, No. 1, 1985, pp. 5-23.

Kling, R., "Social Analyses of Computing: Theoretical Perspectives in Recent Empirical Research," *Computing Surveys,* Vol. 12, No. 1, 1980, pp. 61-110.

Konsynski, B.R., "Model Management in Decision Support Systems," in *Data Base Management Theory and Applications,* C.W. Holsapple and A.B. Whinston, eds., Reidel, Boston, Mass., 1982.

Konsynski, B.R. and R. Sprague, "Future Research Directions in Model Management," *Decision Support Systems,* No. 2, 1986, pp. 103-109.

Konsynski, B.R., "On the Structure of a Generalized Model Management System," *Proc. 14th Hawaii Int'l Conf. System Sciences,* Vol. 1, IEEE CS Press, Los Alamitos, Calif, 1981, pp. 630-638.

Kotter, J.P., "What Effective General Managers Really Do," *Harvard Business Rev.,* Vol. 60, No. 6, 1982, pp. 156-167.

Koubarakis, M., et al., "Telos: A Knowledge Representation Language for Requirements Modeling," *Proc. Int'l Conf. Deductive and Object-Oriented Databases,* 1989.

Kraemer, K.L., ed., *The Information Systems Research Challenge: Survey Research Methods,* Harvard Business School Press, Boston, Mass., 1991.

Kraemer, K.L. and J. King, "Computer-Based Systems for Cooperative Work and Group Decision Making," *Computing Surveys,* Vol. 20, 1988, pp. 115-146.

Krishnan, R., "PM: A Logic Modeling Language for Model Construction," *Decision Support Systems,* 1990.

Kuhn, T.S., *The Structure of Scientific Revolutions,* 2nd ed., The Univ. of Chicago Press, Chicago, Ill., 1970.

Laird, J., P. Rosenbloom, and A. Newell, "Chunking in Soar: The Anatomy of a General Learning Mechanism," *Machine Learning,* Vol. 1, 1986, pp. 11-46.

Laird, J., P. Rosenbloom, and A. Newell, "Towards Chunking as a General Learning Mechanism," *Proc. AAAI-84,* William Kaufmann, Los Altos, Calif., 1984, pp. 188-192.

Laird, J., P. Rosenbloom, and A. Newell, "Soar: An Architecture for General Intelligence," *Artificial Intelligence,* Vol. 33, 1987, pp. 1-64.

Larkin, J.H., "Enriching Formal Knowledge: A Model for Learning to Solve Textbook Physics Problems," in *Cognitive Skills and Their Acquisition,* J.R. Anderson, ed., Lawrence Erlbaum Associates, Hillsdale, N.J., 1981.

Lave and J.G. March, *An Introduction to Models in the Social Sciences,* 1975.

Lawrence, P.R. and J.W. Lorsch. *Organization and Environment,* Harvard Business School Press, Boston, Mass., 1967, 1986.

Leavitt, H.J., "Suppose We Took Groups Seriously," in *Man, Work and Society,* 1975.

Leavitt, H.J., *Managerial Psychology,* Univ. of Chicago Press, Chicago, Ill., 1964.

Leavitt, H.J. and T.L. Whisler, "Management in the 1980's," *Harvard Business Rev.,* Nov.-Dec. 1958, pp. 41-48.

LeBoeuf, M., *Imagineering,* Berkeley Books, New York, N.Y., 1980.

Lee, R.M., A.M. McCosh, and P. Migliarese, eds., *Organizational Decision Support Systems,* North-Holland, Amsterdam, The Netherlands, 1988.

Lehner, P., *Artificial Intelligence and National Defense: Opportunity and Challenge,* Tab Books, Blue Ridge Summit, Penn., 1989.

Lerch, F.J., and M. Mantei, "A Framework for Computer Support in Managerial Decision Making," *Proc. Fifth Int'l Conf. Information Systems,* 1984, pp. 129-139.

Lerch, F.J. and M.J. Prietula, "Designing DSS Interfaces: A Cognitive Perspective," Working Paper, Graduate School of Industrial Administration, Carnegie Mellon Univ., 1990.

Levin, I.P., et al., "Framing Effects in Judgment Tasks with Varying Amounts of Information," *Organizational Behavior and Human Decision Processes,* Vol. 36, 1985, pp. 362-377.

Lewin, A.Y. and J.W. Minton, "Determining Organizational Effectiveness," *Management Science,* Vol. 32, No. 5, 1986, pp. 514-538.

Lewis, F., "Facilitator: A Microcomputer Decision Support Systems for Small Groups," Unpublished Doctoral Dissertation, Univ. of Louisville, 1982.

Lewis, R.L., A. Newell, and T.A. Polk, "Toward a Soar Theory of Taking Instructions for Immediate Reasoning Tasks," *Proc. 11th Ann. Conf. of the Cognitive Science Society,* 1989. In press.

Liang, T.P., "Development of a Knowledge-based Model Management System," *Operations Research,* Vol. 36, No. 6, 1988a, pp. 849-863.

Liang, T.P., "Meta-design Considerations in Developing Model Management Systems," *Decision Sciences,* Vol. 19, 1988b, pp. 72-92.

Liang, T.P., "Reasoning in Model Management Systems," *Proc. 21st Ann. Hawaii Int'l Conf. System Sciences*, Vol. III, IEEE CS Press, Los Alamitos, Calif., 1988, pp. 461-470.

Lichtenstein, S. and P. Slovic, "Reversals of Preference Between Bids and Choices in Gambling Decisions," *J. of Experimental Psychology*, Vol. 89, 1971, pp. 46-55.

Lindman, H.R., "Inconsistent Preference Among Gambles," *J. of Experimental Psychology*, Vol. 89, 1971, pp. 46-55.

Little, J.D.C., "Models and Managers: The Concept of a Decision Calculus," *Management Science*, Vol. 16, 1970, pp. B466-B485.

Little, J.D.C., "Research Opportunities in the Decision and Management Sciences," *Management Science*, Vol. 32, 1986, pp. 1-13.

Lucas, H.C., "An Experimental Investigation of the Use of Computer Based Graphics in Decision Making," *Management Science*, Vol. 27, No. 7, 1981, pp. 757-768.

Mackay, J. and J. Elam, "A Comparative Study of How Experts and Novices Use DSS to Solve Problems in Complex Knowledge Domains," to appear in *Information Systems Research*.

Mackenzie, K.D., "Virtual Positions and Power," *Management Science*, Vol. 32, No. 5, 1986, pp. 622-642.

Main, J. "The Winning Organization," *Fortune*, Sept. 26, 1988, pp. 50-52, 56, 60.

Malone, T. W., et al., "Intelligent Information Sharing Systems," *Comm. of the ACM*, Vol. 30, No. 5, May 1987, pp. 390-402.

Malone, T.W., et al., "Semi-Structured Messages are Surprisingly Useful for Computer-Supported Coordination," *Proc. CSCW '86, Conf. on Computer Supported Cooperative Work*, 1986, pp. 102-114.

Malone, T.W., "Coordination Theory," presented at the TIMS/ORSA Joint Nat'l Meeting, Washington, D.C., April 25-27, 1988.

Manheim, M.L. and D.J. Isenberg, "A Theoretical Model for Solving and its Use for Designing Decision Support Systems," *Proc. 20th Ann. Hawaii Int'l Conf. System Sciences*, IEEE CS press, Los Alamitos, Calif., 1987, pp. 614-627.

Manheim, M.L., "Issues in Design of a Symbiotic DSS," *Proc. 22nd Ann. Hawaii Int'l Conf. System Sciences*, IEEE CS Press, Los Alamitos, Calif., 1989, pp. 14-23.

Mantei, M., "Observation of Executives Using a Computer Supported Meeting Environment," *Decision Support Systems*, Vol. 5, No. 2, June 1989, pp. 153-166.

March, J. and Z. Shapira, "Behavioral Decision Theory and Organizational Decision Making," in *Decision Making: An Interdisciplinary Inquiry*, G. Ungson and D. Braunstein, eds., Kent Publishing Co., Boston, Mass., 1982.

March, J. and H. Simon, *Organizations*, Wiley, New York, N.Y., 1958.

Markus, M.L. and D. Robey, "Information Technology and Organizational Change: Causal Structure in Theory and Research," *Management Science*, Vol. 34, No. 5, May 1988, pp. 583-598.

Marsden, J. and D.E. Pingry, "A Theory of Decision Support Systems Design Evaluation," Kentucky Initiative for Knowledge Management, Paper No. 10, Univ. of Kentucky, Lexington, Kent., 1989.

Marshak, J. and R. Radnor, *Economic Theory of Teams*, Yale Univ. Press, New Haven, Conn., 1972.

Mason, R.O. and I.I. Mitroff, "A Program for Research on Management Information Systems," *Management Science*, Vol. 19, No. 5, 1973, pp. 475-487.

Mason, R.O. and I.I. Mitroff, *Challenging Strategic Planning Assumptions*, Addison-Wesley, Reading, Mass., 1981.

Mason, R.O., "MIS Experiments: A Pragmatic Evaluation," in *The Information Systems Research Challenge: Experimental Research Methods*, I. Benbasat, ed., Harvard Business School Press, Boston, Mass., 1989, pp. 21-32.

McCartt, A. T. and J. Rohrbaugh, "Evaluating Group Decision Support Effectiveness: A Performance Study on Decision Conferencing," *Decision Support Systems*, Vol. 5, No. 2, June 1989, pp. 243-254.

McGoff, C., "Experience at IBM," in *Electronic Meeting System Tutorial*, J.F. Nunamaker et al., eds., presented at Hawaii Int'l Conf. on Systems Science, January 1990.

McGrath, J.E. and I. Altman, *Small Group Research: A Synthesis and Critique of the Field*, Holt, Rinehart and Winston, New York, N.Y., 1966.

McIntyre, S.H., "An Experimental Study of the Impact of Judgement-Based Marketing Models," *Management Science*, Vol. 28, No. 1, 1982, pp. 17-33.

McIntyre, S., B.R. Konsynski, and J.F. Nunamaker, "Automated Planning Environments: Knowledge Integration and Model Scripting," *J. of MIS*, Vol. 2, No. 4, 1986, pp. 49-69.

Meehl, P., *Clinical versus Statistical Prediction*, Univ. of Minnesota Press, Minneapolis, Minn., 1954.

Meeraus, A., "An Algebraic Approach to Modeling," *J. of Economic Dynamics and Control*, Vol. 5, 1983, pp. 81-108.

Messier, W.F. and J.V. Hansen, "Inducing Rules for Expert System Development: An Example Using Default and Bankruptcy Data," *Management Science*, Vol. 34, No. 12, 1988, pp. 1403-1415.

Michie, D., "Current Developments in Expert Systems," in *Applications of Expert Systems: Vol 1.*, J. Quinlan, ed., Addison-Wesley, New York, N.Y., 1987.

Miller, P., *A Critiquing Approach to Expert Computer Advice: Attending*, Pitman Publishing, Boston, Mass., 1984.

Mills, D.Q., *Rebirth of the Corporation*, John Wiley, New York, N.Y., 1990.

Mintzberg, H., D. Raisinghani, and A. Thoret, "The Structure of Unstructured Decision Processes," *Administrative Science Quarterly*, Vol. 21, June 1976, pp. 246-275.

Mintzberg, H., "Managerial Work: Analysis from Observation," *Management Science*, Vol. 18, Oct. 1971.

Moore, J.H. and M.G. Chang, "Design of Decision Support Systems," *Data Base*, Vol. 12, No. 1 and 2, Fall 1980, pp. 8 -14.

Moran, T.P., "The Command Language Grammar: A Representation for the User Interface of Interactive Computer Systems," *Int'l J. of Man-Machine Studies*, Vol. 15, 1981, pp. 3-50.

Mumford, E., et al., *Research Methods in Information Systems*, North-Holland, New York, N.Y., 1985.

Murphy, F.H. and E.A. Stohr, "An Intelligent System for Formulating Linear Programs," *Decision Support Systems*, Vol. 2, No. 1, 1986.

Naylor, T.H., *Corporate Planning Models*, Addison Wesley, Reading, Mass., 1979.

Negroponte, N., "From Bezel to Prosenium: The Human-Computer Interface 25 Years Hence and Beyond the Desktop Metaphor," *Computer Graphics*, Vol. 23, No. 3, July, 1989.

Newell, A. and H.A. Simon, *Human Problem Solving*, Prentice-Hall, Englewood Cliffs, N.J., 1972.

Newell, A., "Heuristic Programming: Ill-Structured Problems," in *Progress in Operations Research,* Vol. 3, J. Aronofsky, ed., John Wiley, New York, N.Y., 1969

Newell, A. and H.A. Simon, "Computer Science as Empirical Inquiry: Symbols and Search," *Comm. of the ACM,* Vol. 19, 1975, pp. 113-126.

Newell, A. and P. Rosenbloom, "Mechanisms of Skill Acquisition and the Law of Practice," in *Cognitive Skills and Their Acquisition,* J. Anderson, ed., Lawrence Erlbaum, Hillsdale, N.J., 1981.

Nilles, J., et al., "The Strategic Impact of Information Technology on Managerial Work," Research Report #R16, Center For Futures Research, Univ. of Southern California, July 1986.

Nolan, R., et al. "Creating the 21st Century Organization," *Stage by Stage,* Vol. 8, No. 4, 1988, pp. 1-11.

Norman, D., *The Psychology of Everyday Things,* Basic Books, New York, N.Y., 1988.

Nunamaker, J., D. Vogel, and B. Konsynski, "Interaction of Task and Technology to Support Large Groups," *Decision Support Systems,* Vol. 5, No. 2, June 1989, pp. 139-154.

Nunamaker, J., et al., "Experiences at IBM with Group Decision Support Systems: A Field Study," *Decision Support Systems,* Vol. 5, No. 2, June 1989, pp. 183-196.

Nunamaker, J.F., L. Applegate, and B.R. Konsynski, "Computer-Aided Deliberatio: Model Management and Group Deliberation Support," *Operations Research,* Nov.-Dec. 1988.

Olle, T., et al., *Information Systems Methodologies,* Addison-Wesley, Reading, Mass., 1988.

Olson, Margrethe H., ed., *Technological Support for Work Group Collaboration,* Lawrence Erlbaum Associates, Hillsdale, N.J., 1989.

Orlikowski, W.J. and V. Dhar, "Imposing Structure on Linear Programming Problems: An Empirical Analysis of Expert and Novice Models," *Proc. Nat'l Conf. Artificial Intelligence, AAAI-86,* William Kaufmann, Los Altos, Calif., 1986, pp. 308-312.

Orlikowski, W.J. and J.J. Baroudi, "Studying Information Technology in Organizations: Research Approaches and Assumptions," *Information Systems Research,* Vol. 2, No. 1, 1991.

Orlikowski, W.J. and J.J. Baroudi, "IS Research Paradigms: Method versus Substance," *Information Systems Research,* Vol. 2, No. 1, 1990.

Orlikowski, W.J. and D. Robey, "Information Technology and the Structuring of Constraints," *Information Systems Research,* Vol. 2, No. 2, June 1991, pp. 143-169.

Palmer R.D., "Senior Managers and Microcomputers: A Study of Use and Behavior," Unpublished Doctoral Dissertation, Claremont Graduate School, 1988.

Panko, R.R. and R.H. Sprague, "Towards a New Framework for Office Support," *ACM Conf. on Office Automation Systems,* 1982.

Panko, R.R., *End User Computing: Management, Applications & Technology,* John Wiley & Sons, Inc., New York, N.Y., 1988.

Panko, R. and R.H. Sprague, "DP Needs New Approach to Office Automation," *Data Management,* 1984.

Park, H.K., "International Group Decision Support System and Intercultural Interface," Unpublished Doctoral Dissertation, Claremont Graduate School, 1990.

Payne, J.W., M.L. Braunstein, and J.S. Carroll, "Exploring Predecisional Behavior: An Alternative Approach to Decision Research," *Organizational Behavior and Human Performance*, Vol. 22, 1978, pp. 17-44.

Payne, J.W., "Task Complexity and Contingent Processing in Decision Making: An Information Search and Protocol Analysis," *Organization Behavior and Human Performance*, Vol. 16, 1976, pp. 366-387.

Payne, J.W., "Contingent Decision Behavior," *Psychological Bulletin*, Vol. 92, No. 2, 1982, pp. 382-402.

Payne, J.W., Personal Interview, 1989.

PC Week, "Phasing Out of Middle Managers May Increase Dependence on EIS," Aug. 21, 1989, pp. 71 and 78.

Peters, T., "The Power of Information," *Portfolio*, May-June, 1989.

Pfeffer, J. and G.R. Salancik, *The External Control of Organizations: A Resource Dependence Perspective*, Harper and Row, New York, N.Y., 1978.

Philippakis, A.S. and G.I. Green, "An Architecture for Organization-Wide Decision Support Systems," *Proc. Ninth Int'l Conf. Information Systems*, 1988, pp. 257-263.

Pinsonneault, A. and K.L. Kraemer, "The Effects of Electronic Meetings in Group Processes and Outcomes: An Assessment of the Empirical Research," *European J. of Operations Research*, Vol. 45, 1990.

Pinsonneault, A. and K.L. Kraemer, "The Impact of Technological Support on Groups: An Assessment of the Empirical Research," *Decision Support Systems*, Vol. 5, No. 2, June 1989, pp. 197-216.

Pollock, J.L., *Contemporary Theories of Knowledge*, Rowman & Littlefield, Totowa, N.J., 1986.

Polya, G., *How to Solve It: A New Aspect of Mathematical Method*, Doubleday/ Anchor Books, Garden City, N.Y., 1957.

Prietula, M. and F. Marchak, "The Effects of Static versus Dynamic Task Representation in Solving an Engineering Problem," working paper, Graduate School of Industrial Administration, Carnegie Mellon Univ., 1990.

Prietula, M. and P. Feltovich, "Expertise as Task Adaptation," working paper, Graduate School of Industrial Administration, Carnegie Mellon Univ., 1990.

Prietula, M., R. Beauclair, and F.J. Lerch, "A Computational Model of Group Problem Solving," *Proc. 23rd Ann. Hawaii Int'l Conf. Systems Science*, Vol. III, IEEE CS Press, Los Alamitos, Calif., 1990, pp. 101-109.

Pylyshyn, Z.W., *Computation and Cognition: Toward a Foundation for Cognitive Science*, The MIT Press, Cambridge, Mass., 1984.

Quinlan, J.R., "Discovering Rules by Induction from Large Classes of Examples," in *Machine Learning: An Artificial Intelligence Approach*, R.S. Michalski, J.G. Carbonell, and T.M. Mitchell, eds., Tioga Publishing Company, Palo Alto, Calif., 1983.

Quinn, R.J. and J. Rohrbaugh, "A Spatial Model of Effectiveness Criteria," *Management Science*, Vol. 29, No. 3, 1983, pp. 363-377.

Quinn, R.J., J. Rohrbaugh, and M. McGrath, "Automated Decision Conferencing," *Personnel*, Vol. 62, 1985, pp. 49-55.

Raghavan, S. and R. Chand, "Exploring Active Decision Support: The JANUS Project: Decision Support and Knowledge Based Systems," *Proc. 22nd Ann. Hawaii Int'l Conf. System Sciences*, Vol. III, IEEE CS Press, Los Alamitos, Calif, 1989, pp. 33-45.

Raghunathan, S., "An Intelligent Decision Support System for Model Formulation," working paper, Univ. of Pittsburgh, 1987.

Raghunathan, S., "An Artificial Intelligence Approach to the Formulation of Quantitative Models," PhD dissertation, Univ. of Pittsburgh, 1988.

Rayna, G., *Reduce: Software for Algebraic Computation*, Springer-Verlag, New York, N.Y., 1987.

Reinfrank, M., "Lecture Notes on Reason Maintenance Systems," Siemens Technical Report INF2 ARM-5-88, Munich, W. Germany, 1988.

Remus, W., "A Study of Graphical and Tabular Displays and Their Interaction with Environmental Complexity," *Management Science*, Vol. 33, No. 9, 1987, pp. 1200-1205.

Riesbeck, C.K. and R.C. Schank, *Inside Case-Based Reasoning*, Lawrence Erlbaum, Hillsdale, N.J., 1989.

Rittel, H. and M. Weber, "Dilemmas in a General Theory of Planning," *Policy Sciences*, Vol. 4, 1973.

Rockart, J.F., "Chief Executives Define Their Own Data Needs," *Harvard Business Rev.*, Mar.-Apr. 1979.

Rockart, J.F. and D.W. De Long, *Executive Support Systems: The Emergence of Top Management Computer Use*, Dow Jones-Irwin, Homewood Ill., 1988.

Rockart, J.F. and M. Treacy, "The CEO Goes On-Line," *Harvard Business Rev.*, Vol. 60, No. 1, Jan.-Feb. 1982, pp. 32-38.

Rockart, J.F., "Critical Success Factors," *Sloan Management Rev.*, Mar.-Apr. 1979.

Rose, T., and M. Jarke, "A Decision-Based Configuration Process Model," working paper, Univ. of Passau, W. Germany, 1989.

Rosenbloom, P.S., A. Newell, and J.E. Laird, "Towards the Knowledge Level in Soar: The Role of the Architecture in the Use of Knowledge," in *Architectures of Intelligence*, K. VanLehn, ed., Lawrence Erlbaum, Hillsdale, N.J., 1989.

Rosenbloom, P. and A. Newell, "The Chunking of Goal Hierarchies; A Generalize Model of Practice," in *Machine Learning: Volume II*, R. Michalski, J. Carbonell, and T. Mitchell, eds., Morgan Kaufmann Publishers, Los Altos, Calif., 1986.

Rosenbloom, P.S., et al., "A Preliminary Analysis of the Foundations of the Soar Architecture as a Basis for General Intelligence," in *Foundations of Artificial Intelligence*, D. Kirsh and C. Hewitt, eds., MIT Press, Cambridge, Mass., 1989.

Rohrbaugh, J., "Demonstration Experiments," in *The Information Systems Research Challenge*, W. McFarlane, ed., Harvard Business School Press, Cambridge, Mass., 1985.

Rumelhart, D.E. and A. Ortony, "The Representation of Knowledge in Memory," in *Schooling and the Acquisition of Knowledge*, R.C. Anderson, R.J. Spiro, and W.E. Montague, eds., Lawrence Erlbaum Associates, Hillsdale, N.J., 1977.

Rumelhart, D.E., J.L. McClelland, and the PDP Research Group, *Parallel Distributed Processing: Explorations in the Microstructure of Cognition*, MIT Press/Bradford Books, Cambridge, Mass., 1986.

Runciman, C. and N.V. Hammond, "User Programs: A Way to Match Computer Systems and Human Cognition," in *People and Computers: Designing for Usability*, M.D. Harrison and A.F. Monk, eds. Cambridge Univ. Press, 1986, pp. 464-481.

Russo, J.E., "Eye Fixations Can Rule the World: A Critical Evaluation and a Comparison Between Eye Fixations and Other Information Processing Methodologies," in *Advances in Consumer Research*, Vol. 5, 1978, pp. 561-570.

Saaty, T.L., *The Analytic Hierarchy Process*, McGraw Hill, New York, N.Y., 1980.

Salamon, G., T. Oren, and K. Kreitman, "Using Guides to Explore Multimedia Databases," *Proc. 22nd Ann. Hawaii Int'l Conf. System Sciences*, Vol. IV, IEEE CS Press, Los Alamitos, Calif., 1989, pp. 3-12.

Schank, R.C. and R. Abelson, *Scripts, Plans, Goals, and Understanding*, Lawrence Erlbaum Associates, Hillsdale, N.J., 1977.

Schkade, D.A. and E.J. Johnson, "Cognitive Processes in Preference Reversals," *Organizational Behavior and Human Decision Processes*, Vol. 44, 1989, pp. 140-168.

Scott Morton, M.S., *Management Decision Systems: Computer Support for Decision Making*, Harvard Univ. Press, Boston, Mass., 1971.

Seward, R., private communication, 1988.

Shafer, D., *Designing Intelligent Front Ends for Business Software*, Wiley, New York, N.Y., 1989.

Shakun, M.F., "Decision Support Systems for Negotiation," *Proc. IEEE Conf. Man, Machine and Cybernetics*, 1985.

Sharda, R., S.H. Barr, and J.C. McDonnell, "Decision Support System Effectiveness: A Rev. and An Empirical Test," *Management Science*, Vol. 34, Feb. 1988, pp. 139-159.

Sharda, R., S.H. Barr, and J.C. McDonnell, "DSS? A Rev. and an Empirical Test," *Management Science*, Vol. 34, No. 2, Feb. 1988, pp. 139-159.

Shaw, M.J., "Applying Inductive Learning to Enhance Knowledge Based Systems," *Decision Support Systems*, Vol. 3, 1987, pp. 319-332.

Shneiderman, B., *Designing the User Interface: Strategies for Effective Human-Computer Interaction*, Addison-Wesley, Reading, Mass., 1987.

Shrivasatave, P., "A Typology of Organizational Learning Systems," *J. of Management Studies*, Vol. 20, No. 1, 1983.

Shu, N., *Visual Programming*, Van Nostrand, New York, N.Y., 1988.

Shwartz, S., *Applied Natural Language Processing*, Petrocelli Books, Princeton, N.J., 1988.

Silver, M.S., "Descriptive Analysis for Computer Based Decision Support," *Operations Research*, Vol. 36, No. 6, Nov.-Dec, 1988, pp. 904-916.

Silver, M.S., "Decision Support Systems: Directed and Non-Directed Change," *Information Systems Research*, Vol. 1, No. 1, Mar. 1990, pp. 47-70.

Silver, M.S., *Systems that Support Decision Makers: Description and Analysis*, John Wiley & Sons, New York, N.Y., 1991.

Simon, H.A., *Models of Man*, Wiley, New York, N.Y., 1957.

Simon, H.A., *The New Science of Management Decision*, Prentice Hall, Englewood Cliffs, N.J., 1960.

Simon, H.A., "Applying Information Technology to Organizational Design," *Public Admin. Rev.*, Vol. 3, No. 3, 1973, pp. 268-278.

Simon, H.A., "Rational Decision Making in Business Organizations," Nobel prize address, 1979.

Simon, H.A., "Information Processing Theory of Human Problem Solving," in *Handbook of Learning and Cognitive Processes*, Vol. 5, W. Chase, ed., Human Information Processing, Lawrence Erlbaum, Hillsdale, N.J., 1978.

Simon, H.A., "Studying Human Intelligence by Creating Artificial Intelligence," *American Scientist*, Vol. 69, 1981, pp. 300-309.

Simon, H.A., *The New Science of Management Decision* (revised ed.), Prentice Hall, Englewood Cliffs, N.J., 1977.

Simon, H.A., "Rationality as Process and Product of Thought," *American Economic Rev.*, 1978.

Sivasankaran, T.R. and M. Jarke, "Logic-based Formula Management in an Actuarial Consulting System," *Decision Support Systems*, Vol. 1, No. 4, 1985, pp. 251-262.

Slovic, P. and S. Lichtenstein, "Preference Reversals: A Broader Perspective," *American Economic Rev.*, Vol. 73, 1983, pp. 596-605.

Sol, H.G., "Simulation in Information Systems Development," PhD Thesis, Univ. of Groningen, Groningen, The Netherlands, 1982.

Sol, H.G. and M.B.M. Van der Ven, "Integrating GDSS in the Organization: The Case of a GDSS for International Transfer Pricing," in *Organizational Decision Support Systems, Proc. IFIP WG 8.3 Working Conf. on Organizational Decisions Support Systems*, North-Holland, Amsterdam, The Netherlands, 1988, pp. 129-138.

Sol, H.G. "Aggregating Data for Decision Support," *Decision Support Systems J.*, Vol. 1, No. 2, 1985.

Sol, H.G., "DSS: Buzzword or Challenge?" *European J. of Operational Research*, Vol. 22, No. 1, 1985.

Sol, H.G. and A.A. Verrijn Stuart, "Information Planning for Personal Computing: Putting the User in Profile," *Proc. Joint Int'l Symp. Information Systems*, Australian Computer Society, Sydney, Australia, 1988.

Sowa, J.F., *Conceptual Structures: Information Structures in Mind and Machine*, Addison-Wesley, Reading, Mass., 1984.

Sprague, R.H., and H.J. Watson, "Model Management in MIS," *Proc. 17th Nat'l AIDS Meeting*, 1975, pp. 213-215.

Sprague, R.H., "A Framework for Decision Support Systems," *MIS Quarterly*, Vol. 4, No. 4, Dec. 1980a, pp. 1-26.

Sprague, R.H., "A Framework for Research on Decision Support Systems," in *Decision Support Systems: Issues and Challenges*, G. Fick and R.H. Sprague, eds., Pergamon Press, London, U.K., 1980b.

Sprague, R.H. and E.D. Carlson, *Building Effective Decision Support Systems*, Prentice Hall, Englewood Cliffs, N.J., 1982.

Sprague, R.H. and H.J. Watson, eds., *Decision Support Systems: Putting Theory into Practice*, 2nd ed., Prentice Hall, Englewood Cliffs, N.J., 1989.

Sproull, L. and S. Kiesler. "Reducing Social Context Cues: Electronic Mail in Organization Communication," *Management Science*, Vol. 32, 1986, pp. 1492-1512.

Stabell, C.B., "Decision Research: Description and Diagnosis of Decision Making in Organizations," in *Proc. Int'l Federation of Information Processing*, North-Holland, Amsterdam, The Netherlands, 1979, pp. 962-966.

Stabell, C.B., *A Decision-Oriented Approach to Building DSS*, Addison-Wesley, Reading, Mass., 1983, pp. 221-260.

Star, S.L. and J.G. Griesemer, "Institutional Ecology, 'Translations,' and Boundary Objects: Amateurs and Professionals in Berkeley's Museum of Vertebrate Zoology, 1907-1939," *Social Studies of Science*, in press.

Star, S.L., "The Structure of Ill-Structured Solutions: Boundary Objects and Heterogeneous Distributed Problem Solving," To appear in *Distributed Artificial Intelligence*, Vol. 2, M. Huhns and L. Gasser, eds., Morgan Kaufman, Menlo Park, Calif.

Stearns, G., "Agents and the HP New Wave Application Programming Interface," *Hewlett-Packard J.*, Vol. 40, Aug. 1989, pp. 32-37.

Stefic, M. and J. Seely Brown, "Toward Portable Ideas," in *Technological Support for Work Group Collaboration*, M.H. Olson, ed., Lawrence Erlbaum Associates, Inc., Hillsdale, N.J., 1989.

Stefik, M. et al., "Beyond the Chalkboard: Computer Support for Collaboration and Problem Solving in Meetings," *Comm. of the ACM*, Jan. 1987.

Stillings, N.A. et al., *Cognitive Science: An Introduction*, The MIT Press, Cambridge, Mass., 1987.

Stitch, S., *From Folk Psychology to Cognitive Science, The Case Against Belief*, The MIT Press, Cambridge, Mass., 1983.

Stohr, E.A. and M.R. Tanniru, "A Database for Operations Research Models," *Int'l J. of Policy Analysis and Information Systems*, Vol. 4, No. 1, 1980, pp. 105-121.

Stone, E.F., *Research Methods in Organizational Behavior*, Scott Foresman, Glenview Ill., 1978.

Strauss, A.L., "A Social World Perspective," *Studies in Symbolic Interaction*, Vol. 1, 1978, pp. 119-128.

Suchmann, L., *Plans and Situated Actions*, Cambridge Univ. Press, New York, N.Y., 1987.

Swartout, W.R., "XPLAIN: A System for Creating and Explaining Expert Consulting Programs," *Artificial Intelligence*, Vol. 21, 1983, pp. 285-325.

Thagard, P., *Computational Philosophy of Science*, The MIT Press, Cambridge, Mass., 1988.

Thagard, P., "Explanatory Coherence," *Behavioral and Brain Sciences*, Vol. 12, No. 3, Sept. 1989, pp. 435-502.

Thagard, P., "The Conceptual Structure of the Chemical Revolution," Cognitive Science Laboratory, Princeton Univ., Report 27, June 1988; forthcoming in *Philosophy of Science*.

The Wall Street Journal, Aug. 21 and Aug. 24, 1989.

Todd, P., "Information Process Decomposition and the Design of Decision Support Systems," Working Paper, School of Business, Queen's Univ., Kingston, Canada, 1989.

Todd, P. and I. Benbasat, "An Experimental Investigation of the Impact of Computer-based Decision Aids on Decision Making Srategies," *Information Systems Research*, Vol. 2, No. 2, June 1991, pp 87-142.

Todd, P. and I. Benbasat, "Process Tracing Methods in Decision Support Systems Research: Exploring the Black Box," *MIS Quarterly*, Vol. 11, 1987, pp. 493-512.

Treacy, M.E., "Future Directions in DSS Technology," in *The Rise of Managerial Computing: The Best of the Center for Information Systems Research*, J. Rockart, and C. Bullen, eds., Dow-Jones Irwin, Homewood, Ill., 1986.

Turban, E., *Decision Support and Expert Systems*, Macmillan, New York, N.Y., 1988.

Turban, E. and D. King, "Building Expert Systems for Decision Support," *DSS-86*

Turban, E. and J.G. Carlson, "Interactive Visual Decision Making," *DSS-88 Trans.*, S. Weber, ed., The Inst. of Management Sciences, Providence, R.I., 1988, pp. 226-236.

Turing, A.M., "Computing Machinery and Intelligence," *Mind*, Vol. 59, Oct. 1950, pp. 433-460.

Tversky, A. and D. Kahneman, "Judgment under Uncertainty: Heruristics and Biases," *Science*, Vol. 185, 1974, pp. 1124-1131.

Tversky, A. and D. Kahneman, "The Framing of Decision and the Psychology of Choice," *Science,* Vol. 211, 1981, pp. 453-458.

Tversky, A., S. Sattath, and P. Slovic, "Contingent Weighting in Judgment and Choice," *Psychological Rev.,* Vol. 95, 1988, pp. 371-384.

Valacich, J., A. Dennis, and J. Nunamaker, "The Effects of Anonymity and Group Size in an Electronic Meeting System Environment," working paper, Univ. of Arizona, 1989.

Van Weelderen, J.A. and H.G. Sol, "The Xpection-Project: Development of an Expert Support System for the Maintenance of Boiler Components Operating in the Creep Range," *Proc. Symp. Expert Systems Application to Power Systems,* Royal Institute of Technology, 1988.

Van Schaik, F.D.J., "Effectiveness of Decision Support Systems," PhD Thesis, Delft Univ. of Technology, Delft, The Netherlands, 1988.

Van der Ven, M.B.M., "A Group Decision Support System for Transfer Pricing in the Pharmaceutical Industry, " PhD Thesis, Delft Univ. of Technology, Delft, The Netherlands, 1989.

Verbraeck, A. and H.G. Sol, "Designing Interactive Production Planning Environments: A Simulation Approach," *Proc. 1989 European Simulation Multiconference,* 1989.

Vogel, D.R. and J.C. Wetherbe, "MIS Research: A Profile of Leading Journals and Universities," *Data Base,* No. 1, 1984, pp. 3-14.

Wagner, G.R., "DSS: Dealing with Executive Assumptions in the Office of the Future," *DSS-81 Trans.,* D. Young and P.G.W. Keen, eds., The Institute of Management Sciences, Providence, R.I., 1981a, pp. 113-121.

Wagner, G.R., "DSS-The Real Substance," *Interfaces,* Vol. 11, No. 2, 1981b.

Watabe, K., C.W. Holsapple, and A.B. Whinston, "Coordinator Support in a Nemawashi Decision Process," Kentucky Initiative for Knowledge Management, Paper No. 4, 1988.

Watson, R.T., "A Design for an Architecture to Support Organizational Decision Making," *Proc. 23rd Ann. Hawaii Int'l Conf. System Sciences,* IEEE CS Press, Los Alamitos, Calif., 1990, pp. 111-119.

Watson, R.T., "A Study of Group Decision Support System Use in Three and Four-person Groups for a Preference Allocation Decision," Unpublished Doctoral Dissertation, Univ. of Minnesota, 1987.

Watson, R.T., G. DeSanctis, and M.S. Poole, "Using a GDSS to Facilitate Group Consensus: Some Intended and Unintended Consequences," *MIS Quarterly,* 1988.

Weber, E.S., "Systems to Think With: A Response to 'A Vision for Decision Support Systems'," *J. of Management Information Systems,* Vol. 2, No. 4, 1986, pp. 85-97.

Weick, K.E. and M.G. Bougon, "Organizations as Cognitive Maps," in *The Thinking Organization,* H.P. Sims, Jr., D. A. Gioia and Associates, eds., Jossey-Bass, San Francisco, Calif., 1986.

Weick, K.E., *The Social Psychology of Organizing,* Addison-Wesley, Reading, Mass., 1979.

Weick, K.E., "Theoretical Assumptions and Research Methodology Selection" in *The Information Systems Research Challenge,* F.W. McFarlan, ed., Harvard Business School Press, Cambridge, Mass., 1985, pp. 111-132.

Weill, P. and M.H. Olson, "An Assessment of the Contingency Theory of Information Systems," *J. of Management Systems,* Vol. 6, No. 1, 1989, pp. 59-85.

Welch, James S., Jr., "PAM—A Practitioner's Approach to Modeling," *Management Science*, Vol. 33, No. 5, May 1987.

Widrow, B. and R. Winter, "Neural Nets for Adaptive Filtering and Adaptive Pattern Recognition," *Computer*, Vol. 21, No. 3, 1988, pp. 25-39.

Wierda, F.W. and H.G. Sol, *Developing Interorganizational Information Systems; A Case in the Port of Rotterdam*, Berlin, 1989.

Wilkins, D., *Practical Planning: Extending the Classical AI Paradigm*, Morgan Kaufman Publishers, San Matao, Calif., 1988.

Will, H.J., "Model Management Systems," in *Information Systems and Organization Structure*, E. Grochla and N. Szyperski, eds., Walter de Gruyter, Berlin, 1975, pp. 468-482.

Winograd, T., *Understanding Natural Language*, Academic Press, New York, N.Y., 1972.

Winograd, T. and F. Flores, *Understanding Computers and Cognition: A New Foundation for Design*, Ablex Publishing, Norwood, N.J., 1986.

Wolfram, S., *Mathematica: A System for Doing Mathematics by Computer*, Addison-Wesley Publishing Company, Reading, Mass., 1988.

Wynn, E., "Office Conversation as an Information Medium," unpublished doctoral dissertation, Univ. of California, Berkeley, 1979.

Young, R.M., R.R.G. Green, and T. Simon, "Programmable User Models for Predicting Evaluation of Interface Designs," *CHI'89 Proc., Human Factors in Computing Systems*, Assoc. for Computing Machinery, New York, N.Y., 1989, pp. 15-19.

Zigurs, I., "Interaction Analysis in GDSS Research: Description of an Experience and Some Recommendations," *Decision Support Systems*, Vol. 5, No. 2, June 1989, pp. 233-242.

Zigurs, I., "The Impact of Computer-Based Support on Influence Attempts and Patterns in Small Group Decision Making," Unpublished Doctoral Dissertation, Univ. of Minnesota, 1987.

Zionts, S. and J. Wallenius, "An Interactive Method for Solving the Multiple Criteria Problem," *Management Science*, Vol. 22, No. 4, 1978.

Zmud, R.W., "Individual Differences and MIS Success: A Review of the Empirical Literature," *Management Science*, Vol. 25, 1979, pp. 966-979.

Zmud, R.W., M.H. Olson, and R. Hauser, "Field Experiments in MIS Research," in *The Information Systems Research Challenge: Experimental Research Methods*, I. Benbasat, ed., Harvard Business School Press, Boston, Mass., 1989, pp. 97-112.

About the Authors

Edward A. Stohr received his BE from the University of Melbourne (Australia) in 1959, and his MBA and PhD in business administration from the University of California (Berkeley) in 1973. Currently professor and chairman of the Information Systems Department at New York University's Stern School of Business, he previously held an appointment in the Graduate School of Management at Northwestern University. His research and teaching interests focus on systems analysis, design, and decision support systems. An associate editor for the *Journal of Information Systems Research*, the *International Journal of Policy Analysis and Information*, the *International Journal of Decision Support Systems*, and the *Journal of Management Information Systems*, he has also published articles in various journals including the *IEEE Transactions on Software Engineering*, *Operations Research*, *Management Science*, *Communications of the ACM*, the *Journal of Management Information Systems*, *MIS Quarterly*, and *Decision Support Systems*. In addition, he has served on several national committees concerned with information systems research and education, presently chairs the International Conference on Information Systems, and has consulted for a number of major corporations.

Benn R. Konsynski is the George S. Craft Distinguished Professor of Business Administration, and area coordinator for decision information analysis, at Emory University's Business School in Atlanta. Before joining Emory, he spent six years at the Harvard Business School, where he taught in the MBA and executive-level programs. Before that, he was a professor at the University of Arizona and a cofounder of that university's multimillion dollar group decision support laboratory. He received his PhD in computer science from Purdue University. His specialty is information technology in relationships across organizations, which involves extensive domestic and international fieldwork. He has spent 20 years investigating development and management issues in the use of computer-aided software engineering, and the emerging use of "out-sourced" (purchased) products, development, and offshore talent to bring software-dependent products to market quickly and economically. He has published in numerous technical journals, and has served as a consultant with IBM, AT&T, Northern Trust, Texas Instruments, the US Army, DEC, Northwestern Mutual Life Insurance, Tessco, MicroAge, Ernst and Young, and the Bank of Montreal.

IEEE Computer Society Press Titles

For further information call toll-free 1-800-CS-BOOKS or write:

IEEE Computer Society Press, 10662 Los Vaqueros Circle, PO Box 3014,
Los Alamitos, California 90720-1264, USA

IEEE Computer Society, 13, avenue de l'Aquilon,
B-1200 Brussels, BELGIUM

IEEE Computer Society, Ooshima Building, 2-19-1 Minami-Aoyama,
Minato-ku, Tokyo 107, JAPAN

Integrated Services Digital Networks (ISDN)
(Second Edition)
Edited by William Stallings
(ISBN 0-8186-0823-4); 406 pages

Knowledge-Based Systems:
Fundamentals and Tools
Edited by Oscar N. Garcia and Yi-Tzuu Chien
(ISBN 0-8186-1924-4); 512 pages

Local Network Technology (Third Edition)
Edited by William Stallings
(ISBN 0-8186-0825-0); 512 pages

Microprogramming and Firmware Engineering
Edited by V. M. Milutinovic
(ISBN 0-8186-0839-0); 416 pages

Modeling and Control of Automated
Manufacturing Systems
Edited by Alan A. Desrochers
(ISBN 0-8186-8916-1); 384 pages

Nearest Neighbor Pattern Classification Techniques
Edited by Belur V. Dasarathy
(ISBN 0-8186-8930-7); 464 pages

New Paradigms for Software Development
Edited by William Agresti
(ISBN 0-8186-0707-6); 304 pages

Object-Oriented Computing,
Volume 1: Concepts
Edited by Gerald E. Petersen
(ISBN 0-8186-0821-8); 214 pages

Object-Oriented Computing,
Volume 2: Implementations
Edited by Gerald E. Petersen
(ISBN 0-8186-0822-6); 324 pages

Parallel Architectures for Database Systems
Edited by A. R. Hurson, L. L. Miller, and S. H. Pakzad
(ISBN 0-8186-8838-6); 478 pages

Reduced Instruction Set Computers (RISC) (Second Edition)
Edited by William Stallings
(ISBN 0-8186-8943-9); 448 pages

Software Engineering Project Management
Edited by Richard H. Thayer
(ISBN 0-8186-0751-3); 512 pages

Software Maintenance and Computers
Edited by David H. Longstreet
(ISBN 0-8186-8898-X); 304 pages

Software Design Techniques (Fourth Edition)
Edited by Peter Freeman and Anthony I. Wasserman
(ISBN 0-8186-0514-6); 730 pages

Software Reuse — Emerging Technology
Edited by Will Tracz
(ISBN 0-8186-0846-3); 400 pages

Software Risk Management
Edited by Barry W. Boehm
(ISBN 0-8186-8906-4); 508 pages

Standards, Guidelines and Examples on System
and Software Requirements Engineering
Edited by Merlin Dorfman and Richard H. Thayer
(ISBN 0-8186-8922-6); 626 pages

System and Software Requirements Engineering
Edited by Richard H. Thayer and Merlin Dorfman
(ISBN 0-8186-8921-8); 740 pages

Test Access Port and Boundary-Scan Architecture
Edited by Colin M. Maunder and Rodham E. Tulloss
(ISBN 0-8186-9070-4); 400 pages

Visual Programming Environments: Paradigms and Systems
Edited by Ephraim Glinert
(ISBN 0-8186-8973-0); 680 pages

Visual Programming Environments: Applications and Issues
Edited by Ephraim Glinert
(ISBN 0-8186-8974-9); 704 pages

Visualization in Scientific Computing
Edited by G. M. Nielson, B. Shriver, and L. Rosenblum
(ISBN 0-8186-8979-X); 304 pages

Volume Visualization
Edited by Arie Kaufman
(ISBN 0-8186-9020-8); 494 pages

REPRINT COLLECTIONS

Distributed Computing Systems:
Concepts and Structures
Edited by A. L. Ananda and B. Srinivasan
(ISBN 0-8186-8975-0); 416 pages

Expert Systems:
A Software Methodology for Modern Applications
Edited by Peter G. Raeth
(ISBN 0-8186-8904-8); 476 pages

Milestones in Software Evolution
Edited by Paul W. Oman and Ted G. Lewis
(ISBN 0-8186-9033-X); 332 pages

Object-Oriented Databases
Edited by Ez Nahouraii and Fred Petry
(ISBN 0-8186-8929-3); 256 pages

Validating and Verifying Knowledge-Based Systems
Edited by Uma G. Gupta
(ISBN 0-8186-8995-1); 400 pages

ARTIFICIAL NEURAL NETWORKS TECHNOLOGY SERIES

Artificial Neural Networks —
Concept Learning
Edited by Joachim Diederich
(ISBN 0-8186-2015-3); 160 pages

Artificial Neural Networks —
Electronic Implementation
Edited by Nelson Morgan
(ISBN 0-8186-2029-3); 144 pages

Artificial Neural Networks —
Theoretical Concepts
Edited by V. Vemuri
(ISBN 0-8186-0855-2); 160 pages

SOFTWARE TECHNOLOGY SERIES

Computer-Aided Software Engineering (CASE)
Edited by E. J. Chikofsky
(ISBN 0-8186-1917-1); 110 pages

Software Reliability Models:
Theoretical Development, Evaluation, and Applications
Edited by Yashwant K. Malaiya and Pradip K. Srimani
(ISBN 0-8186-2110-9); 136 pages

MATHEMATICS TECHNOLOGY SERIES

Computer Algorithms
Edited by Jun-ichi Aoe
(ISBN 0-8186-2123-0); 154 pages

Multiple-Valued Logic in VLSI Design
Edited by Jon T. Butler
(ISBN 0-8186-2127-3); 128 pages

COMMUNICATIONS TECHNOLOGY SERIES

Multicast Communication in Distributed Systems
Edited by Mustaque Ahamad
(ISBN 0-8186-1970-8); 110 pages

ROBOTICS TECHNOLOGY SERIES

Multirobot Systems
Edited by Rajiv Mehrotra and Murali R. Varanasi
(ISBN 0-8186-1977-5); 122 pages

MONOGRAPHS

OPTIC FLOW COMPUTATION:
A Unified Perspective
by Ajit Singh

This monograph provides a new estimation-theoretic framework for optic flow computation and unifies and integrates the existing approaches for this framework. It examines a new framework that views the problem of recovering optic flow from time-varying imagery as a parameter-estimation problem and applies statistical estimation theory techniques to optic flow computation. It also discusses its application for recursive estimation of 3D scene geometry from optic flow using Kalman-filtering-based techniques.

The book addresses five major issues: unification: conservation and neighborhood information, integration of the three approaches, clarification of the distinction between image flow and optic flow, past research on optic flow computation from a new perspective, and incremental estimation of optic flow in real-time applications.

256 pages. January 1992. ISBN 0-8186-2602-X.
Catalog # 2602 $60.00 / $40.00 Member

X.25 AND RELATED PROTOCOLS
by Uyless Black

This monograph presents a tutorial view of X.25, discusses other protocols with which it operates, and provides a convenient reference guide to its protocols. The text contains all original material, including six appendices, over 100 illustrations, and more than 50 tables.

X.25 and Related Protocols explains X.25 operations, the advantages and disadvantages of its use, the concepts and terms of packet networks, and the role other standards play in the operation of X.25. It presents a considerable amount of detailed information about X.25 and its role in various systems such as LANs, PBXs, and ISDNs. The book covers a wide variety of subjects such as switching and routing in networks, the OSI model, physical-layer protocols and interfaces, high-level data-link control (HDLC), X.25 packet structures and types, and internetworking with SNA, DECnet, X.75, LANs, and ISDN

304 pages. 1991. Hardbound. ISBN 0-8186-8976-5.
Catalog # 1976 $70.00 / $45.00 Member

DIGITAL IMAGE WARPING
by George Wolberg

Digital image warping is a growing branch of the image processing field dealing primarily with geometric transformation techniques. Traditionally used for geometric correction in remote sensing and medical imaging, warping has recently enjoyed a new surge of interest stemming from computer graphics use in image synthesis and special effects.

This book, containing all original material, clarifies the various terminologies, motivations, and contributions of the many disciplines involved in this technology. The material is balanced between theory (proofs and formulas derived to motivate algorithms and to establish a standard of comparison) and practice (algorithms that can be implemented). It includes 36 color photographs and contains informative sections on image reconstruction, real-time texture mapping, separable algorithms, 2-pass transforms, mesh warping, and special effects.

340 pages. 1990. Hardbound. ISBN 0-8186-8944-7.
Catalog # 1944 $60.00 / $45.00 Member

BRANCH STRATEGY TAXONOMY
AND PERFORMANCE MODELS
by Harvey G. Cragon

This book provides a taxonomy that classifies and describes strategies in a consistent fashion, presents analytic models that permit the evaluation of each strategy under varying work load and pipeline parameters, and describes a modeling methodology that facilitates the evaluation of new branching strategies. It interprets analytic models that give a designer the capability of evaluating branching strategies while considering the implementation of parameters such as pipeline length and the location of the branch-effective address ALU.

The monograph investigates these six branching strategies along with their subordinate strategies and performance models: baseline strategy, pipeline freeze strategies, branch prediction strategies, fetch multiple paths strategies, instruction sequence alteration strategies, and composite strategies

120 pages. February 1992. Hardbound. ISBN 0-8186-9111-5.
Catalog # 2111 $45.00 / $30.00 Member

from *IEEE COMPUTER SOCIETY PRESS*

To order any of these titles or for information on other books,

call 1-800-CS-BOOKS or order by *FAX* at (714) 821-4010